新 GRE 阅读题源精讲

胡楠 王小丹 李政洁 编著

图书在版编目(CIP)数据

GRE阅读题源精讲 / 胡楠，王小丹，李政洁编著. —
北京：群言出版社，2012（2013.2重印）
ISBN 978-7-80256-353-7
Ⅰ. ①G… Ⅱ. ①胡… ②王… ③李… Ⅲ. ①
GRE—阅读教学—题解 Ⅳ. ①H319.4-44

中国版本图书馆CIP数据核字（2012）第160910号

出版人 范 芳
责任编辑 张 茜
封面设计 大愚设计 + 赵 甜
出版发行 群言出版社(Qunyan Press)
地 址 北京东城区东厂胡同北巷1号
邮政编码 100006
网 站 www.qypublish.com
电子信箱 bj62605588@163.com qunyancbs@126.com
总编办 010-65265404 65138815
编辑部 010-62418641 65276609 65262436
发行部 010-62605019 62263345 65220236
经 销 全国新华书店
读者服务 010-65220236 65265404 65263345
法律顾问 北京市国联律师事务所
印 刷 北京精乐翔印刷有限公司
版 次 2012 年 10 月第 1 版
印 次 2013 年 2 月第 2 次印刷
开 本 880×1092 1/16
印 张 17.25
字 数 327千
书 号 ISBN 978-7-80256-353-7
定 价 40.00元

[版权所有，侵权必究]
如有缺页、倒页、脱页等印装质量问题，请拨打服务热线：010-62605166。

新东方图书策划委员会

主任 俞敏洪

委员 （按姓氏笔画为序）

王　强　　包凡一

仲晓红　　沙云龙

陈向东　　张洪伟

邱政政　　汪海涛

周成刚　　徐小平

谢　琴　　窦中川

前　言

2012年7月，夏夜。

算来自我提笔开始写这本书到现在已经大半年过去了，直到大上个月截稿，在我脑海里回映的画面都是这些年自己和身边朋友们的学习历程。以前我认为：时间是世上最动态的东西，其他的人、物和知识都是相对静态的客观存在；现在则不然：世上万物一切都在不停演变，唯有时间是相对静态的，它为我们带来的每一秒、每一分、每一天的长度永远恒定。在我们都无力改变的时间面前，唯一能做的只有珍惜，只有努力地保持自己和时间的相对静止状态，也许才算是实现了自我的价值。

坦率地说，我从小就不是一个有语言天赋的人，从小学四年级开始学英语一直到初中、高中再到大学，成绩几乎从来没好过。彼时我倒也并不在意，因为我根本就不觉得这个东西会对我有多少影响；在北京生活着，等大学毕业以后找份工作干一些自己喜欢干的事情也就可以了。和我在同一所大学里的同学们毕业后都能找到差不多的工作，我怎么会不能呢？这是我当时的心理写照。时光在蹉跎岁月中过得总是比其他时候要快，一转眼就和别人一起混过去了将近两年大学时光，直到被我最好的朋友生拉硬拽进了新东方GRE课堂，当时连听课证上的名字都不是我。当我刚接触GRE就感到痛苦想要退缩的时候，好朋友劈头盖脸毫不留情地批评了我一顿。人家一个学理工科的女生都有着那么坚韧的毅力，有着永远对自己不满足的饥饿感，更有着对于曾经被我们遗忘的“一分耕耘一分收获”的信条的那般坚持，作为一个马上该上大三的男生又情何以堪？又有何勇气只想着混混日子就能在这个社会上立足？时至今日，我始终都对我的这位朋友心存感激和敬意。人在年轻的时候最宝贵的财富不是年轻和机会，而是能够和许许多多比自己更优秀的朋友始终在一起奋斗，始终在一起做正确的事情！

开始了GRE的学习历程之后，我既深憾多年来自己学习英文的方式和过程似是而非，又感叹身边有那么多同龄的优秀人才，和他们每天七点起床背单词、夜里一点才休息比起来，我之前寄希望于在学校里拿个文凭、找个铁饭碗工作混饭吃的想法有多么卑微鄙俗。人在一个社会团体中生活，或多或少都会受环境的影响，但是真正能决定自我高度的不是智商，而是一个人的情商，特别是坚韧程度。深感未来社会和市场的公平性，亦明白个人立足的本钱取决于其知识和能力，于是我就强迫自己从此和单词书、阅读文章形影不离……

人需要梦想，也需要展开梦想的平台。在如今充满竞争的社会中，有太多无形的压力使我们遵从一些既成的社会规则，有人求速成一步登天，有人求平平稳稳度过一生；有的人为了能博得更高学位获取更多知识毅然选择踏上出国求学的道路；也有人为了避免成为"北漂白领"一族而努力考研、考公务员、进事业单位。不论最终结果如何，至少在生活、学业、未来的几重压力下，人们通过奋斗与坚持总是能够战胜自己。梦想是对自己的一种超越，而展开梦想的平台就是曾经令我们死去活来的恶劣环境，也许正是应了中国非线性哲学中的"福兮祸之所倚，祸兮福之所伏"这句话。因此从低谷中走出的人往往能更好地帮助别人走过相同的道路，和很多人一样我也信奉过程的力量，这也是我写这本书的最重要原因。我见过身边太多人亲手关闭了梦想的天窗，人在遇到困难的时候总是容易怀疑自己的选择，误认为坚持是一种"不撞南墙不回头"的谬误，于是乎他们选择了止步于GRE，甚是可惜。我深知当一个英文基础薄弱的学生读到GRE文章时那种瞠目结舌的无奈，以及对于晦涩难懂的文意产生的厌恶与排斥。所以，自我走上新东方GRE讲台的那一天起，便决心以一种科学、高效的方法帮助每一位选择了这条道路的同学继续走下去，从未敢有一日懈怠。"Courage Never Fades Away"，这也是我始终不变的信念，时间可以带走我们的青春、财富和权力，但是流逝的时间唯一带不走的是那勇气所闪耀的光辉，有了那种泰山崩于前而岿然不动的勇气与从容，我们才有征服一切的机会和可能。

"路漫漫其修远兮，吾将上下而求索"，以我个人之力自然无法做到与每一位拼搏的学子面谈论道，故而希望借此书能为天下莘莘学子提供一条学习GRE阅读的道路。在本书中，我一直着力描述的是一种科学合理解读高端英文文章的能力和方法，以结构化阅读为主线解读整篇文章，帮助考生搭建起由表及里的框架；并以题源阅读为特色，扩展考生在练习本书时的阅读宽度。余谨以至诚，切望考生朋友们能籍由此书切实提高阅读能力。感谢新东方为我们提供了这样的平台，也感谢大愚文化的编辑们的倾心努力。由于笔者个人能力有限，书中如有不足之处敬请考生朋友们指正。

王小丹

使用指南

作为讲解GRE阅读的书籍，《GRE阅读题源精讲》的内容难度和市面上绝大部分关于英文学习的书籍比起来要高出不少，故而考生朋友们在阅读本书的过程中可能需要花费更多的脑力甚至是体力。高端英文的学习讲究档次，也就是说只有当我们的语言能力彻底上升一个层次以后，再去看那些曾经令我们头痛不已的文字时，才能感到容易。因为GRE是一项高端的考试，所以要求考生至少有大学英语六级的基础，在此基础上准备GRE阅读才比较合适。对于阅读实力并不是很强的考生，建议先好好练一练阅读长难句的基本功，或者把单词书背上四五遍，才能谈及如何游刃有余地阅读。

英文学习本身是一个很有趣的过程，有时候我们进行了很长时间的学习训练，却发现自己好像一直在原地兜圈子；而有时候我们只拿出一段时间集中学习，收获的却是突飞猛进的提高。这都是正常人在学习语言过程中的常态，前面的“拖延不进”是在为日后的飞跃打基础。相信阅读本书的考生绝大部分都是在读的大学生，有着扎实的英语基础，现在你们“突飞猛进”的时刻就要到来了。做好准备了吗?

《GRE阅读题源精讲》将从GRE考试本身出发，介绍阅读理解部分的整体形势，然后就英文阅读本身的形态构成、语句形成、单词构建逐一进行剖析，并引入新东方GRE阅读课程的精华内容：结构化阅读，从一个全新的角度和考生一起分享英文阅读的内容及本质。这些内容都是我们的教学中非常重要的部分，也在一定程度上代表着国内英文培训教学的高端方法，不盲目追求“四两拨千斤”的技巧，更不会舍本逐末地总结所谓的“胜经”。如果说GRE是一座大山的话，那我们每一个攀登者都需要一步一步往上走，希望考生朋友们能够踏踏实实地阅读本书，如果没有上过我们的GRE课程，更希望你能认真读三遍左右，这样才能切实体会阅读理解这门“艺术”能够给我们带来的思维——而不仅仅是语言——层面的提升。

本书中另一大特色和亮点就是题源文章。题源文章全部来自英美学术期刊杂志，我们无法全盘照搬也不能统统拿过来，所以在文章的量上无法像很多练习册那样浩如烟海。但是笔者希望考生朋友们能够通过阅读本书的题源文章，养成平时阅读英文原版论文或杂志的习惯，这必将在日后对各位英文能力的提高起到至关重要的作用。所谓“厚积薄发”也好，“不积跬步，无以至千里”也好，我们今日的努力与付出将在未来收到几何倍数的回报。

除此之外，本书中还收录了大量单词，为考生的词汇量武器库做补充。书中第三章给出了GRE阅读文章的高频词汇，是合格的GRE考生必须要掌握的常见单词，也是一个即将进入美国研究生院学习的学生所必备的词汇，请一定要把这些单词牢牢掌握。此外，第四章中每个题材阅读分类的后面也分别列出了自然类、生命类、人文类、社会类四大题材类别的专业词汇。

总的来说，本书在结构、内容以及思路上都具有一定的难度，适应了这种难度的考生朋友们在今后备考GRE的道路上可以更加顺利地走下去。因此，笔者建议考生朋友们最好能将这本书仔细研读三遍左右，切实掌握书中的知识点，并在学习的过程中始终不停地磨练与完善自我，做最好的自己！在学习的过程中完成自我的提高与升华，这也是GRE考试本身带给我们每一个曾经为它战斗过的人最大的财富，因为我们都曾经无怨无悔地“GRE”过！

目 录

本书题源阅读文章分类概览

<table>
<tr><th colspan="2">文章分类</th><th>所选文章</th><th>GRE 阅读题源期刊示例</th></tr>
<tr><td rowspan="3">1. 自然科学类</td><td>1.1 天文</td><td>1.1.1 爱因斯坦的理论在星系团的范围内得到证实
1.1.2 环地球反物质带
1.1.3 星系碰撞创造了类星体</td><td rowspan="3">Science《科学》
PNAS《美国国家科学院院刊》
Journal of Biological Chemistry《生物化学期刊》
National Geographic《国家地理》
Technology Review《技术评论》
Scientific American《科学美国人》</td></tr>
<tr><td>1.2 气候</td><td>1.2.1 气候变化导致文化失落
1.2.2 一天浓雾一天晴</td></tr>
<tr><td>1.3 物理</td><td>1.3.1 中微子没有超光速
1.3.2 葡萄酒漩涡中的物理学
1.3.3 哈勃望远镜发现最遥远的漩涡星系
1.3.4 希格斯玻色子之美</td></tr>
<tr><td rowspan="3">2. 生命科学类</td><td>2.1 动物</td><td>2.1.1 二氧化碳刺激海葵鱼的冒险行为
2.1.2 鸟雀啁啾，可有章法?
2.1.3 为什么一些鸟的羽毛是蓝色的?</td><td rowspan="3">Science《科学》
Wilson Journal of Ornithology《威尔逊鸟类杂志》
Scientific American《科学美国人》
Journal of the American Medical Association《美国医学会杂志》
The New England Journal of Medicine《新英格兰医学杂志》
Cell《细胞》</td></tr>
<tr><td>2.2 植物</td><td>2.2.1 树木为何不会断裂?
2.2.2 感谢植物，让我们的地球与众不同
2.2.3 生物燃料的穷途末路
2.2.4 植物的奇妙私语</td></tr>
<tr><td>2.3 医学</td><td>2.3.1 基因，让干细胞疗法更安全
2.3.2 干细胞与医学：修补受损的心脏
2.3.3 停止大脑的自我损害
2.3.4 鱼、欧米伽和胆固醇
2.3.5 阿司匹林燃烧脂肪的机制已被发现</td></tr>
<tr><td>3. 人文艺术类</td><td>3.1 文学</td><td>3.1.1 在黑暗中翻译
3.1.2 反抗音乐历史
3.1.3 书评：《梵高的人生》
3.1.4《圣经》与美国的文学传承
3.1.5 黑格尔的上帝观</td><td>Los Angeles Times《洛杉矶时报》
The New York Times《纽约时报》</td></tr>
<tr><td rowspan="5">4. 社会科学类</td><td>4.1 政治</td><td>4.1.1 梅隆信条
4.1.2 政治秩序的起源
4.1.3 斯宾诺莎和我们的自由观</td><td rowspan="5">Psychological Bulletin《心理学公报》
MIT Sloan Management Review《麻省–斯隆管理评论》
Los Angeles Times《洛杉矶时报》
The Economist《经济学人》
The New York Times《纽约时报》
Harvard Business Review《哈佛商业评论》</td></tr>
<tr><td>4.2 社会</td><td>4.2.1 公共事务中的风险与草率
4.2.2 女性与阿拉伯觉醒</td></tr>
<tr><td>4.3 经济</td><td>4.3.1 失控的资本主义
4.3.2 自然选择论比亚当•斯密之“看不见的手”更能解释诸多经济现象
4.3.3 解决世界性粮食短缺问题
4.3.4 数据与劳动力市场问题
4.3.5 经济问题与政府干预</td></tr>
<tr><td>4.4 法律</td><td>4.4.1 正义：如何做正确的事</td></tr>
<tr><td>4.5 心理学</td><td>4.5.1 婴儿能判断社交情景
4.5.2 时光缘何放慢脚步
4.5.3 荣格的心理学分类
4.5.4 罗夏墨迹测试</td></tr>
</table>

第一篇　理论篇

导 言

GRE考试的全称为Graduate Record Examination（美国研究生入学考试），这门考试自设立以来，一直都是美国研究生院招生的一项不可替代的重要参考指标；也正是由于这门考试内容的难度与性质，确保了多年以来美国研究生教育的质量一直处于全球最高。GRE考试并非是一门考查语言能力的考试——这一点不同于我们之前参加的考试，而是基于英语语言能力考查考生的逻辑思维能力，并且GRE考试内容的选材一律都是学术科学类，这也就确保了参加这门考试并能取得成功的考生都有足够的资格和潜质完成美国硕士和博士研究生的学业。

然而，这门考试本身并非单独为我们中国考生准备的，世界上任何一个国家的学生（包括美国本土大学生）如果想在北美读研，都要参加GRE考试。考试内容由三个部分组成：写作部分（Analytical Writing）、语文部分（Verbal Reasoning）、数学部分（Quantitative Reasoning）。对于我们中国考生来说，英文基础不如美国学生、英国学生那么深厚，所以多年以来摆在我们面前的"拦路虎"自然就是语文部分（Verbal Reasoning）。因为做学术需要具备的能力大致分为三层：第一层是对于客观世界的普遍认知（Common Sense）——这个部分是东西方教育在基础阶段都已经为我们打好了地基的；第二层是语言能力（Language Level）；第三层是批判性思维（Critical Thinking）。GRE考查的逻辑思维能力就处于第三层，需要以英文为基础顺利高效地完成对于信息的分析和处理。中国考生在国内学了将近十年英语，很多人到了大学一、二年级时词汇量仅为5000左右，若不考GRE的话极有可能一辈子也没有机会再去系统地背单词了。因此，听到"背GRE单词"如闻凶神恶煞，阅读GRE文章更是如品读天书，不禁气为之变、胆为之寒。

究其原因，GRE阅读的难点并非是"由于某些细节不懂"而导致的"文意模糊"，那是国内有些考试通常会给考生留下的印象；而真正的症结在于"看不懂句子和文章的意思"，这是硬实力上的欠缺。说直白些就是，GRE阅读的很多句子对于考生来说即使翻译成中文也搞不懂其到底是什么意思。而这门考试在内容和性质上都决定了一个极其重要也是最基本的要求——精准地理解语句的意思，科学、逻辑方面的内容可是半点含糊不得。因此GRE阅读也就很少出现"繁文缛节"，不追求考生能体会出英语的美感，但求考生能准确理解作者的意思。笔者深知GRE阅读对于中国考生的关键性以及攻坚这座"堡垒"的重要性，接下来我们就从这门考试的命题机构ETS官方给出的"新GRE改革"内容指导部分入手，通过解读阅读理解部分对考生能力的要求，深度剖析GRE阅读。

第一章

解密新GRE阅读

第一节 新GRE考试

美国教育考试服务中心(ETS)在2011年8月6日推出新GRE考试。相较于传统的GRE考试，新GRE在考试内容、考试形式和计分方法上都发生了变化。无疑，这一考试的变革将会深刻影响国内莘莘学子的海外求学准备历程。而语文部分(Verbal Reasoning，又称文字推理)将依然是中国考生的软肋。按照ETS官方的讲法："(新GRE考试将会)减少对于单词意涵背记的孤立考查(如取消类比和反义试题)，更加突出对基于语境的理解能力的考查(如增加阅读理解题目)。"这样可以更加深入并且真实地反映考生的高级认知能力。具体说来，这些能力包括：

- 分析一段论述文字并推导结论；根据不完全的数据做推导；识别作者的前提/假设条件和视角；理解语言文字的多层次含义，包括字面意涵、修辞意涵和作者目的等；
- 挑选重要观点，区别主要论述和次要/相关论述；总结全文；理解文章结构；
- 理解词、句和段落篇章的意涵；理解不同词和概念间的关系等。

那么，新GRE考试语文部分的具体变化主要有哪些呢？随之而来的准备重点的变化究竟是什么呢？我们首先来看看从解题的时间要求上新GRE考试将带给我们怎样的变化(请见表1)。

表1　新老GRE考试语文部分时间对比

传统GRE考试	新GRE考试
两个部分	两个部分
每部分38题	每部分20题
每部分 30 分钟	每部分30分钟

仅从表面上来看，新GRE考试似乎给了考生更多解题时间，这一变化会让粗心大意者欣喜不已。这一理解偏差的根本原因在于没有同时考查GRE题型的显著变化。让我们再来看看传统GRE考试语文部分中的题型分布(请见表2)。

表2　传统GRE考试语文部分各种题型数量对比

传统GRE考试题型	每部分中的题数/总题数
类比/反义词	20/38
句子填空	7/38
阅读理解	11/38

从表2中我们可以看到，传统GRE考试语文部分中阅读理解和句子填空试题所占比重不到二分之一（18/38），而新GRE考试则将之前中国考生主要的一个得分大项“类比/反义”去掉。这表明，我们再也不能仅仅通过勤奋地背记单词而取得考试的优胜；想要在新GRE考试中获得相对优势就必须夯实自己的“实力”。那么新GRE的内容由何组成呢？（请见表3）

表3　新GRE考试语文部分各种题型数量对比

新GRE考试题型	每部分中的题数/总题数
句子填空	10/20
阅读理解	10/20

这个“实力”就是阅读理解的能力！我们看到了新GRE的阅读理解题目数量的比重从原来的**不足33%**上升到了**50%**；对于我们来说还有一个更严峻的问题，那就是阅读文章篇幅的增加：传统GRE语文两个部分的阅读理解总共由“**两篇长文章+两篇短文章**”组成，而新GRE语文两个部分的阅读理解总共由“**两篇长文章+六篇短文章+两道逻辑题**”组成。每个人在考场上碰到的具体题目和数量也许会有一些微调，但整体上的内容基本不变。换句话说，就是新GRE考试语文部分成倍地增加了英文语篇的阅读量，变相缩短了考试时间，实际上增加了考试难度。这将使绝大部分中国大陆考生不堪重负，甚至丧失已有的竞争优势。（请见表4）

表4　新老GRE考试阅读理解篇幅数量对比

传统GRE考试	新GRE考试
阅读理解	阅读理解
两篇长文章	两篇长文章
两篇短文章	六篇短文章
	两道逻辑题

The Verbal Reasoning section of the GRE measures your ability to analyze and evaluate written material and synthesize information obtained from it, to analyze relationships among component parts of sentences, and to recognize relationships among words and concepts.

ETS明确写道，GRE的语文部分是测试考生“analyze and evaluate”（**分析和评估**）书面材料的能力，提炼整合信息的能力，分析句子及其组成部分之间关系的能力，以及理解单词之间、概念之间关系的能力。这里提出一个明确的目的，即“analyze relationships”和“recognize relationships”，强调的是分析清楚元素之间的“关系”。这一点和中国学生多年来习惯的英语考试有着本质区别：很多国内英语考试，外加雅思、托福考试，考查的全是考生读懂语句的能力；而GRE考试考查的是以英语为媒介理解信息与信息之间的关系。更何况新GRE在内容改革以后大大增加了阅读的比重，这对于我们中国学生来说是个不小的难题。

GRE考试自从20世纪90年代在中国大陆“遍地开花”以来，中国学生一直以来的强项是类比/反义词——依靠背词汇就能十拿九稳的一个重头戏，而阅读的状况则不容乐观。对于传统GRE考试中的两篇短文章，有很多考生索性选择战略性放弃，以节约出时间保证类比/反义和句子填空的正确率；而题目数量的分布决定了这种“战略性放弃”往往对考生最后的分数有利。但是，这样就导致很多备考GRE的中国学生对阅读能力重视不够，所以没有取得相应的提高。中国考生GRE阅读能力的不足一时难以用一个可量化的标准予以衡量，但是却明显地体现在ETS官方正式发布新GRE内容改革之后人们对其的反应和态度上：有很多考生看到官方指南给出的阅读文章变成十篇以后，瞬间觉得天旋地转，甚至有些人转而一头扎向了GMAT的"怀抱"。究其原因，大多数同学的问题甚至还不在"analyze relationships"和"recognize relationships"的能力上，而是在于基本功难以达到考试要求。语句的认知是处理句子之间关系的基础，若没有足够的解读单句的能力，一切方法、技巧、套路全都成了无本之木、无源之水；更何况文章的总数量增加以后，原来按套路来快速解决长文章的方法在短文章面前又失去了原有的魔力，所以新GRE考试更多地还是考查考生在英文基础上的硬实力，以及准确高效地构建逻辑关系的能力。

面对新GRE考试的这种情况，我们唯有认真分析其变化规律并且切实提高自己的学术文章阅读水平。下面，笔者将着力谈一下新GRE考试阅读理解部分对于我们的能力要求，以期对各位读者有所启发。

Note

第二节 新GRE阅读要求

The purpose of the reading comprehension questions is to measure the ability to read with understanding, insight, and discrimination. This type of question explores your ability to analyze a written passage from several perspectives, including the ability to recognize both explicitly stated elements in the passage and assumptions underlying statements or arguments in the passage as well as the implications of those statements or arguments. They are designed to test abilities required to read and understand the kinds of prose commonly encountered in graduate school, including:

- Understanding the meaning of individual words
- Understanding the meaning of individual sentences
- Distinguishing between minor and major points
- Summarizing a passage
- Drawing conclusions from the information provided
- Understanding the structure of a text, how the parts relate to one another
- Identifying the author's perspective
- Identifying strengths and weaknesses

以上几个要求是ETS官方列出的GRE阅读要求达到的能力，这些能力也是未来考生能够进入美国研究生院继续攻读浩如烟波的书籍所必备的。GRE文章是ETS的专家学者们精选学术论文，然后进行大量加工改写而成的，所以无论是单句难度还是整体难度都比日后我们要读的学术论文难，把GRE学好对于以后硕士生、博士生的学术生涯也有着极大的好处，能大大提升考生的硬实力。基于此我们也不难看出，GRE阅读对于考生的要求绝不仅仅是把"英语句子读懂"这么简单，语言层面的问题是个人在美国生活学习的基础，属于"经济基础"；而做学术的生涯更多需要的是分析和处理信息的能力，属于"上层建筑"。我们逐个来看看GRE阅读所要求的能力。

1. 理解词汇的意思

毫无疑问这一点是最基本的要求，也是在阅读任何文章时必备的能力。虽说GRE不考查背景知识，一些具有高度专业性和不可替代性的名词无需读者明白：比如像stratocumulus(层积云)，其具体的定义和特性并不需要我们了解，不过作为一个客观存在体，它在文章中和其他信息之间是存在联系的。但是，很多非专业性词汇或者动词是必须认识的：像impetus这个词，词汇书上给的解释是“刺激、推动力”，在GRE阅读中如果出现，如：A is the impetus of B，传递给考生的信息就是“A是B的原因”，这样信息之间的关系已然构建起来了。

2. 理解单句的含义

GRE的单句难度是很高的，它可能没有文学类文章那么多天马行空的点缀修饰，但是许多句子——哪怕是没有难词的句子——蕴含的意思即使翻译成中文也会让人感觉云里雾里，其实这是一种思维上的难度。比如，一句话的中文解释是这样的：**“没有人能够毫不犹豫地说革命党和保皇党之间存在的矛盾不会被任何人发现”**。我们摄取完意思之后，剩下的就是**“革命党和保皇党之间存在矛盾”**！

3. 区分主要观点和次要观点

GRE阅读文章的学术性决定了贯穿其中有许多的论点，那么一个论点是如何成立的、一个论点和另一个论点之间又是什么关系？这样的问题是我们必须面对的。总论点和分论点之间的区分是基于语句认知完成的，确认二者之间的关系就依赖于句间逻辑关系的辨认：比如第一个观点和第二个观点之间是总分关系、第二个观点和第三个观点之间是平行并列关系、第三个观点和第四个观点是因果支持的关系等等。完成对于观点的解读与认知是我们英语语言本身的任务，而判断和分析观点间的联系是大脑逻辑思维的任务。我们将在本书第二章以及第三章的真题解析中重点讲解相关内容。

4. 总结篇章大意

在GRE的长文章阅读当中，考生读完一段后进行总结是很必要的，因为每一段的出现必然有其客观存在的意义。而且，一段话和另外一段话之间的关系也是需要基于对两段话的大意进行总结才能完成的，理解段落意思、看清段落之间的联系对于我们了解作者的行文思路与态度十分重要。

5. 根据已有信息作出推断

这一点体现在考生经常见到的“推断题”上。但关键在于如何进行推断？我们知道，西方学术思维是以线性哲学为根基的，最强调事物之间的因果关系：有因必有果、无因必无果。我们来看一个例子：

▍例1-1▍

原文：公共政策认为：利用民间集资建造公众设施，如果该项目难以收回成本，则难以集资，没有必要修建。比如，弗吉尼亚政府授权开发商建造公路，但开发商没有从民间获得足够的资金，公路也就没建起来。

推论1：该公路的修建在当地居民间颇具争议，一部分民众不喜欢建路。

推论2：该公路即使建成也很难挣到钱。

这两个推论正确的有几个呢？

正确答案只有一个，是推论2。

因为原文的结果是“**公路没有修建起来**”，根据已有信息，我们知道原因一定是“**公路难以收回成本**”，和推论2是一个意思，这才是正确的。而推论1所说的内容从客观上来讲有可能导致“**公路没有修建起来**”这个结果，但是本文中**没有证据**证明该结果一定是由“**民众有意见**”这个原因导致的，所以这个推论不能作为推断题的正确答案。由此我们可见，GRE的推断题是“讲究证据”的，“可能正确”的答案不能选，只能选“必然正确”的答案，这是一个逻辑收敛的过程。

6. 理解文章结构以及各部分之间的关系

这一点体现在两句话或者两个部分之间的逻辑关系上。GRE阅读中的一个句子是有它的客体性的，即“为何要写这句话”？比如：**写第二句是为了说明第一句，那么第一句就是第二句的逻辑上一层**；取逆否命题后依然成立：**如果第一句不存在的话第二句也没有存在的意义，那么第一句是第二句的逻辑上一层**。这种逻辑上下层的关系主要体现在以下几个方面：主题与论点之间、论点与例子之间、观点和细节之间、细节和补充说明之间。其中，前者都是逻辑上一层。把这些东西搞清楚了，GRE阅读文章就不再那么神秘，而成了一个立体的、有机的信息组成体，我们也就自然很容易了解文章的结构和各部分的关系。

7. 了解作者的观点

了解作者观点是在整篇文章的阅读完毕之后必须完成的任务，GRE阅读不是散文，作者一定会在文中列有观点，哪怕只有一个。我们一方面需要从文章逻辑关系的角度去理解各部分的联系及作者意图，另一方面在阅读时要从态度词入手判断作者的态度。常见的态度词以形容词和副词居多，如：seminal(原创性的，开拓性的)、effective(有效的)、treacherously(用心险恶地)等等。

8. 看清文章的优势与缺陷

这一点对于考生的思维能力要求较高，不但需要看出作者在支持其观点方面做得好的地方，同时也要能看到作者在理论论述部分或者举例证明部分的不足之处。比如：某个结果可能是由三个原因共同导致的，而原文只阐述了两个，在题目中极有可能对剩下的一个原因发问：To complete the causal relationship above, the author's premise is that ______. 这就对考生的分析性思维能力提出了更高的要求。

Note

第三节 新GRE阅读题型分析

新GRE考试阅读理解部分的考题形式由三种基本题型组成：单项选择题、不定项选择题、句子选择题。其中后两种题型都是新GRE考试增加的，第一种单选是经典的常规题目。

Multiple-Choice — Select One Answer Choice

- Read all the answer choices before making your selection, even if you think you know what the answer is in advance.
- The correct answer is the one that most accurately and most completely answers the question posed; be careful not to be misled by answer choices that are only partially true or only partially answer the question. Be careful also not to pick an answer choice simply because it is a true statement.

单项选择题比较常见，从五个选项里选择一个正确答案。需要注意以下几点：首先，**一定要仔细阅读所有的选项**。不同于其他英语考试中的一些题目，错误选项能一眼看穿，GRE考试中有些错误选项的迷惑性极强，可能是文中某些信息的"混搭"。不经过分析和判断是无法直接辨别其是否正确的，更无法从语言、语法层面判断了。

其次，**千万要小心判断你心仪的选项是否真正的"正确"**。这一点和之前第二部分GRE阅读要求中的"根据已有信息作出推断"有些相似，"only partially true or only partially answer the question"是个非常重要的点，有些选项中的内容只是和文章内容"不相违背"、"有可能正确"，但是并不一定是从文中推断出来的，这种选项也是错误的。

第三，**要注意题干的要求**。不能因为某个选项所说的内容无误就默认为其一定是正确答案。比如有的题干中问的是"作者行文的主要意图是什么？"或"作者写这篇文章是出于什么目的？"，而有的答案所描述的却是"本文说的主要内容是……"，这显然与题干要求不符，是错误选项。

Multiple-Choice — Select One or More Answer Choices

(Description: These provide three answer choices and ask you to select all that are correct; one, two, or all three of the answer choices may be correct. To gain credit for these questions, you must select all the correct answers, and only those; there is no credit for partially correct answers.)

- Evaluate each answer choice separately on its own merits; when evaluating one answer choice, do not take the others into account.
- One or more correct answer choices accurately and completely answers the question posed; be careful not to be misled by answer choices that are only partially true or only partially answer the question. Be careful also not to pick an answer choice simply because it is a true statement.

不定项选择题，是新GRE阅读中最难做的题目类型，我们必须把三个选项中所有正确的全都选出来，这道题才能得分。这对考生能否准确地理解文意提出了很高的要求。要注意的第一点就是**选项之间的相互独立性**。考生在研究选项时无需考虑其他选项，选项间不存在关联性，要进行独立分析与判断。

此外，和单选题一样的是，要**小心那些"可能正确"的答案**，我们要选择那些"文中信息"必然可以推出的"内容"；而不能选有可能推出"文中信息"的内容。换言之，要选择"文中信息"的必要条件，不能选"文中信息"的充分不必要条件。

Select-in-Passage

(Description.: The question asks you to select the sentence in the passage that meets a certain description. Choose one of the sentences and click on it; clicking anywhere on a sentence will highlight it.)

- Be careful to evaluate each of the relevant sentences in the passage separately before selecting your answer. Do not evaluate any sentences that are outside the paragraphs under consideration.
- A correct answer choice must accurately match the description given in the question; do not select a sentence if the description only partially applies.

句子选择题也是新增题目类型，要求考生点选出符合题干要求的原文句子即可。GRE的句子点选题不提供选项，需要回原文自行选取。这种题目类型考查考生对原文语句的解读，以及理解句子作用和文章结构的能力。

下面，我们举两个ETS官方样题来分析。第一篇例文我们从解题的步骤上为考生做一些解析；第二篇相对有难度，我们给出译文并注解出文章大致逻辑关系。

❙ 例1-2 ❙

Sample questions 1 to 3 below are based on this passage:

Policymakers must confront the dilemma that fossil fuels continue to be an indispensable source of energy even though burning them produces atmospheric accumulations of carbon dioxide that increase the likelihood of potentially disastrous global climate change. Currently, technology that would capture carbon dioxide emitted by power plants and sequester it harmlessly underground or undersea instead of releasing it into the atmosphere might double the cost of generating electricity. But because sequestration does not affect the cost of electricity transmission and distribution, delivered prices will rise less, by no more than 50 percent. Research into better technologies for capturing carbon dioxide will undoubtedly lead to lowered costs.

Sample Multiple-choice Questions — Select One Answer Choice

1. The passage implies which of the following about the current cost of generating electricity?

(A) It is higher than it would be if better technologies for capturing carbon dioxide were available.

(B) It is somewhat less than the cost of electricity transmission and distribution.

(C) It constitutes at most half of the delivered price of electricity.

(D) It is dwelt on by policymakers to the exclusion of other costs associated with electricity delivery.

(E) It is not fully recovered by the prices charged directly to electricity consumers.

解析

首先，我们需要找到题干中的定位关键词“the current cost of generating electricity”。之后，将这个关键词定位到文章中去，发现这组定位词出现在文章当中的第二句话当中：“Currently, technology that would capture carbon dioxide emitted by power plants and sequester it harmlessly underground or undersea instead of releasing it into the atmosphere might double the cost of generating electricity.”接着，文章的下一句话中出现了这样的比例关系。“But because sequestration does not affect the cost of electricity transmission and distribution, delivered prices will rise less, by no more than 50 percent.”这说明“sequestration”所占的比重不超过总费用的二分之一。既然只有“发电”和“减排”两个过程。那么，发电的花费当然是最多只能占到二分之一了。答案C所说正是：“It constitutes at most half of the delivered price of electricity.”故选。

Answer: C

Sample Multiple-choice Questions — Select One or More Answer Choices
Consider each of the three choices separately and select all that apply.

2. The passage suggests that extensive use of sequestration would, over time, have which of the following consequences?

   A The burning of fossil fuels would eventually cease to produce atmospheric accumulations of carbon dioxide.

   B The proportion of the delivered price of electricity due to generation would rise and then decline.

   C Power plants would consume progressively lower quantities of fossil fuels.

解析

首先，从文章中可以看出，没有什么方法可以“停止”大气中二氧化碳的累积，所以A选项中所提到的“The burning of fossil fuels would eventually cease to produce atmospheric accumulations of carbon dioxide.”显然是错误的。另外，整篇文章中也并没有提供一种方法使得电厂可以“减少化石燃料的使用量”，所以C选项显然不符合题意。由于文章中的最后两句话中指出：“But because sequestration does not affect the cost of electricity transmission and distribution, delivered prices will rise less, by no more than 50 percent. Research into better technologies for capturing carbon dioxide will undoubtedly lead to lowered costs.”所以，随着化石燃料使用量的增加，未来可以预期的发电成本将会先增加后减少。应该选择选项B（The proportion of the delivered price of electricity due to generation would rise and then decline.）由此可以看出，尽管新GRE考试中出现了新的多项选择题型，但是并没有在实质上改变原有的命题核心思想，即考查考生理解文章事实和推断进一步信息的能力。

Answer: B

Sample Select-in-Passage Question

3. Select the sentence that explains why an outcome of sequestration that might have been expected would not occur.

Answer:

“But because sequestration does not affect the cost of electricity transmission and distribution, delivered prices will rise less, by no more than 50 percent.”

【例1-3】

Sample questions 4 to 6 below are based on this passage:

Reviving the practice of using elements of popular music in classical composition, an approach that had been in hibernation in the United States during the 1960s, composer Philip Glass (born 1937) embraced the ethos of popular music without imitating it. Glass based two symphonies on music by rock musicians David Bowie and Brian Eno, but the symphonies' sound is distinctively his. Popular elements do not appear out of place in Glass's classical music, which from its early days has shared certain harmonies and rhythms with rock music. Yet this use of popular elements has not made Glass a composer of popular music. His music is not a version of popular music packaged to attract classical listeners; it is high art for listeners steeped in rock rather than the classics.

译文

第一句：在古典音乐创作中使用流行音乐的元素是一种在20世纪60年代已经销声匿迹的做法，作曲家菲利普·格拉斯(生于1937)使这种方法得以复兴：他并没有简单地模仿流行音乐，而是捕捉到了流行音乐的内在气质。

第二句：格拉斯基于摇滚乐手戴维·鲍伊和布赖恩·伊诺的流行音乐创作了两部交响乐，但是它们听起来却和原创作品大相径庭。

(第二句开始的内容是第一句的细节，处于逻辑下一层。)

第三句：流行元素并没有在格拉斯的古典音乐中显得格格不入，在他的早期作品和摇滚乐之中就分享了某些和声和节奏。

(第三句和第二句的内容构成一个整体，说明格拉斯创作的古典乐自成一格。)

第四句：然而，这种流行元素的使用并没有使格拉斯变成一个流行音乐创作者。

(第四句和第三句形成一个对比。)

第五句：他并非简单地将流行音乐包装成新的版本，借以吸引古典音乐的欣赏者；恰恰相反，他在向那些深深浸淫在摇滚乐中的听众展现古典音乐的高雅艺术之美。

(第五句是第三句和第四句对比的原因解释。)

Sample Multiple-choice Questions — Select One Answer Choice

4. The passage addresses which of the following issues related to Glass's use of popular elements in his classical compositions?

(A) How it is regarded by listeners who prefer rock to the classics

(B) How it has affected the commercial success of Glass's music

(C) Whether it has contributed to a revival of interest among other composers in using popular elements in their compositions

(D) Whether it has had a detrimental effect on Glass's reputation as a composer of classical music

(E) Whether it has caused certain of Glass's works to be derivative in quality

解析

文章在谈到关于格拉斯在创作古典音乐中使用流行元素时提到了以下哪个问题?

(A) 那些喜欢摇滚甚于古典音乐的听众对这种做法是如何评价的。
(A不合适。文章没提到摇滚乐迷们对这种做法的反应。)

(B) 这种做法是怎样对格拉斯的音乐在商业上的成功产生影响的。
(B更不对。全文没有一处提到他的音乐在商业上是否成功的问题。)

(C) 这种做法是否有助于其他音乐家重新在创作中使用流行元素。
(C也不合适。本文并未提到其他音乐家是否也会采用这种方式。)

(D) 这种做法是否对格拉斯作为一个古典音乐作曲家的名声产生不利的影响。
(D也属于无关信息。关于格拉斯的名声问题本文没有提到。)

(E) 这种做法是否已经直接衍生出格拉斯的某些作品。
(E才是正确答案。这种"用流行元素创作古典音乐"的方法在其早期的作品中就有所体现，所以本次的作品才显得那么浑然一体、自成一格。)

Answer: E

Sample Multiple-choice Questions — Select One or More Answer Choices
Consider each of the three choices separately and select all that apply.

5. The passage suggests that Glass's work displays which of the following qualities?

A A return to the use of popular music in classical compositions

B An attempt to elevate rock music to an artistic status more closely approximating that of classical music

C A long-standing tendency to incorporate elements from two apparently disparate musical styles

解析

文章表明下列哪个特质在格拉斯的作品之中被展现了出来?

A 一种在古典音乐创作中对于流行音乐使用的回归
(A是正确选项。用流行元素创作古典音乐这种方法在20世纪60年代已经销声匿迹，是格拉斯让其得以复兴的。)

B 试图将摇滚乐提升到一个与古典音乐更加接近的艺术地位上来
(B是个迷惑性选项，错在了"提升摇滚乐档次"这个说法上。若按人们固有的印象，古典乐的艺术地位的确比摇滚乐高，但是在本文中只提到借用摇滚的流行元素创作古典音乐，并未牵涉提高摇滚乐艺术地位的事情，属于无中生有。)

C 一种由来已久的整合两种截然不同的音乐元素的趋势
(C也是正确选项。所谓 "由来已久"，是因为这种借助流行元素创作古典音乐的方法在格拉斯的早期作品中也有体现。)

Answers: A and C

Sample Select-in-Passage Question

6. Select the sentence that distinguishes two ways of integrating rock and classical music.

Answer:

"His music is not a version of popular music packaged to attract classical listeners; it is high art for listeners steeped in rock rather than the classics."

解析

选择一个能将摇滚乐和古典音乐的两种整合方式区分开来的句子。

正确答案："他并非简单地将流行音乐包装成新的版本，借以吸引古典音乐的欣赏者；恰恰相反，他在向那些深深浸淫在摇滚乐中的听众展现古典音乐的高雅艺术之美。"（文章最后一句。）

笔者在第一章的表4中已列出，在新GRE考试当中，除了传统的GRE阅读文章之外，现在还出现了一种新题型：逻辑单题。所谓逻辑单题，其关键在于考查考生能否用题干中的所有信息进行合理的推论、解释、加强观点、削弱观点，以及找出前提假设。新GRE官方指南中明确写道："All the questions can be answered on the basis of the information provided in the passage（回答所有题目需要的全部信息在原文中都已给出）。"因此考生不需要用文章以外的信息进行推理，而是只能根据原文中的逻辑进行推理。原文以外的信息用得越多，推理过程中的漏洞就越大，思维就越不严密，也就非常容易将原本与文章没有关系的选项错选为答案。

新GRE语文部分出现的逻辑单题的类型大致有：

1. 削弱

问题当中出现weaken是削弱题最明显的标志。

削弱题目的实质是找一个选项来反对、驳斥文章，考查运用文章自身的逻辑来削弱文章。在解题时，首先要找到文章的主论点和主论据，再进行反驳。而且，正确选项经常与文章的主论据非常接近与相关，也正因为如此，削弱题很重要的一个技巧就是正确答案必须基于文章的推理，要与文章的结论发生直接的因果关系。

2. 加强

加强题目非常明显的标志就是问题中会出现strengthen这个词。

加强题目的实质是找一个选项来支持、肯定文章。在解题时，同样要在阅读文章时找到文章的主论点和主论据。加强的方式有两种：补充和重复。一般而言，选项但凡能够加强文章论点成立的可能性，均可成为正确答案的备选，而最后选择的答案必须是所有备选选项中与文章的论证发生最直接因果关系的选项。

3. 解释

问题当中的explain是解释题目最为明显的标志。问题既可以要求考生选择一个选项来解释文章当中某一个特定的现象或结果，也可以要求考生选择一个选项来调和文章中出现的矛盾，使这个表面上矛盾的现象合情合理。

既然是要解释，那么首先就一定要明确解释对象。如果是要求解释某一个特定的现象或结果，那么解释对象一定会在问题中直接出现；如果问题是reconciles the apparent discrepancy/paradox presented in the passage，则为调和矛盾，正确答案可以直接导致矛盾调和后出现的现象。

4. 推论

问题当中的conclusions can most properly be drawn from the information above以及infer等是推论题目非常明显的标志。

推论题的实质是考查文章中的信息融合，通过文章的陈述可能得出什么样的结论，与传统阅读题目中的主题题有些类似。

5. 句子作用

文章当中有加粗的句子，以及问题当中的boldfaced portion plays which of the following roles是句子作用题目最明显的标志。

句子作用题的实质是考查考生对于文章推理中每一个句子所表达的态度以及句子自身在文中地位的把握。从选项分析来看，由于这种题型并不考查文章的具体内容，那么句子作用题的解题方法最大的特点就是不用读懂文章的具体意思。做句子作用题时，考生只需一方面根据大型转折词和结论引导词判断**粗体字**句子的态度；另一方面根据因果标志词判断**粗体字**句子自身的角色和地位。

6. 假设

若问题中要求寻找文章论证的assumption，则为假设题目。

假设题目的实质是考查考生对于文章推理成立所需要的必要条件的把握。必要条件顾名思义就是文章推理成立所必须具备的条件，如果这个条件不成立的话，文章推理也是不能够成立的，因此做假设题目最基本、最重要的思想就是“取非削弱”的思想。从理论上来分，假设主要分为两个类型，一种是defender assumption（防守型假设），一种是supporter assumption（支持型假设）。defender assumption（防守型假设）的形式多体现为否定句，而supporter assumption（支持型假设）的形式多体现为肯定句。因defender assumption（防守型假设）更为基本，故而考试中假设题目的答案也多为否定句。

GRE逻辑单题的难度比经典的阅读文章要容易一些，比与GRE类似的GMAT、LSAT考试中的逻辑题难度也要小一些，但是其选项迷惑性较大，外加在考场上时间紧迫，所以这部分内容对于考生来说并非“手到擒来”。需要同学们在课下勤加练习才能稳步地提高正确率。

❙ 例1-4 ❙

During the day in Lake Constance, the zooplankton *D. hyalina departs for the* depths where food is scarce and the water cold. *D. galeata remains near the* warm surface where food is abundant. Even though *D. galeata grows and* reproduces much faster, its population is often outnumbered by *D. hyalina.*

Which of the following, if true, would help resolve the apparent paradox presented above?

(A) The number of species of zooplankton living at the bottom of the lake is twice that of species living at the surface.

(B) Predators of zooplankton, such as whitefish and perch, live and feed near the surface of the lake during the day.

(C) In order to make the most of scarce food resources, *D. hyalina* matures more slowly than *D. galeata*.

(D) *D. galeata* clusters under vegetation during the hottest part of the day to avoid the Sun's rays.

(E) *D. galeata* produces twice as many offspring per individual in any given period of time as does *D. hyalina*.

译文

在白天的Constance湖中，浮游生物Dh启程到湖水深处，湖水深处食物稀少而且水温很低。Dg停留在温暖的湖水表面，湖水表面食物丰富。即便Dg生长和繁殖要快很多，但是它的数量却经常被Dh所超越。

题目

下列的哪一项，如果成立，将会帮助解决上文呈现出的明显矛盾?

(A) 生活在湖内底部的浮游生物物种数量是生活在湖表面浮游生物物种数量的两倍。

(B) 浮游生物的捕食者，比如说白鱼和鲈鱼，白天在靠近湖表面的地方生活和捕食。

(C) 为了充分利用稀少的食物资源，Dh比起Dg要成熟得更慢。

(D) 在一天最热的时候，Dg群落呆在植物下面来躲避太阳的光线。

(E) 在任何给定的时期中，Dg每一个个体都比Dh产生多一倍的后代。

解析

从问题中help resolve the apparent paradox得知题目是解释矛盾类。文章中对于两种浮游生物Dh与Dg在白天的生存情况做了一番描述，Dh生活在湖水深处，食物稀少，水温低，生长繁殖慢；Dg生活在湖水表面，食物丰富，水温暖，生长繁殖快。按道理来说Dh和Dg相比，Dh的数量应该少，Dg的数量应该多，但是文章中给出的现象却是Dh的数量多于Dg，也就出现了表面上相互矛盾的现象。因此，正确答案应该是可以调和矛盾的选项，使得文章中的现象看似矛盾但是有其合理性，即正确选项可以使Dh的数量多，Dg的数量少。

B选项表明浮游生物的捕食者在湖水表面生活和捕食，那么生活在湖水表面的Dg很有可能被捕食者吃掉，因而虽然生活环境良好、生长繁殖也更快，但是死得也快。捕食者直接影响浮游生物数量，B选项为正确答案。

A选项的概念范围与文章不一致。文章中有比较，比得是Dh和Dg两种浮游生物数量的多少，而A选项中比的是生活在湖水表面和生活在湖水底部的浮游生物物种数量的多少，比较对象发生改变，故而排除。C选项表明Dh比Dg成熟慢，则Dh应该数量少。E选项表明Dg产生的后代多，那么Dg的数量应该多，故而排除。D选项与文章中的现象之间没有直接的因果关系，故而作为无关项而予以排除。

Answer: B

| 例1-5 |

In the United States between 1850 and 1880, the number of farmers continued to increase, but at a rate lower than that of the general population.

Which of the following statements directly contradicts the information presented above?

(A) The number of farmers in the general population increased slightly in the 30 years between 1850 and 1880.

(B) The rate of growth of the United States labor force and the rate of growth of the general population rose simultaneously in the 30 years between 1850 and 1880.

(C) The proportion of farmers in the United States labor force remained constant in the 30 years between 1850 and 1880.

(D) The proportion of farmers in the United States labor force decreased from 64 percent in 1850 to 49 percent in 1880.

(E) The proportion of farmers in the general population increased from 68 percent in 1850 to 72 percent in 1880.

译文

在1850到1880年间，美国的农民人口数量一直在上升，但是其增长率低于美国总人口的增长率。

题目

下列哪一项陈述直接反驳了上文呈现的信息?

(A) 在1850到1880这30年当中，美国总人口中农民人口的数量略微增长。

(B) 在1850到1880这30年当中，美国劳动力的增长率和总人口的增长率同时上升。

(C) 在1850到1880这30年当中，农民人口在美国全国劳动力当中所占比例保持稳定。

(D) 农民人口在美国全国劳动力当中所占的比例下降了，从1850年的64%下降到1880年的49%。

(E) 农民人口在总人口当中所占的比例上升了，从1850年的68%上升到1880年的72%

解析

从问题当中的标志词contradict(反驳)得知这是一道削弱题。文章中说“在1850到1880年间，美国的农民人口数量一直在上升，但是其增长率要低于美国总人口的增长率。”这意味着美国农民人口数量在上升，美国总人口数量也在上升，只不过农民人口数增长得没有总人口数快，由此可知农民在总人口中所占比例相对减小。

文章中有隐含比较，即美国农民人口数量与美国总人口数量之间的比较，虽然问题中是选择与文章中信息相反的选项，也同样要围绕农民人口数量和总人口数量来讨论，这是文章总的概念范围。

E选项表示农民人口在总人口当中所占比例增长，而文章中的信息表示农民人口在总人口当中所占比例下降，为信息相反的选项，因而是正确答案。

A选项表示农民人口总数在总人口当中(the number of farmers in the general population)略微增长，与文章中信息一致，不是反驳，故而不选。B、C、D选项均表示农民人口在美国全国劳动力中所占比例的状态，与文章中的概念范围不一致，故而作为无关选项排除。

Answer: E

例1-6

In the past ten years, there have been several improvements in mountain-climbing equipment. These improvements have made the sport both safer and more enjoyable for experienced climbers. Despite these improvements, however, the rate of mountain climbing injuries has doubled in the past ten years.

Which of the following, if true, best reconciles the apparent discrepancy presented in the passage?

(A) Many climbers, lulled into a false sense of security, use the new equipment to attempt climbing feats of which they are not capable.

(B) Some mountain-climbing injuries are caused by unforeseeable weather conditions.

(C) Mountain climbing, although a dangerous sport, does not normally result in injury to the experienced climber.

(D) In the past ten years there have been improvements in mountain-climbing techniques as well as in mountain-climbing equipment.

(E) Although the rate of mountain-climbing injuries has increased, the rate of mountain-climbing deaths has not changed.

译文

在过去的十年中，登山设备有了进步和改良。这些改良使得这项运动对于经验丰富的登山者而言，变得更加安全和愉快。然而，尽管有了这些提升，登山受伤的比例在过去的十年里却变成了之前的两倍。

题目

下列的哪一个选项，如果成立，最好地调和了上文中明显的差异?

(A) 许多登山者陷入一种错误的安全感中，使用新设备去试图攀登他们本没有能力完成的任务。

(B) 一些登山受伤是由于不可预见的天气状况导致的。

(C) 尽管登山是一项危险的运动，(但是)通常不会导致有经验的登山者受伤。

(D) 在过去的十年当中，除了登山设备的改进之外，也有登山技术的提升。

(E) 尽管登山受伤的比例增长了，(但是)登山死亡的比例没有改变。

解析

从问题中best reconciles the apparent discrepancy得知题目为解释题，具体而言是解释矛盾。文章中描述在过去的十年当中登山设备有了进步和提升，使得登山对于有经验的登山者而言更加安全，那么按道理来说登山受伤的比例应该减小，但是却出现了登山受伤的比例反而增加的现象，这就呈现了一个明显的discrepancy。正确答案应该可以调和这个discrepancy，使得文章中的现象看似矛盾但是有其合理性，同时注意解释的是后面叙述的事情，即因为这个选项，所以"登山受伤的比例变成了两倍"。需要关注的一点是，以however为分割线，文章中相互矛盾的现象的主体是不同的，however之前是"经验丰富的登山者"，however之后是"登山受伤"，若however之后为"经验丰富的登山者的受伤"，则前后主体对应严谨。

A选项为正确答案。在登山设备没有提升之前，这些登山者不会进行本没有能力完成的任务；而现在登山设备提升了，就使一些登山者错误地以为登山很安全，从而贸然尝试他们本没有能力完成的任务，这样一来就造成了登山受伤有所增加。

B选项看似可以解释得通：登山受伤是不可预见的天气状况造成的，但这只是说明有其他的原因可能导致登山受伤，却不能解释为什么登山设备提升了以后登山受伤就变成了两倍，因而不是正确答案。C选项表示通常有经验的登山者不会受伤，D选项表示登山技术有所提升，两者能够说明的是登山受伤不应该增加，并没有解释文章中的discrepancy，因而不是正确答案。E选项谈到登山受伤增加而登山死亡没有增加，仅仅是在承认文章中的现象“登山受伤增加了”，而没有给出原因；同时“登山死亡”对于文章而言，属于偏离的概念范围，因此E选项不是正确答案。

Answer: A

通过几篇例文以及题目的解析，考生朋友们已经大致了解了新GRE阅读部分会出现的题目类型。那么面对这几种基本题型，我们需要具备的能力和准备的方向又该是怎样的呢？传统GRE复习过程中对于语篇结构和句法的把握仍然是必备的手段，新GRE阅读篇幅数量的增多，使得即使是英文基本功很好的人也难以靠“纯翻译英文”这种“死打硬拼”的战略来完成考试了，它更要求我们准确把握文章中各个句子之间的逻辑关系。

英文作为一种“形合”的语言，它的起承转合之间有时需要依赖逻辑关系词的介入和辅助。以【例1-2】中第三题为例，此题表面上是考查考生对句子的理解和信息搜索能力，而实际上则是考查问题中所涉及的结论在原文当中是如何被解释的。如果各位能够注意到题干当中的 “...explains why an outcome of sequestration...”，那么，就可以迅速而直接地定位到原文表示原因的句式（...But because sequestration...）当中。这种why和because之间的微妙对应关系可以泛化到广阔的同类命题当中去。

基于此，我们对在学术英文文章中容易出现的句间关系提示词做了大致总结(请见下页表5)，相信这些信号词的总结会给广大考生在应对新GRE考试阅读理解部分时带来帮助。

通过刚才的论述我们不难看出，GRE阅读作为一种学术性的英文考试，并不像托福、雅思考试那样考查考生对于英语本身的认知能力。对于语言的认知只能体现出考生能够明白一句话、一段话的“主体性”，并不能说明考生能够了解其“客体性”。所谓“客体性”，就是指这个句子或段落和其他句子或段落之间的关系。如果一句话只给我们传递出了它本身的信息，和其他的句子或者文章成分没有关系的话，那么我们也可以说它的存在是没有意义的，这种信息叫做静态信息，是孤立的；而信息一旦和其他的信息建立起了联系以后，就变成了动态信息，所谓“牵一发而动全身”。GRE、GMAT、LSAT考试的阅读文章都强调这种信息的动态性，这种动态性固然可以用上述表格中的关联词、提示词来进行判断，但更重要的是通过理解一个句子和其他句子的意思来进行判断，这一点也一直是我们在课上重点讲的内容。

基于此，本书选取了GRE考试曾经出现过的四篇比较经典的文章，从结构化阅读入手，以句间逻辑关系为基础，和考生朋友们做一次深度分享，我们来一起看看经典的GRE阅读文章及题目其 “庐山真面目”究竟是怎样的。

表5 新GRE考试阅读理解中常见句间关系词总结

1	分类式中的标志词		
	categories	classification	groups
	sorts	classes	
2	排序式中的标志词		
	first	now	later
	last		
3	列举式中的标志词		
	next	another	first
	second	also	
4（1）	比较式中的标志词		
	compare	like/alike	resemble
	in the same manner		
4（2）	对比式中的标志词		
	although	however	but
	different		
5（1）	表原因的标志词		
	because	for this reason	since
	attribute to	traceable	
5（2）	表结果的标志词		
	as a result	in effect	therefore
	reflection	motivation	expansion
6	定义式的标志词		
	define	term means	
	defined as	that is	
7	例证式的标志词		
	for example	for instance	illustrate
	specifically	such as	
8（1）	表示问题的标志词		
	problem	duskiness	fogginess
	phenomenon	dilemma	mistiness
8（2）	表示解决的标志词		
	solution	remedy	therapy
	resolve	resolution	

第二章

精讲GRE结构化阅读

第一节 结构化阅读

通过第一章的论述，大家应该已经清楚了解到GRE阅读是学术英文的阅读：一方面体现在词句的解读上相较于普通文章或者文学类文章繁复；更重要的一方面在于，学术文章在阅读的过程中和别的文章有很大差别。阅读学术文章不等同于我们平时习惯的一般英语考试篇章阅读，也不等同于欣赏英美文学作品，它强调的是考生需要分析清楚文章内在的逻辑关系。这也是为何很多考生一开始接触GRE阅读之时会有一些不适应，别的文章是把单句解读明白了以后就可以读懂，而GRE文章不然，需要捋清其中的逻辑关系。为了解决这样的问题，本书在此环节中为考生们着力描述一个重点内容，即“结构化阅读”。

结构化阅读与自然阅读的一个重大区别在于它强调分析句子存在的作用。在大部分的英文考试当中，阅读理解部分考查的只是读明白句子所说的意思，以及把题目做对。而GRE考试中对于句子的把握更深了一层，理解句意是必要条件，而不是考查的内容：在GRE考试中从未出现过一道直接考查句子意思的题目，也没出现过考查句子中指代词(that、this)的题目，真正的考查点是从句意中能够推断出什么，以及某句话的作用等等。这就是GRE考试和其他许多以英语为载体的考试一个重要的不同点。如果说别的很多英文考试是“阅读英文”，GRE更像是在进行“英文阅读”。基于此，我们考生要做到的除了训练基本功以外，应该还要培养一种科学的阅读方法：需要明白每句话存在的作用以及这句话和其他句子的关系——即句间逻辑关系。

在GRE阅读文章当中，常见的句间逻辑关系基本分成三种：

1. 逻辑上下层关系

这种关系是最多的，其特征在于目的性，如：“若写A是为了写B，则B是A的逻辑上一层”。最直接的例子就是For example，后面出现的例子就是“逻辑下一层”，例子之前的理论就是“逻辑上一层”，例子的存在是为了说明“逻辑上一层”的。在GRE阅读当中也有很多时候作者把For example这样的提示词删掉，故而需要考生通过阅读句意把这种关系找到：

例2-1

Indeed a curiously persistent refusal to credit Hansberry with a capacity for intentional irony has led some critics to interpret the play's thematic conflicts as mere confusion, contradiction, or eclecticism. Isaacs, for example, cannot easily reconcile Hansberry's intense concern for her race with her ideal of human reconciliation.

译文

第一句： 诚然，质疑汉斯贝里蓄意安置讽刺细节导致一些文学评论家们误解了该戏剧的貌似冲突的主题，认为这部戏剧的主题很混乱、矛盾，甚至是折中主义。

第二句： **比如**像伊塞克，就难以把汉斯贝里提到的强烈的种族感和全人类和平相处有机地结合起来。

这是逻辑上下层的最基本形式，第二句话作为第一句话的例子。考生也可以把这两句话看成一个整体，称之为一个"逻辑集团"——这个集团的主要意思就是为了说明：有人会误认为"戏剧"的主题是冲突的。在阅读的过程中，即使考生不能准确地辨析第二句的意思，但是起码可以明白不管第二句话有多繁杂，它的作用一定是为了说明第一句话。这对于考生解决阅读理解中的"作用题"会有帮助。

诚然，不是所有时候我们都能够看到句间出现"for example"、"such as"等等这类"可爱"的字眼的。有些时候两句话的内容之间关联紧密，前面一句话是一个总述，后边的句子是细节描述；或者前面是细节，后面是总结性的句子。像这种关系，也属于典型的逻辑上下层：

【例2-2】

Scholars often fail to see that music played an important role in the preservation of African culture in the United States. They correctly note that slavery stripped some cultural elements from Black people—their political and economic systems—but they underestimate the significance of music in sustaining other African cultural values.

译文

第一句： 学者们往往意识不到**音乐**对于保留**非洲文化**的重要性。

第二句： 学者们意识到奴隶制的确剥夺了黑人的一些文化元素，但是仍然低估了**音乐**对于传承**非洲文化**的重要性。

这个例子中的两句话就是"总述与细节的关系"。在GRE阅读文章当中，虽然文章主题是以论述占绝大部分篇幅，但是还是会有一些叙述型内容的出现。这些叙述型内容几乎百分之百都有逻辑上一层，否则文章会变成流水账。所以考生们不但要依靠英文基本功把这些细节读明白，还要分析清楚这些细节的叙述和论述之间的关系。

但是，在阅读文章的过程当中，并非所有的逻辑上下层关系都表现在"举例"、"列举"、"细节"这样的结构上；换言之，有些句子之间即使加上"For example"这样的字眼也无法理出头绪，这就需要我们利用非常重要的反向论证的方法来确定关系了。只需要将**"若写A是为了写B，则B是A的逻辑上一层"**的前半部分进行"逆反"就可以得出非常重要的结论：**"若B不存在的话A存在没有意义，那么B是A的逻辑上一层"**，这种方法也是解决两句话关系的极其重要的手段。

【例2-3】

Although the development of new infrastructure （such public facilities as power plants, schools, and bridges）is usually determined by governmental planning, sometimes this development can be planned more flexibly and realistically by private investors who anticipate profit from the collection of user fees.

Such profits can contribute to the financing of more infrastructure if demand proves great enough, whereas the reluctance of developers to invest in such projects can signal that additional infrastructure is not needed. During the economic boom of the 1980's, for example, the state of Virginia authorized private developers to build a $300 million toll road. These developers obtained the needed right-of-way from property owners, but by 1993 they still had not raised the necessary financing. The unwillingness of investors to finance this project does not negate the viability of privately financed roads; rather, it illustrates a virtue of private financing. If a road appears unlikely to attract enough future traffic to pay for the road, then it should not be built.

译文

第一句： 尽管**基础设施**（如发电厂、学校和桥梁）通常由**政府规划**，但是有时候**私人投资**的建设模式更为灵活并且切合实际，同时私人投资者会从设施使用者的集资中获取一些**利润**。

第二句： 若对基础设施的需求足够多，这些**利润**可有助于以后更多的建造；同样，如果投资者不愿意给钱，则说明没必要再建造了。

本文第一句和第二句的句意并不难，关键在于分析清楚相互的关系。看起来这两句话是顺承连接，可以看做一个整体。这种说法并没有错误，但是忽略了这两句话的内在联系，那就是第一句话中的副词部分：more flexibly and realistically，而私人投资的这种优势就具体体现在第二句话当中。因此，第二句话是对第一句话的细节阐述，属于第一句话的逻辑下一层，是为第一句话服务的。

第三句： 比如，在80年代的经济繁荣期弗吉尼亚州（政府）授权**私人投资者**建造一条市值三亿的收费公路。

第四句： 这些开发商们从地产拥有者手里获得了足够的建筑用地，但是直到1993年他们都**没有**筹到足够的**资金**。

第三句中出现了"for example"的提示词，很明显其中提到的弗吉尼亚州的例子是对第二句话的举例，处于第二句的逻辑下一层。第四句话也是细节，可以作为第三句的逻辑下一层，也可以和第三句合并形成一个"集团"，两句话相当于一句。

第五句： 人们不乐意给钱并非否定**私人投资**公路（修建）这种模式的可行性；恰恰相反，这样一个例子却印证出了私人投资的一个**优点**。

第六句： （优点就是，）如果这条公路难以吸引足够的交通流量来为其付款，那就不应该建它。

本文的逻辑关系分析最难的地方在于第五句和第六句话。这两句的句意很容易，考生也不难看出这两句是对于第三句和第四句弗吉尼亚州例子的补充说明，其意在表明弗吉尼亚案例体现的是私人投资这种方式的优点。那么这里的逻辑关系的分析就需要用到一种分析方法：取反。

首先我们把第三、四句作为一个整体，五、六句作为一个整体（因为他们之间内部的关系更多是叙述，叙述是没有逻辑关系的），看看这两个部分哪一个逻辑层面更高，或者说不可或缺。假设我们将第五、六句删掉的话，那么全文的例子肯定是不完整的。但是，这里的"不完整"指的是文意方面的残缺，和逻辑层面无关。我们要考虑的是，如果没了第五、六句的话，第三、四句存在还有没有意义？答案是肯定的。因为第三、四句描述的例子是为了说明"私人投资具有灵活性"，换言之其最直接的逻辑上一层在于第二句话的理论。缺少了第五、六句的补充说明，文章作者还可以利用别的语句把意思补全。假设我们将第三、四句删掉的话，只看第五、六句，作为第三、四句例子的补充说明，如果没了具体的例子的话，这种补充说明的存在是毫无意义的，因为必须有了例子才有对它“补充说明”的必要。故而，第五、六句是第三、四句的逻辑下一层。

在本书的文章结构化分析过程中，为了使读者能够更加直接明了地回顾文章逻辑关系，我们利用逻辑关系图来予以概括表示。我们运用统一标准，用虚线箭头表示逻辑上下层的关系，虚线的箭头指向逻辑上一层。

所以，【例2-3】的逻辑关系图如下：

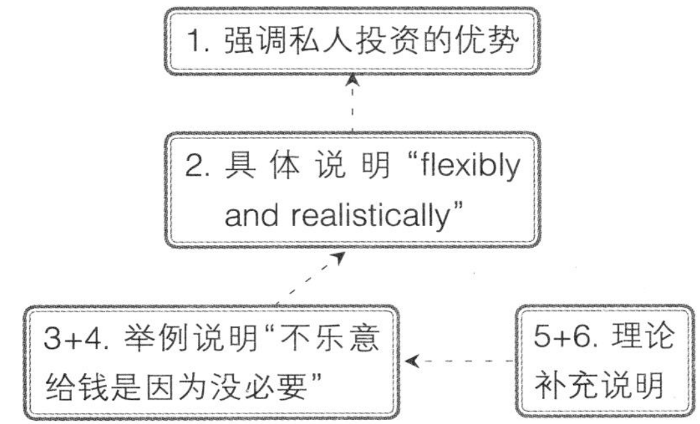

2. 平行并列关系

这是另外一种常见的句间逻辑关系，比如作者为了得出结论A，用了两个分论点B和C，那么B和C就处于同一个逻辑层面上。与此同时，分论点B和C在得出A的过程上，不能有任何的交叉和重合性，相互之间也不能有任何的因果关系，才能说明B和C之间是平行并列的关系。换言之，B或者C两个分论点无论删掉其中的哪一个，都不会影响另一个和A之间的关系，更不会影响另一个分论点存在的意义。如果这样的话，那么我们就称B和C之间是平行并列的关系。

例2-4

The physical properties of most tissues can be matched by careful selection of raw materials: metals, ceramics, or several varieties of polymer materials. Even the requirement that biomaterials processed from these materials be nontoxic to host tissue can be met by techniques. But achieving necessary matches in physical properties across interfaces between living and nonliving matter requires knowledge of which molecules control the bonding of cells to each other—an area that we have not yet explored thoroughly.

译文

第一句：通过精细筛选的各种原材料——金属、陶瓷、其他各种高分子化合物，能够实现与绝大部分人体组织的**生理特性**相匹配。

第二句：即使是“这些生物材料要对机体组织**无毒无害**”这样的要求，也能通过技术手段得以**实现**。

第三句：但是，要使人体组织和移植组织之间连接面的生理特性相互匹配，就涉及“哪些分子控制着细胞之间的连接”这样的知识——这是一个我们还**未搞清楚**的领域。

在这三句话当中，第一句和第二句之间的关系就是一种平行并列。第一句和第二句的存在作用就在于突出转折之后的“问题”所在，故而此二者之间相互不影响，这是比较简单的一种平行并列关系。当然，除了这种平行之外，平行并列关系还可以以其他的表现形式呈现，比如举例：

例2-5

This underappreciation of the social sciences contrasts oddly with what many see as their overutilization. Game theory is pressed into service in studies of shifting international alliances. Models from economics and demography become the definitive tools for examining the financial base of social security.

译文

第一句： 对于**社会科学**的低估和对于其的过度利用形成了奇怪的鲜明**对比**。
第二句： **博弈论**目前在研究国际间盟友关系的变换方面起到了作用。
第三句： **经济学模型和人口统计学模型**对于研究社会稳定的金融基础方面已成为了决定性的方式。

这三个句子的关系相对来说是更为标准的学术文章写法，先写理论然后给出两个例子。很显然这两个例子之间是一种平行并列，如果作者愿意的话，再加两个例子也没有问题。这种也是最简单的一种写法，需要考生在阅读的过程中以及在自己写作的时候能够顺利识别并使用。

3. 因果关系

除了上述两种逻辑关系之外，第三种就是因果关系了。如果说前两种体现更多的是作者的写作思路的话，那么第三种更多体现的就是客观发展规律了。由于像GRE这种学术型文章中每句话传达的意思较多而且严谨，所以文章的发展往往是靠两句话内容之间的因果关系承接的。两句话甚至几句话之间的承接方式往往是没有任何提示词的，只有把句子意思读明白，才能顺利看清其中的逻辑关系。这一点也是GRE阅读没有投机取巧机会的原因所在，在某些考试中考生可以通过各种技巧手段来做到“少读”甚至“不读”就把分数稳稳拿到，那些方法对于GRE、LSAT阅读这种高端文章来说是很难有用的，具体细节我们会在随后的解题方法章节中向大家介绍。基于此，因果关系往往是考生难以瞬间梳理出来的，所以我们就更有必要一方面努力强化自己的长难句阅读能力，另一方面多加训练分析信息的能力。

例2-6

Extended debate concerning the exact point of origin of individual folktales told by Afro-American slaves has unfortunately taken precedence over analysis of the tales' meaning and function. Cultural continuities with Africa were not dependent on importation and perpetuation of specific folktales in their pristine form.

译文

第一句： 不幸的是，目前关于美国黑人民间故事**精确起源的问题**的争论已然超过了对于这些**故事意义和作用**的分析。
第二句： 非洲文化的传承并非依靠引入故事并维持其**原始面貌**来实现的。

对于上面的这两个句子，我相信有50%的人在第一眼看完之后最直接的反应是：“这两句话没啥关系”。这种反应很正常，但是在GRE阅读当中却并没有那么多的“自然而然”，我们之前说过这是一门考查学术性思维的考试，如果有那么多的“想当然”或是“随便”，那是肯定不符合它的水平。第一句话中的“taken precedence over”就是“超越、超过”的意思，整句话所要表达的主要内容是：**关于故事起源的讨论已经超过了关于意义的讨论。**

如果第一句是这个意思的话，那么它的性质是陈述，而非论述，其中没有作者观点态度的表达，也不可能成为主题句。但是，这句话中有一个极其重要的副词“unfortunately(不幸地)”，有了这个副词之后整个句子的性质就发生了变化。先前陈述的意思马上就变成了：**没有必要过分关注故事的准确起源**，这样一来就有了作者的态度。这时再看到第二句话的时候，即“**非洲文化的传承并非依靠引入故事并维持其原始面貌来实现的**”，我们就不难发现第二句话实际上是第一句话的“原因”，作者在第二句话中给出了他发表第一句话观点的理论依据。这种因果关系在本书中用实线箭头来表示，箭头指向表示“结果”，起始端表示“原因”。

逻辑图

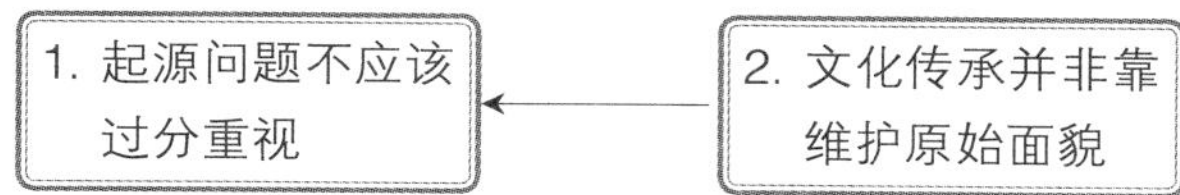

除此之外，因果关系还可以和其他的逻辑关系相结合。GRE阅读是学术英文阅读，考生们在读到文中的信息时，大脑运作的过程应该是客观分析并接受，而不是批判。如果通过原文意思能看出来举例是因果关系还是逻辑上下层关系，考生就没有任何必要去思考“原文的这个例子或者理论作为原因，其关系是否充分并完美?”那是GRE写作环节的要求；对于阅读来说，就是保持头脑空白，将客观分析替代主观批判。而这其中的难点就在于考生能否将其分析清楚。

【例2-7】

African music was based on a total vision of life in which music was not an isolated social domain. In African culture music was pervasive, serving not only religion, but all phases of life. The methods that a community devises to perpetuate itself come into being to preserve aspects of the cultural legacy that that community perceives as essential. Music was so inextricably a part of African culture that it became a crucial means of preserving the culture.

译文

第一句： 非洲音乐是“**全景式俯察生活**”(based on total vision of life)，而非“孤立片段”(isolated social domain)。

第二句： **音乐**遍及非洲生活的每个角落，而不仅仅为宗教服务。

第三句： 一个社会群体用以使自身长存的方式最终得以成形，就是保全该社会群体的核心文化。

第四句： 音乐作为非洲文化中不可分割的一部分，是保存黑人文化极为重要的一种方式。

这四句话当中有着相对明显的因果关系。其提示就在第四句的“so”这个单词，前几句是第四句作者发表观点的原因。在前面的第一句和第二句话很明显是逻辑上下层的关系：第二句话作为第一句的细节，处于逻辑下一层。真正的难点在于第三句话，需要分析它和其他句子之间的逻辑关系。绝大部分读者肯定已经感觉出来了，第三句话应该作为第四句成立的原因，但是还有一个问题：第一句又如何安排呢？在分析因果的过程中需要思考一个关键的问题，那就是：

(因为)第三句，(所以)第四句，这样的逻辑关系是否能够成立?

答案显然是否定的。第三句中连“音乐”的影子都没有，怎么可能得出“音乐是传承文化的重要手段”

呢？实际上，在这一段话当中，第一句和第三句是平行并列的关系，作为两个分论点：

（因为）音乐覆盖非洲生活的全部，（又因为）核心的文化才能作为手段来传承非洲文化，（所以）音乐是传承黑人文化的一个重要手段。

逻辑图

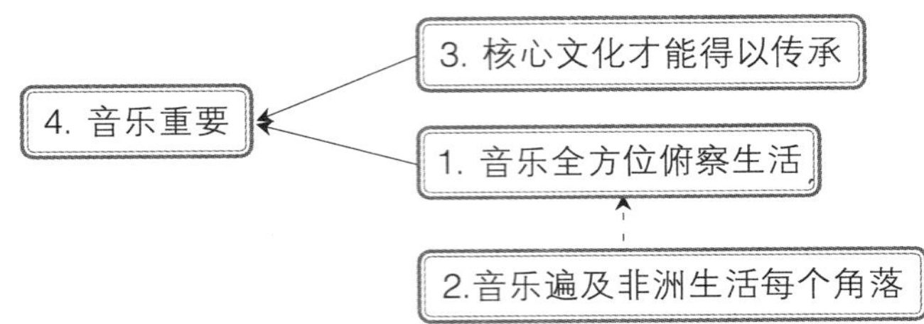

Note

第二节 题目解法剖析

谈到解题的时候，很多考生的第一反应就是：有没有那种看几个关键词甚至连文章都不用看就可以选对答案的方法？大家应该考过包括国内和国外出题的各种各样的英语考试，必须承认的是在很多英语考试当中存在着很多快速并且正确率较高的做题捷径。但是很可惜，在GRE、LSAT、GMAT这些美国研究生院的考试当中，这种情况的可能性几乎就是不存在的：这些考试最基本的一个要求就是要先读完并理解文章之后才能做题。这很好理解，因为GRE阅读部分在设计的原则上就不是为了让考生简简单单找到技巧就能解答问题的，它测试的是考生分析和处理信息的一种能力。鉴于此，对于解题我们是不是就完全没有方法了呢？也并非如此，既然考试要求分析性的思维能力，我们就不妨从思维的角度入手，看看在解题的过程中应当如何思考。

1. 主题题解法

很多文章结束之后往往第一道题就是主题题，常见的问法有以下几种：

(1) Which of the following best describes the passage?

(2) The main idea of the passage is that...

(3) The author is primarily concerned with...

对待这种主题题，很多人的第一反应就是马上回想全文的主要内容。虽不能说错，但是很多时候由于文章较为晦涩，考生难以正确地回忆并总结出原文的主要内容。基于此，从结构化阅读的角度来看，学术类、论述型的文章通常是有主题句的，主题句的特点不在于其句式是否是判断句，也不在于它有多么强烈的态度词，而在于文中的其他句子是否是为之服务的。只要其他句子都是为了这句话而写，那么这句话自然就是主题句。故而，解答主题题的一种方法，就是通过结构化阅读“**找到文章的逻辑最高层**”。

例2-8

Paule Marshall's *Brown Girl, Brownstones* (1959) was a landmark in the depiction of female characters in Black American literature. Marshall avoided the oppressed and tragic heroine in conflict with White society that had been typical of the protest novels of the early twentieth century. Like her immediate predecessors, Zora Neale Hurston and Gwendolyn Brooks, she focused her novel on an ordinary Black woman's search for identity within the context of a Black community. But Marshall extended the analysis of Black female characters begun by Hurston and Brooks by depicting her heroine's development in terms of the relationship between her Barbadian American parents, and by exploring how male and female roles were defined by their immigrant culture, which in turn was influenced by the materialism of White America. By placing characters within a wider cultural context, Marshall attacked racial and sexual stereotypes and paved the way for explorations of race, class, and gender in the novels of the 1970's.

译文

第一句： 葆拉·马绍尔1959年出版的作品 *Brown Girl*, *Brownstones* 中对于**女性角色**的描绘在美国黑人文学史上是个里程碑。

第二句： 马绍尔规避了20世纪初期传统反抗小说中描绘“一个受压迫的悲情**女主角**与**白人社会**斗争”这样的典型桥段。

（第一句是第二句的逻辑上一层，是个结论，第二句是细节的展开。）

第三句： 正如她的前辈们（佐拉·尼尔·赫斯顿和格温德琳·布鲁克斯）一样，马绍尔在小说中着重表现一个寻常的黑人妇女在黑人社会中**追寻自我**的过程。

（第三句实际上可以看做马绍尔的写作特征。）

第四句： 但是，马绍尔同时也拓宽了前辈们对于黑人妇女的分析研究思路：通过与其巴贝多人父辈的关系描绘了女主角的发展过程；探寻男性和女性角色是如何由**移民文化**而界定的，而这种移民文化又被美国**白人社会的物质文化**所影响。

（第四句和第三句形成了一种对比，为了对比突出马绍尔在前人基础之上的突破，这种对比也是第一句话中结论成立的原因。）

第五句： 通过把一个黑人角色置于白人文化背景之下，马绍尔抨击了关于性别和种族的老套模式，还为20世纪70年代小说中对种族、阶级、性别方面的探索铺平了道路。

（第四、五句处于同一个逻辑层面，都是细节。）

逻辑图

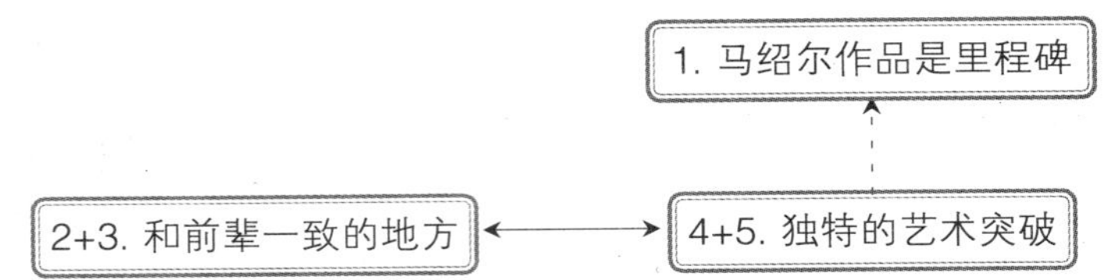

题目

1. The passage is primarily concerned with

(A) comparing the works of three Black American authors

(B) describing common themes in Black American literature

(C) discussing an important work in Black American literature

(D) providing insights about Black American literature in the early twentieth century

(E) providing historical information about the writing of Black American novels in the second half of the twentieth century

解析

本题是典型的主题题，问本文所述的主要内容。本文属于比较典型的结论解释型文章，文章的逻辑最高层也不难寻找。第一句话处于全文的逻辑最高层，而这种论述型的文章中逻辑的最高层就是作者主要关注的内容。

(A) 比较三位黑人作家的作品

（A不正确。典型的鱼目混珠，本文主要谈论的只有马绍尔一个人，另外两位只是为了衬托她而已。）

(B) 叙述美国黑人文学中普遍的主题

（B也不合适。本文主要论述的内容是马绍尔的作品，关于黑人文学的讨论只是对其起到一种衬托的作用。）

（C）谈论美国黑人文学史上一部重要的作品

（C是本题的正确答案。逻辑最高层是本文的第一句话。）

（D）对20世纪初的美国黑人文学给出真知灼见

（D把内容放大了。本文主要讨论的不是黑人文学，而只是一部作品和一位作家。）

（E）针对20世纪后半段的美国黑人文学创作提供了历史性信息

（E也不合适。文章不是在陈列信息，而是借其信息评述马绍尔的作品。）

Answer: C

上述例子是一种非常典型的论述型文章主题题解法。但并非所有文章都是严格的论述，除此之外，还有以叙述为主的文章。由于叙述是没有逻辑关系的，所以对于以叙述为主的文章，考生需要把文章的主要内容多加总结。如果出现主题题的话，其正确答案一定是概括了全文内容的选项。（该内容属于基本功的层面，在本章中暂且不加赘述。）

2. 细节题、推断题解法

说完主题题之后，我们来看另外两种非常常见的题目类型：细节题和推断题。考生可能会想为什么本书要把这两种题目类型放在一起来讲？其原因在于，这两种题目都不牵涉原文中逻辑层面的变化，或者说基本都可以在一个句子当中或一个逻辑集团内部予以解决。如果说GRE阅读总体考查的逻辑思维能力是一座大厦的话，那么细节题就像是构建大厦的水泥混凝土：考查一个考生对于句意等基础语言能力的把握；推断题就像是构建大厦的钢筋结构：其存在令大厦的实体以固定的形态组合起来，工程师只有保证每一处的钢结构稳定，才敢确保整个大厦在工程上是完美无缺的。

对于细节题，我们定位的依据就是题干当中出现的关键词，比如：特定名称、复合词、时间状语、引号内容等等。然后回文定位，这里的定位不光是指定位该关键词出现的句子，实际上该句子所在的整个逻辑集团都有可能成为细节题的答案所在。细节题的题干通常出现的形式有以下几种：

（1）According to the passage, ...

（2）The passage states that which of the following was true...

对待这种细节题，我们一般采用的方法都是进行同义改写，因为这种细节题的答案往往都是**对原文句子进行的语言重现**，包括：变换同义词、变换句型、变换同根词词性等等。比如在原文的句子中出现

Such historians have **broadened** the **conventional** view of feminism.

改写之后为：

Such historians have **expanded** the **traditional** view of feminism.

在这个例子当中，语言改写的特征体现得非常明显。细节题说到底是对考生英语基础能力的一个考量，因此其技巧也比较少，中国考生亟待提高的是词汇量，这样才能在做题的过程中保证速度，至少在读选项时能做到又快又好。

如【例2-8】阅读文章的另外一个题目：

Like her immediate predecessors, Zora Neale Hurston and Gwendolyn Brooks, she focused her novel on an ordinary Black woman's search for identity within the context of a Black community.

2. According to the passage, Hurston, Brooks, and Marshall are alike in that they

(A) did not examine the effects of White culture on their characters' lives

(B) were heavily influenced by the protest novels of the early twentieth century

(C) used Black communities as the settings for their novels

(D) wrote primarily about the difficulties their characters encountered in White culture

(E) wrote exclusively about female characters and the experiences of women

解析

这是一道直接事实题，问"Hurston, Brooks和 Marshall此三人的相似点何在"？这种题目只需要定好位就足够了。本文在第三句话强调的就是马绍尔和这几位前辈们之间的共性，即"关注一个寻常的黑人妇女在黑人社会中追寻自我的过程"。

(A) 都不去考量白人文化对于作品中人物生活的影响

(B) 都深受20世纪早期反抗小说的影响

(C) 都以黑人群体作为行文的背景

(D) 都主要描写人物在白人文化中所经历的艰辛

(E) 都只写女性人物及其经历

Answer: C

本题的答案显而易见，即C选项。由此可见，只要我们能够顺利找到定位点，正确解读题干和选项，做对细节题并不难。

我们再来看推断题。很多人误以为推断题就是会将那种一般正常人都想不到的选项作为正确答案，也有人误把"推断"当成了"推理游戏"，把考生一个个都当做了"柯南"。实际上，GRE阅读理解部分的推断题在很大程度上与细节题极为相似，每道推断题的答案都可以在原文当中找到线索和证据，而不是凭空联想得出或者"想当然"就能符合题目要求的信息。原因在于GRE考试对于考生逻辑思维的要求在于"逻辑收敛"，而非 "逻辑发散"；相比较更趋近于本能的发散来说，收敛更加符合理性分析客观存在的要求——你能读懂这句话吗，并且能在一定程度上满足论证过程中的逆向必要性。对于未来要做学术的人来说，言而有据的推断是非常重要的一种素质。故而本书把推断题和细节题二者统一作一个论述，就是为了让考生意识到：推断题一点也不可怕，只要我们能够找到对应的信息点和逻辑关系就能做对。

还是【例2-8】阅读文章的题目：

3. It can be inferred that the author of the passage would describe *Brown Girl, Brownstones* as being

(A) completely different from novels written before 1959

(B) highly influenced by novels written in the early twentieth century

(C) similar to the protest novels that preceded it

(D) important in the late 1950's but dated today

(E) an important influence on novels written in the 1970's

解析

这是一道态度推断题，问文章作者会怎么描述*Brown Girl, Brownstones*这部作品，下面哪种说法对？

（A）和1959年之前的作品完全不一样
（这个1959是第一句话中提到的该作品的出版时间，作者认为该作品具有里程碑意义，但这并不代表它就和之前的作品完全不一样。况且马绍尔在写作关注点方面和前辈们是一致的。）

（B）受到20世纪早期作品的很大影响
（B也不合适。文章第二句提到，马绍尔规避了20世纪早期作品写作风格的“影响”。）

（C）和之前的反抗小说很是类似
（错的原因和B一致，同样在第二句能找到答案。）

（D）在50年代举足轻重，但是现如今已然过时
（这个选项同样是错误的。作者没提到过时不过时的问题。）

（E）对70年代的作品有着重大影响
（E是本题的正确答案。作者在最后一句话的后半句明确提到这部作品“为70年代的探索铺平了道路”，进行简单的逻辑转化即可得出。）

Answer: E

3. 作用题解法

作用题是GRE阅读常见题型，旨在考查应试者能否判断出作者提到某句话或者某个特定名词的意图。我们在之前的论述中说过，一个句子有它的主体性和客体性，客体性就体现在作者写这个句子的目的所在。常见的作用题题干有如下几种形式：

（1）The author describes something most probably intended to...
（2）The author mentions “XX” primarily in order to emphasize...
（3）The primary purpose of the passage is to...

那么基于这种题目考查的方向，我们也就不难想出解决办法了。既然是问写某句话或者某个词的作用是什么，很明显这种题目的正确答案应该去寻找那句话的**逻辑上一层**。只要找到了逻辑上一层，句子或词汇的客体性就被完全体现出来了。这种题目也是学术型、论述性强的文章所必考的，请考生务必引起重视。

例2-9

This is not to deny that the Black gospel music of the early twentieth century differed in important ways from the slave spirituals. Whereas spirituals were created and disseminated in folk fashion, gospel music was composed, published, copyrighted, and sold by professionals.

题目

1. The author mentions “folk fashion” (line 2) most likely in order to

（A）counter an assertion about the role of improvisation in music created by Black people

（B）compare early gospel music with gospel music written later in the twentieth century

（C）make a distinction between gospel music and slave spirituals

（D）introduce a discussion about the dissemination of slave spirituals

（E）describe a similarity between gospel music and slave spirituals

解析

本题问“作者提到folk fashion（民间风格），其最主要的目的是什么”？定位之后我们发现这个“folk fashion”出现在第二句话，第二句话是对第一句话的举例说明，那么第一句话的内容就是“folk fashion”的逻辑上一层，是其意在表达的东西，即：为了表达“福音音乐和奴隶圣歌有着重大区别”。

（A）反对关于“即席而作在黑人创作的音乐中的地位”的论断

（这并非第二句话的意图，“即席而作”这个信息在第二句中没出现，这个选项却张冠李戴，属于比较低级的错误。）

（B）将早期的福音音乐和20世纪后期有文字记载的福音音乐进行比较

（这个选项中出现了文章中并没有提及的信息，虽然是“进行比较”，但是完全和原文所提及的比较内容不符合。）

（C）把奴隶圣歌和福音音乐作一个区分

（这是本题的正确答案。作者之所以要写到“folk fashion”，就是为了将奴隶圣歌的这个特点和福音音乐的“professional”特点进行对比，以突出二者的不同；就是为了通过这个例子来说明第一句话的内容：二者有着重大区别。）

（D）引入关于奴隶圣歌传播方式的讨论

（本句话的确牵涉到了关于奴隶圣歌的传播，作者也很直接地给出了信息，它的特点就是以一种“folk fashion”的方式来传播。但是，作者写“folk fashion”并非为了就它的传播方式进行讨论，奴隶圣歌的传播方式并非作者所关心的事情，作者关心的是它和福音音乐的区别。）

（E）描述奴隶圣歌和福音音乐的相似之处

（这一点就和我们所分析的结果南辕北辙了，应该是二者的重大区别。）

Answer: C

由此可见，作用题实际上并不难，关键在于分析清楚特定位置的文字处于文章结构的哪一个逻辑层面，至于定位往往并不难找。所以有很多流传甚广的各种各样的阅读做题大法或者技巧，过分强调回文章找到某个特定信息进行定位就能做题，看似举重若轻，实则只是以“做不对是因为你不会找”这样的噱头把考生蒙蔽了，让考生以为自己的问题是出在了“找信息”上，却忽略了阅读的逻辑性和结构性，这是不可取的。

第三节 GRE试题讲解

1. 社会科学类

黑人音乐及传承

Scholars often fail to see that music played an important role in the preservation of African culture in the United States. They correctly note that slavery stripped some cultural elements from Black people—their political and economic systems—but they underestimate the significance of music in sustaining other African cultural values. African music, unlike the music of some other cultures, was based on a total vision of life in which music was not an isolated social domain. In African culture music was pervasive, serving not only religion, but all phases of life, including birth, death, work, and play. The methods that a community devises to perpetuate itself come into being to preserve aspects of the cultural legacy that that community perceives as essential. Music, like art in general, was so inextricably a part of African culture that it became a crucial means of preserving the culture during and after the dislocations of slavery.

Sample Multiple-choice Questions — Select One Answer Choice

1. The primary purpose of the passage is to

(A) analyze the impact that slavery had on African political and economic systems

(B) review the attempt of recent scholarship to study the influence of African music on other music

(C) correct the failure of some scholars to appreciate the significance of music in African culture

(D) survey the ways by which people attempt to preserve their culture against the effects of oppression

(E) compare the relative importance of music with that of other art forms in culture

Sample Multiple-choice Questions — Select One Answer Choice

2. In line 5, the phrase "isolated social domain" refers to

(A) African music in relation to contemporary culture as a whole

(B) music as it may be perceived in non-African cultures

(C) a feature of African music that aided in transmitting African cultural values

(D) an aspect of the African cultural legacy

(E) the influence of music on contemporary culture

Sample Multiple-choice Questions — Select One or More Answer Choices

For the following question, consider each of the choices separately and select all that apply.

3. According to the author, scholars would err in drawing which of the following conclusions?

[A] Slavery stripped the slaves of their political and economic systems.

[B] African music was similar to all other traditions of music in that it originated in a total vision of life.

[C] Music was a crucial part of the African cultural legacy.

译文及解析

第一句： 学者们往往意识不到音乐对于保留非洲文化的重要性。

第二句： 学者们意识到奴隶制的确剥夺了黑人的一些文化元素，但是仍然低估了音乐对于传承非洲文化的重要性。

（第二句是对第一句的举例，第一句是第二句的逻辑上一层。）

第三句： 不同于其他音乐，非洲音乐是“全景式俯察生活”（based on total vision of life），而非“孤立片段”（isolated social domain）。

第四句： 音乐不仅仅是为宗教服务的，而是遍及非洲生活的每个角落，包括出生、死亡、工作和娱乐。

（第四句是对第三句的举例，第三句是第四句的逻辑上一层。）

第五句： 一个社会群体用于使自身长存的方式最终得以成形，就是保全该社会群体的核心文化。

（第五句和第三句的关系：平行并列作为分论点。（因为）音乐覆盖非洲生活的全部，（又因为）核心的文化才能作为手段来传承非洲文化。）

第六句： （所以），音乐作为非洲文化中不可分割的一部分，在黑奴制期间及之后都是保存黑人文化极为重要的一种方式。

（第六句是第三、五句的结果，行文到此结束。）

逻辑图

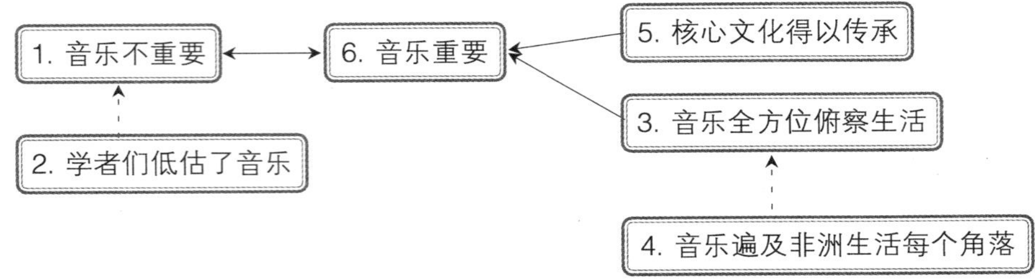

题目及解析

1. The primary purpose of the passage is to

(A) analyze the impact that slavery had on African political and economic systems

(B) review the attempt of recent scholarship to study the influence of African music on other music

(C) correct the failure of some scholars to appreciate the significance of music in African culture

（D）survey the ways by which people attempt to preserve their culture against the effects of oppression

（E）compare the relative importance of music with that of other art forms in culture

这是一道“主旨作用题”，有别于我们印象中的“主题题”。主题题的答案应选择文章的逻辑最高层或者能够概括文章内容的话即可（如非洲音乐很重要）；而主旨作用题需要考生站到高于文章内容的层面去审视，即为何要写这个主题。

（A）分析黑奴制对于非洲政治和经济的影响

本文写关于黑奴制给非洲经济和政治造成的影响，其目的是为了反衬学者们没有意识到音乐的重要性，可以说是一个细枝末节，不是本文的写作目的。出题者只不过用这种比较宏观的概念来迷惑考生而已。

（B）重新审视近期学者们关于非洲音乐对于其他音乐的影响的研究

本文中关于非洲音乐和其他音乐的比较出现在第三句话，目的在于说明非洲音乐俯察生活各个方面的特性。这仅处于一个论点的层面，不可能是本文写作的目的，而且本文不是为了研究非洲音乐对他者的影响而写的。

（C）纠正一些学者在音乐对于非洲文化重要性认识上的错误。

本文主要通过给出理由来说明音乐对于非洲十分重要，这是本文的主题。进一步分析，作者写此文章的目的是为了通过论述得出非洲音乐十分重要这样的结论来纠正之前学者观点的谬误，所以C是正确答案。

（D）调查人们在压迫的环境中是如何保全其文化的

本文对于人们是如何保全文化这一问题进行了探讨，即他们通过保全最核心的文化来使自己的文化得以传承。这一问题的答案只是作者在论述过程中的一个点，并不是行文的目的。

（E）比较音乐相对于其他艺术形式在文化中的重要性

首先，本文探讨的是非洲音乐、非洲文化，这个题干把话题的范围一下子放大，有失偏颇。再者，音乐比其他艺术形式更加重要，这是通过读文章可以了解到的一个信息，不是写这篇文章的目的。

2. In line 5, the phrase “isolated social domain” refers to

（A）African music in relation to contemporary culture as a whole

（B）music as it may be perceived in non-African cultures

（C）a feature of African music that aided in transmitting African cultural values

（D）an aspect of the African cultural legacy

（E）the influence of music on contemporary culture

这是一道细节题，意在考查考生能否根据文中给定的信息理解文章作者的真正意图。“isolated social domain”（孤立的片段）出现在文章第三句话，“African music, unlike the music of some other cultures, was based on a total vision of life in which music was not an isolated social domain.”句子当中提到的信息是：

（1）非洲音乐的特点是全景式俯察生活；

（2）非洲音乐和别的文化的音乐不一样；

（3）从全景的角度俯察生活，音乐不再是孤立的片段。

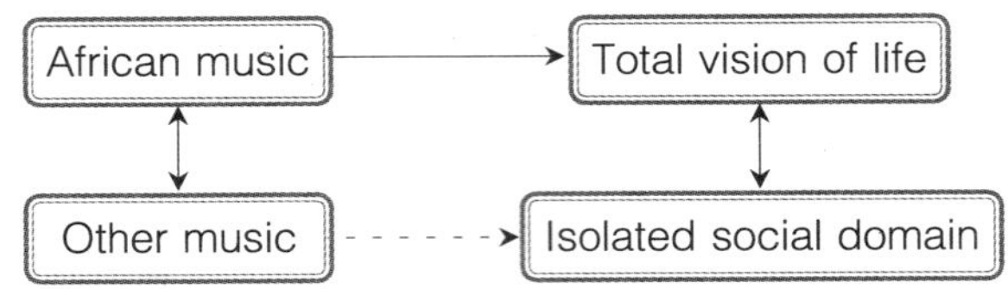

基于以上的分析，不难看出文章作者意在表明“isolated social domain”就是其他文化中的音乐特色。

(A) 非洲音乐与整体当代文化相联系而构成一个整体

(B) 在非洲文化之外的其他文化当中的音乐

(C) 帮助非洲文化传播的非洲音乐的一种特性

(D) 非洲文化遗产的一个方面

(E) 音乐对于当代文化的影响

故而正确答案就是选项B了。本题还体现了GRE阅读无需背景知识的特点，即根据文章给定的信息就可以得出符合要求的答案。

For the following question, consider each of the choices separately and select all that apply.

3. According to the author, scholars would err in drawing which of the following conclusions?

A Slavery stripped the slaves of their political and economic systems.

B African music was similar to all other traditions of music in that it originated in a total vision of life.

C Music was a crucial part of the African cultural legacy.

这是一道不定项选择题，这种题目要求考生对于信息的理解要十分透彻，很难有投机取巧的方法，是检验考生阅读水平的好题目。更重要的是，这种不定项选择题是**GRE阅读的新题型**。在新GRE考试中，这种不定项选择题会在阅读中经常出现。

题干的解读需要注意一下，作者在此处用了一个虚拟语态would err in drawing...，即“如果学者们得出以下哪个/哪些结论，那么学者们就会是错的？”这里的“学者”虽然和文章中的学者都用的是scholars这个词，但是并非指文中的学者们，而是指广义的研究这方面内容的研究者。试想：如果这里的scholars指的是文中的学者，那么他们已经犯了错误，又何必再用虚拟语态呢？所以，这道题我们需要选择的是和文中所说的正确观点不同的错误信息就可以了。

A 黑奴制使得奴隶们失去了他们的政治体系和经济体系。
(这是文章中第二句话提到的信息，是正确的信息。)

B 非洲音乐和其他文化当中的音乐甚为相似，都是源自对生活的全方位俯察。
(这显然和文章中第三句所说的内容相反。)

C 非洲音乐是非洲文化中十分重要的一个部分。
(这是本文的重要论点，在最后一句话中得以体现，肯定是正确的信息。)

所以本题正确答案只选B。

2. 自然科学类

地幔分层学说是与非

Geologists have long known that the Earth's mantle is heterogeneous, but its spatial arrangement remains unresolved—is the mantle essentially layered or irregularly heterogeneous? The best evidence for the layered mantle thesis is the well-established fact that volcanic rocks found on oceanic islands, islands believed to result from mantle plumes arising from the lower mantle, are composed of material fundamentally different from that of the mid-ocean ridge system, whose source, most geologists contend, is the upper mantle.

Some geologists, however, on the basis of observations concerning mantle xenoliths, argue that the mantle is not layered, but that heterogeneity is created by fluids rich in incompatible elements (elements tending toward liquid rather than solid state) percolating upward and transforming portions of the upper mantle irregularly, according to the vagaries of the fluids' pathways. We believe, perhaps unimaginatively, that this debate can be resolved through further study, and that the underexplored mid-ocean ridge system is the key.

Sample Multiple-choice Questions — Select One Answer Choice

1. Which of the following best expresses the main idea of the passage?

(A) Current theories regarding the structure of the Earth's mantle cannot account for new discoveries regarding the composition of mantle xenoliths.

(B) There are conflicting hypotheses about the heterogeneity of the Earth's mantle because few mantle elements have been thoroughly studied.

(C) Further research is needed to resolve the debate among geologists over the composition of the mid-ocean ridge system.

(D) There is clear-cut disagreement within the geological community over the structure of the Earth's mantle.

(E) There has recently been a strong and exciting challenge to geologists' long-standing belief in the heterogeneity of the Earth's mantle.

Sample Multiple-choice Questions — Select One or More Answer Choices
For the following question, consider each of the choices separately and select all that apply.

2. It can be inferred from the passage that the supporters of the layered-mantle theory believe which of the following?

[A] The volcanic rocks on oceanic islands are composed of material derived from the lower part of the mantle.

[B] The materials of which volcanic rocks on oceanic islands and mid-ocean ridges are composed are typical of the layers from which they are thought to originate.

[C] The differences in composition between volcanic rocks on oceanic islands and the mid-ocean ridges are a result of different concentrations of incompatible elements.

译文及解析

第一句： 一直以来，地质学者们认同地球地幔的性质是不尽相同的，但是关于其空间排布悬而未解的难题是：地幔究竟是分层的呢？还是不规则地异质构成的呢？

（提出本文要探讨的问题，看似是一个疑问句，实际上本句是一个结论，后面的内容都围绕其展开，在全文中起到主题句的作用。）

第二句： 对于地幔分层的观点来说，最好的证据就是这样一个确认的事实：在那些海洋岛屿——被认为是生成于下层地幔升上来的地幔柱状熔岩流——上发现的火山岩石，是由与海洋中部山脊系统的物质完全不同的物质所构成的；而关于海洋中部山脊系统的形成源头，大多数地质学家认为是上层地幔。

（地幔分层就是第一句话中提到的第一种理论。）

第三句： 但是，某些地质学家，以对地幔捕虏岩体所作的观察为依据，指出地幔并非分层排列；相反，地幔具有异质性，是由那些富含不相容成分的流质构成的，这些成分趋向于流体而非固体的状态，自下而上渗透扩散，并且由于这些流质流向的任意性，不规则地将上部地幔的某些部分予以改变。

（地幔异质性是第二种理论。）

第四句： 并非戏言，我们相信通过更深入的研究，这样的争论能够得到解决，而还有待研究的海洋中脊系统就成了关键。

（最后一句是在第二句、第三句的基础上对未来前景的展望，也是在对第一句话进行补充解释，也说明了现阶段对于地幔空间分布还存在问题。）

逻辑图

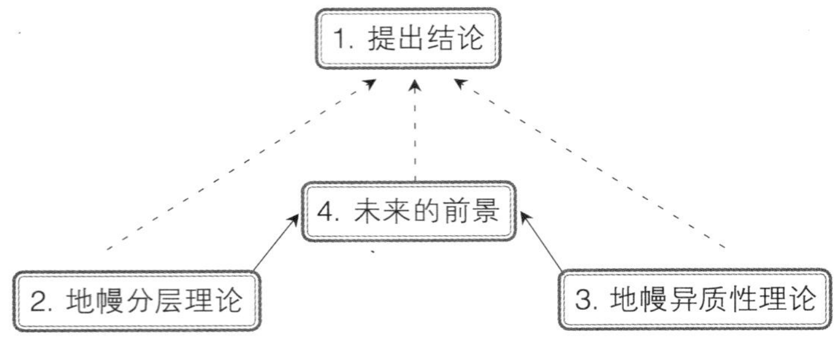

题目及解析

1. Which of the following best expresses the main idea of the passage?

   (A) Current theories regarding the structure of the Earth's mantle cannot account for new discoveries regarding the composition of mantle xenoliths.

   (B) There are conflicting hypotheses about the heterogeneity of the Earth's mantle because few mantle elements have been thoroughly studied.

   (C) Further research is needed to resolve the debate among geologists over the composition of the mid-ocean ridge system.

(D) **There is clear-cut disagreement within the geological community over the structure of the Earth's mantle.**

(E) There has recently been a strong and exciting challenge to geologists' long-standing belief in the heterogeneity of the Earth's mantle.

这是一道主题题，问“以下哪个选项表达了全文的中心意思?”短文章的主题题有时比长文章要复杂，原本就不多的几句话，再加上每句话都很长、信息量大，经常会难以抉择。考生处理这种题目的时候，只要考虑清楚某个句子的存在对于其他句子的作用。比如本文中，写第二句和第三句都是为了解释第一句话中说的“but its spatial arrangement remains unresolved—is the mantle essentially layered or irregularly heterogeneous?”，所以第一句一定是第二句、第三句的逻辑上一层，因此第二、三句以及其中包含的关于地幔的具体细节肯定不会是本文的主题句。有人轻易地认为本文的第四句话是主题句，这实际上忽略了第四句话说到“未来的研究有望能解决这个争论”实际上也就是在说“现阶段的争论问题的确存在”，第四句还是在为第一句话服务。因此，本文的第一句话作为整个文章的逻辑最高层，便成为了本文的主题句。

(A) 现有的地幔结构理论无法解释关于地幔捕虏岩体的成分的新发现。

(B) 因为地质成分研究不完全，所以现有的关于地幔异质性的假说自相矛盾。

(C) 解决地质学家们关于海洋中脊系统成分的争论，需要未来进一步的研究。

(D) 地质学界对于地球的地幔结构存在明显的争议。

(E) 地质学家们长期以来关于地幔异质性的理论最近受到了强有力的冲击和挑战。

毫无疑问本题的正确答案为选项D。C是个迷惑选项：文章中说的是未来的研究能够帮助学者们解决关于“地幔到底是分层的还是不规则异质性”的问题，而不是解决“海洋中脊系统成分”的问题。

For the following question, consider each of the choices separately and select all that apply.

2. It can be inferred from the passage that the supporters of the layered-mantle theory believe which of the following?

[A] **The volcanic rocks on oceanic islands are composed of material derived from the lower part of the mantle.**

[B] **The materials of which volcanic rocks on oceanic islands and mid-ocean ridges are composed are typical of the layers from which they are thought to originate.**

[C] The differences in composition between volcanic rocks on oceanic islands and the mid-ocean ridges are a result of different concentrations of incompatible elements.

从题目形式上看，这是一道推断题，而且还是不定项选择。但是通过题干“支持地幔分层理论的人会同意下面哪些选项?”我们发现其更像是一道细节题。支持地幔分层理论的人，一定同意文中所说的关于的地幔分层的信息，所以本题的关键就在于立足文章中地幔分层理论中的信息选择答案。

[A] **海洋岛屿上的火山岩石是由源于下层地幔的物质材料组成的。**

[B] **海洋岛屿的火山岩石和海洋中脊系统的组成物质材料源自(各个)地幔层。**

[C] 海洋岛屿的火山岩石和海洋中脊系统在组成成分上的差异是由“不兼容的成分”的浓度不同所导致的。

这道题对于考生把握长难句的能力提出了较高的要求。本文的第二句话可以算得上是自然科学类文章中非常晦涩难懂的句子，其中的宾语从句里包含了很多名词，通过这些名词之间的关系反映出主句的含义。主句当中说到"对于layered mantle thesis(地幔分层学说)来说，最好的支持性证据就是这样一个事实……"，这里的关键在于分析清楚后边的宾语从句。

宾语从句中说道："volcanic rocks(火山石)found on oceanic islands"，在海洋岛屿上发现的火山岩石，给考生传递的信息是二者具有核心的同质性，即：火山岩石具有海洋岛屿所具有的核心特征；"islands believed to result from mantle plumes"，海洋岛屿是由柱状熔岩流生成的，那么海洋岛屿具有柱状熔岩流的核心特征。

"mantle plumes arising from the lower mantle"柱状熔岩流是由下层地幔上升而形成的，这说明柱状熔岩流的源头在于下层地幔，则其具有下层地幔所拥有的核心特征。至此，宾语从句的前半句给考生传递的是一串源头在下层地幔的名词信息，因此火山岩石代表着下层地幔。再看宾语从句的主句部分："volcanic rocks are composed of material fundamentally different from that of the mid-ocean ridge"(火山岩石是由某些物质构成的，而这些物质与构成海洋中脊系统的物质有本质上的区别)。既然构成二者的材料有着本质上的区别，那么火山岩石和海洋中脊系统一定有着本质上的不同。

后文中说到，"mid-ocean ridge system, whose source, most geologists contend, is the upper mantle"专家们认为海洋中脊系统源于上层地幔，那么海洋中脊系统有上层地幔的核心特征。根据文章传递的信息，我们就能够构建下面的关系：

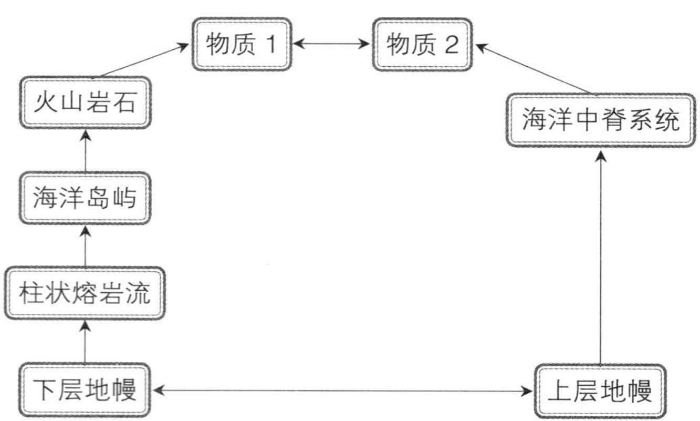

在这句话当中，文章是利用物质1和物质2的本质上的不同，来反映下层地幔和上层地幔在本质上的不同，由于二者存在根本上的差异，所以地幔不是同质性的而是分层的，于是地幔分层理论就得到了验证。

因此，此题的答案就很明显了，应该是选项A、B。可见，只要把文章第二句话的意思弄明白并不难选。

3. 生命科学类

生病与发烧的关系

Warm-blooded animals have elaborate physiological controls to maintain constant body temperature (in humans, 37°C). Why then during sickness should temperature rise, apparently increasing stress on the infected organism? It has long been known that the level of serum iron in animals falls during infection. Garibaldi first suggested a relationship between fever and iron. He found that microbial synthesis of siderophores-substances that bind iron-in bacteria of the genus Salmonella declined at environmental temperatures above 37°C and stopped at 40.3°C. Thus, fever would make it more difficult for an infecting bacterium to acquire iron and thus to multiply. Cold-blooded animals were used to test this hypothesis because their body temperature can be controlled in the laboratory. Kluger reported that of iguanas infected with the potentially lethal bacterium A. hydrophilia, more survived at temperatures of 42°C than at 37°C, even though healthy animals prefer the lower temperature. When animals at 42°C were injected with an iron solution, however, mortality rates increased significantly. Research to determine whether similar phenomena occur in warm-blooded animals is sorely needed.

Sample Multiple-choice Questions — Select One Answer Choice

1. The passage is primarily concerned with attempts to determine

   (A) the role of siderophores in the synthesis of serum iron

   (B) new treatments for infections that are caused by A. hydrophilia

   (C) the function of fever in warm-blooded animals

   (D) the mechanisms that ensure constant body temperature

   (E) iron utilization in cold-blooded animals

Sample Multiple-choice Questions — Select One Answer Choice

2. Which of the following can be inferred about warm-blooded animals solely on the basis of information in the passage?

   (A) The body temperatures of warm-blooded animals cannot be easily controlled in the laboratory.

   (B) Warm-blooded animals require more iron in periods of stress than they do at other times.

   (C) Warm-blooded animals are more comfortable at an environmental temperature of 37°C than they are at a temperature of 42°C.

   (D) In warm-blooded animals, bacteria are responsible for the production of siderophores, which, in turn, make iron available to the animal.

   (E) In warm-blooded animals, infections that lead to fever are usually traceable to bacteria.

Sample Multiple-choice Questions — Select One Answer Choice

3. If it were to be determined that "similar phenomena occur in warm-blooded animals" (line 11), which of the following, assuming each is possible, is likely to be the most effective treatment for warm-blooded animals with bacterial infections?

(A) Administering a medication that lowers the animals' body temperature

(B) Injecting the animals with an iron solution

(C) Administering a medication that makes serum iron unavailable to bacteria

(D) Providing the animals with reduced-iron diets

(E) Keeping the animals in an environment with temperatures higher than 37°C

译文及解析

第一句： 温血动物拥有精密的调控机制来保持体温恒定(比如，人类体温是37°C)。

第二句： 但是为何在生病期间体温会升高，从而加重染病机体的负担呢?

(第二句话提出了问题，是本文要回答的。第一句是个条件，即"既然"有第一句的情况，"为何"会有第二句的情况呢？)

第三句： 我们知道，动物在生病时，体内血清中的铁含量是下降的。

第四句： 加拉巴迪率先提出铁的含量和发烧的关系。

第五句： 他发现，沙门氏菌中的一种细菌（亲水性致命病菌A)，在其所处的环境温度高于37°C时，其含铁细胞的合成是下降的，而当温度到达40.3°C时就会停止(合成)。

(第四、五句作为一个整体细节。)

第六句： 所以，发烧使得这些感染性细菌难以获得铁，也就难以繁殖了。

(第六句是第四、五句的结果，是因果关系。第六句和第三句是平行并列的关系，用来解释第二句中的问题。)

第七句： 为了验证假说，我们利用在实验室中能够控制体温的冷血动物来做实验。

(第七句是用来支持第六句的结论的，是第六句的逻辑下一层。)

第八句： 克卢格发现，感染了致命病菌A的美洲大蜥蜴在42°C的存活率比在37°C的时候高（虽然平时它习惯于37°C)。

第九句： 但是，当在42°C给蜥蜴注射铁元素溶剂之时，蜥蜴死亡率猛然高了起来。

(第八、九句是第七句的细节，证实了第六句的假说。)

第十句： 我们现在急需做的调查研究就是证明温血动物是否也有这样的表现。

逻辑图

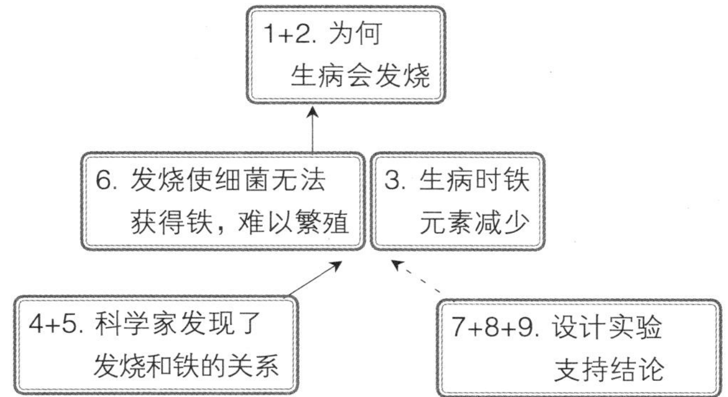

题目及解析

1. The passage is primarily concerned with attempts to determine

（A）the role of siderophores in the synthesis of serum iron

（B）new treatments for infections that are caused by A. hydrophilia

（C）the function of fever in warm-blooded animals

（D）the mechanisms that ensure constant body temperature

（E）iron utilization in cold-blooded animals

从题干我们很容易看出这是一道主题题，问本文主要探讨的内容是确定什么东西。这是一篇问题解决型文章，解决这个问题最核心的点就在于研究证明 **“发烧之后铁元素含量下降，使得病菌无法繁殖”**，所以本文主要想确定的点一定和“发烧”有关。

（A）含铁细胞对于血清中铁合成的作用

（B）对于亲水性致命病菌A引起的流感的新型治疗方法

（C）发烧对于温血动物的影响

（D）使机体维持恒定体温的方法

（E）冷血动物对于铁元素的使用

本题的正确答案相对明显，是选项C。其他几个答案都是在讨论细枝末节(如A)或者无中生有(如B)。

2. Which of the following can be inferred about warm-blooded animals solely on the basis of information in the passage?

（A）The body temperatures of warm-blooded animals cannot be easily controlled in the laboratory.

（B）Warm-blooded animals require more iron in periods of stress than they do at other times.

（C）Warm-blooded animals are more comfortable at an environmental temperature of 37°C than they are at a temperature of 42°C.

（D）In warm-blooded animals, bacteria are responsible for the production of siderophores, which, in turn, make iron available to the animal.

（E）In warm-blooded animals, infections that lead to fever are usually traceable to bacteria.

本题的问法比较常规，问“以下哪个关于温血动物的说法可以从文中信息推出?”这是典型的推断题问法。在本文中温血动物共出现了两次：一处是在开头第一句话；另一处是在结尾最后一句话。整篇文章中关于做实验的过程以及理论的推断都没有和温血动物直接相关，所以本题算是一道有难度的推断题目。

（A）温血动物的体温在实验室环境中不容易被控制好。

关于在实验室环境中控制动物的温度出现在文章的第七句。冷血动物的特征是体温容易控制，因此科学家拿冷血动物做实验来证明第六句的观点。但是最后一句作者提到“我们需要知道温血动物是否也有这样的表现”，说明科学家希望研究清楚的是温血动物，但是为何没有选用温血动物而用冷血动物作为实验对象呢？因为文中提到的冷血动物的体温容易控制。据此，我们可以推断出“温血动物的体温难以在实验室环境中被轻易控制”。A是正确答案。

（B）温血动物在压力大时比在其他时候获取铁元素的量更大。

B是文章没有提到的信息。贸然出现的比较级往往是错误选项。

（C）温血动物在37°C时比在42°C时感觉要更舒服。

这是本题的一个迷惑性选项，选项当中所说的细节是关于冷血动物的。但这是个特定的细节，而不能直接归结为温血动物的特点。在文中，两个温度的横向比较出现在第八句。因此，这里属于肆意推断，文章并没有给出相应的信息。

（D）在温血动物中是细菌引起含铁细胞的合成，从而使得铁元素能够为机体所用。

D也错了，含铁细胞的合成这一细节是出现在第五句的，和温血动物不属于同一个逻辑集团，考生也无证据证明温血动物中含铁细胞的合成是由细菌引起的。

（E）在温血动物中，引起发烧的感染往往是由细菌引起的。

细菌引起感染，再导致发烧，这是个常理。E选项把貌似常规的信息串连在一起迷惑考生。首先，作者在前两句提到了温血动物发烧，但并没有说是由病菌引起的。由病菌引起的感染出现在冷血动物(美洲大蜥蜴)身上。因此，这个选项的错误在于将文章中的信息进行混搭。错误的关键在于“往往”这个概念，在文中没有给出这种信息的前提下，这种概念在某种程度上等同于极端词汇。

3. If it were to be determined that “similar phenomena occur in warm-blooded animals” (line 11), which of the following, assuming each is possible, is likely to be the most effective treatment for warm-blooded animals with bacterial infections?

（A）Administering a medication that lowers the animals’ body temperature

（B）Injecting the animals with an iron solution

（C）Administering a medication that makes serum iron unavailable to bacteria

（D）Providing the animals with reduced-iron diets

（E）Keeping the animals in an environment with temperatures higher than 37°C

本题的题干属于GRE阅读当中比较长的，问道：为了要验证“温血动物也有类似的反应”的话，那么对于一个感染了病毒的温血动物最有效的治疗手段是什么呢？此处题干中的“最”字需要注意，这种极端词汇的出现标志着我们在解决这个问题的时候必须抓住核心才可以，一切的手段、间接的路径都不合适。

我们先来看看作者引用冷血动物作为例子的用意何在。只要分清楚逻辑层面就可以。本文第七句说到"为了验证假说"，该假说就是第六句"发烧使得细菌难以获得铁，难以繁殖"。如此，一切例子的论述都是要证明这一观点，这也是有待证明的关于温血动物的"类似反应"。那么治疗的手段当中：

（A）给动物用药以使其体温下降

降温并不治病，一降温，细菌就容易繁殖，而温血动物就容易一命呜呼。

（B）给动物注射含有铁元素的溶剂

B更不行了，打入铁元素之后动物就更加无法存活了。

（C）加入药物使得细菌无法利用机体内的铁元素

C才是本题的正确答案。任何方法的关键都是让细菌无法获得铁，这才是核心。

（D）给动物吃低铁餐

D也不行，不是最直接、最有效的。

（E）让动物身处高于37°C的环境之中

E也不行，首先温血动物的体温不受外界环境的直接影响，而且这种做法也不是核心，只是希望通过温度来使得细菌无法获得铁，不合适。

4. 人文艺术类

瓦格纳与黑人诗歌

Jean Wagner's most enduring contribution to the study of Afro-American poetry is his insistence that it be analyzed in a religious, as well as secular, frame of reference. **The appropriateness of such an approach may seem self-evident for a tradition commencing with spirituals and owing its early forms, rhythms, vocabulary, and evangelical fervor to Wesleyan hymnals.** But before Wagner a secular outlook that analyzed Black poetry solely within the context of political and social protest was dominant in the field.

It is Wagner who first demonstrated the essential fusion of racial and religious feeling in Afro-American poetry. The two, he argued, form a symbiotic union in which religious feelings are often applied to racial issues and racial problems are often projected onto a metaphysical plane. Wagner found this most eloquently illustrated in the Black spiritual, where the desire for freedom in this world and the hope for salvation in the next are inextricably intertwined.

Sample Multiple-choice Questions — Select One Answer Choice

1. The primary purpose of the passage is to

（A）contrast the theories of Jean Wagner with those of other contemporary critics

（B）document the influence of Jean Wagner on the development of Afro-American poetry

（C）explain the relevance of Jean Wagner's work to the study of Afro-American religion

（D）indicate the importance of Jean Wagner's analysis of Afro-American poetry

（E）present the contributions of Jean Wagner to the study of Black spirituals

Sample Multiple-choice Questions — Select One Answer Choice

2. In the argument given, the role that the portion in **boldface** played could be most exactly described as which of the following?

 (A) It weakens the prominence of Wagner on the development of Afro-American poetry.

 (B) It contrasts with Wagner's view that Black poetry should be analyzed within the context of political.

 (C) It explains why author considered Wagner's view about Black poetry is appropriate.

 (D) It undermines the author's positive attitude about the Wagner's method of analyzing Black poetry.

 (E) It presents details to explore the development of Black Poetry.

译文及解析

第一句： 瓦格纳对于研究美国黑人诗歌最大的贡献是他坚持的观点，即：黑人诗歌应该利用宗教的框架来分析，而不仅仅用世俗的方法分析之。

第二句： 因为黑人诗歌起源于圣歌，而且早期从“韦斯利赞美诗集”中借鉴形式、韵律、辞藻以及狂热的激情，从这些方面看来，（瓦格纳的）分析方法是非常合适的，这一点不言自明。
（第二句是第一句的原因，但在本文写作中，作者是为了突出第一句的结论，所以第二句应该是第一句的逻辑下一层。）

第三句： 但在瓦格纳之前，在学术界占统治地位的一种世俗观点是：黑人诗歌就应该单纯被置于政治和社会抗议这样的背景下进行分析。
（第三句的转折是对第二句的一次转折，和第二句处于同一逻辑层面，都是为了说明第一句话的结论。）

第四句： 正是瓦格纳率先指出种族与宗教的情感在黑人诗歌中的有机结合。
（第四句是第一句结论的细节，也处于第一句的逻辑下一层，但和第二、三句并非是同一内容。）

第五句： 瓦格纳认为，种族和宗教此二者构成了一种共生共栖的状态：宗教情感往往应用在种族问题之中；种族问题也经常被投射到形而上的玄学层面上讨论。
（第五句是第四句的细节，指出种族问题与宗教问题的相互关系。）

第六句： 瓦格纳发现这一特性在黑人圣歌当中表现最为明显：对于今生自由的渴望和对于来世涅槃重生的希望，二者交织缠绕，不可分割。
（第六句是对第五句的一个举例支持。）

逻辑图

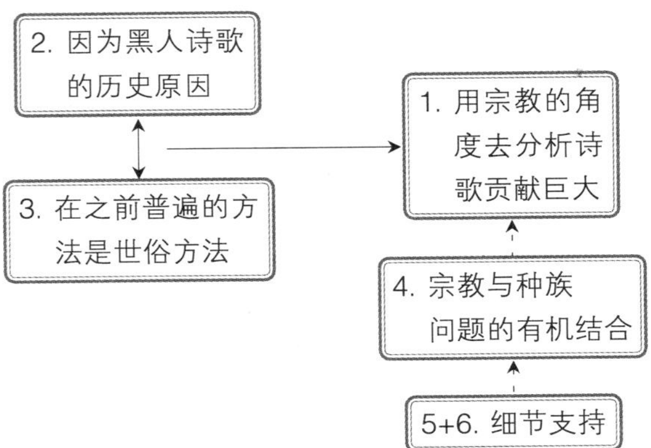

题目及解析

1. The primary purpose of the passage is to

(A) contrast the theories of Jean Wagner with those of other contemporary critics

(B) document the influence of Jean Wagner on the development of Afro-American poetry

(C) explain the relevance of Jean Wagner's work to the study of Afro-American religion

(D) indicate the importance of Jean Wagner's analysis of Afro-American poetry

(E) present the contributions of Jean Wagner to the study of Black spirituals

这是一道主题作用题，问"这篇文章的写作意图何在"。在本文中，作者的行文结构是很明显的：一开始给出一个结论，然后给出原因上的论证以及细节上的支持。这种写法从套路来说属于结论解释型文章，作者的写作意图当然在于阐明自己的一个结论：瓦格纳对于黑人诗歌的研究有重要影响。

(A) 将瓦格纳和同时期的评论家们的理论作对比

A不正确。文中并没有提到同时期的学者，虽然有对比，但那是和在瓦格纳之前的理论进行对比。

(B) 记录瓦格纳对于美国黑人诗歌的重要影响

B也不合适。本文是通过描绘这些影响来说明瓦格纳的理论颇具价值，而并非诗歌本身的发展。B选项中的文字内容没错误，但是不符合本题的要求。

(C) 阐明瓦格纳的作品和美国黑人宗教的关联性

C错误，属于概念上的混淆。瓦格纳和美国黑人的宗教文化的确有联系：即瓦格纳运用宗教的角度来分析黑人诗歌。本文虽是在通过这样的联系来行文的，但本文并非是在解释为何瓦格纳和宗教问题会有联系。

(D) 证明瓦格纳对于美国黑人诗歌的研究的重要意义

D是本题的正确答案。作者写了六句话其目的就在于证明第一句话的正确性，所以第一句是文章的逻辑最高层。

(E) 陈述瓦格纳对于黑人圣歌研究的贡献

E犯了张冠李戴的错误。文章的主要内容并不是瓦格纳研究黑人圣歌。

2. In the argument given, the role that the portion in **boldface** played could be most exactly described as which of the following?

(A) It weakens the prominence of Wagner on the development of Afro-American poetry.

(B) It contrasts with Wagner's view that Black poetry should be analyzed within the context of political.

(C) It explains why author considered Wagner's view about Black poetry is appropriate.

(D) It undermines the author's positive attitude about the Wagner's method of analyzing Black poetry.

(E) It presents details to explore the development of Black Poetry.

这是一道句子作用题，问 "第二句话的作用何在?" GRE阅读这种作用题的一大特点就是难以通过单纯地排查选项、选择合适的态度词就可以选出正确答案。更何况题干中还有"most"这样的极端词汇，预示着题干的干扰性会更强一些。

（A）削弱了瓦格纳在黑人诗歌发展历史中的地位。

A不正确。文中并没有提到对瓦格纳的负评价。

（B）该句与瓦格纳的“诗歌应该从政治的角度予以分析”的观点形成了对比。

B也不合适。“诗歌应该从政治的角度予以分析”这个观点并非是瓦格纳所持有的，而是之前的学术界普遍流行的一种看法。

（C）解释了为何作者认为瓦格纳关于黑人诗歌研究的观点是合适的。

C是本题的正确答案。从句间逻辑关系上不难看出这一点。

（D）该句削弱了作者对于瓦格纳分析诗歌的方法的赞同态度。

D也是错在了态度上，同选项A。undermine这个词的意思是“破坏、削弱”。

（E）陈列细节来描述黑人诗歌的发展过程。

E也不合适。该句并非是为了陈列细节而写的。其内容本身并没有错误，但是不符合第二句话客观存在的作用，也不符合题干中的“most”这个词对答案的要求。

通过上述的例文以及例题，我们大致呈现了新GRE阅读题的基本面貌。那么GRE阅读题与一般考试的阅读题最大的区别在于何处？在判断选项的过程中又需要注意什么内容呢？我们通过解读ETS官方指南得到：

Reading passages are drawn from many different disciplines and sources, so you may encounter material with which you are not familiar. Do not be discouraged when this happens; all the questions can be answered on the basis of the information provided in the passage, and you are not expected to rely on any outside knowledge. Sometimes your own views or opinions may conflict with those presented in a passage; if this happens, take special care to work within the context provided by the passage. You should not expect to agree with everything you encounter in the reading passages.

Read and analyze the passage carefully before trying to answer any of the questions, and pay attention to clues that help you understand less explicit aspects of the passage.

- Try to distinguish main ideas from supporting ideas or evidence.
- Try to distinguish ideas that the author is advancing from those he or she is merely reporting.
- Try to distinguish ideas that the author is strongly committed to from those he or she advances as hypothetical or speculative.
- Try to identify the relationship between different ideas.

Read each question carefully and be certain that you understand exactly what is being asked.

ETS在文中提到一个概念“not expected to rely on any outside knowledge”，不牵涉背景知识，为何？因为参加GRE考试的考生可能来自各个不同的专业，如果文章出现的信息需要背景知识才能读懂的话，这门考试的公平性显然就丧失了。比如：作为一个化学系的同学，你也许知道“量子贯穿反应”的原理，但是考试原文会把这个“贯穿反应”的过程及机理大致做出描述，足够所有考生解题。此外，“Sometimes your own views or opinions may conflict with those presented in a passage”也需要引起考生注意，从这一点我们也可以确认ETS对于考试内容的公平性的把握，不要盲目地认为对文中出现的内容有大致了解，就可以利用背景知识直接去做题，GRE文中的内容可能和考生已知的知识细节是不一致的。

除上述信息之外，考生在具体解题的过程中，还需要注意以下几点：

（1）分清主要观点和支持性细节或观点

对于支持性细节或观点，是很多细节题的出题处，也是很多作用题出题的点，典型的问法就是："The author cited...in order to...?"解决这种作用题，我们比较直接的做法就是寻找其逻辑上一层。这类观点或细节的存在，必然是为了其逻辑上一层而服务的。

（2）分清作者认同的观点和仅处于假设阶段的观点

第二点和第三点具有共通性：作者认同的观点往往都予以展开；而作者并不确定、处于假设阶段的观点，往往仅是陈列而已，用以和其他观点做横向比较。考生在阅读过程中一定要注意哪些是主、哪些是次。针对假设型的观点，文章之后可以出现正改善题，典型的问法是这样的："The XX conclusion mentioned in the passage would be more convincing if which of the following is true?"我们的解决方法也很简单，找到原文中观点不足的地方予以改正，或是将缺乏的条件予以补充即可。

（3）了解观点之间的联系

观点之间的关系是GRE考查的一个亮点所在。我们都知道一般论述性的文章大部分是以事实细节来支持观点，但是高端的学术文章中不但有细节支持观点，几个观点之间的相互联系也非常重要。比如：观点A是观点B成立的前提条件，观点C是观点A的另一个分支，和观点D呈平行并列关系等等。找到观点之间的联系对于我们解读整个文章非常重要，它能反映出作者行文的思路和意图。

但是，中国考生必须注意的一点是：**无需背景知识不等于可以一无所知**。GRE这门学术化考试的考查对象是具有大学本科学历的考生，这些考生都需要拥有扎实的**英文基本功和学术思维习惯**，以及**阅读学术性题材读物**的能力，这三者缺一不可。英文的基本功是托福级别的考试就能够帮助我们达到的水平，GRE的语言虽说和托福、雅思等考试不在一个水平上，但也还不至于遥不可及。学术思维的习惯以及阅读能力需要我们通过大量阅读英美学术论文期刊杂志才能得以强化，否则在考场上见到一大堆瞠目不识的信息时，正常人是很难在规定时间之内完成GRE阅读考题的。这也是笔者为何运用本书后面的大量篇幅来引入"**题源阅读**"的原因，因为笔者自从2006年教授GRE阅读以来，已经接触过太多由于平时积累不够在考场上栽跟头的同学了。故而万望考生朋友们要认识到这一点学术底蕴的重要性。

第三章
深入浅出说阅读

通过第二章对于四篇文章的解析，相信考生朋友们已经对GRE阅读理解文章的特色有了一些认识。GRE考试是一门学术化的考试，其措辞、语句、笔法全都有明显的学术性文章的特色。既然强调学术性，它的难度自然会比较高，而且也不是我们单纯地靠“好好学英语”就能搞定的——这一点我们在之前的篇章中曾经说过。笔者经常会收到类似这样内容的邮件：

> 老师您好：
>
> 我是您暑假班的学生，非常感谢您精彩的讲解。我现在感觉自己的GRE阅读水准有了突飞猛进的提高。可是，最近在做一些文章的时候发现单词基本都认识，但整个文章读下来就是觉得晕乎乎的，不知所云。我马上就要面临考试了，学校的课业又非常忙，所以请教老师有木有绝招？谢谢谢谢！

我相信，可能考生朋友们有相当一部分人曾经或者现在就有类似这位同学的困惑：为什么我把上课布置的单词、材料和文章认认真真学了那么久，但是还不能像当年高考那样做到游刃有余？是的，这是一个非常关键的问题，这也在一定程度上决定了为何GRE阅读总是中国同学最害怕、发怵的一个环节。单词也背了、长难句也看了、句间逻辑关系也学会了，还是没有足够信心把阅读搞定。其原因就在于六个字：**学术底蕴不足！**

首先，请大家通读下面这篇文章：

Scientists typically advocate the analytic method of studying complex systems: systems are divided into component parts that are investigated separately. But nineteenth-century critics of this method claimed that when a system's parts are isolated its complexity tends to be lost. To address (to deal with: TREAT "intrigued by the chance to address important issues I. L. Horowitz") the perceived weakness of the analytic method these critics put forward a concept called organicism, which posited that the whole determines the nature of its parts and that the parts of a whole are interdependent.

Organicism depended upon the theory of internal relations, which states that relations between entities are possible only within some whole that embraces them, and that entities are altered by the relationships into which they enter. If an entity stands in a relationship with another entity, it has some property as a consequence. Without this relationship, and hence without the property, the entity would be different—and so would be another entity. Thus, the property is one of the entity's defining characteristics. Each of an entity's relationships likewise determines a defining characteristic of the entity.

One problem with the theory of internal relations is that not all properties of an entity are defining characteristics: numerous properties are accompanying characteristics—even if they are always present, their presence does not influence the entity's identity. Thus, even if it is admitted that every relationship into which an entity enters determines some characteristic of the entity, it is not necessarily true that such characteristics will define the entity; it is possible for the entity to enter into a relationship yet remain essentially unchanged.

The ultimate difficulty with the theory of internal relations is that it renders the acquisition of knowledge impossible. To truly know an entity, we must know all of its relationships; but because the entity is related to everything in each whole of which it is a part, these wholes must be known completely before the entity can be known. This seems to be a prerequisite impossible to satisfy.

Organicists' criticism of the analytic method arose from their failure to fully comprehend the method. In rejecting the analytic method, organicists overlooked the fact that before the proponents of the method analyzed the component parts of a system, they first determined both the laws applicable to the whole system and the initial conditions of the system; proponents of the method thus did not study parts of a system in full isolation from the system as a whole. Since organicists failed to recognize this, they never advanced any argument to show that laws and initial conditions of complex systems cannot be discovered. Hence, organicists offered no valid reason for rejecting the analytic method or for adopting organicism as a replacement for it.

如果你读完之后的感觉是懵懵懂懂一头雾水，那么，你与绝大部分GRE考生显然处于同一个阵营。现在，我们来告诉你：在西方心理学史上有这样一个学派，叫做格式塔学派。他们的主张是“整体大于部分之和”。简单地说，就是整体是不可以被拆分的，拆分之后的各个部分的简单加和并不能实现之前整体的功能。举个例子，通常猫走路是用四条腿的，如果有一天它少了一条腿的话，它通常还是能够走路，但是走路的方式就与之前用四条腿走路的方式大不相同了。现在，请各位再费心读一遍上面的文章，你就会发现，几句背景知识的点拨，已经足以使你非常顺利并且自信满满地读完这篇文章了吧！

很多考生把备考GRE阅读文章简单地还原为单词的问题，笔者觉得这种想法有失偏颇。因为有一个问题摆在眼前，如果想要在规定时间内保质保量地完成GRE阅读部分，还需要一定的学术底蕴。诚然，GRE考试并不需要我们依靠背景知识来解题，但是这并不等同于我们可以完全不读不看英美的学术论文；而且我们考GRE的目的是出国留学，最终还是要每天和这些学术文章做伴。有的同学在思想上有误区，认为只把新东方GRE课上发的学习材料翻来覆去地学好就能把阅读搞定，这是不合适的。谈到学术知识，我们往往想把自己变成维基百科；其实，这种想法既不现实也没有必要，GRE阅读常涉及的学术背景知识以及其阅读理解文章的题源材料笔者已在本书中列出。如果说我们之前绝大部分时间都是在“招式”上修炼自己的话，那么希望各位能从读完本书开始，切实地从“内功”上提升自己的档次，做到“形神兼备”才能从根本上解决这一令考生发慌的问题。

第一节 词——高频词列表

既然所有GRE阅读文章的文体都是议论文，那么在编制的过程中会选择什么样的文章？文章中高频的单词又会有哪些呢？笔者在本书中明确给出了一份详细的关键词表，由ETS和计算机软件专家测试后得出，可以更好地帮助考生夯实议论文学术化词汇的基础。

这部分基础词汇出现的频率是非常高的。如paradox, plausible, controversial，因为对这些词汇的理解不到位，这些重要词汇已经成为考试中很多题目做错的“元凶”。再有，对于approach, hypothesis, theory, fact, evidence, confirm, refute, evaluate等这些特定词汇的准确把握也将成为做好结构题、作用题和一些其他相关题型的基本保障。考生值得花时间把这份词表详细研究一遍，然后把自己不甚了解或者看起来模棱两可的关键词从韦氏大词典中仔细查其英文解释，该词典中的解释也是GRE出题所秉承的依据。

说到单词，很多人都很关心英文单词是怎么来的。英文在演化过程当中融合了古代的希腊语、拉丁语，其中还有古法语等欧罗巴大陆主流语系的介入。所以组成英文单词的词根通常都是拉丁语或希腊语，还有很多看似“没道理”的词汇，可能是其他语言的单词通过变形得出的。鉴于此，本书在本章中先把英文单词形成的四种主流路径与各位考生做一个分享，由于篇幅的限制笔者无法列举出太多的词汇做例子，希望考生朋友们在日后学习的过程中，如果遇到不懂的单词时，多利用手中的韦氏词典或者维基百科，把功课切实做到家。

▶ 由词根词缀构成

这种构词方法适合大部分常见的学术单词，通常都是一个英语词根外加前缀或者后缀形成一个单词。英文大约有700个词根，其中常用的只有250个左右：比如aer(空中)、cap(头部)、cid(切)、fic(做)。这些词根是需要备考GRE的考生们好好学习的，现在市面上的图书，尤其是新东方北美考试类相关词汇书，在词根词缀方面功夫做得非常足，十分值得一读。词根是一个单词的核心，是单词的生命力所在，抓住了词根就能帮助考生大大提高背词的效率。

除词根以外，单词中用于修饰、完善词根的部分就是词缀。英文单词的前缀共有约150个，常见的像pre-(在前)、pro-(向前)、dis-(分离)、apo-(离开)、intra-(内部) 等等。前缀的作用在于表示词根所代表的动词发出动作的特性，或者是词根所代表的名词的某种状态性动作。与之相对应的是后缀，后缀的作用在于表明该单词的词性，或者是一种主动或被动的状态。英文中后缀共约有220个，包括常见的：-ous(形容词后缀)、-ible(被动后缀)、-ion(抽象名词后缀)等等。考生只要在背单词的过程中勤于总结，牢记常用的词根和词缀，一定可以让自己的词汇量突飞猛进。

▶ 从古代语言演变而成

之前我们说过，英文是从古希腊语、古拉丁语、古法语等语言演化过来的，那么英文单词中从其他语言演化而成的自然也就不在少数了，其中还包括很多从古代英语演化而成的现代英语单词。比如：

(1) lobster(龙虾)：这个词源于拉丁语中的的locasta，是“蝗虫”的意思；又因为在古代人们认为龙虾这种动物的长相有点类似于“蜘蛛”，而古英语中的“蜘蛛”是loppe。因此这两个单词结合就成了现代英语当中的lobster了。

（2）female（女性）：这个词源于中世纪的法语femelle，是指“年轻的女子”。随着这个词在14世纪进入英语以后，它的形态成为femelle、femal等等，等到了14世纪末的时候人们将其与male“男性”这个词相联系，于是就固定下来female这样的写法并一直沿用至今。

（3）test（考试）：这个词源于古法语中的testum，指的是一种用于检验鉴定贵重金属的器皿。人们把含有杂质的金属放到testum当中加热，然后就可以提纯出比较纯净的贵重金银。在14世纪的时候，test这个词进入了英语，人们把“器皿”这样的意思抛弃掉了，只剩下了“提纯”、“精化”这样的含义，久而久之就形成了如今“考试、测试”这样的意思。

（4）history（历史）：这个词的直接起源是拉丁语当中的historia，原意是“the recording of the things past”（对过去事件的记载）。通常来说指的是时间跨度较长的事情；而形近词story指的是时间跨度较短的事件，因此就有了“故事”这个含义。

▶ 从历史事件演化而成

正如中国古代很多故事总结为成语一样，在欧洲历史中很多事件以及神话故事慢慢演化而形成了单词，这些单词往往没有标准的词根和词缀，也没有很强的记忆规律，因此在背很多这样的词汇之时，除了选择“过遍数”以外，再无他法。勤奋是人与人之间最大的比较优势，只有踏踏实实地把单词背三五十遍，才能确保这些知识全都属于自己。比如echo“回音”，这个词就起源于古希腊神话：Echo是天后赫拉的侍女，当赫拉的丈夫宙斯和情人幽会的时候，Echo就不停地和赫拉说话，使赫拉无暇去监视丈夫的行为。后来赫拉发现上当了之后怒气冲天，就施法令Echo失去了独立说话的能力，只能重复别人谈话的尾音。慢慢地这个词流入英语当中，随着历史的演化就有了“回音、共鸣”这样的含义。

笔者切望考生能够通过这个部分的训练，扎实提高阅读词汇量。考生一方面需要通过背GRE红宝书踏踏实实提高自己的词汇量，另一方面也需要在阅读难词、高频词中扩展提高，毕竟仅靠通用的、基础的（英文叫fundamental）词汇并不足以帮助考生制胜。因此单词始终都是摆在我们每一个考生眼前的拦路虎、绊脚石，GRE作为学术性的英文考试，测试的对象是即将进入美国研究生院读书的学生，因此对于词汇量的要求必然相当高：在老GRE考试中，世人皆知“得单词者得天下”。考生们在初次面对GRE要求的将近13000的词汇量时，恐惧和退缩的心态是最正常的。而且这么多词汇当中绝大部分全都是用法严谨、高度稳定的学术词汇，不光是靠平时多在英语环境中交流就能积累起来的。所以如何能够过好单词这一关也就成了能否在前往美国留学的道路上继续前行的首要决定性因素。上过新东方GRE课程的同学应该都清楚：

“背单词唯一有效的手段就是过遍数！”

我们利用数据库分析技术，以新GRE已考真题和官方指南为分析对象进行了词频分析，并去除了四六级和托福考试中大家已经掌握的词汇，剩下了如下“干货”，332个新GRE必考高频单词。希望能对紧张备考GRE阅读理解部分的同学有所裨益。

新GRE阅读高频词汇表

词汇	释义
abate	消减
aberrant	异常的
abeyance	中止
abscond	逃匿
abstemious	节制的
admonish	告诫
adulterate	掺杂
aesthetic	美学的
aggregate	聚集
alacrity	敏捷
alleviate	缓和
amalgamate	合并
ambiguous	模糊不清的
ambivalence	正反感情并存
ameliorate	改善
anachronism	不合时代的事
analogous	相似的
anarchy	无政府(状态)
anomalous	反常的
antipathy	憎恶
apathy	漠然
appease	平息
apprise	告知
approbation	认可
appropriate	侵吞
arduous	艰巨的
artless	单纯的
ascetic	禁欲的
assiduous	刻苦的
assuage	缓和
attenuate	减轻
audacious	大胆的
austere	简朴的
autonomous	自治的
aver	断言
banal	平庸的
belie	掩饰
beneficent	行善的
bolster	鼓励,支持
bombast	大放厥词
boorish	粗野无理的
burgeon	迅速生长
burnish	改善(形象)
buttress	支持
cacophonous	刺耳嘈杂的
capricious	变幻莫测的
castigation	斥责
catalyst	诱因
caustic	尖刻的
chicanery	诈骗
coagulate	(液体)凝结
coda	【音】结尾
cogent	令人信服的
commensurate	(比例)相当的
compendium	概要
complaisant	恳切的
compliant	服从的
conciliatory	调停的
condone	容忍
confound	使困惑
connoisseur	鉴赏家
contention	观点
contentious	有争议的
contrite	悔悟的
conundrum	难题
converge	汇集
convoluted	费解的
craven	懦弱的
daunt	使胆怯
decorum	端庄得体
default	不履行
deference	敬重
delineate	刻画
denigrate	诋毁
deride	嘲弄
derivative	衍生的

词汇	释义
desiccate	使脱水
desultory	散乱的
deterrent	威慑的
diatribe	抨击
dichotomy	天壤之别
diffidence	羞怯
diffuse	传播
digression	偏离主题
dirge	挽歌
disabuse	使省悟
discerning	有识别力的
discordant	不协调的
discredit	败坏名声
discrepancy	差异
discrete	分离的
disingenuous	不诚恳的
disinterested	公正的
disjointed	不连贯的
dismiss	不考虑
disparage	贬低
disparate	完全不同的
dissemble	掩饰
disseminate	散布
dissolution	解散
dissonance	不和谐
distend	(使)膨胀
distill	提炼
diverge	相悖
divest	剥夺
document	证明
dogmatic	武断的
dormant	蛰伏的
dupe	愚弄
ebullient	热情奔放的
eclectic	兼收并蓄的
efficacy	功效
effrontery	厚颜无耻
elegy	哀歌
elicit	引出
embellish	润色

词汇	释义
empirical	经验主义的
emulate	仿效
endemic	地方性的
enervate	使衰弱
engender	导致
enhance	增加
ephemeral	短暂的
equanimity	平静
equivocate	含糊其辞
erudite	博学的
esoteric	深奥的
eulogy	颂词
euphemism	委婉说法
exacerbate	使恶化
exculpate	开脱
exigency	紧急情况
extrapolation	推断
facetious	滑稽的
facilitate	促进
fallacious	谬误的
fatuous	愚蠢的
fawning	逢迎
felicitous	恰当的
fervor	热情
flag	疲乏
fledgling	刚开始的
flout	藐视
foment	煽动
forestall	预先阻止
frugality	节俭的
futile	无用的
gainsay	反驳
garrulous	饶舌的
goad	刺激
gouge	挖凿
grandiloquent	夸张的
gregarious	爱交际的
guileless	忠厚的
gullible	轻信的
harangue	高谈阔论，努力说服

词汇	释义
homogeneous	同性质的
hyperbole	夸张(法)
iconoclastic	有悖传统的
idolatry	盲目崇拜
immutable	永恒的
impair	损害
impassive	喜怒不形于色的
impede	阻碍
impermeable	不可渗透的
imperturbable	沉着的
impervious	无动于衷的
implacable	无法平息的
implicit	含蓄的
implode	向心聚爆
inadvertently	无意的
inchoate	才开始的
incongruity	不适宜
inconsequential	不重要的
incorporate	包含
indeterminate	不明确的
indigence	贫乏
indolent	怠惰的
inert	静止的
ingenuous	坦率的
inherent	固有的
innocuous	无害的
insensible	无知觉的
insinuate	含沙射影地说
insipid	枯燥无味的
insularity	孤立保守的状态
intractable	难以驾驭的
intransigence	不妥协
inundate	泛滥
inured	习惯于
invective	猛烈抨击的
irascible	性情暴躁的
irresolute	犹豫不决的
itinerary	旅程
laconic	言简意赅的
lassitude	困乏倦怠

词汇	释义
latent	潜在的
laud	称赞嘉许
lethargic	慵懒的
levee	堤
levity	轻浮
log	正式地记载
loquacious	喋喋不休的
lucid	明晰的
luminous	发光的
magnanimity	宽宏大量
malingerer	装病以逃避责任的人
malleable	可塑的
maverick	标新立异的人
mendacious	虚伪捏造的
metamorphosis	彻底的变化
meticulous	小心谨慎的
misanthrope	遁世者
mitigate	减轻
mollify	抚慰
morose	阴郁的
mundane	平凡普通的
negate	取消
neophyte	初学者
obdurate	顽固不化的
obsequious	奉承的
obviate	消除
occlude	堵塞,阻隔
officious	爱管闲事的
onerous	繁重的
opprobrium	责难抨击
oscillate	摆动
ostentatious	豪华铺张的
paragon	典范
partisan	有倾向性的
pathological	走极端的
paucity	贫乏
pedantic	迂腐的
penchant	嗜好
penury	赤贫
perennial	永恒持续的

词汇	释义
perfidious	背信弃义的
perfunctory	敷衍的
permeable	可渗透的
pervasive	四处弥漫的
phlegmatic	沉着冷静的
piety	虔诚
placate	安抚
plasticity	可塑性
platitude	陈词滥调
plethora	过多，过剩
plummet	骤然下跌
porous	能渗透的
pragmatic	实用主义的
preamble	序言
precarious	不稳定的
precipitate	仓促的
precursor	先驱
presumptuous	自以为是的
prevaricate	搪塞推诿
pristine	一尘不染的
probity	正直
problematic	有问题的
prodigal	挥霍的
profound	深刻的
prohibitive	禁止的
proliferate	激增
propensity	（性格上的）倾向
propitiate	劝解抚慰
propriety	礼貌得体
proscribe	禁止
pungent	一针见血的
qualified	有资质的
quibble	争辩
quiescent	沉寂的
rarefied	过于高雅的
recalcitrant	顽抗的
recant	公开放弃
recluse	隐居者
recondite	深奥艰涩的
refractory	难以控制的

词汇	释义
refute	驳斥
relegate	贬黜
reproach	责备
reprobate	行为不检的人
repudiate	批判驳斥
rescind	废除
resolution	正式决议
resolve	决定
reticent	沉默寡言的
reverent	恭敬虔诚的
sage	睿智的
salubrious	舒适宜人的
sanction	正式批准
satiate	使充分满足
saturate	使饱和
savor	滋味，气味
secrete	隐匿
shard	（玻璃、陶器、金属的）碎片
skeptic	怀疑的
solicitous	关怀的
soporific	催眠的
specious	似是而非的
spectrum	范围
sporadic	零星的
stigma	耻辱
stint	限制
stipulate	规定
stolid	冷漠的
striated	有条纹状的
strut	炫耀
subpoena	（以传票）传唤
subside	平息缓和
substantiate	证实
supersede	取代
supposition	假定设想
tacit	默认的
tangential	间接相关的
tenuous	牵强的
tirade	长篇的批评性发言
torpor	麻木迟钝

词汇	释义
tortuous	曲折的
tractable	易处理的
transgression	违反
truculence	暴躁，野蛮
vacillate	踌躇
venerate	崇敬
veracious	诚实的
verbose	冗长的
viable	切实可行的
viscous	(液体)黏稠的
vituperative	责骂的
volatile	不稳定的
warranted	担保的
wary	小心提防的
welter	翻滚
whimsical	异想天开的

Note

第二节 句——长难句理解

1. ETS行文困难重重

> The text features implemented in the Source Finder prototype were intended to allow users to screen source text for length, content, clarity, density, and level of argumentation. Length filtering is extremely important, since copyright constraints dictate that the number of words in a reading comprehension passage must be less than 10% of the total number of words in the source document from which the passage was extracted. For example, the source document for a 450-word GRE passage must include at least 4,500 words.

上面一段话是笔者在Source Finder的研究论文中找到的。Source Finder 软件对文章的判断是基于原文章长度、内容、清晰性、密度以及论证程度等各种因素。这些因素对于计算机来说并不困难；真正“困难”的是，GRE文章的长度永远是架在ETS身上的枷锁，出于版权限制，**ETS用于实际考试的GRE文章最多只能引用10%的原文内容**，这种“带着镣铐跳舞”的结果是大量文章的改写、重写和删节。

难句理论的提出正是针对这种背景的深刻分析。在传统的四六级阅读中，考生对于难句的感受可能还不明显、不突出；但是在GRE阅读中，这些恐怖的难句不仅是难点，更是很多题目产生的温床。出于字数限制，ETS在GRE考试中自愿或是被迫使用了大量改写，把单位句子的长度和难度大大提高。有的GRE难句长度甚至堪比一段；很多句子中大量插入修饰补充说明内容，把整个句子主干分割得支离破碎；有的句子修改后各部分比例严重失衡，所以引入了很多特殊的倒装结构等等。GRE中的难句不是阅读老师渲染出来的，而是考生实践检验体会出来的。这些繁难的长句、复合句和复杂修饰句又很容易成为考试题目集中的重点。对于难句概念，论文中给予了统计学上的支持佐证。

> As the data indicate, there is a wide disparity between the feature values calculated in the 33 original sources and in the passages that were eventually developed from those sources. For example, the average sentence length of the five original sources is 23.2 words, compared with 35.0 words for the corresponding GRE passages. Similarly, the average type-token ratio for the five sources is .26, compared with .56 for the corresponding GRE passages.
>
> As noted earlier, the Source Finder feature labeled UniqWordPerWord is a measure of the size of the vocabulary used in a given document. This feature is also called type-token ratio because it is a ratio of the total number of word in a document to the total number of word tokens in the document. The type-token ratio calculated for a particular document can range from 1, in the case of all unique words, to 1/N where N is the total number of words in the document. Certain word types occur relatively more frequently than so-called content words.

通过上述的材料我们不难看出，GRE句子的长度已经是其特有的一种“符号”了，人们戏谑GRE为“God Read English”。句子长度长容易理解，而文中提到的参数type-token ratio比较专业，是指全文中独特单词占总文字字数的比例。根据语言学专家的研究结论，句子以及文章中独特单词越多，专业术语和复杂内容一般就更多，最后导致全文理解难度提高。可见，GRE文章经过原材料的加工和改写后其基本特点就是：句子更长，句子之中包含的不可替代的信息更多，因此更难理解。由此可见，顺利地解读难句是征服GRE阅读的必要条件之一，而提炼句子主体词的训练则有效地针对了type-token ratio参数提示的必要能力：考生需要在充满了学术专业名词的长句子中提出关键词、观点等有价值的信息。

我们通过一个例句来看：

【例3-1】

Many readers are convinced that the compelling mysteries of each plot conceal elaborate structures of allusion and fierce, though shadowy, moral ambitions that seem to indicate metaphysical intentions, though efforts by critics to articulate these intentions have generated much controversy.

译文

许多读者认为，各(剧本)引人入胜的神秘情节掩饰了其构思精巧的文意暗示，也遮盖了那看似朦胧实则激进的道德感——这种道德感向人们表明了形而上学的意图（虽说为了使这种形而上学的意图得以更加清晰地表达，文学评论家们的努力已经引发了诸多争议）。

解析

看到这句话时，想必很多读者首先映入眼帘的是一个提示词“though”(尽管)，可能接下来马上就反应出“反义转折”这样的概念，但是仔细一想，这个“though”到底转折的是谁？整个句子的意思又是在哪一个点上进行的转折？该提示词对于真正令人们困惑的问题实际上帮助甚微。

首先辨析句子结构。本句有着标准的由“that”引导的宾语从句结构，而主句也简单：Many readers are convinced...(许多读者认为……)。光是这个主语和谓语部分，我们无法得出任何的信息，这就体现了GRE句子的一大难点：宾语复杂。因为宾语是人对客观存在世界的第一印象表述，所以**客观存在越复杂，宾语就越复杂**。

分意群。我们把宾语部分的意群做一个划分：“the compelling mysteries of each plot”(各(剧本)引人入胜的神秘情节)、“conceal”(掩盖)、“elaborate structures of allusion”(构思精巧的文意暗示)、“fierce, though shadowy”(看似模糊实则强烈)、“moral ambitions”(道德感)、“seem to indicate metaphysical intentions”(表明形而上学的意图)、“though”、“efforts by critics”(评论家们的努力)、“to articulate these intentions”(阐明形而上学的意图)、“have generated much controversy”(产生了诸多争议)。

前三个意群是标准的主谓宾结构：“各(剧本)引人入胜的**情节**掩盖了构思精巧的文意暗示”。第四个意群实际上是对第五个意群的修饰，是形容词性结构。第三和第五两个意群“构思精巧的文意**暗示**”和“**道德感**”是平行并列关系，都是被掩盖的对象。故而前面的意思是：情节掩盖了暗示以及道德感。

接下来出现的一个定语从句提示词“that”提示我们后文的内容都是在具体描述“moral ambitions”。“seem to indicate metaphysical intentions”(表明形而上学的意图)。作为承接性谓语动词，“indicate”往往表明两个名词之间的关系，即“moral ambitions”和“metaphysical intentions”二者属于“一根绳上的蚂蚱”。

再往后我们又看到了一个由“though”引导的让步状语从句，那么其必然和刚才的“seem to indicate metaphysical intentions”形成一种让步转折关系。从句中的一个动词“articulate”的意思是“使……得以清晰的表达”；让步状语从句的主语部分“efforts by critics to articulate these intentions”(评论家们努力阐明形而上学的意图)这件事承接的谓语宾语部分是“have generated much controversy”(引发了诸多争议)。这个让步状语从句本身的意思不难理解，但问题是这个部分到底和前文有什么转折？在这个从句部分中，其核

心意思是 "形而上学的意图没能得以清晰、准确、唯一的传递"，由此我们不难看出这个意思是和"moral ambitions that seem to indicate metaphysical intentions"形成反义关系的：前面说"道德感表明了形而上学的意图"，后面说"形而上学的意图没能得以清晰的传递"。其原因在于前半句：道德感被"神秘的情节"掩盖住了。

通过上例我们不难看出，学术文章容易出现难点的地方往往都是宾语部分：因为客观存在越复杂，需要予以表述清楚的信息就越冗长混乱；再加上语言层面的变换，很容易把考生迷倒。有人问我GRE的句子为什么难读？我的回答一律是"**即使翻译成中文你也看不懂**"。英语语言本身绝非是GRE的亮点所在，只不过由于ETS出题的专家学者们本身的英语水平太高，故而其设计出的考试内容在语言关上就能把很多人拒之于千里之外。所以考生在学习GRE的过程中，重点在于训练自己的头脑，使其始终保持在一种高速运转的状态之中。而这种GRE级别的句子就是ETS通过大量的语句改写、压缩之后得出的产物。也许把句子变得这么难并非ETS考官们的初衷，但在客观现实要求的面前，GRE的句子就已经变成了甚至连原作者也瞠目不识的面貌，并且多年以来已经形成了属于GRE考试的定式成规。所以，考生们欲征服GRE，解读难句是必过的关卡。

GRE考试是一门具有高度学术性、严谨性以及抽象性的考试，所针对的人群都是以英语为母语的考生。对于中国考生来说，认知学术英文的困难程度很大，阅读时的晦涩感也很强，这让很多从小英文基础很好的孩子感觉碰上了一座难以逾越的大山。说到英文的难，高端的英文阅读，其难度大致分为两种路线：一种是语言要素色彩缤纷的艺术路线，另一种是严密稳定的学术路线。可以说这两种路线取并集之后就构成了英文阅读的全部精华，然而能把这两条路线融会贯通从本质上就不是一件容易的事，当然，对于GRE的考生来说也不是必要的。

GRE阅读理解的难度并非如大部分考生想象的那种天马行空的繁杂，单纯靠辞藻修饰来增加难度绝非是GRE的测试方向，更不是一个未来做学术的学者所必备的水平。它要考查的是把一个抽象复杂的事情解析清楚的能力，是一个深入浅出的过程；而伟大的英文著作、散文、诗歌等，它的任务是利用曼妙的辞藻把平淡的生活艺术化、美化，是一个化简为繁的过程，在这一点上它和学术英文刚好是相反的两种路径。所以，考生在面对GRE阅读理解部分的时候，真正最大的难题是"在认知词汇的基础上精确理解句子的意思"，强调意思的准确性和唯一性。而如果像阅读散文小说那样 "一千个人有一千个哈姆雷特"的话，那必然是"天下大乱"。

对于大部分中国考生来说，首要问题出现在"认知词汇"上。因为很多同学词汇量不够大，而一般的说法也是GRE阅读文章难得根本就看不懂，这导致了部分人错以为只要词汇量特别高的话，GRE的阅读也不在话下。实际上当词汇量能达到一万三千左右的时候，才会发现GRE文章的真正难度是体现在句子意思理解和句间逻辑关系的把握上。而寻找句间逻辑关系又是基于准确解读单句的基础之上，故而笔者在书中此环节着力为考生描绘的就是如何解读好单个句子。

2. 为何中国同学阅读速度慢

根据我们长时间以来的调研和教学互动，我们不难看清一个现实，就是中国同学阅读英文的速度很慢。以所有中国同学最为重视的考试——高考为例，在我们对大一刚刚入学的700位同学所做的调查中发现，几乎有42%的同学在高考时英语阅读是没有全看完的。我们抛开应试问题不谈，单纯从阅读的角度来说，这种现象的普遍性和持久性不难说是个公认的问题。那么，为何会产生这样的问题？一个非常主要的原因在于"中国同学的阅读习惯不正确"。而这个主要问题又可以从两个角度来谈：

第一，中国同学理解文字信息的重点并非英文的本质。

第二，中国同学接受文字信息方式的不正确。

我们先看第一个问题，为何说中国同学理解文字的重点并非是英文的本质呢？因为大部分中国同学在做的工作是一种**“蹩脚的翻译“**，更有甚者是在**“背单词然后拼凑句意”**。这在很大程度上是多年以来的应试教育给同学们造成的不良影响，因为高考硬性规定需要掌握“定语从句”、“虚拟语态”、“同位语从句”、“强调句式”、“反义疑问句”等等，所以很多同学自从学习英文以来，上过的课、学过的课本和做过的练习册，所处的英文学习环境相对被动、局限性大，这就从客观上阻碍了同学从文字的本身去理解英文。总是习惯于背会讲过的语法、句式，然后拿到练习册和考卷上一做题，发现做对了，于是乎完成任务。所以很多时候同学们都是在进行一个人为设计好的游戏，熟悉的是相对固定的游戏规则，而非英文领域的天然规则。这也能够解释两个现象：1. 为何很多同学拿到选自外国文献的文章就一筹莫展，看到GRE、LSAT更如洪水猛兽一般。2. 为何很多同学自从上了大学以后英文阅读水平如股市一般震荡下挫。他们一旦脱离了长久以来别人为其设计好的游戏规则，需要从更真实的角度去探索高端英文时必然会造成不习惯，而这种不习惯以及没有老师像中学时期一样为他们描绘框架、设计游戏规则，才导致很多同学遭受打击之后灰心丧气，放弃了对于知识的探索，甚是可惜。

那么我们有必要探讨一下英文信息的本质是什么，不妨思考如下几个问题：

第一：英文在19世纪前的演化过程中有没有中文的因素掺杂其中？

第二：自己在看到英文的时候，第一反应是什么？

对于第一个问题答案是明确的，那就是：没有。可以说，在19世纪及工业革命资本主义扩张以前，古老的东方和西方世界几乎是隔绝的，青藏高原和万里长城从形态上隔绝了中国与西方的联系，封建体制的国家从思想上禁锢了国民与外界的交流。因此，中华民族与希腊人、日耳曼人、波斯人、匈奴人不同，中华文明一点也没有参与到英文的发展过程当中，那么英文的发展必然不会牵涉到中华文明的元素。而一个民族的文化元素可以概括为一个民族对于世界的认知过程，尤其是语言，代表着这个民族对于客观世界的认识、接受并理解的方式。所以说，西方的英文所代表的是另外一种认知世界的方式，当然也就表明即使你一点中文都不会，也可以从西方人认识世界的角度来体会英文的本质。所以对于英文阅读很困难的同学们来说，我们的第一步就是要有意识地消除自己头脑中固有的中式思维，准备以一个欧美人的角度去理解文字。

这就说到了第二个问题，语言在我们眼里到底应该是什么？在所有语言传递的过程中，最重要的两步就是解码和吸收，而中国同学在此基础之上必须再进行一次编码的过程，就是把英文编成中文(无论现在的水平如何，任何人都会有这样的习惯，这就是母语的影响)，因此导致了同学们阅读速度的下降。我在之前说到很多中国同学阅读速度很慢，并非仅仅是单纯意义上的时间长，更重要的是“发挥不出应有的速度”。为何我们习惯于把编码再编成中文呢？因为中文对于我们来说是最直接最简单的，用英文讲叫“accessible”。那么为了解决这一情况，我们必须要找到的一个答案就是，到底什么东西能比中文简单？什么东西是英美人将英文传递进大脑的载体？上一段我们说到语言是人类认知世界的方式，这个答案很清晰了，英国人传递进大脑的信息不是字母，而是他们对于客观世界的认识和印象，说通俗点，叫做**“画面感”**。没有人会对画面感感到陌生，这也是人类幼年的时候对于万物的认识方式，既然我们要打破长久的中式思维，从西方的角度理解英文，那么从最基本、最初始的状态和方式开始训练是有必要的。

举个例子来看：比如读到一个单词eject，我们基本上都认识它，意思为“弹射出”。如果反应中文才能理解的话未免太慢，比较正确的阅读习惯应该是看到它脑海当中出现一幅图画：某物A扔出去了一个东西，那个东西在空中飞……。这个A一定是eject前面的主语，动词后边承接的一定是宾语B，所以在读完B之后基本的画面就形成了。你肯定想要知道这个B被扔到哪里去了，于是乎就有了A eject B to somewhere。那个somewhere就是目的地所在。如果你还想知道A为什么要把B扔到那个地方的话，原因自然就会在somewhere后面的in order to 或者for引导的信息当中提示给你。学术英文的句子毫无例外都是这样组建起来的，也符合人类认知世界方式的顺序。大家也许会有一个疑惑，就是“如果我读到的信息不是单纯的一个一个词构成的画面意思，而是几个词串在一起，又怎么办呢？”这就牵涉到了接下来要讨论的一个方法，叫做“分意群”。

3. 意群是什么

“意群”很多同学应该都听过，但是利用意群来阅读英文难句却未必人人都做过。关于分意群的方法有很多种，但是一个意群最重要的特色不是语法特点，而是“一幅不可简化的画面”。举个最简单的例子：如果你想表达“窗户上有只猫”，那么最直接的对于名词的描述应该是“a cat on the window”。这五个单词可以说就构成了一个画面，几乎无法再简化，也没有其他的任何一个单词能表述出这样一个画面，而接下来这只猫有什么样的动作和状态等等就又有谓语、宾语或者系表结构予以修饰了。因此，我们可以把这五个单词看做一体，即称之为一个“意群”。

我们不妨拿这样一个例句来看：

❙ 例3-2 ❙

This preference for exogamy, Gutman suggests, may have derived from West African rules governing marriage, which, though they differed from one tribal group to another, all involved some kind of prohibition against unions with close kin.

这句话是GRE阅读长度中等的句子。第一行出现了一个插入语“Gutman suggests”(古特曼认为)，这个插入语出现的位置非常准确，为何？因为它之前的四个单词正好是一个意群：“This preference for exogamy”(对于异族通婚的偏好)，出现在考生脑海当中的信息是一种客观存在的事情，“某些人结婚都和外族人结婚”，这个事情也就作为本句的核心主语。而这个插入语的位置是不能出现在前四个单词的任何两个之间的，否则意思会发生混淆。如果插在preference的后面，就成了“古特曼提出的偏好”，意思就是古特曼只是对于“偏好”有某种概念，而非对于“异族通婚的偏好”有何见解，意思自然大变。

再往后看到谓语的部分：“may have derived”(也许发源于)。这时候一定有读者心里有疑惑，觉得derive from是一个经典的短语，意为“源于”，为何意群只分到derive就停止了？这就牵涉到关于短语的问题：介词到底跟着谁？

大家大概都背过这样的短语：compare A with B，意思是“把A和B进行比较”，实际上with 表示前后两个名词处于平行并列的关系，属于同一个逻辑层面，这个短语直译也就是“把A放在和B同等的平台上进行比较(compare)”。而另一个短语，compare A to B，意思是“把A比作B”，为何只改变了一个介词，整个短语的意思就大变了呢？全在于对于介词的理解上，to这个介词是一种表明指向性的介词，其后往往伴随“目的”的出现。在这里直译就是“为了达到B，我们把A和B比一下”，也就是希望A能像B一样，使二者具有共性，因此称做“把A比作B”，显然B是对A发出动作的目标。

这两个短语之所以在意思上大相径庭，全都是因为介词的存在使得B的地位和意义不同。因此，我们需要说明的一点是：**介词是跟着后面的名词的!** 它要表达的是“其他事物所发出的动作或状态与介词之后名词的关系”。再有一点也可作为明证，介词的英文为“preposition”，pre- 表示“在……之前”的意思，“pos”表示“放置”，“-ition”是个名词后缀，因此“preposition”直译应该译为“放在前面的东西”。既然是“放在前面”的，那么自然是放在名词前面，因此介词是随着后面的名词的。

我们再看一下这句话的谓语部分：“may have derived”(发源)，本句的主语和谓语构建的画面感是“对外通婚这件事情作为……结果”，接下来出现的自然就该是原因了：“from West African rules governing marriage”(源于西非关于婚姻的规矩)。到此为止，整个事件的因果关系已然交代清楚了：一个抽象概念的规则控制着人们的婚姻习惯。

在本句后面出现了which 引导的定语从句，用来修饰“West African rules governing marriage”。看到“which”之后，我们的大脑已经做好了准备接受关于“西非婚姻规矩”的信息。就在此时，出现了一个让步转折“though they differ”(尽管它们有所区别)，由此可知这些婚姻的规矩和某事物有所差别，接下来需要了解的就是这些规矩到底与何物“不一样”，也就出现了“from one tribal group to another”(从一个部落到另一个部落)这样一个介词短语作为differ这个动词的修饰，在我们眼前的画面感应该就是“西非婚姻的规矩在各个部落间都不一样”(当然这个很抽象也很简单)。然后出现的是宾语从句的主干部分：“all involved some kind of prohibition”(所有的规矩都牵涉到某一个特定的禁忌)，画面感就是这些规矩“都”反对某事物，具体的事物就由“against”引导的名词予以表述了：“unions with close kin ”(近亲结婚)。

到此为止，定语从句中的画面感也就比较清晰了，“西非各个婚姻规矩千差万别，但都禁止近亲结婚!”或者更简单一些“西非部落的人各种结婚的组合都有，就是没有近亲的!”这都可以。此定语从句所说的内容是用来修饰“West African rules governing marriage”的，故而不论从句里面的信息说什么，都不影响主句的意思。

整句话的含义相对很明朗了：“人们之所以和外族人结婚，是因为受西非的传统影响，在西非，近亲结婚是不允许的。”这个画面感虽然很简单，但是这样的分析有助于考生减少语法现象的混杂对于理解句意的困难。

我们再看这样一个句子：

▎例3-3 ▎

An impact (on the Mars) capable of ejecting a fragment of the Martian surface into an Earth-intersecting orbit is even less probable than such an event on the Moon, in the view of the Moon's smaller size and closer proximity to Earth.

在这句话中先读到的部分是“An impact (on the Mars)”。我们有必要对impact这个词的概念进行一下澄清。impact这个词在韦氏词典上的解释为：“an impinging or striking especially of one body against another”，强调的是一种“冲击”，而大部分同学背过的意思应该是“影响”，也就容易认为这个词是“一词多义”。实则不然，impact的解释第二条写道：“the force of impression of one thing on another”，某物对于另一个事物造成的“影响”，这种“影响”实质上是“冲击”所造成的，是“冲击”这个事件的结果，是一种process与result的关系。因此这个词描述的实际上是一个客观存在的事件，而非两件事；读到此处我们头脑中反映出的画面应该是“火星被某物撞击了”。

大家可能会有一系列疑问：这样的撞击有什么特征呢？就出现在后边的一个意群中，“capable of ejecting a fragment”（能够弹射出碎片）；弹射出什么碎片呢？继续往后出现的意群是“of the Martian surface”（弹射出火星表面的碎片）；那么把碎片弹到什么地方呢？就出现在后边几个单词中“into an Earth-intersecting orbit”（弹到与地球的交叉运行轨道之中）。到此为止，这个画面感构建得已经比较完整了，而且原文给我们提供的主语部分的信息也完整了。

这样一个主语（表示一个事物）怎么样了呢？也就出现了后边的系表结构“is even less probable”（可能性不如其他事情的大）。我们需要了解的是什么样的事情比这件事发生的几率还大，即“than such an event on the Moon”（不如在月球上发生这样的事情可能性大），这里的“such an event”指的自然是本句主语中出现的“impact”了。至此，本句中出现了一个关于发生概率的比较；后文出现了一个短语“in the view ”，直译为“就……的观点来看”，而这种翻译显然太复杂，剖析其实质的话应是“原因”的意思，其后引导的内容表示的应该是前半句之所以成立的原因：“of the Moon's smaller size and closer proximity to Earth”（因为月球体积更小，而且离地球更近）。这种因果关系的存在，就构成了GRE阅读可能出现的题目风格，即推断题。

我们有理由相信，GRE的出题人员完全可以根据【例3-3】这句话出这样一道题：

根据原句所述，现在有一个行星，其体积介于火星与月球之间，距离地球的距离也介于火星和月球跟地球的距离之间，请问在该行星上发生类似碎片弹射的概率比起火星与月球如何？

答案很显然应该是这种概率也介于火星和月球的概率之间。这是通过信息之间的相关性自然而然可以推断出来的，信息一旦建立了相关性之后，就成了动态的信息。GRE的阅读是一种动态化的阅读，其文字之间是有逻辑关系的。有因有果才能构建起映射关系，这个风格和大部分做“presentation”（陈述）的英文阅读是不同的。能够在信息之中剖析清楚来龙去脉、因果关系，这是日后作为一个顶级人才所必须掌握的重要素质，也是ETS考试设计者们所秉持的初衷。

4. 如何训练

刚才利用两个例句大致描述了一下什么叫做“构建画面感”，实际上画面感才是人类共通的、最直接、最简单甚至最原始的理解方式，既然中英文之间存在天然隔阂，那么我们为何不利用画面感作为桥梁纽带，来疏通自己与陌生英文之间的关系呢？基于此，就涉及最关键的一个谈论环节，即：如何科学地进行训练？

1. 登泰山而小天下，重视水平档次，千万不宜细水长流。
2. 不追求过遍数，印象消失之后再看学过的句子。

这是在练习GRE阅读基本功过程当中最重要的两点，我们先说第一点。有很多同学总发信问我这样的问题：

“老师，我是一个英语基础不太好的学生，在学校时英语课上得也是马马虎虎，上次考四级勉强考过。对于我来说英语阅读很多时候是在靠做题的常规方法把该拿的分拿到。经过一个月的学习之后，我把词汇背了三遍，但是还没信心开始复习阅读。就我现在的情况来看，您觉得我应该先读些什么材料，再看GRE比较好呢？”

诚然有很多同学在刚接触GRE阅读的时候会萌生这样的想法，认为以自己现在的功力还驾驭不了这个级别的句子。在这一群体之中，实不乏有这样一批词汇背得很好的同学，却依然对阅读心怀恐惧。这种未战先怯的心态从主观意识上来讲是源于我们多年以来的一种学习习惯，叫“由浅入深、循序渐进”。我承认这种习惯在绝大部分时间内对同学们的学习是不无裨益的，但是，作为一个学习GRE的同学来说，需要的不是循序渐进。

对于学习理科的同学来说，最重要的任务是打好基础，才能学习并掌握好更深一层次的理论内容。比如只有学好了代数公式才能明白二次方程、学会了向量方程才能去做立体几何、弄懂了微积分才会理解常微分方程，在学习进步的过程中最忌讳的是有漏洞而不补救，只要把每一部分知识掌握得滚瓜烂熟，就一定能够学会更难的知识。然而文科却不是如此，我没见过有谁能做到把高考辅导书、考研辅导书的语文、英语、政治部分做七八遍然后在考场上就能得满分的。因为文科最讲究的是提升档次，也就是我刚才说到的第一条“登泰山而小天下，不宜细水长流”。语言和文字归根结底其作用在于使人们“用以前人曾拥有过的方式去理解世界”，试问如果一个人几年时间内都总是在阅读同一个级别的文字，他的水平会有多少提升呢？

本书的读者都有着十几年的学习经历，真正最需要的应该是最高端的知识以及人文社会所共同认可的文字信息，而非在某一个圈子中逡巡不前，最终白白浪费掉大好的时光。所以，对于大部分接触GRE的同学来说，眼前就摆着一个机会，你们需要利用GRE的阅读来提升自己，不光会在英文功底上有所飞跃，还会在逻辑思维上百尺竿头更进一步。当你们将GRE级别的文章烂熟于胸以后，再看之前自认为困难而不肯花时间去学习的英文，那种阅读起来的畅快感才会体现得淋漓尽致。不要怕读不明白GRE长难句，只要能达到大学英语四六级的水平，更重要的是只要付出艰苦卓绝的努力，就一定可以在阅读理解能力上在相对短的时间内取得飞跃。于此，笔者为各位考生隆重推荐一本久经市场考验的GRE系列丛书：《GRE/GMAT阅读难句教程》，杨鹏编著。各位备考GRE的考生一定要拿出相当多的时间来好好练习此书，付出的努力一定和你最终的收获成正比！

谈到“努力”二字，有的人一定还关心与之辅助的“方法原则”，没有方法和原则的努力只能是徒耗心力，到头来是竹篮打水。之前我说过“阅读的本质在于熟悉表达习惯”，关键在于通过反复阅读以达到熟悉的地步。在新东方的课堂上我们讲到GRE词汇的背法，上课的同学一定也记得，那就是三个字“过遍数”。但是，GRE阅读训练的“过遍数”和背单词完全不一样：背单词讲究记忆和印象，只要能认识就可以；而阅读需要的是一种分析和处理信息的能力，所以有时候把文章内容记得一清二楚对于分析文章反倒不利。因此，这就说到了我们刚才提出的第二条“不追求过遍数，印象消失之后再看学过的句子”，尽量做到每次看句子的时候大脑中都会在分析作者写这句话的意图何在，以及诸如此类的逻辑信息。我们所一直强调的GRE阅读的关键在于疏通逻辑，单纯的记忆对于提高考生解读单句的能力是不利的，最佳状态是每次都能以全新的状态读明白作者是怎么写出一句话的。基于此，我建议考生们在自己练习时能保持：

1. 每天至少读懂15个长难句。
2. 每天至少分析清楚两篇文章。

完成这些工作看起来不过举手之劳，但学过GRE的同学都明白满篇生涩的难词对于初学乍练者的难度。更何况完成这些工作主要的难点是在思维上，学习越是到了高端的地步，想要有进境就越难，故而希望本书的读者们能在学习的过程中不骄不躁，用毅力来克服GRE阅读这个摆在眼前的大山。

5. GRE长难句解析

刚才我们介绍了关于句子应该如何分意群去阅读的问题，介绍这一环节的目的在于分意群作为基本功能够帮助我们更高效地完成对于长难句的剖析。故而在本章的这一个环节，我们重点讲解如何解读清楚GRE长难句。

这是我在2012年2月寒假班的时候收到的一位同学给我写的信：

“老师你好！我是一个大三的学生。从小学开始我一直辛辛苦苦学了将近十年英语之后接触到了GRE考试，可是迎接我的文章句子却每每令人望而生畏。我发现大学以前我们那么多年学习的语法、固定搭配、词组等等在GRE的句子里用得极为灵活，以至于让我应接不暇；更头疼的事情是我发现无论我怎么分析这个句子的结构语法，总会在随便某个地方蹦出一句我又看不懂的话——即使我把里面的单词都查了一遍；除此之外最要命的是有的句子我已经把词汇和语法搞定了，可是翻译不出来，总觉得自己总结出来的意思有些不成人话。这应该怎么办呢？”

像这位同学一样有着相同痛苦的朋友估计不在少数。首先在语法方面，GRE的句子绝对可以保证符合规范，甚至可以说GRE、GMAT、LSAT是世界上对于英语语法的使用最为严谨的考试，这一点从考试的专业方向上就可以窥见一斑：学术、商业、法律。你也许可以在盖斯凯尔、狄更斯等人的小说里看到天马行空的语句，但是你不会在GRE阅读里看到有歧义的句子。学术型文章的语言表达都是规范并且相对稳定的，所以考生只要打好英语语法的基本功，就没有理由读不懂GRE长难句。

那么GRE长难句当中经常出现的基本语法有哪些呢？比如：

- 定语从句
- 宾语从句
- 同位语从句
- 主语从句
- 宾语倒装
- 插入语修饰
- 双重否定结构

以上七种语法现象可以大致涵盖GRE长难句中经常出现的情况，其实同学们在初中高中以及大学的学习过程中都学过。很多人批评我国的英语教育体系残缺、设计不当。但是平心而论，我认为初中和高中这六年间的基础英语教育为我们打下了非常坚实的语法基础；如果没有这些基本功的话，我们在阅读GRE这样的文章时就更难以招架了。可是，就算我们能熟练掌握这些基本语法，就能保证一定可以把句子读明白吗？不妨来看一眼下面这个句子：

▎例3-4▐

Such variations in size, shape, chemistry, conduction speed, excitation threshold, and the like as had been demonstrated in nerve cells remained negligible in significance for any possible correlation with manifold dimensions of mental experience.

译文

神经元细胞间在尺寸、形状、化学成分、传导速度、兴奋阈值以及相似度上有差异，这已得到证实；(但)这些差异和人类各种各样的神经感觉建立联系时，其作用微乎其微。

解析

按照传统的英语学习方式，我们看到一个句子的时候都要找出主、谓、宾语，然后译出来，再根据意思拼凑出句意；随着学习年头增长，头脑中逐步消除中英文的翻译过程，直接根据词汇拼出句意。我们从小到大在攻克英语考试的征途上，熟练掌握到第二步的时候应该已经能够应付一般英语考试、阅读国外学术文章了。但是，由于GRE长难句是由ETS的专家们从国外学术期刊杂志上摘下来的，再进行语法变换，把两三句合并成一句，也就凭空多了许多的插入、倒装、省略、逆向指代。这些语法拼凑起来，也就构成了冗长、意思复杂、语法晦涩的GRE长难句。

在本句中"Such variations in size, shape, chemistry, conduction speed, excitation threshold, and the like as had been demonstrated in nerve cells"，这么长的成分可以说是本句的全部主语，但其核心就在于"variations"，至于后边的尺寸、形状、化学成分、传导速度等等都是对"差异"的修饰，以及后边的补充：说明这些差异在神经细胞例子中得到了验证……这些描述的都是variations。

本句从"remain negligible" 开始出现谓语和宾语部分，对于表达句子核心意思的谓语部分固化翻译，难以辨析具体意思。GRE长难句的谓语部分经常给人一种似曾相识的感觉，但翻译过来非常别扭。这不光是因为ETS出题人员增加了句子难度，也是要照顾到该句逻辑关系上的准确性。句中"remained negligible in significance"，挨个词理解的话：remain保持，negligible微不足道，significance重要性，串起来就是某事物"在重要性的程度上，依旧保持着微不足道的状态"。但是在训练GRE阅读的时候，看到这一串词，脑子里只需要有一个意思："不重要"。

到了本句的宾语部分的时候，一个介词"for"表示"对于……"的意思，承接前后，表示"这些差异对于某事物来说不重要"，只需看清楚后面的事物："any possible correlation"(相关性、关联性)，到此为止句意是"差异对于建立相关性不重要"，那么我们有必要知道的是"差异和什么东西建立不起来相关性"，即"manifold dimensions of mental experience"(神经感觉的各个方面)。读到此处就不难理解了：神经元的差异不能解释人类各种不同的神经感觉(如冷、热、酸、甜等)。

通过【例3-4】我们不难看出来，GRE的句子实际上只是把最基本的语法规则进行线性的合成产生的，而正是由于各式各样语法的组成形式是无限的，所以会让我们觉得很晦涩。我们一直不提倡靠死记硬背语法的方式来学习句子，在上一个部分中我们给大家说过英语的受众范围有自己理解世界的方式，所以我们的任务是学会如何按照别人的角度来思考语言：其中最重要的手段就是通过切分意群来构建画面感——读到哪儿反映到哪儿的意思，直到句子读完，一个完整的画面感才得以呈现。为了能够帮助读者更高效地读懂句子，我们可以大致把句子讲解的过程分成以下几步：

第一步：迅速识别主谓宾，辨析句子结构。

第二步：分割意群。

第三步：找出核心意思，理解意群之间的关系。

也许每个人都有自己习惯的阅读方法，但在这里我们要强调的是：不管你以前习惯用哪种方法来读英文句子，只有能够把句中每一个语素解读清楚的方法才是科学的方法。考生在初期勿要为了追求速度而忽略了对句子意思的把握，只要有科学的阅读方式，假以时日，阅读速度一定会逐渐加快。

| 例3-5 |

The appreciation of traditional oral American Indian literature has been limited, hampered by poor translations and by the difficulty, even in the rare culturally sensitive and aesthetically satisfying translation, of completely conveying the original's verse structure, tone, and syntax.

译文

对于美国印第安传统口语文学的欣赏，一直受制于蹩脚的翻译，即使是那种不可多得的既体现出文化的敏锐感、又给人以美感的译作，也难以完整地传递出原作的诗体结构、语调和句法。

解析

第一步，辨析句子结构。本句当中一个由even引导的插入语表示让步，在GRE长难句阅读中需要第一时间反应出来此插入语的作用——反义重复，反向补充说明difficulty。

第二步，分意群："the appreciation"、"of traditional oral American Indian literature"、"has been limited"、"by poor translation"、"and by the difficulty"、"of completely conveying"、"the original's verse structure, tone, and syntax"、"even"、"in the rare sensitive and aesthetically"、"satisfying translation"。对于插入语的解释，统一放在主句之后。至于介词，也统一分给后边的名词，因为英文表达信息的方式从来都是先主体、后修饰，所以动词引导的介词短语，传递的信息永远都先是动词概念，而后再跟随名词概念予以补充，介词的作用在于更加准确地传达宾语和主语或者主谓的关系，所以英美人脑子里很少有"词组"这个概念。

第三步：合并词汇。"appreciation"+"traditional oral literature"+"limited"+"poor translation"+"difficulty"+"conveying"+"structure, tone, syntax" / "even"+"sensitive and satisfying"。前边三个意群实际上主要是appreciation的意思：对于什么的欣赏呢？→ traditional oral literature。这样的欣赏如何了呢？→ limited被限制了，hampered造成损害了。为何造成的呢？→ poor translation and difficulty。什么样的difficulty？→ 难以completely conveying完整地传递信息。关于什么的信息呢？→ structure，tone，syntax结构、语调、语法方面难以完整传递。这就是最为基础的理解信息的能力，因为英美读者接受信息传达的习惯方式是这样的。英美人脑子中并没有固定的意思，ETS的出题者也没有人会背韦氏大词典的解释从而将句子拼凑而来，所以借助语法而不依靠语法、理解词汇而不记忆词汇，做到了这两点才有可能摆脱长难句的框架。

然后再看插入语：even引导的插入语表示让步，所以可以判断出其句意一定和全句的核心意思相反，全句说某些信息难以完整地传递，即使translation既有文化上的敏锐感，也在审美感觉上能够令人满意，也不能完成这样无法完成的任务。

可能很多读者认为limited、hampered这些词是核心，那只是停留在句子的表层，放到文中。**"不能欣赏这样的文字"**只是表象，是**结果**。我们需要找到这个结果的逻辑上一层，是什么导致了这样的结果发生呢？正是由于**翻译印第安文学的文字**，所以才欣赏不了这些文学作品。

GRE阅读难句是由英美的学术论文加工改造而成，论文讲究的学术性自然就是GRE句子和篇章的根本特性：也许没有华丽曼妙的辞藻，也许用不到天马行空的意识流，但是想把GRE的句子读明白的话，要求考生的头脑必须十分清楚。把一个句子准确地读懂——而非大致明白它的“意境”——可能会是我们考生长久以来需要面对的难题。基于此，我们把长难句的难点陈列如下：

- 宾语复杂
- 句子结构混乱
- 修饰复杂

例3-6

It is possible to demonstrate by other methods refined structural differences among neuron types; however, proof was lacking that the quality of the impulse or its condition was influenced by these differences, which seems instead to influence the developmental patterning of the neural circuits.

译文

（诚然）我们能够用其他方法证实在不同神经元之间存在严格的结构性差异；但是，（我们）缺乏证据说明神经冲动的性质或状态被这些差异所影响，而这些差异影响的却是神经回路的发育模式。

解析

第一步：辨析句子结构。本句中间有分号，表示顺承连接，但后面有一个however，预示着可能出现的逻辑态度转折。从大体上划分句子非常重要。再往后有一处逗号，接着定语从句修饰前句。到此即可。

第二步：从前半句开始逐步阅读，先分意群：“it is possible”、“to demonstrate by other methods”、“refined structural differences among neuron types”；**词汇合并，找出核心意思**：“可行”、“证实”、“差异”、“存在于神经元类型之间”。第二组意群中的demonstrate是个典型的承接性动词，看到它脑中马上应该要准备接受后面宾语的信息，下文会说“证明”了什么事情，此宾语是内容的**核心**。所以，快速准确地判断动词是否是承接性动词能够节约阅读的时间、提高速度，让考生在阅读的过程中思路更清晰，知道该吸收什么信息。

前边几个单词综合起来的意思是“通过其他方法来证明某某事物是可行的”，这个某某事物就在“refined structural differences”中，核心词是differences，前面两个词和后面的补语是对它的修饰，为了使其更严谨、具有科学性。refined的词性当然是形容词，解释为：fastidious、cultivated、precise，可以翻译成“严格的”；后面的修饰语只要能看明白就可以了，一带而过。

第三步：后半句很长，不过根据我们的经验判断，这个长度是用一个定语从句撑起来的，属于虚假繁荣、纸老虎，大可不必害怕。

首先一个非常重要的词however，表示转折，作者从此开始否定前句说的内容观点。However属于**强转折**，和**强对比、强因果**一起归为GRE阅读的**三强词汇**，当它们出现的时候，要格外注意文章意思的理解。

接下来分析后半句，最主要的方法还是**分意群、合并词汇**，“proof was lacking”“that the quality of the impulse or its condition”“was influenced by these differences”。第一组直译为“证据是缺乏的”，但在阅读时出现在脑子中的信息当然就是“没证据、行不通、不行”表示否定，所以前三个词传递的信息就是否定后面的内容，到此为止就可以了。第二组就简单多了，核心就是impulse的condition和quality（神经冲动的性质或者状态）。第三组亦然，知道“被differences影响”就可以了。后半句在脑子中处理的时间非常短，只需要三秒钟就能完成，大脑中反映出的直接意思应该是“impulse的condition和quality并不受differences影响”。这样翻译，就已经把这句话要传达的意思和事物对象表述清楚了。

第四步：处理后置定语从句的取舍。本句最后部分的定语从句直接修饰differences，那么在阅读的过程中，我们对它应该是“从轻处理”的，但是决不能舍掉不看。如果时间够用，就大致判断一下这个从句的内容；如果时间紧，就记住这里有一处对于differences的内容补充说明，如果有题考查到就能迅速找到出处。

我们阅读一下这个定语从句：难点在前面几个单词“seems instead to influence....”，实际上seem和instead表达“看起来却又如何”，这两个词的使用是为了使表述更严谨准确，承接后面的宾语部分。基于前句句意，可翻译为“differences并不影响quality of the impulse or its condition，而像是影响了某某”，instead的意思已经在转折中带出。这个“某某”就是后面的“developmental patterning of the neural circuits”。至此，从句的意思已经分析清楚。在本句话中，虽然出场频率最高的词汇是difference，但是本句话所围绕展开的核心内容却是“impulse”(神经冲动)。作者希望能够证明“神经冲动的性质或状态受神经元之间差异的影响”，但不巧的是作者失败了，神经冲动并不受这些差异的影响，所以本句话的核心在于“神经冲动”，解读单句到了这个地步，对于考生来说再阅读任何的文章也就轻车熟路了。

例3-7

Traditionally, pollination by wind has been viewed as a reproductive process marked by random events in which the vagaries of the wind are compensated for by the generation of vast quantities of pollen, so that the ultimate production of new seeds is assured at the expense of producing much more pollen than is actually used.

译文

传统观点看来，风媒传粉被视做一种随机性的繁殖过程，在这个过程中风的不确定性靠植物产生的大量花粉予以弥补，所以新种子的产生需要以比实际需求的量多很多的花粉为代价才可以实现。

解析

首先判断一下句子的大致结构，本句话在中间由“so that”隔开，表示“如此……以至于……”，显然“so that”后面出现的内容是前半句内容的结果。先看前半句：前两个意群“pollination by wind”(风媒传粉)、“has been viewed as a reproductive process”(是一种繁殖过程)，到这里交代了关于“风媒传粉”的概念，可是此概念还不够全面，于是就有了接下来的定语修饰：“marked by random events”表明“风媒传粉其特点在于随机性”。这就是说无需背景知识原则，GRE会把需要考生了解的客观信息呈现出来。风媒传粉是怎样的一种随机过程呢？就在其后的定语从句中继续说明：“the vagaries of the wind are compensated for ”(风的不确定性得到了弥补)，“by the generation of vast quantities of pollen”(依靠产生大量的花粉)。读完前半句，作者才算把“风媒传粉“的概念交代清楚，是一种“依靠大量产生花粉来弥补风的不确定性的繁殖过程”，说简单点儿叫做“以量取胜”。

前半句是对概念及特征的描述，到了后半句，“so that”后面引导的就是前半句“以量取胜”的结果：“the ultimate production of new seeds”(新种子的产生)、“is assured”(得到了保证)。然而在后面的意群中：“at the expense”、“ of producing much more pollen”、“ than is actually used”。“at the expense”直译为“以……为代价”，连接前两个意群就表示“新种子的产生以某物为代价”，实则是一种条件关系：有了后者才会有前者，而二者又不可能同时存在。这个"代价"就是"producing much more pollen"(产生更多的花粉)、" than is actually used"(比实际需要的花粉还要多)。到此为止句义已经表达完毕，后半句所说的内容是"以量取胜"的细节，在句子内部概念和细节的因果逻辑关系就由"so that"承接了起来。

【例3-8】

Because the potential hazards pollen grains are subject to as they are transported over long distances are enormous, wind-pollinated plants have, in the view above, compensated for the ensuing loss of pollen through happenstance by virtue of producing an amount of pollen that is one to three orders of magnitude greater than the amount produced by species pollinated by insects.

译文

由于种子在长距离传输过程中所面临的潜在风险是巨大的，基于上述观点，风媒植物是通过产生比虫媒植物多一到三个数量级的花粉的特性来弥补随之而来的花粉损失。

解析

这句话的句子结构相对也很明显，一开始出现"because"引导的原因状语，后半句作为结果。先看前半句"the potential hazards"(潜在威胁)，什么样的"潜在威胁"呢？省略掉"that"的定语从句跟在后边："pollen grains are subject to"(花粉种子要面对的)，"as they are transported over long distances"(在它们长距离传输的过程中)，到此为止前半句的主语部分意思已经比较明晰了，就是"花粉种子需要面对在传输过程中的潜在威胁"。考生在阅读时会有这样的疑问：为何这些种子会面对潜在威胁呢？答案就在第一句话中曾经告诉过我们的"风的随机性"。前半句是系表结构："the potential hazards are enormous"(风险是巨大的)。到此为止前半句句意已经明朗了，其作用是作为后半句的原因。因为"风险巨大"，所以："wind-pollinated plants have compensated for the ensuing loss of pollen through happenstance"(风媒植物需要弥补随之而来的花粉损失)。那么"风媒植物弥补损失"所采取的方法就是"by virtue of producing an amount of pollen"(产生花粉)，其所产生的花粉特点是"that is one to three orders of magnitude greater"(风媒植物产生的花粉比别的要多一到三个数量级)，这种花粉比谁要多呢？答案就在最后一个意群中："than the amount produced by species pollinated by insects"(比虫媒传粉植物产生的花粉数量多一到三个数量级)。因此，这句话所表述的意思就是"由于不确定性较大，所以风媒植物需要产生比虫媒植物多一到三个数量级的花粉才可以"。作为文章的第二句话，其作用是作为第一句的例子，来说明"风媒植物以量取胜"，是【例3-7】的逻辑下一层。

通过刚才几个句子，相信读者们也已经大致适应了GRE句子的长度、难度。在以上三个难点中，最容易出问题的是修饰复杂。"修饰复杂"一般指的都是对核心主语或者宾语所添加的一系列修饰性成分，主要包括：形容词、动词过去分词、从属性名词，以及起着状语作用的从句。这种类型的句子对于考生者来说最大的难点在于不容易找到核心的意思，比如像：经常找错谓语动词、找错动词作用的目标名词、分辨不清修饰的主体是谁，诸如此类问题在阅读中屡见不鲜。

对于个人学习者来说，为了能够改善这种情况，大家往往喜欢借助词汇书或语法书去巩固基础。我承认这种做法无可厚非，但我不认为这是最有效率的解决方法：往往考生在考场上或者在练习中见到的句子都是全新的，即使你花费了两周的功夫强化语法，可能见到的句子还会令你不知所云。究其原因在于，GRE长难句把复杂的信息和思想以精炼的语句予以表达，这在本质上就决定了它不会太容易读懂；

如果我们以语法分析的习惯去阅读这种句子的话，难免容易掉到墨守成规、纸上谈兵的怪圈当中。对待这种句子，我们应该学会从思维上进行调整：英美人能够读懂的句子，我们也一定能够读懂。我们需要做的是从英美人阅读这个句子的角度来解读，在本章的第一部分我们给大家论述了培养构建画面感的习惯，一个不可分割的画面感就是一个意群，读完一个部分大脑反应出一个部分的意思，等所有的意群全都读完时整个一幅画面构建完毕，当做到这一点的时候才能保证拿到句子时心中不慌。语言不是借助语法简单拼凑词汇的工具，而是用于准确、优美、高效地传递思想的媒介，GRE这个级别的语言强调的是准确和高效地传递复杂的思想，所以我们在有了大学英语语法的基础之上，应该勇于抛弃语法，轻装前进。读这种句子的原则就是理解作者的思维和想法，故而我们强调“**阅读的本质在于熟悉文法的表达习惯**”。只有做到“熟悉”，考生才能在对付繁复晦涩的长难句时做到循序渐进、稳步提高。

Note

第三节 章——文章结构模式

2006年，GRE考试命题方在一篇研究论文中披露其阅读文章选材主要基于ETS自行开发的Source Finder网络文本识别软件，并对其测试信度和效度进行了严格的分析和评估。Source Finder的开发是为了帮助ETS在网络上自动检索数字论文库EBSCO中的文献，从中提炼出符合ETS各种考试风格要求的样本文章。根据开发的初衷，软件希望达到的主要目标有五个：

第一，减少ETS寻找合适文章的时间。由于在GRE考试设计过程中，寻找、改写学术材料和出题的过程需要许多专家学者花费相当多的时间才能做到文题对应、准确无漏，所以编写GRE的考题相对来说是一个很长的过程。为了提高工作效率，ETS就利用电脑软件的搜索功能快速找到原材料，节约时间成本。

第二，扩大现有备用文章的储备。正是由于设计GRE考试的成本所耗颇大，所以ETS会储备一些曾经被用来出GRE题目的文章原材料，有必要时可以对其重新改写加工、重新出题，提高工作效率。

第三，加快从笔考到机考的正规化转变过程。原来传统的GRE考试变成了机考以后，平均每个月都会有一到两次考试机会。在这么短的时间周期内想每次都从"寻找原材料"开始设计考题显然成本太高，故而有必要借助Source Finder软件储备可用的源文章。

第四，提供管理层对item writer(负责审查文章是否符合GRE风格的工作人员)评估文章重新考查的机会。这一点接触过GRE的考生应该都很了解：GRE的阅读文章选自英美学术期刊、论文，其学术特征非常明显，其用语最大限度地规避了英语本身语言层面的内容：如双关语、暗喻等文学类写作手法都不符合学术的要求；而且所用的单词大部分都是学术类词汇，尤其对于文中信息之间的承接上，更是慎之又慎。此外，GRE阅读文章的客观性很强，我们即使读上20篇文章，可能都不会出现一个像"I"这样的单词。所以，GRE阅读文章无论是内容的科学性、逻辑的严谨性、用语的规范性都堪称世界一流，ETS在其内容上的把关做得非常严格。

第五，Source Finder由哥伦比亚大学教授Rebecca Passonneau负责，该教授曾着力研究时态和语法规范的语义学计算模型。项目资金由GRE委员会和ETS方面提供，最后也由他们负责验收。可见该软件开发的相对重要性，以及在ETS整体考试发展规划中的地位。此报告中透露出很多关于GRE阅读考试的秘密和背景，笔者认为这些内容对教学研究的深入以及广大同学对考试的多角度认识，都有一定的帮助作用。除去关于该软件评测机理和实际使用效果的评估等内容外，笔者对论文的重要内容会做一定介绍和分析。

1. GRE文章的整体结构

GRE文章的源材料是浩如烟波的学术论文，那么Source Finder软件是如何选材的呢？它又会先从哪个角度入手判断某一篇文章是否适合被用来改编成为GRE文章呢？设计人员首先瞄准了文章整体的结构，一篇学术科研论文的段落和篇章结构是否符合GRE考试习惯的文章结构，就成了其是否适合用来出题的第一判断因素。

（1）GRE文章的信息强调相关性

客观地说，即使到了复习中后期的GRE考生，也并非所有人都能够做到分析性阅读，完全理解通原文并借此来回答好之后的题目。这一方面是考试对阅读水平要求太高，另一方面，ETS处心积虑地设置种种障碍破坏了理解全文的可能性。在内容上，文章通常有针锋相对的观点所产生的矛盾，有新发现对已有观点和认识的挑战，也有对一个问题解决方案的分歧等。不仅如此，文章还有充分的细节和逻辑论证推理支持这些分歧和对比。例子多如牛毛：比如令考生谈之色变的、独占GRE阅读文章难度"亚军"宝座的著名文章："伊斯兰法与其他法律的比较"，全文就是介绍伊斯兰法、犹太法和罗马天主法三种宗教法的不同。通过交织在一起的"求同存异，大同小异"，全文难度徒然飙升，在考试现场几乎难以理解。其他类似的细节还有如龙虾左螯右螯，比目鱼左眼右眼，蜗牛壳左旋右旋……

我们发现，细节越多，逻辑越纠缠。因为单纯简单线性发展的文章不能成为GRE阅读文章。比如高级口译中的阅读文章很长，时间压力也很大，但是和GRE文章的风格是完全不同的。GRE文章强调的是出现的信息之间是有关系的，考试本身不需要考生能通过阅读文章"学"到新知识，而需要考生利用阅读文章"分析"知识信息。若要"分析信息"，又不牵涉背景知识，那么唯一的途径就只有通过信息之间的关系比如因果、平行、逻辑上下层等等来出题，这就是GRE强调的信息之间的相关性。既然GRE在这方面考查我们的逻辑思维能力，那么其本身就必然作为一个充分的逻辑载体呈现在我们眼前，必须让我们考生有逻辑关系可找才行。那么这就牵涉到GRE出题者对于文章论述性的把握，西方的线性哲学思想最重要的、也是最基本的逻辑关系就是因果关系，强调"有因必有果"，GRE的命题过程必然也遵循着以因果关系为基础的逻辑。

（2）GRE阅读文章套路总结

★ 结论解释型

结论解释型在学术文章中出场频率比较高，先给出结论再辅以证据论证，主题句就是"结论"。总体来说文章结构不难，但是文章考查考生能否把论点和论据分清楚，题目主要考查考生能否分析明白论据是如何支持论点的。

【例3-9】

A mysterious phenomenon is the ability of over-water migrants to travel on course. Birds, bees, and other species can keep track of time without any sensory cues from the outside world, and such "biological clocks" clearly contribute to their "compass sense." For example, they can use the position of the Sun or stars, along with the time of day, to find north. But compass sense alone cannot explain how birds navigate the ocean: after a flock traveling east is blown far south by a storm, it will assume the proper northeasterly course to compensate. Perhaps, some scientists thought, migrants determine their geographic position on Earth by celestial navigation, almost as human navigators use stars and planets, but this would demand of the animals a fantastic map sense. Researchers now know that some species have a magnetic sense, which might allow migrants to determine their geographic location by detecting variations in the strength of the Earth's magnetic field.

例文【3-9】中主要描述的内容是关于动物跨越水面按固定轨迹飞行。通读全文之后，我们能够从第五句中找到线索，本文想说的是"动物是如何跨越水面按固定轨迹飞行"这件事人类目前还解释不清。全文六句话印证了开头的总括"A mysterious phenomenon"(一个神奇的现象)，故而这种文章的写法套路就称为**"结论解释型"**。对于这种文章的处理，最科学的方法就是寻找其句子之间的逻辑关系，分析清楚作者是如何支持自己的观点的；判断出作者到底是在做叙述还是论述。在结论解释型文章中，考生需要注意表达作者态度的副词，以及句子之间的关联词，这些地方都是推断题或者态度题的出题点。

★ 问题解决型

问题解决型文章最明显的特征就是文中会出现一般疑问句，在接下来的段落中对这个问题予以回答，全文的主题句就是该问题的“解决方法”。这种文章的关键在于读明白哪些部分是在做陈述、哪些部分是在做论述；分清楚解决问题的方法和问题存在的条件。

【例3-10】

Although the hormone adrenaline is known to regulate memory storage, it does not pass from the blood into brain cells. We are faced with an apparent paradox: how can a hormone that does not act directly on the brain have such a large effect on brain function?

Recently, we tested the possibility that one of the hormone's actions outside the brain might be responsible. Since one consequence of adrenaline release in an animal is an increase in blood glucose levels, we examined the effects of glucose on memory in rats. We found that glucose injected immediately after training enhances memory tested the next day. Additional evidence was provided by negative findings: drugs called adrenergic antagonists, which block peripheral adrenaline receptors, disrupted adrenaline's ability to regulate memory but did not affect memory enhancements produced by glucose that was not stimulated by adrenaline. These results are as they should be if adrenaline affects memory modulation by increasing blood glucose levels.

例文【3-10】中的第一段就很直接地提出了一个问题“荷尔蒙是怎样在不直接作用于大脑的前提下对脑功能产生重大影响的呢?”接下来的内容就在解释这个问题，从荷尔蒙在脑外的一个作用说起，借助“葡萄糖”这一参量来证明了荷尔蒙的释放能够间接影响记忆力。并利用反证法证明了“葡萄糖”和“记忆力”之间关联的独立性，直到全文的倒数第二句话说完，才算真正解释清楚了第一段所提出的问题。类似这种问题解决型文章在英美的学术期刊论文上出场频率不可谓不高，因此在GRE阅读中这种套路的文章也是屡见不鲜。考生在处理这种文章的过程中最关键的点就是找文中给我们提供的因果关系，西方线性思维的本质就是因果关系的建立与梳理，学术皆从之起源。只要分清楚到底是哪个要素和哪个要素之间能构建这种关系，问题解决型文章就解决了一大半。

★ 现象解释型

现象解释型文章在某种程度上和问题解决型文章有类似之处，前文以叙述的方式提出了一个现象、一种情况，在后文中基于此现象给出一个解释。考查的一方面是考生阅读信息的能力，另一方面更多的是关注这个解释和之前的现象之间的关系，即“解释的来龙去脉”。在这种文章当中，主题句就是解释的句子。一般来说，人文科学类文章在解释之后就会结束行文，而自然科学类文章在解释之后还要设置对照实验过程。

【例3-11】

Extended debate concerning the exact point of origin of individual folktales told by Afro-American slaves has unfortunately taken precedence over analysis of the tales' meaning and function. Cultural continuities with Africa were not dependent on importation and perpetuation of specific folktales in their pristine form. It is in the place that tales occupied in the lives of the slaves and in the meaning slaves derived from them that the clearest resemblances to African tradition can be found. Afro-American slaves did not borrow tales indiscriminately from the Whites among whom they lived. Black people were most influenced by those Euro-American tales whose functional meaning and aesthetic appeal had the greatest similarity to the tales with deep roots in their ancestral homeland. Regardless of where slave tales came from, the essential point is that, with respect to language, delivery, details of characterization, and plot, slaves quickly made them their own.

例【3-11】之所以说是一篇现象解释型文章，其根本的破解点就在于第一句话和第二句话之间的关系上。第一句话的字面意思是“不幸的是，对于黑人民间故事起源问题的讨论已超过了对于其意义和作用的讨论”，而其要表达的核心意思是“人们不该过分地讨论黑人故事的起源问题”，这是个现象。第二句话说“黑人文化的传承并非是依靠保持原始面貌完成的”显然应该是对第一句话的一个解释。这种套路就是现象解释型，因果关系当然也是重中之重，考生需要注意文章中出现的逻辑关系提示词，如：although、thus、as for等等。在现象解释型文章后作者是非常喜欢出推断题的，解决这种推断题的方法就要从“解释”和“现象”之间的关系入手。如果是自然科学类的现象解释型，在最后的验证实验部分中还需要注意可能出现的细节作用题，要搞清楚某个要素存在的意义到底是什么。

★ 新老观点对比型

GRE的文章既然选材于学术论文，那么作为论文的作者，为了在学术上有所突破，必然会在研究的过程中对前人提出的老观点产生一些反驳，这是不可避免的。故而也就出现了新老观点对比型文章，这种套路重点要求考生读出新观点与老观点对比的地方，老观点不是完全错误，而一定是在某一“点”上有失偏颇，才有了本文的论述，这往往是出题点。在这种套路的文章当中，新观点是主题句，文章围绕之展开。

【例3-12】

Writing of the Iroquois nation, Smith has argued that through the chiefs' council, tribal chiefs traditionally maintained complete control over the political affairs of both the Iroquois tribal league and the individual tribes belonging to the league, whereas the sole jurisdiction over religious affairs resided with the shamans. According to Smith, this division was maintained until the late nineteenth century, when the dissolution of the chiefs' council and the consequent diminishment of the chiefs' political power fostered their increasing involvement in religious affairs.

However, Smith fails to recognize that this division of power between the tribal chiefs and shamans was not actually rooted in Iroquois tradition; rather, it resulted from the Iroquois' resettlement on reservations early in the nineteenth century. Prior to resettlement, the chiefs' council controlled only the broad policy of the tribal league; individual tribes had institutions—most important, the longhouse—to govern their own affairs. In the longhouse, the tribe's chief influenced both political and religious affairs.

本文作为典型的新老观点对比型文章，第一段提出学者史密斯的观点，第二段提出了作者的新观点，认为史密斯没有准确注意到“酋长”在易洛魁民族当中的作用，全文否定了老观点，肯定新观点，这是新老观点对比型文章的固定模式。如果在后面有主题作用题，那么答案一定是“correct the failure of scholar”、“question the assumed claim that”这类的字眼，这是解题的技巧。

新老观点对比型、问题解决型、现象解释型和结论解释型，这是对ETS文章内容准确的、几乎完全一致的总结。可见，对套路感和文章结构的强调是必要的，而且它是ETS判断一篇文章是否符合GRE阅读文章这个身份的重要评价标准。从根本上说，Source Finder软件的职责就是用程序找到这些符合要求的文章。

2. GRE文章的题材分类

在本章开始部分，笔者说过GRE文章来源于学术期刊论文，那么对于这些英美学术论文、期刊中浩如繁星的文章，ETS究竟会偏好于选取哪些题材的文章，以及这些文章经过出题人员的改编以后又会倾向于哪些方面，这就是我们在本章节所要讨论的重点。

笔者通过对从1990年以来的GRE阅读理解文章的总结，发现GRE考试中出现的题材大致分为四类：

- 自然科学类
- 生命科学类
- 人文艺术类
- 社会科学类

大家心中肯定有疑问："为何ETS选用这些题材来作为GRE的阅读文章？GRE阅读文章的特点是什么？"想弄明白这些问题，我们需要从GRE阅读的设计要求入手。

(1)GRE阅读设计初衷

首先，GRE阅读理解部分设计的初衷是希望参加这门考试的考生能够拥有分析和处理信息的能力。但是，这种能力每个人从小都在不停地训练，单纯地所谓考查"能力"是没有优劣标准的，故而ETS的出题者们就在文字的难度上进行变化，看考生是否有能力把繁杂晦涩的文字转化成简单的信息，再进行正常处理。所以，在GRE考试中，文字功底是基础，分析和处理信息的能力是出题者想考查的素质，此二者缺一不可。对于大部分中国考生来说，分析和处理信息的能力是足够的，大家相差无几，关键就是英文基本功这一关过不去。就像打篮球抢篮板时，其技术动作要领不过寥寥：双脚卡位、重心下沉、支起肩膀、用躯干挡住对方球员，简单得很。但是让你去和德怀特·霍华德抢几个篮板的话，你就发现这些技术帮不上你的忙，因为你的身体素质的基础根本不行。这和考GRE是一个道理：再聪明的同学，如果英文基础不够好的话，想得高分也只能是水中月镜中花。

既然GRE考查的是考生分析和处理信息的能力，那么应试者对于考试内容的背景知识并不是掌握得越多越好。"信息量的积累不是最重要的"，分析能力才是最重要的素质。而且由于参加GRE考试的考生来自各个不同的学术背景，所以ETS设计考试时秉持的一个原则就是"头脑空白原则"，考生在阅读句子和文章时不需要了解这些信息与文外信息的联系。比如文章提到爱因斯坦和量子力学，考生无需清楚量子力学的任何公式或者其所需的微积分基础；句子中提到作者对于狄更斯的评价，考生也无需知道学术理论界对于狄更斯的历史评价。当然，这也体现了这门考试的公平性，尽力让所有考生处于同一平台上进行考试才能最大限度地反映出应试者的能力。

基于此，GRE的文章在选材的过程中就需要出题者琢磨：什么样内容的学术文章既能考查考生的理解能力，同时又不过分涉及背景知识？因为学术文章从大的方向上分类，应该分为自然科学和人文科学两种。而此两种学科包罗甚广，更何况人文科学类写作风格和题材范畴不拘一格，自然科学类牵涉许多原理和实验，如何保证所有学科的考生都能应对呢？这就需要GRE出题人员把原版的论文进行改装。改装的主要手段有两个：

1. 词句的同义改写
2. 把文章中的信息建立相关性

我们对于把词句进行同义改写的做法并不陌生：用高端的学术词汇替代常见的词汇或短语，把一个整句压缩成从句加在另一个主句中构成长难句等。总而言之，经过GRE改写之后的句子无论是中文还是英文都令人不容易理解，比如下面这个句子：

“《阳光下的葡萄干》中对于黑人自立和人类和谐的一致性的复杂思想一点都不比杜波依斯那著名的、深思熟虑的有关民族自尊和人类团结一致的思想以及法侬对于一个和民族特性及地位相和谐的国际主义思想的强调要更为不一致。”

不知道有着多年中文阅读经验的考生看到这样一句话的时候，心里作何感想？经过反复分析之后我相信大部分人能够读出这句话的核心意思在于：“《阳光下的葡萄干》的主题并不矛盾”，这也是这句话希望考生最终得出的结论。我们从这些中文当中得出这样一个比原句直接很多的意思，就是“分析和处理信息能力”的一种表现，只不过我们是在进行中文的处理，那英文又该如何呢？GRE不是为中国人设计的考试，它假定参加这门考试的人们都能够用英文自如地学习和交流，这就是为何美国本科生也必须要考好GRE才能进入研究生院继续学习。

经过了对于词句的改写，正常的语句被修改成了文意晦涩的长难句。但这还不够，因为一个学者在其学术生涯中几乎每天都要面对的是新的信息、以及新信息与已知信息之间的关系，故而GRE考试的设计过程中还有一个非常重要的环节就是把文章内部出现的信息建立关联性。这样一来，就做到了既需要考生能解读清楚文中所出现的信息，又需要考生能够把出现的信息之间的关系梳理清楚——这种关系就取代了信息原有的背景知识，成为了考查关键点。比如下面这个句子：

例3-13

The predictions of quantum mechanics, however, give only the probability of an event, not a deterministic statement of whether or not the event will occur. Because of this probabilism, Einstein remained strongly dissatisfied with the theory throughout his life, though he did not maintain that quantum mechanics is wrong.

译文

但是，量子力学只能预测出某事件发生的可能性，不能确定事件是否一定发生。正是由于这种不确定性，爱因斯坦一生都对量子力学抱负评价的态度，尽管他也并非认为量子力学是谬误的。

解析

这句话给我们传递的信息是“quantum mechanics”（量子力学）的特征是“只能给出一个事件发生的概率”，作者要告诉考生的是“量子力学”和“概率”此二者挂钩。在第二句话中，出场的人物是爱因斯坦，而爱因斯坦和前一句中信息的关系是这种“不确定性”，所以“爱因斯坦”对“量子力学”不满意。这样一来我们读完这两句话之后脑子当中有的信息就是“量子力学”、“概率”、“爱因斯坦”此三者，其关系说通俗点就是：前两者属于一根线上的蚂蚱，和后者是分离的，后者反对前者。由此我们不难看出GRE的文章最大限度地规避了背景信息，我们无须知道爱因斯坦在学术生涯中到底支持不支持量子理论，仅凭这两句话就已经将这个问题交代得很清楚了。

这句话并不算难，甚至可以说是GRE阅读中比较简单的句子，随着考生学习进度的深入，慢慢会碰到越来越多困难的词和句子。直到能够读懂GRE和LSAT中词汇抽象、句意艰涩、关系繁杂、逻辑缜密的文章，那时考生不禁回头望去颇感今日之所学与往昔让自己难以自拔的英语天差地别，人言世界上最高端的英文难度莫过于斯。

(2)GRE阅读题材选择

在大致了解了GRE阅读文章的形成过程之后，我们也就不难弄懂为何GRE考试喜欢选用**社会科学、生命科学、自然科学和人文艺术**四类作为主要题材了。首先，这四类题材中学术用语的频率和密度是相对较高的，这利于出题者对文章进行改写。比如“autonomous”这个词，既可以在人文学科中表示某人或某一团体的“自主性”；也可以在生物文章中表示某种生物“相对独立的个体性”。其次，这四类题材的逻辑构架相对比较严谨，出题者在改编文章的过程中容易建立相关性信息。比如在人文艺术类的文章当中，常见的是某些学者对于某个作品的态度，以及其他因素与学者态度的关系。基于此，ETS出题者可以很容易地把这样的信息合并在一句话之内，既增加阅读难度，又保留其原有的关联性。我们来看下面这句话：

例3-14

The implication of the papyrus administered a severe shock to the vast majority of classical scholars, who had confidently asserted that not only the role of the chorus but also language, metrics, and characterization all pointed to an early date.

译文

莎草纸上的提示给了众多传统学者们极大的震撼，这些人之前曾信誓旦旦地宣称，不光是合唱团的地位，包括像语言、韵律、人物角色都表明(该作品)处于更早的时期。

解析

上面这句话出自GRE阅读中一篇难度非常高的文章《莎草纸上的希腊戏剧》。这句话中信息的关联是相对比较简单的。一开始“莎草纸上的提示”作为整句的主语部分，连接谓语部分“给了”以及宾语部分“极大的震撼”，合起来传递的信息就是“莎草纸上的某些提示给了学者们极大的震撼”；直接点说就是“莎草纸的信息”和“学者们的观点”必然是相反的，这就是信息之间的相关性。在后半句中作者用定语从句连接“classical scholars”，其内容说的是这些学者们的观点，他们认为“(某个戏剧中的）合唱团、语言、韵律、人物角色等等都表明其处于一个很早的年代”。这样一来，“莎草纸”上的信息内容我们也就不难得知了，其内容必然是证明“该戏剧所处的年代并不早”。在这句话中出现的三个信息，其中的关联性就是“莎草纸“和“学者”之间的对立关系，“后半句的信息”又是对“学者”的具体说明。

GRE的阅读文章当中，作者不会把写作重点放在作品的内容上，更多的是以第三人称的视角来论述其他学者关于这个作品的学术观点，然后让考生去理解各个观点之间的关联性。如此一来，GRE考试既做到了不涉及背景知识，又考查了考生理清信息之间关系的能力。故而**人文艺术类**一直是GRE阅读文章选材的主要方向之一。与之相类似，很多的社会问题以及学术界对于社会问题的看法也可以用对人文艺术类相似的处理方法进行处理，做成一篇**社会科学类**的文章。社科类文章与人文类文章不同的地方就在于二者的文字风格不同，人文类的单词较难而且生僻，社科类的词汇相对容易，但是句内和句间逻辑关系更为复杂。除此以外，GRE文章还经常会涉及关于微观社科类的内容，比如心理学、博弈论等近来的社会话题。此外，美国学术界还喜欢研究社会中的一些特殊人群、弱势群体，包括：黑人、妇女、老幼等，这些人群在GRE的文章中也是屡见不鲜，而且每次作者的态度毫无疑问都是正评价，我们也将予以关注。由于这些话题相对于社会科学来讲主题更为单一，而且其研究方法与宏观社会学科略显不同，不过整体上依旧隶属于社会科学类。

以上几种都属于研究人文艺术和社会科学的范畴，除此之外，GRE阅读理解文章还喜欢从自然科学范畴选择题材。而自然科学与人文科学的文章除了在词句方面风格不同以外，更重要的区别在于自然科学的文章容易考查考生对于某自然过程的理解，以及该自然过程发生发展的原因。比如下面这几个句子：

❙例3-15❙

Researchers are finding that in many ways an individual bacterium is more analogous to a component cell of a multicellular organism than it is to a free-living, autonomous organism. Anabaena, a freshwater bacteria is a case in point. Among photosynthetic bacteria, Anabaena is unusual: it is capable of both photosynthesis and nitrogen fixation.

这一小段话包含了三个句子，其中第一句的核心信息是“an individual bacterium is more analogous to a component cell of a multicellular organism”，即“个体细菌和多细胞生物的某一个组成部分十分相似”，后半句说其并非是一个独立的生命个体。这句话从英文角度并不难理解，其中的名词也只有“multicellular”并不常见，但是根据词根拆解我们可以很容易得知该词是“多细胞”的意思，但理解本句的逻辑关系及内容并非那么容易，难点就在于第二句和第三句话：第二句说“鱼腥藻是一个例子”，第三句说“在光合细菌当中，鱼腥藻算是一个特例了，因为其既能进行光合作用又能进行固氮作用”。严格来说，第二句和第三句可以看做一个整体，作为一个例子来支持第一句话的论点；作者是在进行一个论述的过程，其真正的难点在于这个例子是如何支持第一句话的论点的？

破解这三句话的关键在于弄懂“Anabaena”到底是什么东西，才能搞明白它到底是作为第一句话中哪个名词的例子。有人可能认为“Anabaena”一定是第一句话中所说到的“个体细菌”，但这样一来即使读完全文也不会搞清楚为何说“Anabaena”的例子能支持第一句话；因为“Anabaena”(鱼腥藻）根本不是“an individual bacterium”，而是一种“multicellular organism”(多细胞生物)。这种多细胞生物之所以“不寻常”，能够进行光合作用和固氮作用，其原因就在于原文中接下来就要写到这个多细胞生物中有两种个体细菌，分别用于光合作用和固氮作用，作者借此来说明“个体细菌是多细胞生物的一个组成部分”。有人一定有疑惑：GRE不是不要求背景知识吗？我不知道鱼腥藻是多细胞生物怎么办？这并非是背景知识，而是通过第二句话中一个词“bacteria”体现出来的，“bacteria”不能单纯地翻译成“细菌”，这个词是bacterium的复数形式，中文解释叫做“菌群”，这样一来意思就一目了然了。

通过刚才的例子，大家不难发现自然科学在单词、句子的把握上要求也颇高。自然科学类文章除了描写天文、地质、生物圈、大气层、动物习性等等宏观方面之外，还有很多文章的题材描写的是生物细胞（就像刚才的例子)、神经系统、生命技术等等微观层面。因此，在自然类学科范围内，根据描述的内容不同，可分为宏观自然科学类文章和生物科学类文章。

第四节 GRE题源阅读材料列表

我们已经了解了ETS机构是如何通过Source Finder软件寻找学术型关键词，遴选文章，然后把语句进行大幅度改写，进而使GRE文章形成一定的套路，最终成为GRE阅读考试的文章。本书的讲解从文章模式到最基本的学术特征词遴选，以一种从宏观到微观、从表象到根基的方式与各位读者做了一次分享。那么还有一个重要的问题，就是Source Finder软件在选择文章的时候，其样本会从什么地方选择呢？

在课上时，有很多勤奋的同学问及课下应该阅读什么文字材料来提高GRE阅读的能力。简单地读普通报纸杂志比如*China Daily*，收获是非常有限的。最根本原因是从这些文字中读不出最关键的信息相关性和逻辑关系，相反只是一种放松的阅读。除了课堂上推荐的GMAT，LSAT等同类型风格的全真试题之外，笔者从参考论文中找到了ETS命题组在编制GRE文章考题时采用的材料来源。这部分学术期刊就是**GRE阅读理解的"题源"**，Source Finder软件在选择文章的时候，其样本就会从以下的学术期刊中选择。

1. *Science*

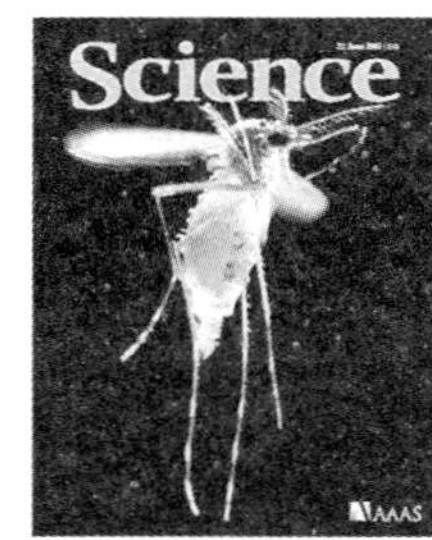

1880年，纽约新闻记者约翰·麦克尔创立了*Science*(《科学》)杂志，这份杂志先后得到了托马斯·爱迪生以及亚历山大·格拉汉姆·贝尔的资助。此后，由于财政困难*Science*于1882年3月停刊。一年后，昆虫学家塞缪尔·斯卡德使其复活并取得了一定的成功。然而到了1894年，*Science*重新陷入财政危机，随后被以500美元的价格转让给心理学家詹姆斯·卡特尔。1944年Cattell去世后，AAAS成为*Science*的新主人。

Science(《科学》)于1894年10月10日成为美国最大的科学团体"美国科学促进会"——American Association for the Advancement of Science（AAAS)的官方刊物。全年共51期，为周刊，全球发行量超过150万份。*Science*主要刊登最新的科学研究成果、各个学科的原创论文，以及科学新闻、科技政策、科学家对感兴趣事务的观点，是全世界最权威的著名学术杂志之一，影响因子高达31.364。*Science*杂志发表的论文涉及所有科学学科，特别是物理学、生命科学、化学、材料科学和医学中最重要的、最激动人心的研究进展。目前，*Science*的主要竞争对手是英国出版的*Nature*杂志。

2. *Nature*

Nature(《自然》)是世界上历史悠久的、最有名望的科学杂志之一，首版于1869年11月4日。*Nature*是科学界普遍关注的、国际性、跨学科的周刊类科学杂志。2010年它的影响因子为36.101。*Nature*每周刊载科学技术各个领域中具有独创性的、重要性的，以及跨学科的研究，同时也提供快速权威的、有见地的新闻和评论，还有关于科学界和大众对于科技发展趋势的见解的专题。与其他专业的科学杂志一样，在*Nature*上发表的文章需要经过严格的同行评审。在发表前编辑选择其他在同一领域有威望的、但与作者无关的科学家来检查和评判文章的内容。作者要对评审做出的批评给予反应，比如更改文章内容，提供更多的试验结果，否则的话编辑可能拒绝该文章。*Nature*是一份在英国发表的周刊，其出版商为自然出版集团，这个集团属于麦克米伦出版有限公司，而它又属于格奥尔格·冯·霍茨布林克出版集团。*Nature*在伦敦、纽约、旧金山、华盛顿哥伦比亚特区、东京、巴黎、慕尼黑和贝

辛斯托克都设有办公室。自然出版集团还出版其他专业杂志，如《自然神经科学》、《自然生物学技术》、《自然方法》、《自然临床实践》、《自然结构和分子生物学》和《自然评论》系列等。

3. *Scientific American*

Scientific American（《科学美国人》）是美国的一本科普杂志，始于1845年8月28日，起先是每周出版，后改为每月出版，为美国历史最久的、一直连续出版的杂志。*Scientific American*在2005年12月时每个月约有555,000份美国国内发行量，以及90,000份的国际发行量。虽然被认为是高水平的期刊，但这本杂志并不采用类似*Nature*杂志同行评审的方式审查稿件，而是提供一个论坛来呈现科学理论和科学新发现。

*Scientific American*一开始是由鲁弗斯·波特所发起的单页报纸。早期主要报道美国专利局所登记的项目，如永动机。Porter后来在1846年将这份报纸卖给阿尔弗雷德·比奇及奥森·米恩。1986年卖给德国的Holtzbrinck集团。

中文版的文章大多数都是翻译自英文版的文章，中文版杂志曾为 *Scientific American*在中国大陆的中文版。《电脑报》杂志社后获得了美国*Scientific American*杂志社新的授权，在2006年1月，与*Scientific American*版权合作的简体中文月刊《环球科学》创刊。现在，《环球科学》于每月5日出版。中国的硕士研究生入学考试公共英语科目试题中的阅读理解经常使用该杂志的文章来设置考题。

4. *Psychological Bulletin*

Psychological Bulletin（《心理学公报》）是一份心理学学术期刊，由美国心理学会主办并出版，是享誉国际的心理学领域顶级期刊，研究及评论心理学的最新发展情况，影响因子达10.905。所载论文既反映了心理学研究领域的最新发展，同时也成为沟通心理学所属各研究领域、心理学与相关学科关系的桥梁。研究内容涉及实验心理学的社会影响、心理学的目标建设，大脑不对称的视觉空间频率模式、精神分裂症的社会认知、宗教和心理治疗过程及心理治疗成果方面的实验研究。

*Psychological Bulletin*由约翰·霍普金斯大学的心理学家詹姆斯·马克·鲍德温创刊于1904年，当时他刚刚收购了他和詹姆斯·麦基恩·卡特尔两人在10年前创办的*Psychological Review*（《心理学评论》）。1909年，鲍德温由于丑闻被迫从约翰·霍普金斯大学辞职，并将两份杂志的主编位置让给了约翰·布罗德斯·华生。*Psychological Bulletin*的所有权转给了霍华德·沃伦，最后又捐赠给了美国心理学会，直到今日。

5. *Astronomy*

Astronomy（《天文学》）是美国出版的天文学杂志，以月刊形式出版。*Astronomy*是由位于威斯康辛州沃基肖（Waukesha）的卡姆巴克出版社（Kalmbach Publishing）出版，读者主要是对天文学有兴趣的业余人士，这些读者大多希望能知道未来天象、天文仪器的新科技、天文摄影等。*Astronomy*于1973年8月发行第一期，该期总共有48页；创办人是威斯康辛大学史蒂文斯角波因特分校（University of Wisconsin–Stevens Point）毕业的业余天文学家斯蒂芬·瓦尔特。1985年*Astronomy*成为卡姆巴克出版社旗下一

员。1990年成立了独立的网站，Astronomy.com。*Astronomy*目前是世界发行量最大的天文杂志，主要的竞争者是*Sky & Telescope*（《天空与望远镜杂志》）。

*Astronomy*每一期前半部分的文章都是由专业天文学家撰写的天文知识介绍，后半部分则适合天文爱好者阅读。专业文章包含天文学各领域，如宇宙论、天文生物学等，以及天文台介绍、天文学家介绍。适合天文爱好者的文章则有深空天体观测、行星观测以及天文摄影等介绍。

*Astronomy*每期都附有当月星图、行星位置图。并有一个单元"Ask Astro"专门接受各地读者对天文相关问题的询问，并由专业天文学家或编辑群回答。此外还有关于天文书籍、活动信息、仪器等的介绍。同时也刊出由读者投稿的天文摄影照片。

6. *The Lancet*

The Lancet（《柳叶刀》）是世界上最悠久以及最受重视的同行评审性质之医学期刊，主要由爱思唯尔（Elsevier）出版公司发行，部分是由里德·爱思唯尔(Reed Elsevier)集团协同出版。1823年由托马斯·瓦克利(Thomas Wakley)创刊，他以外科手术刀"柳叶刀"(Lancet)的名称来为这份刊物命名，而"Lancet"在英语中也是"尖顶穹窗"的意思，借此寓意著期刊立志成为"照亮医界的明窗"(to let in light)。*The Lancet*始终在一些重大的医学议题上以直言不讳闻名，例如：批评世界卫生组织，拒绝让顺势疗法的功效正式成为众多治疗法选择中的一种，发表2003年美伊战争平民伤亡的统计，以及不赞成里德·爱思唯尔(Reed Elsevier)集团与军需产业(Arms industry)有所关联。

*The Lancet*在全世界拥有高影响因子，有一群重要的读者阶层的支持。本期刊登载有原创性的研究文章、评论文章("小组讨论"及"评论")、社论、书评、短篇研究文章，也有其他一些在刊内常登载的文章，诸如：特刊消息、案例报道等。*The Lancet*被视为一种核心的医学综合期刊，同样亦是世界医学权威杂志；其他同性质的刊物有新英格兰医学期刊、美国医学协会期刊以及英国医学期刊。

7. *Technology Review*

Technology Review(《技术评论》)创刊于1899年，距今已有110年的历史，是美国第一本专业的科技评论杂志。如今的*Technology Review*已远非一份仅限麻省理工学院校友交流的内部刊物，而是发扬一贯的科技创新理念，重点关注新兴科技及其对商业与社会的巨大影响力，为科技和商业领袖提供及时、前瞻性的资讯、独到深入的研究以及行业趋势分析，助其创造更多的经济财富和社会价值。

Technology Review(《技术评论》)美国版杂志的读者数量高达48万余人，其网站Technologyreview.com每月的访问者数量在62万以上；国际版本的总发行量达22万；其简报的订阅数量在16万以上。在全球范围内，*Technology Review*至少达及140万科技和商业领域的专业人士与领袖。

麻省理工《科技创业》是*Technology Review*独家授权的中文版杂志，旨在为科技创业者、企业及政府高管、MBA和科技类学子提供最新科技资讯与研究成果，并着重介绍科技的商业化过程。麻省理工《科技创业》将通过杂志、网站、简报、论坛和展会等全方位媒体平台向读者提供权威、前瞻、深入的科技资讯。

8. *Harvard Business Review*

Harvard Business Review，简称HBR(《哈佛商业评论》)是自1922年起，由哈佛商学院集结专家、教授，针对管理事务的研究而出版的专业杂志。HBR是一份专门为专业经理人及工商管理者提供参考的月刊，其主要读者群是产业领袖、学者、高阶管理者及管理顾问等。*Harvard Business Review*是哈佛商学院的标志性杂志，月发行量达到25万，它几乎没有新闻图片，也没有事实报道。创刊80多年来，*Harvard Business Review*始终致力于发掘和传播工商管理领域中最前卫的思想理论、观点和方法，帮助管理者们不断更新理念、开阔视野、适应变化，与时代共进。

目前*Harvard Business Review*在全球有250,000本的发行量、11个版本的授权，包括两种中文版、德文版、波兰文版、匈牙利文版、葡萄牙文版(在巴西发行)，及一种发行于南亚(印度)的英文版。这份杂志由哈佛商学院独立编辑，与各学者完成相关企业或个案研究后即将其发表于HBR，其目的是使著者的新文章出版及时而增加其参考价值。

9. *Cell*

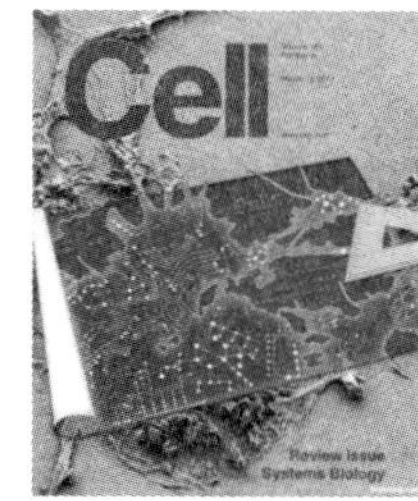

Cell(《细胞》)为爱思唯尔出版公司旗下Cell Press(细胞出版社)发行的一份同行评审科学期刊，出版历史由1974年至今。*Cell*主要发表生命科学领域中的最新研究发现。*Cell*刊登过许多重大的生命科学研究进展，与*Nature*和*Science*并列，是全世界最权威的学术杂志之一。其2010年的影响因子为32.401，高于*Science*的影响因子(31.364)，接近*Nature*的影响因子(36.101)，表明它所刊登的文章广受引用。

从20世纪末开始，细胞出版社在*Cell*之后陆续推出一系列学术期刊，包括：

1997年创刊　细胞生物学、分子生物学
2001年创刊　发育生物学
2002年创刊　癌症领域
2005年创刊　代谢领域
2007年创刊　感染症领域、微生物学
2007年创刊　干细胞领域、再生医学

10. *PNAS*

Proceedings of the National Academy of Sciences of the United States of America，通常简称为PNAS（《美国国家科学院院刊》）是美国国家科学院的官方科学周刊杂志。创刊于1915年。院刊提供具有高水平的前沿研究报告、学术评论、学科回顾及前瞻、学术论文以及美国国家科学学会学术动态的报道和出版。该刊覆盖生物学、化学、物理学、数学和社会科学等领域。该刊拥有广泛的读者群，尤其是世界各地从事基础科学领域研究的科学工作者。与*Nature*和*Science*一样，是世界上最负盛名的基础科学领域的学术杂志之一。2009年影响因子为9.432，在SCI(Science Citation Index)综合科学类排名第三位，已成为全球科研人员不可缺少的科研资料。

11. *The Economist*

The Economist(《经济学人》)是一份以报道新闻与国际关系为主的英文刊物，每周出版一期，采用杂志专用的光面纸印刷，由伦敦的经济学人报纸有限公司出版。虽然它的发行方式更像是周刊，但是*The Economist*将自己定位为报纸，因此，它每一期除了提供分析与意见外，还报道整周发生的所有重要政经新闻。*The Economist*从1843年9月由创办人詹姆斯·威尔逊首次发行至今，2007年的全球发行量据报道约为每期140万份，其中有半数销往北美洲，20%在欧洲大陆，15%在英国，10%在亚洲。杂志的写作风格十分有特色，注重于如何在最小的篇幅内告诉读者最多的信息，大多数文章写得机智、幽默、有力度，严肃又不失诙谐。*The Economist*的报道内容并非完全专注于经济事务，该刊的创办目的是“参与一场推动前进的智慧与阻碍我们进步的胆怯无知之间的较量”，这句话被印在每一期*The Economist*的目录页上。*The Economist*主要关注政治和商业方面的新闻，但是每期也有一两篇针对科技和艺术的报导，以及书评。除了常规的新闻之外，*The Economist*每两周还会就一个特定地区或领域进行深入报道。*The Economist*的报道体裁多为倡导新闻，文章一般没有署名，而且往往带有鲜明的立场，社论立场根植于自由贸易和全球化，无论是在经济还是政治上的立场都是倾向保守派，反对政府在经济和政治方面过度的介入。

12. *Neuron*

Neuron(《神经元》)是神经科学的顶极期刊，Cell Press(细胞出版社)出版的*Cell*杂志的姐妹期刊。Cell Press 数据库的期刊是生物医学方面的权威学术期刊。1974 年 Benjamin Lewin 先生创建*Cell*期刊，当时属于MIT出版社旗下。1986 年Cell Press 成立，并陆续出版*Neuron*(1988)、*Immunity*(1994)和*Molecular Cell*(1997)。1998年Cell Press 被爱思唯尔公司收购。之后，又分别于2001 年、2002 年和2005 年创建以下期刊：*Developmental Cell*、*Cancer Cell*、*Cell Metabolism*。同时，原来爱思唯尔的期刊*Current Biology*、*Structure* 和*Chemistry & Biology*归入Cell Press。1997 年cell.com 网站创建，以后各个期刊也建立了自己的网站。2004 年，Cell Press 的期刊在Science Direct 平台上提供服务。Cell Press 数据库收录的生物学方面的9 种期刊全部被SCI 收录，影响因子都非常高，并且Cell Press 数据库会进行实时更新。

我曾经接到过二十几位同学给我发过类似这样的邮件：

> “老师您好，上完GRE课之后我按着上课布置的学习计划学了七个月，现在我发现做过GRE的文章已经基本没什么问题了，讲长难句的书籍也看了三遍，GRE单词背了二十几遍。但是一模拟考试就发现自己还是有很多不会的地方，一碰到新文章还会发晕，请问应该怎么解决呢?”

这封信和第三章开始笔者列出的邮件何其相似？诚然，这些同学在课下付出的努力毋庸质疑，而且他们其实也已经走到了距离成功顶峰非常接近的地方：无论是逻辑思维能力、英文单词量、做题的方法都应该已经炉火纯青。那么对于GRE阅读他们仍然无法达到“信手拈来”，其原因就在于自身所学的知识过于固化，底蕴不够深厚。打个比方，这些同学好比《笑傲江湖》中的令狐冲、《三国演义》里的蜀国：令狐少侠空有天下第一的高明剑法却手无缚鸡之力，对付草莽流寇绰绰有余而碰到任我行一招即败；蜀汉王朝徒具两川之险坐拥良子强将，而本国经济生产基础不足曹魏三分之一，纵然六出祁山依然无果，亦非巧合也。故而，长期稳步提高自己在学术英文方面的功底是极其重要的一个环节。以上我们给读者列举的12种学术期刊，是GRE阅读文章的题源，是能从本质上帮助我们提升学术底蕴的材料。勤奋的同学只要能养成坚持定期阅读这些学术杂志的习惯，一定会极大提高自己的英文阅读能力、逻辑思维能力，还会使自己的专业背景知识得到进一步的充实，能够时刻了解到世界上最高端最前沿的学术信息。“书山有路勤为径，学海无涯苦作舟”，希望考生朋友们都能在知识的海洋里不断地超越自我，才算是真正实现了学习的价值。

本书第四章包括按题材分类的GRE真题讲解及题源扩展阅读，为考生准备了GRE阅读真题解析以及充足的题源文章和对照译文。其中，GRE真题阅读理解部分配有详细的解析，每篇文章都有对应的译文，还有对句间关系的分析以及逻辑简图，以助考生培养分析和处理信息的能力。

每个分类的真题之后还附带有扩展题源阅读文章，这些文章都是选材于英美学术期刊论文，所讨论的题材范畴也隶属于本书分类。这些文章虽然未经ETS之手加工，其逻辑框架并不如GRE阅读文章那么严密精妙，但是其整体行文紧凑、用词准确精炼以及基本句间关系的应用对于备考都有极大的好处。GRE阅读的考题正是从这样的题源文章中选材并予以加工得以形成的，其中语句的难度并不亚于GRE、GMAT阅读文章的语句，希望考生能从其中得到切实的能力提高。

Note

第二篇　题源篇

GRE阅读题源精选

第四章 GRE题源阅读

第一节 自然科学类

自然科学类文章历来是GRE阅读喜欢采用的题材，包括量子力学理论、运动原理理论等等。这一点从考试本身的学术属性就可以明确：GRE考生在未来三年内走的都是学术路线，那么研读其他学者或者大贤的学术论文自然是必不可少的基本功。和考生平时所读的学术论文相比，GRE的科学理论类文章除了在单句的难度和全文的精度上要高出一个层次以外，另外一点就是GRE文章当中所涉及的为人们所熟知的科学家、学者的理论往往有可能是遭到反驳和质疑的。因为GRE所选取的有时很多是近期发表的学术论文，作为论文的作者，他们需要的是科学界新的研究成果，而非拾人牙慧、人云亦云。

GRE的自然科学类文章包罗甚广，像量子力学理论、进化博弈论、运动原理理论等等。相对容易理解的题材是社会科学类的理论，比如博弈论、运动原理、某某主义的学说等；较难读懂的文章大多涉及抽象的概念，像宏观与微观世界的转化、量子理论、冰河世纪间冰期等，我们需要理性地分析和处理信息的能力。比如：迅速利用关键词搞清单句的核心意思；通过有些句子中存在的有感情色彩的副词或动词判断作者或某学者对于理论的态度；借助一系列逻辑承接词找到理论中要素与要素之间的因果逻辑关系。此外，考生在做题的时候一定要谨慎读题干，看题目问的是作者还是某个学者对于特定理论的态度。

在自然科学领域，与探索发现相关的专题是从学术论文当中最容易寻找到的题材，也会是新GRE考试的阅读部分——特别是长文章——以后选材的侧重方向。首先，这类题材的文章对于大部分考生来说并不算很难，最重要的一个原因在于题材的性质：探索发现类的文章无论其涉及的学科是天文地理还是花鸟鱼虫，都必然含有“老知识”与“新知识”的对应；文中信息点之间的对照在某种程度上缓解了未接触过的信息带给考生的生疏感。除了难度之外，更重要的是这类有着“信息对照”的文章能够最大限度地规避“背景信息”，使得考试对于大部分考生来说更加公平。

对于考生来说，在处理这种类型的文章时，要注意知识点之间的新老对比，以及出现或可能出现新现象的原因所在。GRE考试不会完全依照文章内容进行语言层面的考查，而会借助文章中给出过的信息及与之相联系的因果关系考查考生能否正确判断出未知或者未定的信息内容。除此之外，对于这种类型文章的阅读，考生还要更多关注文中的动词。按照规律，如果是句子比较晦涩的文章，破解它的关键点就在于把握清楚名词之间的关系；若是单句和逻辑关系并非那么复杂的文章全文中叙述内容的比例相对较高，而在叙述的句子当中，动词是不可或缺的。希望考生千万不要因为哪些关键的动词不认识或盲猜而导致对整个句子或者某一个部分的理解产生偏差。

Exercise 1

量子力学领域中爱因斯坦的决定论

Quantum mechanics is a highly successful theory: it supplies methods for accurately calculating the results of diverse experiments, especially with minute particles. The predictions of quantum mechanics, however, give only the probability of an event, not a deterministic statement of whether or not the event will occur. Because of this probabilism, Einstein remained strongly dissatisfied with the theory throughout his life, though he did not maintain that quantum mechanics is wrong. Rather, he held that it is incomplete: in quantum mechanics the motion of a particle must be described in terms of probabilities, he argued, only because some parameters that determine the motion have not been specified. If these hypothetical "hidden parameters" were known, a fully deterministic trajectory could be defined. Significantly, this hidden-parameter quantum theory leads to experimental predictions different from those of traditional quantum mechanics. Einstein's ideas have been tested by experiments performed since his death, and as most of these experiments support traditional quantum mechanics, Einstein's approach is almost certainly erroneous.

Sample Multiple-choice Questions — Select One Answer Choice

1. It can be inferred from the passage that the author's conclusion that Einstein's approach is "erroneous" (line 11) might have to be modified because

   (A) it is theoretically possible to generate plausible theories with hidden parameters within them

   (B) some experimental tests of Einstein's theory do not disconfirm the hidden-parameter theory of quantum mechanics

   (C) it is possible for a theory to have hidden parameters and yet be probabilistic

   (D) traditional quantum mechanics has not yet been used to analyze all of the phenomena to which it could be applied

   (E) there are too many possible hidden parameters to develop meaningful tests of hidden-parameter theories

Sample Multiple-choice Questions — Select One Answer Choice

2. According to the passage, Einstein posed objections to the

   (A) existence of hidden parameters in quantum theory

   (B) probabilistic nature of quantum mechanics

   (C) idea that quantum mechanics is incomplete

   (D) results of experiments testing quantum theory

   (E) importance accorded quantum mechanics in physics

Sample Multiple-choice Questions — Select One Answer Choice

3. The passage suggests that which of the following would have resulted if the experiments mentioned in lines (9-11) had not supported the predictions of traditional quantum mechanics?

(A) Einstein, had he been alive, would have revised his approach to quantum mechanics.

(B) Hidden-parameter theories would have been considered inaccurate descriptions of real-world phenomena.

(C) A deterministic description of the motion of a particle might still be considered possible.

(D) Quantum mechanics would have ceased to attract the attention of physicists.

(E) Einstein, had he been alive, would have abandoned attempts to specify the hidden parameters that describe motion.

译文及解析

第一句： 量子力学是一个很成功的理论：它帮助人们精准地计算出各种实验的结果，尤其是关于微粒子的实验。

第二句： 但是，量子力学只能预测出某事件发生的可能性，不能确定事件是否一定发生。

第三句： 正是由于这种不确定性，爱因斯坦一生都对量子力学抱负评价的态度，但他也并非认为量子力学是谬误的。

第四句： 他认为量子力学存在缺陷：只是因为有些决定粒子运动的参量并没有明确，所以量子力学只能靠概率研究粒子的运动。

第五句： 如果这些理论上的“隐形参量”能够得以确认，那么粒子的运行轨道就能准确无疑地被判断出来了。

（第三、四、五句处于第二句的逻辑下一层，给出关于量子力学负评价的细节。）

第六句： 关键是，根据“隐形参量理论”，实验结果的预测和传统量子力学有很大不同。

第七句： 自爱因斯坦辞世后，他提出的理论被实验检验了多次，结果几乎全部都支持传统量子力学，所以爱因斯坦之言我们基本可以肯定是谬误的了。

（第六、七句和前面的二、三、四、五句形成对比，用事实说明爱因斯坦的理论存在谬误。从第二句话一直到第七句作为一个整体是第一句话的逻辑下一层。）

逻辑图

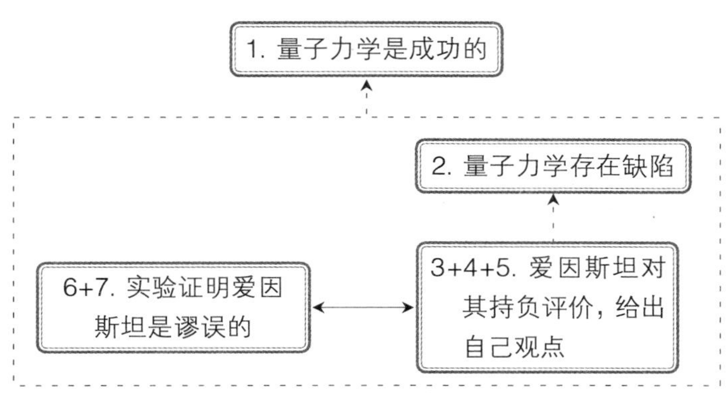

题目及解析

1. It can be inferred from the passage that the author's conclusion that Einstein's approach is "erroneous"（line11）might have to be modified because

（A）it is theoretically possible to generate plausible theories with hidden parameters within them

（B）some experimental tests of Einstein's theory do not disconfirm the hidden-parameter theory of quantum mechanics

（C）it is possible for a theory to have hidden parameters and yet be probabilistic

（D）traditional quantum mechanics has not yet been used to analyze all of the phenomena to which it could be applied

（E）there are too many possible hidden parameters to develop meaningful tests of hidden-parameter theories

解析

这是一道推断题，问"如果以下哪个选项成立的话，'爱因斯坦之言存在谬误' 这样的论断就值得商榷了？" 本文给出了作者反对爱因斯坦理论的原因，即：做出来的实验结果和根据爱因斯坦理论所得出的结果相违背。根据这样一个信息，我们可以知道如果实验结果和爱因斯坦理论所得出的结果不违背的话，那么我们就不能抨击爱因斯坦了。

（A）根据"隐形参量"能得出一些理论上可行的结论

（本选项错在了"得出结论"上，爱因斯坦也得出了一个结论，但光得出结论是不能帮助爱因斯坦的，必须要拿事实说话才可以。）

（B）一些根据爱因斯坦理论得出的实验结果并不违背"隐形参量"的理论

（有事实来支持爱因斯坦的理论，自然我们就不能够抨击爱因斯坦的理论了，B毫无疑问是正确的。）

（C）一个理论当中的确可能存在"隐形参量"，但也仅仅是可能

（从理论层面上说，爱因斯坦理论的可能性是没法帮助他的，必须要有实验的结果来证实，所以C不对。）

（D）传统量子力学理论还没有对每个可行的现象进行检验

（本选项是对传统量子力学理论的质疑，看似否定另一个理论来帮助爱因斯坦的理论。实际上这种质疑也帮助不了爱因斯坦，因为爱因斯坦的理论需要的是与之相符合的实验结果，而不是去否定它的"对手"。）

（E）有很多"隐形参量"可以让我们用来对"隐形参量理论"做有意义的实验

（还和之前的错误一致，理论上的成立、可能的实验结果帮不了爱因斯坦，我们需要的是明摆着的事实，E肯定也不行。）

可见，做GRE阅读的这种推断题，关键在于找到问题的实质。对于本题来说，要抓住正确答案应该包含的核心，即要有实验结果来支持爱因斯坦的理论，然后再进行逐个选项的分析，才能从根本上避免考生出现"被各式各样的选项信息牵着鼻子走"的情况。

2. According to the passage, Einstein posed objections to the

（A）existence of hidden parameters in quantum theory

（B）probabilistic nature of quantum mechanics

（C）idea that quantum mechanics is incomplete

（D）results of experiments testing quantum theory

（E）importance accorded quantum mechanics in physics

解析

这是一道细节题，题干当中的关键词在于“objection”(反对)，问“爱因斯坦反对以下哪个内容？”

（A）“隐形参量”在量子力学理论当中的存在性

（爱因斯坦认为：由于“隐形参量”存在却不能搞清楚，才使得粒子的运动轨迹不确定。他不可能反对A的内容。）

（B）量子力学理论本质上的概率性、不确定性

（这正是爱因斯坦所否认的东西，他认为只要“隐形参量能够得以确认”，粒子的运动轨迹就可以唯一确定，而不以概率来描述了。）

（C）关于“量子力学理论不完整”的观点

（这种观点就是爱因斯坦提出的，他不可能否认这个。）

（D）验证量子力学理论的实验的结果

（本篇文章提到的检验型实验是在爱因斯坦逝世后才做的，他不可能否认这个。）

（E）量子力学在物理学中的重要性

（爱因斯坦从未说过量子力学是错的，也从未质疑过量子力学是否重要，他只是认为理论中存在着缺陷和未知因素。）

本题并不难做，选项B为正确答案。这种细节题提高正确率的关键不在于回文找关键词的能力有多强，而在于分析清楚文章给考生传递的信息，根据所阅读到的信息和题干，就已经能把正确答案大致猜出来。回文定位的意义在于检验自己的答案是否肯定是正确的，而非全凭回文找答案。这种英文阅读的考试技巧在GRE这种级别的阅读中没什么用处，只会给考生造成信息混乱。

3. The passage suggests that which of the following would have resulted if the experiments mentioned in lines（9-11）had not supported the predictions of traditional quantum mechanics?

（A）Einstein, had he been alive, would have revised his approach to quantum mechanics.

（B）Hidden-parameter theories would have been considered inaccurate descriptions of real-world phenomena.

（C）A deterministic description of the motion of a particle might still be considered possible.

（D）Quantum mechanics would have ceased to attract the attention of physicists.

（E）Einstein, had he been alive, would have abandoned attempts to specify the hidden parameters that describe motion.

解析

这又是一道推断题，提示词是“suggest”(暗示)。这是一种条件推断，根据条件的变化得出相应的可能发生的情况，考查读者寻找给定信息之间逻辑关系的能力。题干问“根据原文内容，如果9行至11行中提到的实验结果并不支持传统量子力学理论的话，会发生以下哪件事?”

原文传递的信息之间是有因果关系的：因为“实验结果都支持传统量子力学理论”+“爱因斯坦的‘隐形参量’理论预测结果和传统理论相反”，所以“爱因斯坦的理论是谬误的”。现在题目中把刚才的因果关系中的原因更改了，既然现在实验结果都不支持传统量子力学理论，那么爱因斯坦的“隐形参量”理论就该受到人们的认可了。

(A) 爱因斯坦如果还在世的话，就会修改他对量子力学的研究。.
(不正确。如果真如题干所说，那么爱因斯坦的理论就是正确的，何必要修改呢?)

(B) “隐形参量理论”对于真实世界现象的描述是不准确的。
(不正确。如果真如题干所说，隐形参量是不会有负评价的。)

(C) 准确描述出粒子运动的轨迹是可行的。
(这是本题的正确答案。爱因斯坦的理论就是粒子运动轨迹是可以被确定下来的。)

(D) 量子力学不再受到物理学家的关注。
(不正确。题干只是说实验结果不支持传统量子力学，不能推出此理论就失去重视，推断过度。)

(E) 爱因斯坦如果还在世的话，将会放弃用“隐形参量”来描绘粒子的运动。
(不正确。如果他还在世，一定会就“隐形参量”进行继续研究。)

Note

Exercise 2

贯穿效应与宇宙中生命的起源

About a century ago, the Swedish physical scientist Arrhenius proposed a law of classical chemistry that relates chemical reaction rate to temperature. According to the Arrhenius equation, chemical reaction are increasingly unlikely to occur as temperatures approach absolute zero, and at absolute zero (zero degrees Kelvin, or minus 273 degrees Celsius) reactions stop. However, recent experimental evidence reveals that although the Arrhenius equation is generally accurate in describing the kind of chemical reaction that occurs at relatively high temperatures, at temperatures closer to zero a quantum-mechanical effect known as tunneling comes into play; this effect accounts for chemical reactions that are forbidden by the principles of classical chemistry. Specifically, entire molecules can "tunnel" through the barriers of repulsive forces from other molecules and chemically react even though these molecules do not have sufficient energy, according to classical chemistry, to overcome the repulsive barrier.

The rate of any chemical reaction, regardless of the temperature at which it takes place, usually depends on a very important characteristic known as its activation energy. Any molecule can be imagined to reside at the bottom of a so-called potential well of energy. A chemical reaction corresponds to the transition of a molecule from the bottom of one potential well to the bottom of another. In classical chemistry, such a transition can be accomplished only by going over the potential barrier between the wells, the height of which remains constant and is called the activation energy of the reaction. In tunneling, the reacting molecules tunnel from the bottom of one to the bottom of another well without having to rise over the barrier between the two wells. Recently researchers have developed the concept of tunneling temperature: the temperature below which tunneling transitions greatly outnumber Arrhenius transitions, and classical mechanics gives way to its quantum counterpart.

This tunneling phenomenon at very low temperatures suggested my hypothesis about a cold prehistory of life: the formation of rather complex organic molecules in the deep cold of outer space, where temperatures usually reach only a few degrees Kelvin. Cosmic rays (high-energy protons and other particles) might trigger the synthesis of simple molecules, such as interstellar formaldehyde, in dark clouds of interstellar dust. Afterward complex organic molecules would be formed, slowly but surely, by means of tunneling. After I offered my hypothesis, Hoyle and Wickramasinghe argued that molecules of interstellar formaldehyde have indeed evolved into stable polysaccharides such as cellulose and starch. Their conclusions, although strongly disputed, have generated excitement among investigators such as myself who are proposing that the galactic clouds are the places where the pre-biological evolution of compounds necessary to life occurred.

Sample Multiple-choice Questions — Select One Answer Choice

1. The author of the passage is primarily concerned with

   (A) describing how the principles of classical chemistry were developed

   (B) initiating a debate about the kinds of chemical reactions required for the development of life

   (C) explaining how current research in chemistry may be related to broader biological concerns

   (D) reconciling opposing theories about chemical reactions

   (E) clarifying inherent ambiguities in the laws of classical chemistry

Sample Multiple-choice Questions — Select One Answer Choice

2. The author's attitude toward the theory of a cold prehistory of life can best be described as

   (A) neutral

   (B) skeptical

   (C) mildly positive

   (D) very supportive

   (E) pointedly critical

Sample Multiple-choice Questions — Select One Answer Choice

3. Which of the following best describes the organization of the first two paragraphs of the passage?

   (A) The author cites a basic principle of classical chemistry and then describes the research from which that principle was developed.

   (B) The author cites an apparent contradiction to the principles of classical chemistry and then explains the process of a chemical reaction to show there is in fact no contradiction.

   (C) The author describes the role of heat in chemical reactions and then offers a detailed explanation of its function.

   (D) The author presents a law of classical chemistry in order to introduce a kind of chemical reaction that differs from it and then explains the essential difference between the two.

   (E) The author presents the fundamental rules of classical chemistry in order to introduce an explanation of a specific chemical reaction.

译文及解析

第一段

第一句： 大约在一个世纪以前，瑞典物理学家阿列纽斯提出了有关化学反应速率和温度之间关系的经典化学理论。

第二句： 根据阿列纽斯的公式：愈是趋近于绝对零度，化学反应愈是难以发生；当温度达到绝对零度之时，化学反应停止。（注：绝对零度指的是开氏温度，相当于-273摄氏温度）

（第二句是第一句的细节，这是传统的关于化学反应的观点。）

第三句： 但是，近期实验研究表明，阿列纽斯的理论在温度相对较高的环境中是适用的；但当温度趋近于绝对零度时，某种称之为“贯穿”的量子效应便开始发挥作用。这种效应可以解释一系列有悖于常规化学理论的反应。

（第三句和第一句形成对比。）

第四句： 具体来说就是，整个分子在能量不足的情况下（按照经典化学理论的说法）依然能够穿过其他分子的阻碍，进行化学反应。

（第四句是第三句的逻辑下一层。）

第二段

第一句： 除去温度不予考虑，化学反应的速率通常取决于一个非常重要的参量，即反应能量。

第二句： 我们可以假设任何一个分子都处于“势井”的底部。

第三句： 化学反应就相当于分子从一个“势井”的底部转移到另一个“势井”的底部。

（前三句都是在对化学反应进行基础的理论剖析。）

第四句： 在经典化学中，分子在“势井”之间的转移是通过跨越其间的障碍来得以实现的，此障碍的高度是恒定的，即反应能量。

第五句： 然而，在“贯穿”化学反应中，分子无须升起跨越障碍就能从一个“势井”底部穿过到另一个的底部。

（第四、五句进行了对比，是前三句的逻辑上一层，前三句的目的在于说明量子理论与传统理论有区别。）

第六句： 近期，研究者们给出了“贯穿”温度的概念：在某特定温度之下，“贯穿”反应的数量将远超阿列纽斯反应的数量，经典化学理论让步于量子化学理论。

（第六句是第四、五句的逻辑上一层，正是为了得出第六句的结论，作者才会对比传统化学反应和量子化学反应。）

第三段

第一句： 在极低温环境下的“贯穿”化学反应能够印证本人对于史前生命起源的假说：即在遥远寒冷——温度通常仅达到几开氏温度——的外太空环境中复杂有机分子的形成过程。

第二句： 宇宙射线（高能量质子和其他微粒）能够激发星际之间灰尘团中的简单分子——如甲醛分子——的合成。

第三句： 之后，慢慢地通过“贯穿”作用，复杂的有机分子得以成形。

（第二、三句都是第一句的细节，属于逻辑下一层。）

第四句： 在本人提出自己的假说之后，霍伊尔和威克二人认为星际间的甲醛的确逐步形成了稳定的多糖，比如纤维素和淀粉。

第五句： 尽管他们的理论争议颇多，但是对于像我这样——认为生命所需化合物的原始形成之地就是银河星云——的研究人员来说，毫无疑问是令人振奋的。

（作者写第四、五句的目的在于，通过另外两个人提出的观点来支持自己对于史前生命起源的假说，所以是第二、三句的逻辑下一层。）

逻辑图

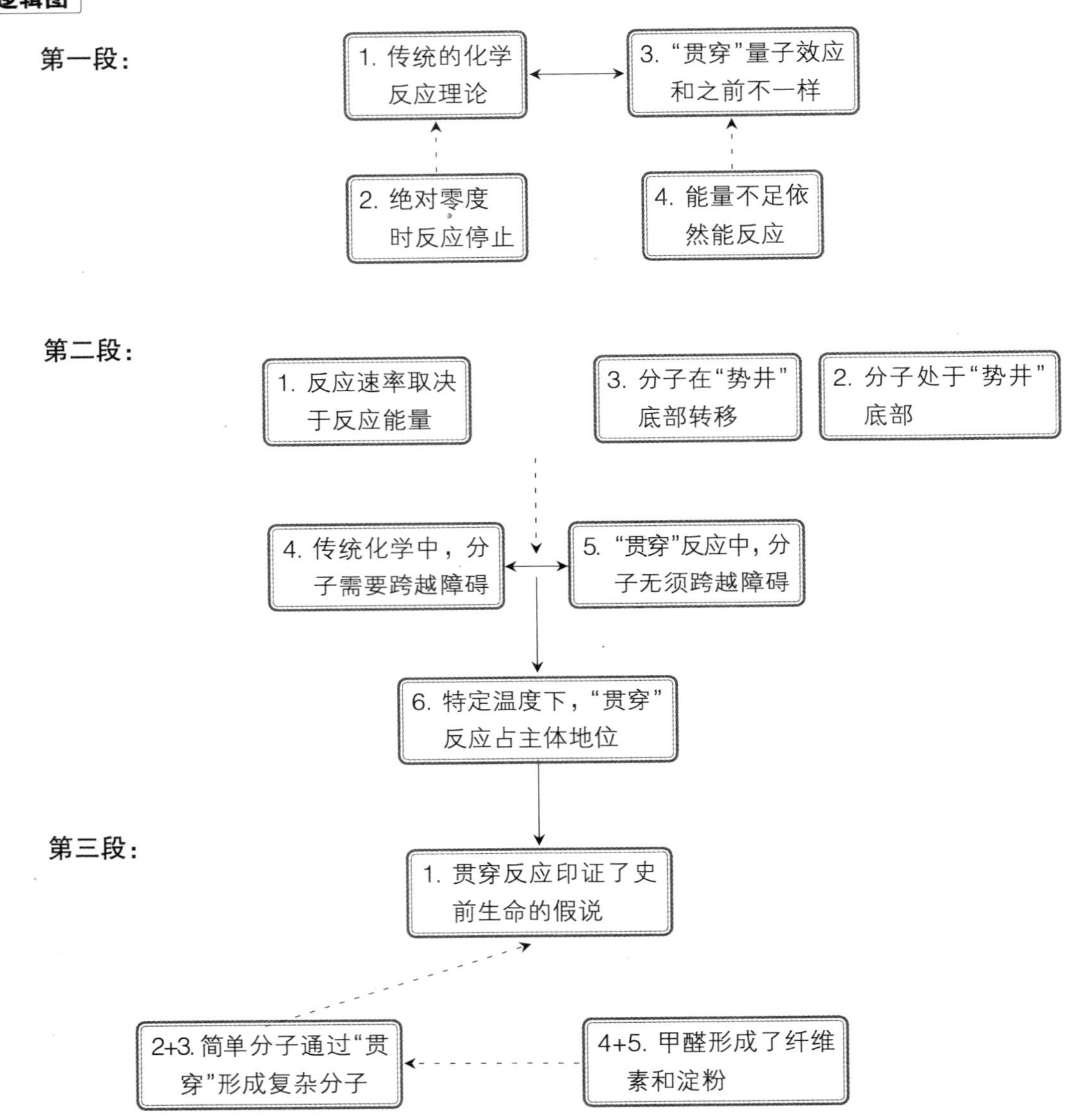
第一段：
1. 传统的化学反应理论
3. “贯穿”量子效应和之前不一样
2. 绝对零度时反应停止
4. 能量不足依然能反应
第二段：
1. 反应速率取决于反应能量
3. 分子在“势井”底部转移
2. 分子处于“势井”底部
4. 传统化学中，分子需要跨越障碍
5. “贯穿”反应中，分子无须跨越障碍
6. 特定温度下，“贯穿”反应占主体地位
第三段：
1. 贯穿反应印证了史前生命的假说
2+3. 简单分子通过“贯穿”形成复杂分子
4+5. 甲醛形成了纤维素和淀粉

题目及解析

1. The author of the passage is primarily concerned with

(A) describing how the principles of classical chemistry were developed

(B) initiating a debate about the kinds of chemical reactions required for the development of life

(C) explaining how current research in chemistry may be related to broader biological concerns

(D) reconciling opposing theories about chemical reactions

(E) clarifying inherent ambiguities in the laws of classical chemistry

解析

这是一道主题题，问“本文主要关注的内容是什么?”这种主题题真正的难点不是总结各段的内容然后选择一个最全面的答案，而是需要考生通过每段话所陈述的信息判断出作者的态度。这篇文章看似大都是在陈述，实则具有极强的议论文色彩。本文在第一段讨论了与常规的化学反应理论不同的“贯穿”反应，其目的在于引出第二段关于“贯穿”反应原理的描述；而本文描述“贯穿”反应的原理，其意图不是为了说明这种反应存在的合理性，而是为了通过印证这种原理的存在性来证明作者自己关于史前生命起源问题的合理性。所以，第二段是第一段的逻辑上一层，第三段又是第二段的逻辑上一层，本文的行文最终的目的在于通过“贯穿”的原理说明史前生命起源假说。

(A) 描绘经典化学理论是如何形成的

(A选项错。关于经典化学的描述只是论述过程的一个环节而已。)

(B) 引发关于生命起源所必需的化学反应的种类的争论

(B选项也不正确。本文不是为了就传统化学反应还是“贯穿”化学反应提出争论，而是为了证明“贯穿”反应对于生命起源的重要意义。)

(C) 阐述当前化学领域的研究是如何与生物界相联系的

(C是本题的正确答案。“当前研究”就是“贯穿”反应，“贯穿”反应对于生命起源的重要意义就是作者最终要论证的内容。)

(D) 调和关于化学反应的两种对立理论

(典型的断章取义，作者不是为了“调和”而行文的，是借用两种理论的区别得出作者需要的理论依据，即：在绝对零度之时，传统化学让步于量子化学。)

(E) 澄清传统化学理论中内在的混乱之处

(E选项错误比较低级。“inherent ambiguities”这个说法有失偏颇。)

2. The author’s attitude toward the theory of a cold prehistory of life can best be described as

(A) neutral

(B) skeptical

(C) mildly positive

(D) very supportive

(E) pointedly critical

解析

这是一道态度推断题，也是ETS设计的一种经典题型。题干问“作者关于史前生命论的态度”。很容易定位到第三段，作者利用“贯穿”化学反应理论的真实性来为自己提出的史前生命假说做理论支持；但是能够看出来作者的态度并非那么肯定，因为他也承认和他属于同一个阵列的两个学者的假说在学术界争议颇多。故而应该选择一个偏正评价的态度。

（A）不偏不倚
（B）怀疑
（C）略表支持
（D）坚定不移
（E）明确批评

因此，正确答案为选项C。

3. Which of the following best describes the organization of the first two paragraphs of the passage?

（A）The author cites a basic principle of classical chemistry and then describes the research from which that principle was developed.

（B）The author cites an apparent contradiction to the principles of classical chemistry and then explains the process of a chemical reaction to show there is in fact no contradiction.

（C）The author describes the role of heat in chemical reactions and then offers a detailed explanation of its function.

（D）The author presents a law of classical chemistry in order to introduce a kind of chemical reaction that differs from it and then explains the essential difference between the two.

（E）The author presents the fundamental rules of classical chemistry in order to introduce an explanation of a specific chemical reaction.

解析

这是一种非常规性的题目，问“以下哪个选项最好地勾勒出了前两段的结构?”在题干当中出现极端词汇“best”，意味着选项当中内容正确的只有一个。先看看前两段作者的写作意图，第一段提出了量子化学和经典化学之间的对比，其目的在于引出第二段对于造成这种对比的理论的阐述。再根据选项来判断：

（A）作者给出了一个经典的化学原理，并描绘出该原理的研究推导过程。
（A并不正确。作者并没有叙述经典化学原理的推导过程。）

（B）作者列举了一个与经典化学相矛盾的现象，并解释了这个现象，目的在于说明其实根本没有矛盾。
（这个与经典化学相矛盾的现象就是量子力学的“贯穿”效应，作者也的确解释了为何会有所谓的“矛盾”，即在绝对零度的时候传统化学让步于量子化学。看起来天衣无缝，实际上这是本题最具迷惑性的答案。这个选项如果用来概括前两段内容的话很好，但要说到文章结构就不合适了，因为作者不是为了说明“二者之间不存在矛盾”而行文的，而是要借用“不矛盾”的原理来为第三段铺垫，所以B不正确。）

（C）作者描绘了“热”在化学反应中的作用并给出了详细解释。

（“热”只是在反应中的一个变量而已，根本不是作者行文的目的或基础。）

（D）作者提出经典化学理论，其目的在于引出另一种与之不同的化学理论，然后再解释它们之间最基本的区别。

（D是本题的正确答案。它把作者所写的几个实体信息之间手段和目的的关系表述得很清楚。作者写经典化学正是为了引出量子化学，写量子化学在“势井”底部转移正是为了得出二者区别的原因，然后在第三段再借用此原因来支持自己的理论。）

（E）作者给出经典化学的基本原理，其目的在于引出一种特定的化学反应的解释。

（E选项也属于迷惑性选项。经典化学的原理是分子在绝对零度之时就停止运动了，另外一种“特定化学反应”的现象不是经典化学的原理能解释清楚的，而是通过研究与经典化学不一致的现象进行解释。故而不能说“贯穿”反应的解释是根据经典化学原理得出来的。）

本题属于比较难的题目类型，题干当中出现“best”时常需要考生在几个选项之间进行横向比较。

Note

Reading Comprehension 1

Galaxy Clusters Validate Einstein's Theory
爱因斯坦的理论在星系团的范围内得到证实

Testing gravity is simple: walk out of a second-floor window and see what happens. It's a lot tougher to test Albert Einstein's theory of gravity—the general theory of relativity—which says that the gravity of an object warps space and time around it. Although researchers have proved general relativity on the scale of the solar system, validating it on cosmic scales has been more challenging.

检验万有引力现象很简单：从二楼的窗户走出去（禁止付诸实践），看看会发生什么！但是要想检验爱因斯坦的万有引力理论——广义相对论，难度就要大得多。该理论的内容是：一个物体的重力会使其周围的空间和时间扭曲。尽管研究人员在太阳系范围内证明了广义相对论，但是在整个宇宙范围内验证该理论是更具挑战性的。

The researchers, led by Radek Wojtak of the Niels Bohr Institute at the University of Copenhagen, set out to test a classic prediction of general relativity: that light will lose energy as it is escaping a gravitational field. The stronger the field, the greater the energy loss suffered. As a result, photons emitted from the center of a galaxy cluster—a massive object containing thousands of galaxies—should lose more energy than photons coming from the edge of the cluster because of the strongest gravity. Based on the former theory, light emerging from the center should become longer in wavelength than light coming from the edges, shifting toward the red end of the light spectrum. The effect is known as gravitational redshifting.

在哥本哈根大学尼尔斯·波尔研究所的拉德克·沃杰塔克的带领下，一组研究人员着手检验广义相对论的一个经典预测：光在逃离引力场的时候会损失能量；引力场越强，光损失的能量就越多。因此，从星系团中心散发出来的光子应该比星系团边缘散发出的光子损失的能量更多，因为星系团中心区的引力最强。星系团是包含了成千上万个星系的大型天体系统。根据之前的理论，在波长上，来自星系团中心的光比来自边缘的光变得更长，移向光谱的红色端。这个效应被称为“引力红移现象”。

Wojtak and his colleagues knew that measuring gravitational redshifting within a single galaxy cluster would be difficult because the effect is very small and needs to be teased apart from the redshifting caused by the orbital velocity of individual galaxies within the cluster and the redshifting caused by the expansion of the universe. The researchers approached the problem by

沃杰塔克和他的同事知道，测量单个星系内的引力红移会很困难，因为星系内引力红移效应非常小，而且需要将这种红移效应和星系的轨道速度以及宇宙膨胀造成的红移效应分离开来。研究人员从“斯隆数字巡天计划”中搜集了8000个星系团的数据，并通过平均这些数据解决了这个问题。“这样做是希望通过研究

averaging data collected from 8,000 galaxy clusters by the Sloan Digital Sky Survey. The hope was to detect gravitational redshift "by studying the properties of the redshift distribution of galaxies in clusters rather than by looking at redshifts of individual galaxies separately," Wojtak explains.

星系团中星系之间的红移分布特点来发现引力红移效应，而不是分别查看各个星系的红移效应，"沃杰塔克解释说。

Sure enough, the researchers found that the light from the clusters was redshifted in proportion to the distance from the center of the cluster, as predicted by general relativity. It's possible to measure small differences in the redshift of the galaxies and see that the light from galaxies in the middle of a cluster had to "crawl" out through the gravitational field, while it was easier for the light from the outlying galaxies to emerge.

果然，研究人员发现，正像广义相对论预测的那样，星系团中的光发生了红移，而且和到星系团中心的距离成比例。(并且)可以测量出星系之间红移效应的微小差别，看得出来自星系团中心区星系的光不得不"费力爬出"那里的引力场，而来自边缘星系中的光则可以较为轻松地散发出来。

Besides confirming general relativity, the results strongly support the Lambda-Cold Dark Matter model of the universe, an already popular cosmological model according to which most of the cosmos is made up of invisible stuff that does not interact with matter constituting stars and planets. The test also lends support for dark energy, the mysterious force that appears to be pushing the universe apart.

除了证实广义相对论之外，这些研究结果也有力地说明了拉姆达冷暗物质宇宙模型。这个已经流行于世的宇宙模型表明，宇宙的大部分是由不可见物质构成的，这种物质与构成恒星和行星的物质不发生相互作用。这项研究也支持了暗能量的存在，暗能量似乎是正在使宇宙膨胀的一种神秘力量。

David Spergel, an astrophysicist at Princeton University, compliments Wojtak and his colleagues on "cleverly combining" a large cluster data set to detect a "subtle effect." Spergel says, "This is another victory for Einstein. ... This cluster test suggests that we do live in a strange universe with dark matter and dark energy, but one in which Einstein's theory of gravity is valid on large scales."

普林斯顿大学的天体物理学家戴维·斯博格尔赞扬了沃杰塔克及其同事的研究。他们"聪明地结合了"大型的星系团数据集来探测"微小的红移效应"，斯博格尔说，"这是爱因斯坦的又一次胜利……此次对星系团的检验表明，我们的确生活在一个拥有暗物质和暗能量的奇怪宇宙中，而在这个广大的范围中，爱因斯坦的万有引力理论仍然有效。"

Reading Comprehension 2

Galaxy Collisions Give Birth to Quasars
星系碰撞创造了类星体

Peering behind thick clouds of cosmic gas and dust, researchers believe they have finally determined the origins of quasars, the brightest and most powerful objects in the universe. X-ray and infrared observations of over 200 distant galaxies, coupled with images taken in visible light, reveal that quasars form when two galaxies smash into each other and their central black holes merge. The new observations also suggest that quasars were more common in the early universe than previously thought.

研究人员将视线深入到由宇宙气体和尘埃构成的浓密云团后面，他们认为类星体的起源终于可以确定了。类星体是宇宙间最为明亮、最具威力的天体。通过对200多个遥远的星系进行X射线和红外线观测，结合在可见光下拍摄的图像，结果显示，当两个星系互相碰撞、其中心的黑洞融合在一起的时候，类星体就形成了。这些新观测还表明，早期宇宙中的类星体更为常见，这一点是始料不及的。

Astronomers discovered quasars, short for quasi-stellar objects, in the 1950s. Only about the size of our solar system, quasars easily outshine entire galaxies and can burn for 100 million years. For decades, however, astronomers could not figure out what generated these cosmic beacons. The obvious suspects were supermassive black holes, which anchor the cores of practically all galaxies, can devour gigantic amounts of matter, and are known to produce huge jets of particles and energy. But many galaxies—including the Milky Way—host supermassive black holes yet don't generate quasars.

天文学家们在20世纪50年代发现了类星体，类星体是“类似恒星的天体”之缩略语。类星体仅仅相当于我们太阳系的大小，可是它们可以轻而易举地照亮整个星系，可以燃烧一亿年。然而几十年来，天文学家们一直不明白是什么创造了这些宇宙明灯。最可能的目标就是超大质量的黑洞，它们稳居在几乎所有星系的中心，可以吞噬大量的物质，而且据了解它们能够产生巨大的粒子和能量射流。但是很多星系——包括银河系在内——都拥有超大质量的黑洞，然而并没有产生类星体。

Perhaps the younger quasars were hiding. At least, that's what astronomers began to suspect in the late 1990s when they noticed that some galaxies whose central cores were obscured by huge clouds of dust seemed to emit the same kind of radiation and produced similar levels of energy as quasars.

或许，较为年轻的类星体隐匿起来了！至少在20世纪90年代末期，天文学家们就开始这么认为了。当时，他们注意到一些星系的核心被巨大的尘埃云团所遮掩，但所释放出的射线似乎跟类星体一样，散发出的能量水平也近似于类星体。

To peek behind the dust, astronomer Ezequiel Treister and colleagues first selected about 200 candidate galaxies out of 100,000 images. Then they trained the

为了观察到尘埃后面的情况，天文学家埃塞基耶尔·特雷斯特及其同事首先从10万张图像中选择了大约200张。然后，他们将钱德拉

Chandra and Spitzer space telescopes, which can see in x-ray and infrared light, respectively, on the galaxies' obscured cores. The candidates ranged out to a distance of about 11 billion light-years. The new observations revealed hidden quasars in every one of the galaxies. What's more, by studying the shape of the galaxies, the astronomers found that they all had arisen from the mergers of two massive galaxies and their central black holes. Additional, in the early universe, collisions—and hence quasars came into being—occurred more often because galaxies were packed much more closely together.

太空望远镜和斯必泽太空望远镜对准这些星系被遮挡的核心。这两个望远镜分别可以在X射线和红外线状态下进行拍摄。这些目标星系的距离范围延伸到大约110亿光年。这些新的观测显示，每个星系中都有隐藏的类星体。并且，通过研究星系的形状，天文学家们发现，类星体全部产生于两个巨型星系及其中心黑洞的合并。另外，在早期宇宙中，星系碰撞以及因此而形成类星体的情况发生得更加频繁，因为当时星系之间的距离要近得多。

Reading Comprehension 3

Climate Change Has Helped Bring Down Cultures
气候变化导致文化失落

Humanity has weathered many a climate change, from the ice age of 80,000 years ago to the droughts of the late 19th century that helped kill between 30 and 50 million people around the world via famine. But such shifts have transformed or eliminated specific human societies, including the ancient Sumerians and the Ming Dynasty in China.

从8万年以前的冰川时期至干旱的19世纪晚期，人类经历了很多气候变化，这些气候变化使得全球3000万至5000万的人口死于饥荒。但是，这样的变化改变和淘汰着人类社会，包括古苏美尔人和中国明朝人等特定的人类群体。

Epidemiologist Anthony McMichael of Australian National University surveyed how human societies fared during previous episodes of extreme weather brought on by climate shifts. The big threat is changes to food production, or as McMichael puts it "the drought-famine-starvation nexus." And we've never weathered a climate change so big, so rapid and so widespread as the one we are now busily creating by burning fossil fuels, notes McMichael.

澳大利亚国立大学的流行病学家安东尼·麦克迈克尔研究了在不同历史时期的极端气候条件下，人类社会是如何挨过的。其中，巨大的威胁是粮食产量的变化，或者就像麦克迈克尔指出的"干旱—饥荒—饥饿连锁反应"。然而，他认为，我们人类从来没有像现在这样，由于燃烧化石燃料，致使气候发生很大、很快以及非常广泛的变化。

Long-running climate changes have often brought about the downfall of cultures, including foiling the earliest human attempts at settled farming nearly 13,000 years ago. Around that time, a major millennia-long climate cooling event known as the "Younger Dryas" coincides with the end of most settlements along the Nile Delta and in modern-day Syria. Skeletons from the era evince "an unusually high proportion of violent deaths, many accompanied by remnants of weapons," McMichael noted.

长期的气候变化往往会带来文化的衰落，包括阻碍13000年以前人类早期的农耕业。在那个时期，气候变冷持续了1000年，被称之为“新仙女木事件”；同时，在尼罗河三角洲地区以及今天的叙利亚地区，大部分定居终结。麦克迈克尔指出，那个时期的骨骼显示出“极高的暴力死亡率，并伴有大量的武器残留”。

Shorter-term climate changes have proven equally devastating. Decade-long droughts in 17th century China led to starvation, internal migration and, ultimately, the collapse of the Ming Dynasty. A seven-year span of torrential rains, attendant floods and cold in the early 1300s helped cause a famine that may have killed as much as 10 percent of the people in northern Europe—a generation that would then face the Black Death a few decades later.

更短时期的气候变化同样证明了其破坏力。17世纪的10年干旱使得中国饥馑丛生，国内移民频繁，最终导致明朝灭亡。而14世纪早期延续7年的暴雨，以及随之而来的洪水泛滥和寒冷，引起了严重饥荒，北欧大约10%的人口死于饥饿——而这一代人在几十年后又面临了黑死病的侵袭。

Even a single bad summer can be enough—like the hot summer of 1793 in Philadelphia that, paired with an influx of refugees from modern day Haiti, saw an outbreak of yellow fever that killed tens of thousands.

甚至一个噩梦般的夏天也足以带来这种厄运(气候致死)：美国费城1793年的夏天极其炎热，同时由于来自现在海地地区的流亡者们大量涌入，这导致成千上万人死于黄热病。

Of course, none of these societies had the benefits of modern technology or modern energy, whether medicine or air conditioning. But even that may not be enough to offset the roughly 2 to 4 degrees Celsius of warming in average global temperatures the world is on pace to achieve via emissions of greenhouse gases. "Such a change will surely pose serious risks to human health and survival," McMichael wrote, "impinging unevenly, but sparing no population."

当然，上述社会中没有哪个社会能够享有现代技术或是现代能量带来的好处，不论医药或是空调。但是，这些也没办法抵消温室气体排放造成的约2–4度的全球平均温度的提升。“这种变化必将给人类健康和生存带来严重的威胁，”麦克迈克尔写道，“虽然这种冲击是不均衡的，但是人类也很难免于劫难。”

Reading Comprehension 4

Early Earth Hazy One Day Clear the Next
一天浓雾一天晴——早期地球大气化学成分的震荡性变化

A new study of ancient South African rocks indicates Earth may have experienced huge swings in the composition of its early atmosphere. The study in the journal *Nature Geoscience* indicates Earth's atmosphere transitioned between an oxygen rich environment and a thick methane hydrocarbon haze similar to what is now seen on the Saturnian moon Titan.

一项关于古代南非岩石的最新研究表明，地球早期大气的组成可能发生过巨大的振荡。这项来自《自然地质科学》期刊的研究表明，地球大气在富含氧气的环境和含有高浓度甲烷碳氢化合物的浓雾之间转变，而后者和我们今天在土星的卫星Titan上所观测到的情况相似。

The work by scientists including Dr. Aubrey Zerkle analysed marine sediments deposited in the Campbellrand-Malmani carbonate platform in South Africa's Ghaap Group which is one of the oldest platform on Earth with rocks dating back to between 2.65 and 2.5 billion years ago. The analyses allowed Zerkle and colleagues to reconstruct the ocean and atmospheric chemistry of the period, finding evidence of oxygen production by microbes.

整个研究工作由包括奥布里·热尔科博士在内的人员完成，他们分析了Campbellrand-Malmani碳酸盐平台中存留的海洋沉积物，这个平台在南非的Ghaap Group，是地球上最古老的平台之一，其岩石生成于26.5到25亿年以前。通过这个分析，热尔科及其同事得以重构那一时期的海洋和大气的化学组成，并发现了微生物产生氧气的证据。

They also found carbon and sulphur isotopes indicating the oxygen was made in a reduced atmosphere that was periodically rich in methane. Zerkle and colleagues believe the findings are consistent with previous theories of Earth's early atmosphere having a thick organic haze similar to that on Titan.

他们还发现了碳和硫的一些同位素，表明氧气是在周期性富含甲烷的密度减小的大气中产生的。热尔科及其同事相信，这些发现和先前关于地球早期大气的理论是一致的，即像Titan一样具有很浓的有机烟雾。

However, their simulations suggests Earth's atmosphere repeatedly transitioned between two main atmospheric states, one haze free, the other thick in hydrocarbons. Zerkle and colleagues attribute the transitions to changes in the rate of methane production by microbes. They say the hydrocarbon haze didn't permanently retreat until the oxygenation of the atmosphere some 100 million years later.

但是，这种模拟表明，地球大气在两种主要状态间频繁转换，一种没有浓雾，另一种则充满碳氢化合物。热尔科及其同事将这种变化归因于微生物产生甲烷的速率的变化。他们说，碳氢化合物的浓雾在大气氧气化发生约一亿年以后才永久性退去。

Professor Malcolm Walter from the Australian Centre for Astro-biology at the University of New South Wales says the paper confirms a very large change in the chemistry of the Earth's surface about 2.65 billion years ago. "We've known about the basic elements of this for a while, but they've refined the processes that took place at the time," says Walter. "It's hard to read the record in rocks this old."

来自澳大利亚新南威尔士大学天文生物学中心的马尔科姆·沃尔特教授说：这份论文证明了地球表面的化学组成在26.5亿年前有过非常大的变动。"我们对这件事情的基本了解已经有些时候了，但是他们将当时发生的过程研究得更明确了，"沃尔特说，"从这么古老的岩石中读出这些记录是非常困难的。"

Walter says the findings are consistent with previous research into 2.7 billion year old stromatolite fossils from the Pilbara region of Western Australia conducted by his team. "They've done a good job of trying to pin down exactly when things happened, just what happened, how long it happened for and what the chemical processes were."

沃尔特说，这项研究与先前他自己的团队对来自27亿年前澳大利亚西部皮尔巴拉地区的叠层化石的研究是一致的。"他们干得非常好，努力搞清楚事情什么时候发生、发生了什么、发生了多久以及发生的化学过程是什么。"

Reading Comprehension 5

The Physics of Wine Swirling
葡萄酒漩涡中的物理学

Meet the new flavor of wine: fruity with a hint of fluid dynamics. Oenophiles have long gotten the best out of their reds by giving their glasses a swirl before sipping. Twirling a wineglass gently creates smooth arcs in the liquid that then circle, coating the sides of the glass and then mixes oxygen into a red, enhancing its flavor. A new study has revealed the physics behind that sloshing, showing that three factors may determine whether your merlot arcs smoothly or starts to splash.

葡萄酒中的新口味：果味中带着一丝流体力学的味道。一直以来，品酒师在抿一口酒之前先摇晃酒杯(使酒产生漩涡)，就能使红酒散发出最佳气味。轻轻地快速转动葡萄酒杯，使液体产生平滑的圆弧，并覆盖在玻璃杯边缘，然后此漩涡运动就能够将氧气混合到红酒中，增强红酒的口味。一个新的研究揭示了在这个晃动背后的物理学，展示出可能是决定你的梅洛(一种来自法国波尔多产区的红葡萄酒)会在杯中平滑地形成圆弧还是开始飞溅的三个因素。

Three factors seemed to determine the swirling movement of wine: the ratio of the level of wine poured

似乎有三个因素决定了葡萄酒旋转运动：倒入的葡萄酒的水平面与葡萄酒杯直径的比

in to the diameter of the glass; the ratio of the diameter of the glass to the width of the circular shaking; and the ratio of the forces acting on the wine. Those forces affecting the wine were the centrifugal force pushing the liquid to the outside of the glass and the gravitational force shoving the liquid back down. By tweaking these factors a notch—for instance, by pouring a bit more wine into a glass or shaking that glass in tighter circles—researchers found that if they kept all three ratios identical, they began to spot the same waves forming again and again, even in cylinders of very different sizes.

率；葡萄酒杯的直径与圆周晃动的宽度的比率；和施加在葡萄酒上的力的比率。这些影响着葡萄酒的力是将葡萄酒推出葡萄酒杯的离心力和将液体拉回来的重力。将这些因素作一些小调整，比如多倒一些葡萄酒到杯子里或者在更紧凑的圆轨道上晃动杯子，研究者发现，如果他们保持这三个比率完全相同，就会反复观察到同一种波形一次又一次地形成，甚至在尺寸迥异的圆桶中也是一样。

Another important discovery was also landed: how overly enthusiastic wine swirlers manage to splash their drinks. Just like an ocean crest, wine waves begin to break, turning frothy, if they're moving too quickly. The breaking acceleration for a merlot is about 40% of the force of gravity or nearly 4 meters per second. That acceleration, in turn, is dependent on the volume of wine in the glass, the force of shaking, and other factors.

另一个重要的发现是：葡萄酒“旋流器”是多么狂热地想将这些酒洒出去。就像海浪的波峰，如果移动过快，葡萄酒波就开始瓦解，变为泡沫。使梅洛的波瓦解的加速度大约是重力的40%，或者近4米/秒。反观这个加速度，它取决于玻璃杯中葡萄酒的体积、使玻璃杯晃动的力和其他一些因素。

The analysis seemed simple but did make sense, and the study illustrated how seemingly everyday physics, such as the swirling of a glass of wine, might help scientists and engineers develop as well as ameliorate lab tools: When growing bacterial cultures, biologists often mix cells in with nutrients in one big jar, then swirl. That rotation distributes the bacterial food throughout the slurry and also removes excess carbon dioxide.

这个分析似乎很简单但是确实有意义，它很好地解释了日常生活中的物理学，比如玻璃杯中葡萄酒的漩涡，可能会帮助科学家和工程师发明和改善实验室工具：生物学家进行细菌培养时，通常将细胞和营养物质混合在一个大的广口瓶里，然后打旋。这种旋转将食物分散在细菌混合液中，并且挤出了多余的二氧化碳。

Reading Comprehension 6

Neutrinos Not Faster Than Light
中微子没有超光速

Neutrinos obey nature's speed limit, according to new results from an Italian experiment. The finding contradicts a rival claim that neutrinos could travel faster than the speed of light.

根据意大利研究人员最新的实验结果，中微子依然遵守自然界的速度限制。这个实验结果反驳了之前提出的一个相反观点——中微子可以超越光速。

Last September, an experiment called OPERA turned up evidence that neutrinos travel faster than the speed of light by detecting neutrinos sent from CERN, Europe's premier particle-physics laboratory near Geneva, Switzerland. According to the group's findings, neutrinos made the 731-kilometre journey 60 nanoseconds faster than predicted if they had travelled at light speed. Although the announcement made international headlines, but physicists were deeply skeptical because the axiom that nothing travels faster than light was first formulated by Albert Einstein and was a cornerstone of modern physics.

去年九月，名为"OPERA"的实验得出证据，证明中微子的移动速度超过了光速。该实验检测的中微子来自欧洲核子研究中心(CERN)——欧洲首席粒子物理实验室，位于瑞士的日内瓦附近。根据此实验结果，中微子在60纳秒内移动了731公里，要比光速快。尽管这个结论一下子成了国际头条，但是物理学家们都深表怀疑：爱因斯坦最早提出这个公理，即没有什么可以超过光速，这也是现代物理的基石。

Now another experiment located just a few metres from OPERA has clocked neutrinos travelling at roughly the speed of light, and no faster. The rival group monitored a beam of neutrinos sent from CERN in late October and early November of last year. The neutrinos were packed into pulses just 4 nanoseconds long, which could be measured far more accurately than the former measurement. The distance over which neutrinos covered within just 4 nanoseconds of the time seemed equal to that of light travelling in the same time, well within the experimental margin of error.

如今，离OPERA实验组所在地不远的另外一个实验组重新检测发现，中微子基本按照光速运动，并不比光速快。该实验组在去年十月底到十一月初期间监测一束由欧洲核子研究中心发射出的中微子。他们使用四纳秒脉冲计时器捕获了这些中微子，这意味着计时器所测量的时间比之前OPERA测量得要准确很多。在考虑实验误差的情况下，测定了中微子在四纳秒的时间内穿过的距离，这和光速基本一致。

Reading Comprehension 7

Antimatter Belt Found Circling Earth
环地球反物质带

A newly discovered belt of antimatter circling Earth could be an astronaut's best friend. The belt, which consists of antiprotons trapped by Earth's magnetic field several hundred kilometers above the planet's surface, may ultimately become a key source of fuel for missions venturing beyond the solar system.

一个新发现的环地球反物质带可能会为宇航员提供最有用的帮助。该反物质带由反质子构成，被地表以上几百公里处的地球磁场所捕获，最终可能为太阳系以外的航天探险行动提供重要的燃料源。

Researchers analyzing data from the PAMELA (Payload for Antimatter/Matter Exploration and Light-nuclei Astrophysics) satellite, a joint mission among scientists from Italy, Germany, Russia, and Sweden, reported the findings 26 July on arXiv.org and in the 20 August *Astrophysical Journal Letters*.

研究人员分析了来自"物质/反物质探索与轻核天体物理研究有效载荷"(简称为PAMELA)卫星的资料，该卫星是意大利、德国、俄罗斯和瑞典等国科学家们的联合航天项目。7月26日，研究人员将该发现发表在arXiv.org网站上；于8月20日发表在《天体物理学期刊快报》上。

"The results are credible and are consistent with models that previously predicted (the belt's) existence," says James Bickford, senior member of the technical staff at the Draper Laboratory in Cambridge, Massachusetts, who was not part of the study. Bickford's own research predicts that other planets, including Jupiter, Saturn, Neptune, and Uranus, should have similar antiproton belts. Saturn may produce the greatest number of antiprotons because of interactions between cosmic rays—energetic charged particles from space—and the planet's icy rings.

"这些研究结果跟以往预测反物质带时所做的模拟是一致的，"马萨诸塞州剑桥市德雷珀实验室的资深技术员詹姆斯·比克福德说，但他并没有参与这项研究。比克福德根据自己的研究预测出，其他的行星包括木星、土星、海王星和天王星也应该有类似的反质子带。由于宇宙射线（来自太空的高能带电粒子流）和土星冰冷的光环之间进行相互作用，土星上产生的反质子数量可能最多。

Antiprotons are particles with the same mass as more familiar protons but with opposite charge. To hunt for them, the PAMELA team analyzed data the craft gathered from July 2006 to December 2008 during the first 850 days of its science mission. The researchers, who include Alessandro Bruno of the University of Bari in Italy and the INFN in Bari, focused on a region known as the South Atlantic Anomaly, where Earth's inner Van Allen

反质子跟我们比较熟悉的质子质量相同，但是所携带的电荷相反。为了寻找这些粒子，PAMELA研究小组分析了2006年7月至2008年12月期间PAMELA卫星收集到的数据，这是该卫星在其科学使命中前850天所完成的任务。研究人员中包括意大利国家核物理学学会会员、巴里大学的亚历山德罗·布鲁诺。他们的研究集中于一个被称为"南大西洋异常区"

radiation belt comes closest to the planet's surface and the density of particles encountered by the craft would likely be the highest. In its low Earth orbit, PAMELA regularly plows through this region.

的区域，在那里，地球近围的范艾伦辐射带和地球表面最接近，而PAMELA卫星在该区域遇到的粒子浓度可能是最高的。PAMELA卫星绕地球低轨道定期地穿越该区域。

The team identified 28 antiprotons with kinetic energies between 60 million and 750 million electron volts. That number is far higher than scientists would expect to see shooting toward Earth from distant reaches of the galaxy. The antiparticles appear to form a thin belt around Earth, gyrating around Earth's magnetic field lines and bouncing back and forth between the planet's north and south magnetic poles, the team notes. The belt, which extends from a few hundred to about 2,000 kilometers above Earth, "constitutes the most abundant source of antiprotons in Earth's vicinity," Bruno says.

研究小组发现了28个反质子，动能在6000万至7.5亿电子伏特之间，这个能量比科学家们所预期的、从遥远星系射向地球的能量高出许多。这些反粒子好像在地球周围形成一条细带，环绕着地球的磁力线运动，并在地球的南北磁极之间来回穿梭。这条带在地球上空从几百公里一直延伸到大约2000公里处，"构成了地球附近最为丰富的反质子储存库，"布鲁诺说。

Most of the antiprotons come from antineutrons, which are generated when energetic cosmic rays strike the upper atmosphere tens of kilometers above Earth's surface, Bruno notes. The antineutrons escape the atmosphere and then decay into antiprotons at much higher altitudes. Pairs of protons and antiprotons are also directly produced in the cosmic ray collisions with the atmosphere. The antiprotons tend to congregate several hundred kilometers above Earth, where ordinary matter is so scarce that they are unlikely to meet up with their particle counterparts—protons—and destroy each other on contact.

布鲁诺指出，多数反质子来自反中子。反中子是高能宇宙射线袭击了地球表面以上几十公里处的上层大气时产生的。反中子逃离大气，然后在更高的区域衰变为反质子。另外，宇宙射线撞击大气时，也会直接产生成对的质子和反质子。这种反质子往往汇集在地球上空几百公里处，那里普通物质是极为稀少的，不大可能遇到与它们对应的粒子——质子，也不会通过互相接触而发生湮灭现象。

Changes in the energy of particles in the belt could help verify and calibrate models that attempt to quantify the effect on Earth's environment of solar flares and other outbursts from the sun, Bickford notes.

比克福德指出，反物质带中粒子能量的变化可以帮助检验和校准科学模型，以便更加精确地量化太阳耀斑和其他类型的爆发对地球环境造成的影响。

More provocatively, antiprotons in the belt might one day be harvested to fuel missions that would travel far beyond the solar system, Bickford says. The best concepts for antimatter propulsion require that the antiprotons be collected and isolated. At the right moment, the

比克福德说，更加令人兴奋的是，有朝一日反物质带中的反质子可以被收集起来，为奔向太阳系外的远距离航天行动提供燃料。至于反物质推进，最好的想法是将反质子收集起来并实施隔离。在合适的时刻，使反质子和质子

antiprotons would mix with protons and annihilate them to produce highly energetic charged particles to propel the craft. The number of antiprotons needed, however, would exceed the amount in the newly discovered belt or even the much larger belt that may circle Saturn, Bickford says.

混合，发生湮灭，产生高能带电粒子，推进飞船运行。然而比克福德说，需要的反质子数量会超过反物质带中新发现的数量，甚至会超过潜在的、数量更大的环木星反物质带中反质子的数量。

But Bickford says some researchers have proposed that a smaller supply of antiprotons, comparable to the population of the belt, could be used as a catalyst to trigger nuclear reactions that would release charged particles. (The antiprotons in this scheme would be gathered into a vast fuel tank, a nearly weightless cloud hundreds of meters long surrounding the craft.)

但是，比克福德说，一些研究人员提出，较少的反质子，类似于反物质带中的反质子数量，可以用来作为催化剂，引发释放带电粒子的核反应。(在这一计划中，反质子会被收集起来装进一个巨大的燃料箱，该燃料箱实际上就是环绕在飞船周围长达几百米的无重量云团。)

Travelling at nearly the speed of light, the charged particles produced by the nuclear reactions would fly out of the back end of the craft, propelling it beyond the solar system. In contrast, Bickford notes, a spacecraft using chemical propellant to journey well past the fringes of the solar system at high speed would need a fuel supply more massive than the observable universe.

核反应产生的带电粒子以近光速穿行，将会飞离飞船的末端，将飞船推进至太阳系之外。比克福德指出，相比较而言，使用化学推进剂的宇宙飞船要想以高速度远远地离开太阳系的边缘，所需要的燃料供应量将会极其巨大，在可见宇宙中是无法得到的。

“Antiprotons are incredibly expensive and difficult to produce and store on Earth,” and even the world’s most powerful atom smashers could produce and trap only nanograms of the stuff each year, Bickford adds. That’s why the antiprotons in the belt are nearly a trillion times more valuable than diamonds, he says.

“反质子是极为昂贵的，在地球上难以生产和存储，”甚至世界上最具威力的核粒子加速器每年可生产和捕获的反质子也只不过有几毫微克，比克福德接着说。所以说，反物质带中的反质子要比钻石贵重将近一万亿倍！

Reading Comprehension 8

Hubble Spots the Farthest Spiral Galaxy Ever Seen
哈勃望远镜发现最遥远的漩涡星系

Like a beautiful rose sprouting from a field of weeds, a spectacular spiral galaxy has emerged near the edge of the observable universe, where most galaxies are ragged

就像杂草地里冒出的一朵玫瑰，一个壮观的漩涡星系出现在可观测宇宙的边缘附近，那里的多数星系呈现出不规则的团状。这个新发

blobs. The newfound galaxy is the most distant spiral ever seen and may offer clues to the origin of spiral structure in galaxies elsewhere. Today about two-thirds of all bright galaxies, including the Milky Way and Andromeda, are spirals which have fast-spinning disks whose stars and gas clouds nevertheless move slowly relative to their neighbors—a condition that favors the formation of spiral patterns. In the distant past, however, spirals were rare, because stars and gas clouds moved fast relative to one another, suppressing spiral structure; so as astronomers peer out at great distances, they look back to a time before these glowing pinwheels existed.

现的星系是目前观测到的最遥远的漩涡星系，或许它可以为其他漩涡状星系的起源提供线索。当今，在所有的星系中大约有三分之二是漩涡星系，其中包括银河系和仙女座星系：这些漩涡星系拥有快速旋转的圆盘，而其中的恒星和气团相对于其相邻恒星和气团来说旋转较慢，这种状况有利于漩涡形状的形成。然而在遥远的过去，漩涡星系很稀少，因为恒星和气团之间的相对运动很快，阻止了漩涡形状的形成。因此，当天文学家们凝望遥远的宇宙空间时，他们所看到的是这些发光转轮形成之前的情况。

Researchers used the Hubble Space Telescope to examine 306 far-off galaxies, finding one that had three spiral arms just popped out, looking like a spiral. That galaxy astounded researchers.

研究者们利用哈勃太空望远镜仔细观察了306个遥远的星系，有一个星系脱颖而出，该星系有三条旋臂，看起来像漩涡星系。当研究者们看到这个星系的时候感到异常惊讶。

With the Keck II telescope in Hawaii, the astronomers then detected Doppler shifts from different parts of the galaxy's disk, indicating it spins as fast as the Milky Way does. The galaxy is 50,000 light-years across—less than half the diameter of the Milky Way's stellar disk—but harbors more gas and spawns far more new stars. It seems to be possibly a new manifestation of spirality because the galaxy's stars and gas clouds move fast relative to their neighbors; yet despite the turbulence the galaxy has been able to form spiral arms.

后来，研究人员利用夏威夷的凯克二号望远镜，在星系圆盘的不同位置探测到多普勒频移，说明该星系的旋转速度跟银河系是一样的。这个星系直径为5万光年，不到银河系恒星盘的一半，但是其中拥有更多的气体，产生的新恒星也要多得多。这可能是一种新的螺旋形式，因为这个星系中的恒星和气团比相邻的恒星和气团运动得更快，而且尽管星系中的涡流强劲，仍然能够形成旋臂。

So how did this far-off galaxy create its spiral pattern? Law says the galaxy has a small companion whose gravity may have stirred up the spiral structure. However, Elmegreen questions this idea, noting that most spirals stirred up by companion galaxies have two arms, not three. Instead, he says the large amount of gas in the galaxy may be responsible. Although the stars and gas clouds in the galaxy move fast relative to their neighbors, Elmegreen says the gravity of all the gas may overwhelm the high velocity dispersion and mold a spiral pattern.

那么这个遥远星系的漩涡形状是如何形成的呢？劳说，该星系拥有一个小型伴星系，这个伴星系的引力可能促成了漩涡结构。然而，厄尔姆格林对这个观点表示质疑，他提出，多数由伴星系引起的漩涡的旋臂只有两条，而不是三条。他说，相反地，星系中大量的气体可能是形成漩涡形状的原因。厄尔姆格林称，尽管星系中的恒星和气体云团比临近的恒星和气体云团运动得快，但是所有气体的引力可能会限制高速外散，形成漩涡状。

Reading Comprehension 9

The Beauty of the Higgs Boson
希格斯玻色子之美

The dust is beginning to settle—a new particle has been discovered using the Large Hadron Collider. Discovering new particles of nature is not an everyday occurrence and we are reasonably entitled to proclaim that this is the arrival of the Higgs. We aren't certain, though: more careful examination of the particle's properties is needed before we can be—we want to know that it has spin zero and that it couples to other particles with a strength that is in proportion to their mass. Answers to those questions and to many others will follow over the coming months and years. This is all very important—but why? Why is the discovery of a new type of particle something to get so excited about?

尘埃开始落定——一种新的粒子在大型强子对撞机中得以发现。发现自然界新粒子这种事不是每天都能发生，我们有理由说这意味着希格斯玻色子的到来。然而，我们对此不是很确信，我们需要就这种粒子的属性进行更为细致的验证——我们想确认它自旋为零，并且它与其他粒子的相互作用是通过与它们质量成正比的力实现的。这些问题的答案在接下来的几个月或几年将会出现。这非常重要——但为什么，为什么一种新粒子的发现会让人如此激动？

The best way to appreciate the beauty of a discovery is to get stuck in, learn some mathematics and see those dazzling equations in all their glory. Examples include Einstein's equation of general relativity, Dirac's equation for the electron and the Lagrangian at the heart of the standard model of particle physics. But it is possible to get the gist of what a physicist means when they speak of a beautiful theory without the hard work. Before doing that let's be clear—this is a kind of life-changing beauty. This is not titillation and it is not a conceit of the human mind—it leaves everyone who has studied these things with an overwhelming sense that the natural world operates according to some beautiful rules and that we are very fortunate to be able to appreciate them. To spend time contemplating this is thrilling. We believe that these are universal rules that would also be uncovered by sufficiently intelligent aliens on a distant planet: we are discovering something at the heart of things.

鉴赏发现之美的最好方式就是深陷其中，探索其数学本源，观察光环之下让人眼花缭乱的方程式，比如粒子物理学中标准粒子模型的核心理论涉及爱因斯坦的广义相对论方程、迪拉克电子方程以及拉格朗日函数。这时你可能会发现，当物理学家们说优美的理论不需要付出艰苦的工作才能得到时，他们想表达的意思是什么。在此之前我们要知道，这是一种能改变生活的美，而不是一种人类狂妄的愉悦。它给予每个研究者一种无与伦比的感觉——自然世界原来是通过遵循这些优美的法则运行的，我们又是如此幸运能够对此进行欣赏。花点儿时间想想这些真让人激动。我们相信，在某个遥远的星球上有着足够智慧的生物也可能会发现这些普适的法则，因此我们正在揭示一些核心的东西。

The situation is extreme enough for greats such as Einstein and Hawking to invoke God. But they were certainly using the word to express the intimate relationship between the human mind and the glorious intelligibility of the universe. It feels like a personal thing—like we are relating to something very special. This is the sense in which Hawking once spoke of knowing the mind of God, but it doesn't really have anything to say about the existence or not of a creator.

对于像爱因斯坦和霍金这样的伟人，知道这些已经足以唤醒上帝了。他们当然会用言语表达人类意识与宇宙的可理解性之间的密切关系。这让人感觉有点私人化，似乎我们与一些特别的东西相互联系着。就像霍金曾说过他知道上帝的意志，但并非说上帝是否存在的问题。

A beautiful piece of physics is elegant. An elegant theory has the capacity to explain many apparently different things simultaneously—it means that rather than needing a library full of textbooks to explain the workings of the universe we can manage with just one book. In fact the situation is better than that—the fundamental equations that underpin all known natural phenomena can be written down on the back of an envelope. That is really true—the nature of light, the workings of the sun, the laws of electricity and magnetism, the explanation for atoms, gravity and much more can all be expressed with breathtaking economy. It is like we are in the business of discovering the rules of an elaborate game and we have figured out that they are really very simple, despite the rich variety of phenomena we see around us. Uncovering the rules of the game is exciting, and maybe one day we will know all of the rules accessible to us—that is what people are referring to when they speak about a "theory of everything". It sounds very arrogant to speak about a theory of everything but those in pursuit of it are not so dumb. They are well aware that knowing the rules is not the whole story. A child can know the rules of chess but exploiting them to produce a classic game is far from easy. This is an illustration of how simple rules can lead to something very complicated. The study of complex phenomena and their emergence is another very exciting area of modern physics.

物理之美的一个侧面是简洁。一个简洁的理论具有同时解释很多种明显不同事物的能力——这意味着要解释宇宙的运行，我们并不需要一整座装满教科书的图书馆，而只需要一本书。实际上还会更简洁，写下解释所有已知自然现象的基本方程组只需要信封背面那么大的地方。真的，光的本质、太阳的运行、电磁定律、原子的解释、重力等等都能得到令人吃惊的简明解释。这就像我们正在参与一场要求发现规律的精巧游戏，虽然我们身边的现象如此的纷繁复杂，但我们发现这些规律本质上相当简单。揭示游戏规则的确令人激动，或许有一天我们会知道支配身边所有一切的规则——这种规则就是人们所谈及的“万能理论”。万能理论听起来有些狂妄自大，不过追寻这一理论的人并不是这样的，他们很清楚地了解规则并不是全部。一个小孩子也许会知道国际象棋的规则，但利用这些规则下一局好棋绝非易事。这就是简单规则会导致复杂结果的一个例子。研究复杂现象及其成因是现代物理学中另一个令人振奋的研究领域。

Beautiful physics is also compelling. It is as if nature possesses a kind of perfection that is guiding us in our pursuit of the rules of the game. The result is that we very often have little or no choice when figuring out what equations to write down. That is a very satisfying situation to be in. It means that when we try to figure out an equation to describe something important, such as how an electron behaves, instead of saying, "Well... the equation might look like this... or maybe it looks like that... or..." we have no choice and nature simply screams out at us: "The equation simply must look like this." Dirac's beautiful equation is just like that—it describes the electron and predicts the existence of its anti-matter partner, the positron. Our understanding of the origins of inter-particle interactions (aka force) is like this too—starting from a very dull theory in which particles do not interact with one another (so no stars or people) and the idea that nature is symmetric in a certain way we are absolutely compelled to introduce interactions into the theory—the symmetry forces our hand and dictates how the theory should look. Symmetry is so often the device that leads to elegant and compelling theories. A snowflake is symmetric—if I draw part of one you could probably do a good job of sketching the rest. Likewise equations can be symmetric, which means we only need part of one in order to figure out the rest. In the case of particle interactions, symmetry means we can infer their necessary existence starting from the simpler equations that describe a world without any interactions at all... and that really is beautiful.

优美的物理也具有强制性，似乎是自然过程的完美性来指引我们追寻游戏的规则。结果是，当要搞清该写下哪些方程时我们几乎总是没有多余的选择，这种情况很令人满意。这意味着当我们试图利用方程描述一些重要的事情时，比如电子的行为，不是说“嗯……方程可能像这样……或者可能像那样……或者……”，我们没有选择余地，自然会大声告诉我们：“方程只会像这样。”迪拉克优美的方程就是这样——它描述了电子，并预测了其反物质正电子的存在。我们所理解的粒子间作用(也就是力)也是如此——这源于一个粒子并非一定彼此互动（星体和人类也是这样)的理论以及自然界是具有对称性的想法，这使我们不得不将交互作用引入理论——对称性通过指挥我们的手来引导着理论如何成型。对称性经常是通向简洁的、强制性的理论的途径。雪花是对称的，如果我画出一部分你或许就会画出剩下的部分。同样的，方程也可以是对称的，我们只需要知道一部分就可以解出其余的部分。对于粒子相互作用，对称性意味着，我们从描述不存在任何相互作用的世界的简单方程组就可以推断出粒子相互作用实际存在的样子……这的确很美。

The genius of Peter Higgs and the other physicists who proposed the existence of the Higgs boson was to take the idea of symmetry seriously. The same symmetry that gives us "for free" the theory of inter-particle interactions also appears, at first glance, to predict that nature's elementary particles should all be without mass. That is flatly wrong and we are faced either with ditching a symmetry that has delivered so much (although that

提出希格斯玻色子存在的彼得·希格斯和其他物理学家，这些天才们认真地采纳了对称性的构想。对称性也给了我们关于粒子间相互作用的“免费”理论，乍看之下，自然界元粒子应当没有质量。这绝对是错误的，我们面对两种情况：其一是甩开对称性（尽管在20世纪60年代早期希格斯的先驱们尚不知晓对称性），其二是想出更精巧的解答。

was not known when the Higgs pioneers were beavering away in the early 1960s) or figuring out an ingenious solution.

The Higgs idea is that solution—it says empty space is jammed full of Higgs particles that deflect otherwise massless particles as they move—the more a particle is jiggled by the Higgs particles the more it has mass. As a result, the fundamental equations maintain their precious symmetry while the particles gain mass. Faith in the idea that nature's laws should be elegant and compelling has, yet again, delivered insight. The Higgs discovery is the jewel in the crown of particle physics and a worthy testament to nature's astonishing beauty.

希格斯的想法就是这个（精巧的）解答——它认为真空中充满了会使其他无质量粒子偏转的希格斯粒子。一个粒子被希格斯粒子偏转越严重，它的质量就越大。结果是，基本方程组在粒子获得质量的同时，仍维持其对称性。自然法则应当具有简洁性和强制性这一信念也又一次得以验证。希格斯的发现是粒子物理学王冠上的钻石，它证实了自然界那令人赞叹的美。

自然科学类题源单词补充

分类	编码	真题原词	真题背景精确注释
地理	001	abyss	深渊
地理	002	achondrite	无球粒陨石
地理	003	advection	水平对流
地理	004	Aleutian Deep	阿留申海沟
地理	005	Aleutian Islands	阿留申群岛
地理	006	alluvial gold	沙金
地理	007	alluvial	冲积层
地理	008	Alpine glaciation	阿尔卑斯山脉的冰蚀
地理	009	Andean	安第斯人
地理	010	Archean Age	太古代
地理	011	asthenosphere	岩流圈
地理	012	atoll	环礁
地理	013	Barbados	巴巴多斯岛
地理	014	basin	盆地
地理	015	bauxite	铝矾土
地理	016	bearings	方位
地理	017	bed	河床
地理	018	Benioff Zone	贝尼奥夫带
地理	019	Bering Strait	白令海峡
地理	020	calcite	方解石
地理	021	Cambrian	寒武纪的
地理	022	canyon	峡谷
地理	023	Carboniferous	石炭纪
地理	024	cartographer	地图绘制员
地理	025	chondrite	球粒陨石
地理	026	cirque	冰斗，冰雪坑
地理	027	clay	黏土
地理	028	clayey	黏土的
地理	029	climatic	气候的
地理	030	coke	焦炭
地理	031	compass	罗盘
地理	032	conglomerate	砾岩
地理	033	continental shelf	大陆架
地理	034	continental	大陆的
地理	035	coral	珊瑚
地理	036	core	岩心
地理	037	corundum	刚玉

分类	编码	真题原词	真题背景精确注释
地理	038	crater	陨石坑
地理	039	crust	地壳
地理	040	crustal plate	地壳板块
地理	041	declination	磁偏角
地理	042	denude	剥蚀
地理	043	deposit	矿床
地理	044	depositional	沉积的
地理	045	displacement	错层
地理	046	earthquake focus	震源
地理	047	eddy	涡流
地理	048	El Nino	厄尔尼诺海流
地理	049	epicenter	震中
地理	050	epoch	新纪元
地理	051	erosion	侵蚀
地理	052	eruption	喷发
地理	053	estuary	海河口
地理	054	exogenous	外成的
地理	055	fairway	航道
地理	056	fault	断层
地理	057	floe	大片浮冰
地理	058	flow	岩石流
地理	059	formation	地质岩层
地理	060	fossil fuel	矿物燃料
地理	061	fracture	断裂面
地理	062	furrow	狭沟
地理	063	garnet	石榴石
地理	064	geographic	地理的
地理	065	geohydrology	地质水文学
地理	066	geophysical	地球物理的
地理	067	geothermal	地热的
地理	068	geyser	间歇泉
地理	069	glaciation	冰蚀
地理	070	glacier	冰川
地理	071	gneiss	片麻岩
地理	072	gold quartz	金乳石英
地理	073	graded	坡度平缓的
地理	074	granite	花岗石
地理	075	gravel	沙砾层
地理	076	gypsum	石膏岩
地理	077	gyre	环流

分类	编码	真题原词	真题背景精确注释
地理	078	hydrogeology	水文地质学
地理	079	Ice Age	冰河时代
地理	080	igneous rock	火成岩
地理	081	igneous	火成的
地理	082	inclusion	包体
地理	083	intensity	强度
地理	084	interface	分界面
地理	085	interglacial period	间冰河期
地理	086	interglacial	间冰期的
地理	087	interstratified	间层的
地理	088	intrusive	侵入的
地理	089	islet	小岛
地理	090	kimberlite	角砾云母橄岩
地理	091	lagoon	咸水湖
地理	092	latitude	纬度
地理	093	latitudinal	纬度的
地理	094	lava	熔岩
地理	095	layer	地层
地理	096	limestone	石灰石
地理	097	lithosphere	岩石圈
地理	098	loam	肥土
地理	099	lode	矿脉
地理	100	magma	岩浆
地理	101	magmatic fluid	岩浆流体
地理	102	magnetic field	磁场
地理	103	magnetic sense	地磁感觉
地理	104	magnetic	磁化的
地理	105	mantle plume	地幔热柱
地理	106	mantle	地幔
地理	107	Mediterranean	地中海的
地理	108	meridian	全盛时期
地理	109	Mesozoic	中生代的
地理	110	metamorphic fluid	变质流体
地理	111	midocean ridge system	中央海岭
地理	112	mineral	含矿物的
地理	113	mineralogical	矿物学的
地理	114	Miocene	中新世
地理	115	molten	熔解的
地理	116	moraine	冰碛
地理	117	mound	土墩

分类	编码	真题原词	真题背景精确注释
地理	118	neap current	最低潮
地理	119	offshore	离岸的
地理	120	Oligocene	渐新世
地理	121	olivine	橄榄石
地理	122	ore	矿石
地理	123	orebody	矿体
地理	124	Paleocene	古新世
地理	125	paleoclimatologist	地质气候学家
地理	126	pebble	圆石
地理	127	peneplain	准平原
地理	128	peninsula	半岛
地理	129	perigean	近地点的
地理	130	permafrost	永久冻结带
地理	131	pillow	枕状熔岩
地理	132	plateau	高原
地理	133	Pleistocene glaciers	更新世冰川
地理	134	Pleistocene	地质更新世
地理	135	Pliocene	上新世
地理	136	plume	地柱
地理	137	Pluvial	洪积世
地理	138	polar	近极的
地理	139	postglacial period	后冰河期
地理	140	postglacial	冰期后的
地理	141	pristine	太古的
地理	142	prospecting	勘探
地理	143	proterozoic	元古代的
地理	144	pyroxene	辉石
地理	145	ridge	分水岭
地理	146	rift	断裂
地理	147	rugged	崎岖的
地理	148	schist	页岩
地理	149	secondary(S) wave	地震横波
地理	150	sediment	沉积物
地理	151	sedimentary rock	沉积岩
地理	152	sedimentary	沉积的
地理	153	seismic	地震的
地理	154	seismologist	地震学家
地理	155	semitropical	亚热带的
地理	156	shale	泥板岩
地理	157	stratum	地层

分类	编码	真题原词	真题背景精确注释
地理	158	substratum	下层土壤地基
地理	159	suture	板块缝合
地理	160	system	地层系
地理	161	tectonics	构造地质学
地理	162	temperate	温带的
地理	163	terrestrial	陆地的
地理	164	tidal	潮水的
地理	165	topographical	地形学的
地理	166	tsunami	海啸
地理	167	tundra	冻土带
地理	168	upland	高原
地理	169	variation	磁偏角
地理	170	vein	矿脉
地理	171	volcanic cone	火山锥
地理	172	volcanic	火山的
地理	173	watershed	分水岭
地理	174	weathering	风化
地理	175	xenolith	捕虏岩
地质	001	active volcano	活火山
地质	002	altitude	高度
地质	003	Antarctic	南极地区
地质	004	arctic	北极的
地质	005	arid	干旱的
地质	006	aseismic	耐震的
地质	007	cavern (cave)	巨洞
地质	008	channel	海峡
地质	009	cliff	悬崖
地质	010	coastland	沿海地区
地质	011	continent	大陆
地质	012	continental drift	大陆漂移
地质	013	continental island	大陆岛
地质	014	contour	轮廓
地质	015	crack	裂缝
地质	016	crest	山顶
地质	017	crevice	裂缝
地质	018	delta	三角洲
地质	019	dormant volcano	休眠火山
地质	020	elevation	海拔
地质	021	equator	赤道
地质	022	erode	侵蚀

分类	编码	真题原词	真题背景精确注释
地质	023	Eurasian	欧亚的
地质	024	extinct volcano	死火山
地质	025	fieldstone	卵石
地质	026	frost heaving	冻胀现象
地质	027	gorge	峡谷
地质	028	Grand Canyon	大峡谷
地质	029	hemisphere	半球
地质	030	high latitudes	高纬度地区
地质	031	hillside	山坡
地质	032	horizon	地平线
地质	033	hypocenter	震源
地质	034	insular	海岛的
地质	035	ledge	矿脉
地质	036	leeway	风压差
地质	037	low latitudes	低纬度地区
地质	038	lowland	低地
地质	039	magnitude	震级
地质	040	margin	边缘
地质	041	marine	航海的
地质	042	maritime	海上的
地质	043	meridian	子午线
地质	044	mountain chain	山脉
地质	045	oasis	绿洲
地质	046	parallel	纬线
地质	047	plain	平原
地质	048	plate tectonics	板块构造论
地质	049	plate	板块
地质	050	prairie	大草原
地质	051	precipice	悬崖
地质	052	range	山脉
地质	053	sea-floor spreading	海床扩张
地质	054	seismology	地震学
地质	055	semi-arid	半干旱的
地质	056	stratigraphical	地层学的
地质	057	stratigraphy	地层学
地质	058	subterrane	表层下基岩
地质	059	subterranean	地下的
地质	060	summit	顶峰
地质	061	temperate latitudes	温带地区
地质	062	terrain	地形

分类	编码	真题原词	真题背景精确注释
地质	063	terrestrial magnetism	地磁
地质	064	theodolite	经纬仪
地质	065	time zone	时区
地质	066	topsoil	表层土
地质	067	transatlantic	横跨大西洋的
地质	068	tributary	支流
地质	069	tropical	热带的
地质	070	valley	峡谷
化学	001	additive	添加剂
化学	002	alchemy	炼金术
化学	003	Alkali	碱
化学	004	Aluminium	铝
化学	005	amalgam	混合物
化学	006	Calcium	钙
化学	007	carbohydrate	碳水化合物
化学	008	catalyst	催化剂
化学	009	caustic	腐蚀性的
化学	010	cement	胶粘剂
化学	011	coagulant	凝结剂
化学	012	combustible	易燃的
化学	013	compost	混合肥料
化学	014	compound	复合物
化学	015	corrosive	腐蚀性的
化学	016	defoliant	脱叶剂
化学	017	defoliator	落叶剂
化学	018	dehydrate	脱水
化学	019	desalinize	除去盐分
化学	020	detergent	清洁剂
化学	021	disinfectant	消毒剂
化学	022	emollient	润肤剂
化学	023	filter	滤纸
化学	024	flammable	易燃的
化学	025	germicide	杀菌剂
化学	026	herbicide	除草剂
化学	027	hydrate	水化
化学	028	icing	糖霜
化学	029	ingredient	成分
化学	030	insecticide	杀虫剂
化学	031	Iodine	碘
化学	032	leaven	发酵剂

分类	编码	真题原词	真题背景精确注释
化学	033	lubricant	润滑剂
化学	034	miscellany	混合物
化学	035	molecule	分子
化学	036	noxious	有毒的
化学	037	nucleus	核
化学	038	oxidize	氧化
化学	039	pesticide	杀虫剂
化学	040	pigment	天然色素
化学	041	precipitant	沉淀剂
化学	042	saccharin	糖精
化学	043	saliferous	含盐的
化学	044	soluble	可溶的
化学	045	solvent	溶剂
化学	046	toxin	毒素
化学	047	yeast	酵母
天文	001	aerial	航空的
天文	002	aerodynamicist	空气动力学家
天文	003	Andromeda	仙女座
天文	004	asteroid	小行星
天文	005	astrology	占星术
天文	006	astronomer	天文学家
天文	007	astronomical	天文的
天文	008	astronomy	天文学
天文	009	astrophysics	天体物理学
天文	010	atmospheric	大气的
天文	011	big bang	创世大爆炸
天文	012	black hole	黑洞
天文	013	Callisto	木星的第四颗卫星
天文	014	camelopardalis	鹿豹星座
天文	015	celestial navigation	星体导航法
天文	016	celestial	天空的
天文	017	circumstellar	环绕恒星运转的
天文	018	cluster	星团
天文	019	comet	彗星
天文	020	constellation	星座
天文	021	corona	日冕
天文	022	cosmic	宇宙的
天文	023	cosmology	宇宙生成学
天文	024	cosmos	宇宙
天文	025	dwarf star	矮星

分类	编码	真题原词	真题背景精确注释
天文	026	envelope	包层
天文	027	equatorial	赤道附近的
天文	028	extraterrestrial	地球外的
天文	029	flare	耀斑
天文	030	galactic	银河的
天文	031	galaxy	星系
天文	032	Geminorum	双子座
天文	033	helium	氦
天文	034	interstellar	星际的
天文	035	ionosphere	电离层
天文	036	Jovian	木星的
天文	037	Jupiter	木星
天文	038	magnetosphere	磁圈
天文	039	Mars	火星
天文	040	Mercury	水星
天文	041	meteorite	陨星
天文	042	Milky Way	银河
天文	043	nebule	星云
天文	044	Neptune	海王星
天文	045	neutron star	中子星
天文	046	nova	新星
天文	047	orb	球体
天文	048	orbit	轨道
天文	049	ozone	臭氧
天文	050	perigee	近地点
天文	051	perturbation	摄动
天文	052	planetesimal	星子
天文	053	Pluto	冥王星
天文	054	pole star	北极星
天文	055	probe	探测器
天文	056	pulsar	脉冲星
天文	057	quasar	类星体
天文	058	radio galaxy	射电星系
天文	059	red giant	红巨星
天文	060	satellite	卫星
天文	061	Saturn	土星
天文	062	solar system	太阳系
天文	063	solar	太阳的
天文	064	spatial	空间的
天文	065	sphere	天体

分类	编码	真题原词	真题背景精确注释
天文	066	spiral galaxy	螺旋星云
天文	067	spiral nebula	涡状星云
天文	068	stellar	星球的
天文	069	stratify	分层
天文	070	stratocumulus	层积云
天文	071	sunspot	太阳黑子
天文	072	supernova	超新星
天文	073	tropic	回归线
天文	074	tropopause	对流顶层
天文	075	troposphere	对流层
天文	076	ultraviolet	紫外线辐射
天文	077	updraft	向上的气流
天文	078	Uranus	天王星
天文	079	variability	(亮度)变化
天文	080	Venus	金星
天文	081	white dwarf	白矮星
物理	001	agglomerate	凝聚
物理	002	aggrandize	增大
物理	003	airborne	空气传播的
物理	004	axis	轴线
物理	005	band	收音机波段
物理	006	brake	减速
物理	007	buoyant	有浮力的
物理	008	carat	克拉
物理	009	centrifugal	离心的
物理	010	centripetal	向心的
物理	011	chafe	摩擦生热
物理	012	circuit	电路
物理	013	clot	凝块
物理	014	coagulate	使凝结
物理	015	concentrate	浓缩
物理	016	concrete	具体存在的
物理	017	concrete	有形事物
物理	018	condense	浓缩
物理	019	congeal	凝固
物理	020	cord	木堆体积
物理	021	curdle	变稠
物理	022	decibel	分贝
物理	023	diffuse	漫射
物理	024	dilute	冲淡

分类	编码	真题原词	真题背景精确注释
物理	025	dissolve	溶解
物理	026	distill	蒸馏
物理	027	dynamo	发电机
物理	028	emulsify	使乳化
物理	029	evaporate	蒸发
物理	030	explosive	爆炸性的
物理	031	fathom	水深单位
物理	032	friction	摩擦
物理	033	gallon	加仑
物理	034	galvanize	电镀
物理	035	gasification	气化
物理	036	generator	发电机
物理	037	gravitational	万有引力的
物理	038	inelasticity	无弹性
物理	039	lever	杠杆
物理	040	liquefy	液化
物理	041	mechanical	机械的
物理	042	mechanics	力学
物理	043	metrical	测量的
物理	044	mote	微粒
物理	045	neutron	中子
物理	046	nonradioactive	非放射性的
物理	047	ossify	硬化
物理	048	permeate	渗透
物理	049	projectile	抛射物
物理	050	quantum	量子
物理	051	reactant	反应物
物理	052	reflect	反射
物理	053	refraction	折射
物理	054	rotundity	圆形物
物理	055	sonic	音波的
物理	056	spatial	有关空间的
物理	057	spectrum	光谱
物理	058	strength	强度
物理	059	tensile	张力的
物理	060	thaw	解冻
物理	061	thermal	热气流
物理	062	torque	转矩
物理	063	trajectory	弹道轨道
物理	064	vaporization	气化

分类	编码	真题原词	真题背景精确注释
物理	065	vaporize	使气化
物理	066	velocity	速度

Note

第二节 生命科学类

生命科学类文章作为GRE阅读理解部分的重要题材，已经为广大考生所熟知。多年以来，生物题材的文章一直是绝大部分中国考生所畏惧的：其中生僻的名词、混乱的关系令人“望而生畏”，被很多人视为洪水猛兽。在过去几年中，ETS在生物类文章方面的选材日趋多样化：从80年代90年代被“重点照顾”的基因技术、病毒、生物化学方面，到21世纪前十年的生态发展、人体生理平衡等内容。作为中国考生，这种文章里最令我们头疼的地方毫无疑问就是生词多，由于生词多导致文章读不懂。GRE无需考生能够“真真切切”地明白文章所讨论的学术内容是何物，破解它最需要的，就是能够准确地找到文中出现的名词、意群和句子之间的相互关系。名词的把握不是最主要的，处理名词之间的关系才是我们最需要的能力。比如：“A技术的发展受到B问题的限制”，我们可以马上反应出“B是A的决定因素，处于逻辑上一层”。类似的情况会有很多，除了事物发展规律上的逻辑关系，还有句子与句子之间的关系，这些内容都需要考生靠结构化阅读的能力不断予以完善、提高。

生命科学类题材中关于各种各样的实验研究、生长规律的调查等层出不穷，占据着GRE阅读部分中相当大的比例。对于动物类的题材，基本上分成两种：其一是关于动物的实验，其二是关于动物习性的研究。关于植物的研究，基本上集中在对植物形态特征及其形成原因的探索上。相较于人文社会科学强调规律的内在发展与联系来说，生命科学类更加强调探索客观存在体的外相、特性的内在原因，强调因果关系的建立。一般来说，在GRE文章中无论是动物类还是植物类的题材，涉及常见的动植物题材不多，这是为了尽量规避很多人了解其背景知识的可能性。既然这些文章所涉及的内容较为偏僻，那么其难点就在于对单词的认知和内容细节的解读。

在出题方面，生命科学类文章常考的题型有细节题和推断题。考查细节题很好理解，例如，在对某个物种的描述中必然会出现使其区别于其他对照个体的因素，这种地方很容易作为细节题的出题点。另外，由于这种题材的文章必然存在叙述成分，而叙述部分中又存在着对于现象的原因剖析，所以也很容易出推断题。比如，文章中出现这样的细节：由于某方面的情况，所以导致了某个问题的出现；题目就可以考查：“如果以下哪个选项成立，作者就可以认为某事物会更好？”这属于典型的改善推断题。

综上所述，生命科学类文章的总体难度属于中等，题目的难度也属于中等，考生在做题时需要注意文中表达唯一性的提示词(only、uniquely、solely)，以及表达差异性的提示词(different、identify)和一些容易出现虚拟语气的地方(as if、assumed、would like)。

Exercise 3

生物移植技术

Currently, the paramount problem in the field of biomaterials, the science of replacing diseased tissue with human-made implants, is control over the interface, or surface, between implanted biomaterials and living tissues. The physical properties of most tissues can be matched by careful selection of raw materials: metals, ceramics, or several varieties of polymer materials. Even the requirement that biomaterials processed from these materials be nontoxic to host tissue can be met by techniques derived from studying the reactions of tissue cultures to biomaterials or from short-term implants. But achieving necessary matches in physical properties across interfaces between living and nonliving matter requires knowledge of which molecules control the bonding of cells to each other—an area that we have not yet explored thoroughly. Although recent research has allowed us to stabilize the tissue-biomaterial interface by controlling either the chemical reactions or the microstructure of the biomaterials, our fundamental understanding of how implant devices adhere to tissues remains woefully incomplete.

Sample Multiple-choice Questions — Select One Answer Choice

1. According to the passage, the major problem currently facing scientists in the field of biomaterials is

(A) assessing and regulating the bonding between host tissue and implants

(B) controlling the transfer of potentially toxic materials across the interface of tissue and implant

(C) discovering new materials from which to construct implant devices

(D) deciding in what situations implants are needed

(E) determining the importance of short-term implants to long-term stability of tissue implant interfaces

Sample Multiple-choice Questions — Select One Answer Choice

2. The author's primary purpose is to

(A) answer a theoretical question in the field of biomaterials

(B) discuss the current state of technology in the field of biomaterials

(C) resolve a research dispute in the field of biomaterials

(D) predict an ethical crisis for biomaterials researchers

(E) suggest some practical benefits of biomaterial implants

译文及解析

第一句： 如今在生物材料领域最大的问题就是，如何控制人体组织和移植组织之间的连接面。

（第一句是全文的逻辑最高层，是要予以论述的结论。）

第二句： 通过精细筛选的各种原材料——金属、陶瓷、其他各种高分子化合物，能够实现与绝大部分人体组织的生理特性相匹配。

第三句： 即使是“这些生物材料要对机体组织无毒无害”这样的要求，只要利用通过研究机体组织对生物材料的反应或者研究短期移植而发明的技术手段，也能得以满足。

第四句： 但是，要使人体组织和移植组织之间连接面的生理特性相互匹配，就涉及“哪些分子控制着细胞之间的连接”这样的知识——这是一个我们还未搞清楚的领域。

（第二、三句是平行并列的关系，作为整体与第四句形成对比，说明“分子控制细胞间的连接还没搞清楚”这样一个事实，所以第四句是逻辑上一层。）

第五句： 尽管现在我们能够通过控制化学反应或者生物材料的微结构来维持人体组织和移植组织之间连接面的稳定，但是对于移植组织是如何连接人体组织的基本认识还很不足。

（第五句和第四句是一种因果关系，因为人们对于分子技术还不够了解，所以人们对移植技术的根本认识还不足。综合第二、三、四、五句这些具体细节，说明了第一句的结论。）

逻辑图

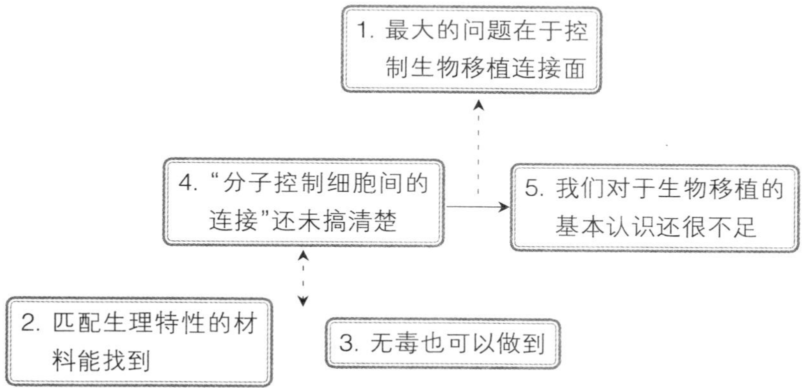

题目及解析

1. According to the passage, the major problem currently facing scientists in the field of biomaterials is

(A) **assessing and regulating the bonding between host tissue and implants**

(B) controlling the transfer of potentially toxic materials across the interface of tissue and implant

(C) discovering new materials from which to construct implant devices

(D) deciding in what situations implants are needed

(E) determining the importance of short-term implants to long-term stability of tissue implant interfaces

解析

这是一道细节题，问“目前在生物材料领域最主要的问题是什么”。纵观全文，我们不难得知，整篇文章就是为了阐述第一句话的结论“the paramount problem in the field of biomaterials is control over the interface, or surface, between implanted biomaterials and living tissues"(最大的问题就是对于移植材料和人体组织之间的连接控制)。

(A)确定并调整移植组织和人体组织之间的连接

(B)控制潜在有毒材料在人体组织和移植组织之间连接面上的交换

(C)发现用以制造移植器材的新型材料

(D)明确什么时候需要使用移植技术

(E)确认短期移植技术对于人体组织和移植组织连接面长期稳定性的重要意义

本题的正确答案是选项A，关键词就是"bonding"(连接)。本文提到，最终的学术问题关键在于分子的相互控制上，即哪些分子控制着人体组织和移植组织的连接就成了这个学术问题的核心。B选项用"control"这个词来迷惑考生，实际上阅读文章关键是要抓住实体信息之间的关系，如果选项中的实体信息有误，就必然是错误的。而B选项中就错把"分子的连接"换成了"有毒材料"，与原文不符。其他三个选项也都不是最主要的问题。

2. The author's primary purpose is to

(A) answer a theoretical question in the field of biomaterials

(B) discuss the current state of technology in the field of biomaterials

(C) resolve a research dispute in the field of biomaterials

(D) predict an ethical crisis for biomaterials researchers

(E) suggest some practical benefits of biomaterial implants

解析

这是一道主题题，通过作者写作的逻辑态度判断其为何要写这篇文章。本文的逻辑最高层是目前生物移植领域存在的主要问题，其他信息都是为了支持这一论点而服务的。

(A)回答有关生物材料领域的一个理论问题
(A不正确。因为本文并没有就这个问题进行回答，这不是一个question，而是一个problem。)

(B)谈论当今生物材料界的技术现状
(这是本题的正确答案。当今生物材料的现状既有乐观的地方(如二、三句)，也存在根本的问题(如第一句)。)

(C)解决在生物材料研究方面的争议
(C也不正确。本文所讨论的问题并未得到解决。)

(D)预言生物材料研究人员面临的道德危机
(D更不正确。属于肆意上升主题高度。)

(E)表明生物移植的一些实际好处
(E选项有失偏颇。文中提到的是目前生物移植领域的一些利好的进展，而非生物移植技术的实际好处。)

Exercise 4

花粉的传播方式

Traditionally, pollination by wind has been viewed as a reproductive process marked by random events in which the vagaries of the wind are compensated for by the generation of vast quantities of pollen, so that the ultimate production of new seeds is assured at the expense of producing much more pollen than is actually used. Because the potential hazards pollen grains are subject to as they are transported over long distances are enormous, wind-pollinated plants have, in the view above, compensated for the ensuing loss of pollen through happenstance by virtue of producing an amount of pollen that is one to three orders of magnitude greater than the amount produced by species pollinated by insects.

However, a number of features that are characteristic of wind-pollinated plants reduce pollen waste. For example, many wind-pollinated species fail to release pollen when wind speeds are low or when humid conditions prevail. Recent studies suggest another way in which species compensate for the inefficiency of wind pollination. These studies suggest that species frequently take advantage of the physics of pollen motion by generating specific aerodynamic environments within the immediate vicinity of their female reproductive organs. It is the morphology of these organs that dictates the pattern of airflow disturbances through which pollen must travel. The speed and direction of the airflow disturbances can combine with the physical properties of a species' pollen to produce a species-specific pattern of pollen collision on the surfaces of female reproductive organs. Provided that these surfaces are strategically located, the consequences of this combination can significantly increase the pollen-capture efficiency of a female reproductive organ.

A critical question that remains to be answered is whether the morphological attributes of the female reproductive organs of wind-pollinated species are evolutionary adaptations to wind pollination or are merely fortuitous. A complete resolution of the question is as yet impossible since adaptation must be evaluated for each species within its own unique functional context. However, it must be said that, while evidence of such evolutionary adaptations does exist in some species, one must be careful about attributing morphology to adaptation. For example, the spiral arrangement of scale-bract complexes on ovule-bearing pine cones, where the female reproductive organs of conifers are located, is important to the production of airflow patterns that spiral over the cone's surfaces, thereby passing airborne pollen from one scale to the next. However, these patterns cannot be viewed as an adaptation to wind pollination because the spiral arrangement occurs in a number of non-wind-pollinated plant lineages and is regarded as a characteristic of vascular plants, of which conifers are only one kind, as a whole. Therefore, the spiral arrangement is not likely to be the result of a direct adaptation to wind pollination.

Sample Multiple-choice Questions — Select One Answer Choice

1. The author of the passage is primarily concerned with discussing

 (A) the current debate on whether the morphological attributes of wind-pollinated plants are evolutionary adaptations

 (B) the kinds of airflow patterns that permit wind-pollinated plants to capture pollen most efficiently

 (C) the ways in which the reproductive processes of wind-pollinated plants are controlled by random events

 (D) a recently proposed explanation of a way in which wind-pollinated plants reduce pollen waste

 (E) a specific morphological attribute that permits one species of wind-pollinated plant to capture pollen

Sample Multiple-choice Questions — Select One or More Answer Choices
For the following question, consider each of the choices separately and select all that apply.

2. According to the passage, true statements about the release of pollen by wind-pollinated plants include which of the following.

 A The release can be affected by certain environmental factors.

 B The amount of pollen released increases on a rainy day.

 C Pollen is sometimes not released by plants when there is little wind.

Sample Multiple-choice Questions — Select One Answer Choice

3. It can be inferred from the passage that the claim that the spiral arrangement of scale-bract complexes on an ovule-bearing pine cone is an adaptation to wind pollination would be more convincing if which of the following were true?

 (A) Such an arrangement occurred only in wind-pollinated plants.

 (B) Such an arrangement occurred in vascular plants as a whole.

 (C) Such an arrangement could be shown to be beneficial to pollen release.

 (D) The number of bracts could be shown to have increased over time.

 (E) The airflow patterns over the cone's surfaces could be shown to be produced by such arrangements.

Sample Multiple-choice Questions — Select One Answer Choice

4. Which of the following, if known, is likely to have been the kind of evidence used to support the view described in the first paragraph?

 (A) Wind speeds need not be very low for wind-pollinated plants to fail to release pollen.

 (B) The female reproductive organs of plants often have a sticky surface that allows them to trap airborne pollen systematically.

(C) Grasses, as well as conifers, generate specific aerodynamic environments within the immediate vicinity of their reproductive organs.

(D) Rain showers often wash airborne pollen out of the air before it ever reaches an appropriate plant.

(E) The density and size of an airborne pollen grain are of equal importance in determining whether that grain will be captured by a plant.

译文及解析

第一段

第一句： 传统观点看来，风媒传粉被视做一种随机性的繁殖过程，在这个过程中风的不确定性靠植物产生的大量花粉予以弥补，所以新种子的产生需要以比实际需求量多很多的花粉为代价才可以实现。

（第一句话是一种传统观点，作为结论。）

第二句： 由于种子在长距离传输过程中所面临的潜在风险是巨大的，基于上述观点，风媒植物是通过产生比虫媒植物多一到三个数量级的花粉的特性来弥补随之而来的花粉损失。

（第二句是第一句的细节，属于逻辑下一层。先理论后细节，这是典型的学术文章写法。）

第二段

第一句： 但是，风媒植物还有一些特性能够帮助其减少花粉的浪费。

（这是一个新观点，与第一段第一句话相对，新老观点对比型写法。）

第二句： 比如，很多风媒植物在风速低或者湿度大的环境下不释放花粉。

（第二句是第一句的例子，是减少花粉浪费的特性之一。）

第三句： 近期研究表明，风媒植物有另外一种方法来弥补其传粉效率不高的问题。

（第三句和第二句是平行并列的关系，是又一种特性。）

第四句： 研究显示，风媒植物往往在其雌蕊附近创造某种特定的空气动力环境，以利用花粉的运动轨迹。

（第四句是第三句的细节。）

第五句： 正是这种器官的形态决定了花粉在传播过程中空气的流向。

第六句： 空气流动的方向和速度结合花粉的物理特性造就了花粉着蕊的一种特殊方式。

第七句： 鉴于花粉着蕊的地点是特定的，空气流向与花粉特性的结合能够极大提高雌蕊捕捉花粉的效率。

（从第五句到第七句都是对于第四句的细节支持，是其逻辑下一层。）

第三段

第一句： 有一个亟待回答的问题：风媒植物雌蕊的这种形态特性是在进化过程中对于风媒传粉的适应呢？还是仅仅是一种巧合？

（这句话提出了一个问题，接下来的内容对该问题进行解释。因为第一句话是基于第二段的内容提出的，故而第三段处于第二段的逻辑下一层。）

第二句： 这个问题至今无法得到彻底的回答，因为若想证明“适应性”，就必须把每个品种的独特特性进行一一检验才可以。

第三句： 然而，不得不说的是，尽管有些证据表明这些特性是风媒植物进化中适应性的表现，但若说(雌蕊的)形态是进化适应的表现，还是要慎之又慎。

(第二句和第三句形成一种平行关系，目的在于强调第三句话。)

第四句： 例如，带有雌蕊的松球的螺旋形鳞苞复合体对于产生气流十分重要；气流在松球表面呈螺旋型上升，然后把花粉从一个鳞苞传递到另一个鳞苞上。

(第四句在具体阐述雌蕊形态及气流运动，目的在于支持第三句的结论。)

第五句： 但是，这样的形态不能视为适应性的结果，因为这种螺旋结构存在于很多非风媒传粉植物中，而且还是维管植物的特性之一，比如针叶树。

(第四句和第五句是一种平行并列关系。)

第六句： 所以，很难说螺旋形结构是适应风媒传粉的直接结果。

(第四句和第五句作为原因，得出第六句的结论。实际上第六句和第三句本质是一样的。)

逻辑图

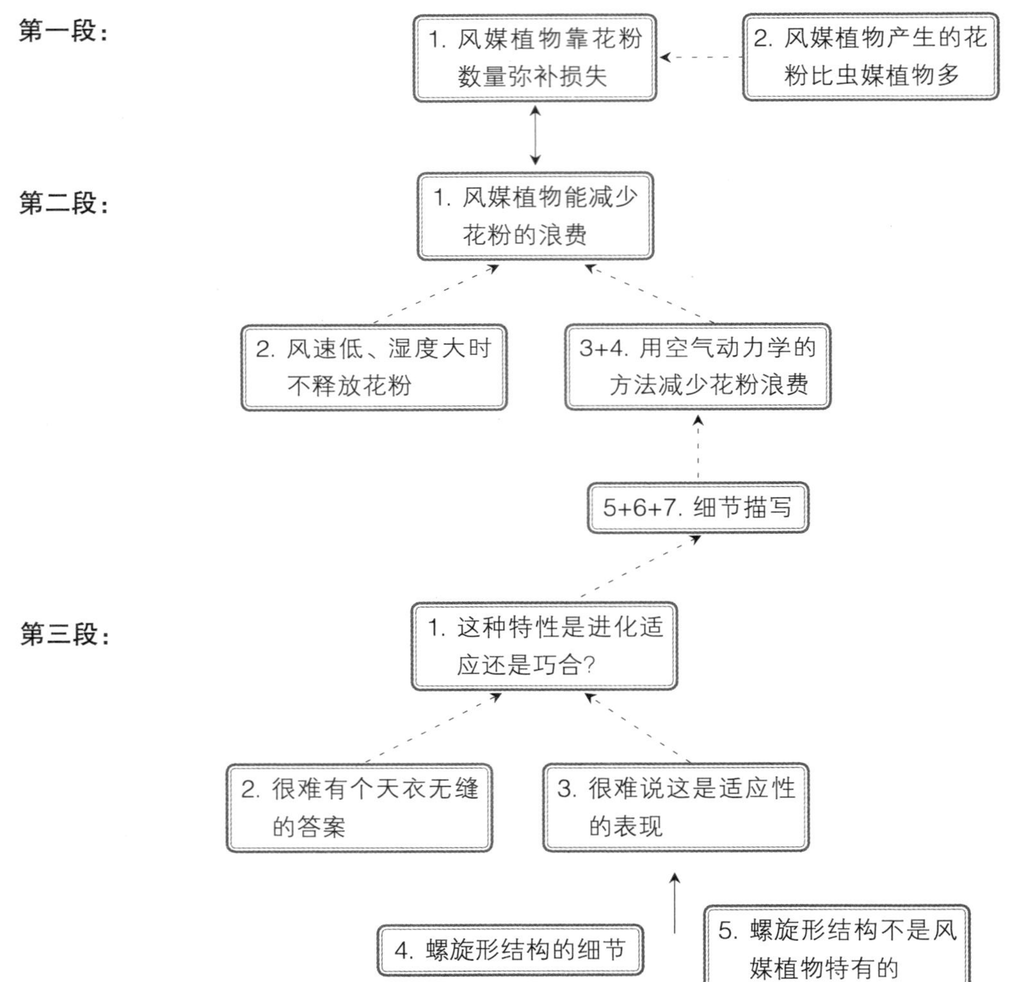

题目及解析

1. The author of the passage is primarily concerned with discussing

(A) the current debate on whether the morphological attributes of wind-pollinated plants are evolutionary adaptations

(B) the kinds of airflow patterns that permit wind-pollinated plants to capture pollen most efficiently

(C) the ways in which the reproductive processes of wind-pollinated plants are controlled by random events

(D) a recently proposed explanation of a way in which wind-pollinated plants reduce pollen waste

(E) a specific morphological attribute that permits one species of wind-pollinated plant to capture pollen

解析

这是一道典型的主题题，问本文主要探讨的是什么问题？从行文结构上看，本文第一段提出了老观点，然后从第二段开始阐述新观点，这些观点所说的内容都是关于风媒植物传粉的问题，但是核心的点是“风媒植物减少传粉浪费的方法”。

(A) 当前关于“风媒植物的形状特性是否是进化中适应性表现”的争论
(A不正确。这是第三段的主要内容，而非全文的主要内容。)

(B) 帮助风媒植物高效捕捉花粉的气流的种类
(B错误。这只是文章谈论过程中涉及的一个因素而已，逻辑层面不对。)

(C) 风媒植物繁殖过程中受随机事件影响的方式
(C也错误。这个内容只在文中第一段提到。)

(D) 近期提出的关于“风媒植物减少花粉浪费的方式”的解释
(D是正确答案。)

(E) 使得风媒植物捕捉花粉的某种形态特征
(E也不正确。这个形态特征只是作为讨论内容的一个重要部分。)

For the following question, consider each of the choices separately and select all that apply.

2. According to the passage, true statements about the release of pollen by wind-pollinated plants include which of the following?

A The release can be affected by certain environmental factors.

B The amount of pollen released increases on a rainy day.

C Pollen is sometimes not released by plants when there is little wind.

解析

这是一道不定项选择题，也是新GRE考试当中出现的一种新题型，需要考生细心分析题干，避免漏选、错选。本题问道“本文关于风媒植物释放花粉的叙述中，下列哪个或哪些选项是正确的？”

A 花粉的释放受到环境因素的影响。
(A是正确的。第二段的第二句话中有体现。)

B 在雨天花粉的释放量会增加 。

（B错误。第二段第二句明确说道，湿度大或风速低的时候不释放花粉。）

C **几乎没风的时候植物不释放花粉。**

（C正确。同样在第二段第二句能找到证据。）

3. It can be inferred from the passage that the claim that the spiral arrangement of scale-bract complexes on an ovule-bearing pine cone is an adaptation to wind pollination would be more convincing if which of the following were true?

（A）**Such an arrangement occurred only in wind-pollinated plants.**

（B）Such an arrangement occurred in vascular plants as a whole.

（C）Such an arrangement could be shown to be beneficial to pollen release.

（D）The number of bracts could be shown to have increased over time.

（E）The airflow patterns over the cone's surfaces could be shown to be produced by such arrangements.

解析

这是一道推断题，问到"如果以下哪个选项正确的话，螺旋型鳞苞复合体就能被视为对于风媒传粉的适应?"这道题定位到第三段的第四句和第五句，二者共同作为第六句结论的原因。如果要想使结论取反的话，需要把支持论点的原因取反：在第五句中作者提到"这种螺旋型结构并非是风媒植物特有的"，把它取反之后自然就可以使结论取反。

（A）这样的螺旋结构只有在风媒植物中才有。

（B）这种螺旋结构在所有维管植物中都出现。

（C）这种螺旋结构对于花粉的释放是有利的。

（D）苞叶片的数量呈上升趋势。

（E）松球表面气流是由这种螺旋结构形成的。

本题的正确答案很明显，是选项A。

4. Which of the following, if known, is likely to have been the kind of evidence used to support the view described in the first paragraph?

（A）Wind speeds need not be very low for wind-pollinated plants to fail to release pollen.

（B）The female reproductive organs of plants often have a sticky surface that allows them to trap airborne pollen systematically.

（C）Grasses, as well as conifers, generate specific aerodynamic environments within the immediate vicinity of their reproductive organs.

（D）**Rain showers often wash airborne pollen out of the air before it ever reaches an appropriate plant.**

（E）The density and size of an airborne pollen grain are of equal importance in determining whether that grain will be captured by a plant.

解析

本题是一道论据题，需要考生找出能够支持第一段论点的论据。这种题目的答案无需从文中找，只要选项中所描述的现象能够支持理论就可以。第一段的论点是“花粉传播过程中需要以量取胜”。

（A）风媒植物不释放花粉的时候，风速并不是特别低。
（A不正确。这个内容与第一段的论点无关。）

（B）雌蕊的表面有黏性，因此能够捕捉到花粉。
（B也不正确。关于雌蕊的信息也是在第二段中提到的，况且文中也没提到黏性的问题。）

（C）草和针叶树一样都会在其雌蕊附近产生特定的空气动力学环境。
（C涉及的依然是第二段出现的信息。）

（D）花粉在传播到植物的过程当中通常会被雨水冲走。
（D是本题的正确答案。这个例子支持了第一段中“花粉有损失”的论点。）

（E）在花粉能否被植物接收的问题上，花粉的密度和尺寸也同等重要。
（E的内容不符合题干要求，因为第一段没有讨论花粉有效接收的问题。）

Note

Reading Comprehension 10

Carbon Dioxide Encourages Risky Behavior in Clownfish
二氧化碳刺激海葵鱼的冒险行为

Carbon dioxide in the ocean acts like alcohol on fish, leaving them less able to judge risks and prone to losing their senses. The intoxication—around 2.3 billion tonnes of human-caused CO_2 emissions dissolve into the world's oceans every year—adds to the threats that global warming and ocean acidification pose to marine ecosystems.

对于鱼类来说，海洋里的二氧化碳就像酒精，可以让它们减少对危险的判定和感知。二氧化碳中毒——每年由人类排放的大约23亿吨二氧化碳溶于海洋中——增加了全球变暖和海洋酸性对海洋生态系统的威胁。

Philip Munday have previously found that if you put reef fish into water with more CO_2 than normal in it—similar to the levels expected in oceans by the end of the century—they become attracted to odors they would normally avoid, including those of predators and unfavorable habitats. Setting the pair reared clownfish larvae in seawater with normal (450 microatmospheres) and elevated (900 microatmospheres) CO_2 levels, when they reached adulthood, the fish were given a choice between a water stream containing the odor of common predators or a stream lacking predatory odors. Those reared in high levels of CO_2 swam towards predator's scent around 90 percent of the time, whereas those that had enjoyed normal levels of CO_2 avoided the predator's scent more than 90 percent of the time.

菲利普·芒迪教授很早就发现如果将岩礁鱼类放在含有高浓度二氧化碳的水里——类似于到本世纪末海洋中预计所能达到的浓度，他们会变得喜欢正常情况下不喜欢的味道，包括其捕食者和不喜欢的栖息地所散发的味道。将一组海葵鱼(俗名“小丑鱼”)的幼体分别放在含有正常浓度的二氧化碳和二氧化碳浓度高一倍的海水中成长，当它们成年后，让它们分别选择有捕食者气味的水流和没有捕食者气味的水流。那些放在高浓度二氧化碳海水中成长的成鱼游向有捕食者气味的水流的机会是90%，而那些在正常二氧化碳浓度中成长的成鱼躲过有捕食者气味的水流的次数高达90%。

Through a great number of experiments and analysis, Munday has now discovered that CO_2 leads to riskier behavior by interfering with a neurotransmitter receptor called GABA-A. Treating the clownfish bred under CO_2-rich conditions with gabazine, a chemical that blocks the GABA-A receptor, helped them to regain their senses, though: fish treated this way swam towards the predatory smell only 12 percent of the time. The fact that we could use a specific blocker for the GABA-A receptors to

通过多次实验以及分析，芒迪发现二氧化碳导致这种危险行为是通过干扰受体的神经传递素来实现的，称为GABA-A(氨基丁酸–A型)。对幼年生活在高浓度二氧化碳下的海葵鱼使用受体阻断剂，这种化学物质可以阻止GABA-A受体，来恢复它们的感知。用这种方法治疗后的成鱼游向捕食者气味的次数仅为12%。事实证明，我们对GABA-A接受者使用特殊的封阻剂可以扭转其行为，也就证明接受

reverse the behavioural alterations proves that this receptor is involved in the CO_2 effects.

者是受二氧化碳的影响。

The GABA-A receptor sits on dendrites, the wiry projections of a neuron that detect chemical signals from other neurons. When the neurotransmitter GABA binds to its receptor, the receptor opens and a flood of negatively charged chloride and bicarbonate ions rush into the cell and prevent it from firing. This means that GABA has an inhibitory effect on the neuron.When CO_2 accumulates in the fish, it alters the distribution of ions. Now, when the receptor opens, chloride and bicarbonate ions escape out of the cell, exciting the neuron instead. This would have strong effects on the function of neural circuits in the brain and may ultimately make the fish behave in a way that increases its likelihood of being eaten.

GABA-A受体在神经树突上，神经树突是神经元的细长投影，探测其他神经元中的化学信号。当GABA神经传递素绑在受体上，受体便打开，带负电荷的氯化物和重碳酸盐离子快速进入细胞并阻止其抵抗。也就是说GABA有抑制神经元的作用。当二氧化碳积聚在鱼类体内，它会改变离子的分布。这种情况下，当受体打开时，氯化物和重碳酸盐离子逃离细胞，这将对脑部的神经回路功能产生很强的作用，从而增加鱼被吃的概率。

Reading Comprehension 11

Are Birds' Tweets Grammatical?
鸟雀啁啾，可有章法？

Are humans the only species with enough smarts to craft a language? Most of us believe that we are. Although many animals have their own form of communication, none has the depth or versatility heard in human speech. We are able to express almost anything on our mind by uttering a few sounds in a particular order. Human language has a flexibility and complexity that seems to be universally shared across cultures and, in turn, contributes to the variation and richness we find among human cultures.

只有人类才智超群能创造出语言吗？大多数人认为确实如此。尽管许多动物有它们自己的交流方式，但就深度和多功能性而言，都不足与人类语言相提并论。通过发出一串有特定排序的声音，我们就能表达出头脑中几乎所有的想法。人类虽有多种不同的文化，但语言都同样地灵活、复杂，并且这种灵活性和复杂性又促使文化更加多样、更加丰富。

But are the rules of grammar unique to human language? Perhaps not, according to a recent study, which showed that songbirds may also communicate using a

但是不是只有人类语言讲究语法规则？可能并非如此。最近一项研究显示，鸣禽交流也用复杂的语法，这种特征连我们最近的亲

sophisticated grammar—a feature absent in even our closest relatives, the nonhuman primates.

戚——其他灵长类——身上也没有。

Kentaro Abe and Dai Watanabe of Kyoto University performed a series of experiments to determine whether Bengalese finches expect the notes of their tunes to follow a certain order. To test this possibility, Abe and Watanabe took advantage of a behavioral response called habituation, where animals zone-out when exposed to the same stimulus over and over again.

京都大学的安倍太郎和渡边大进行了一系列实验，目的是确定白腰文雀（一种小的雀类）所鸣出的曲调的音符是否遵循某种顺序。为了试验这种可能性，安倍和渡边做了一个“习性形成”的行为反应实验。所谓习性形成就是对动物反复使用同一刺激信号，令它们产生条件反射。

In each experiment, the birds were presented with the same songs until they became familiarized with the tune. The researchers then created novel songs by shuffling the notes around. But not every new song caught the birds' attention; rather, the finches increased response calls only to songs with notes arranged in a particular order, suggesting that the birds used common rules when forming the syntax of that song. When the researchers created novel songs with even more complicated artificial grammar—for example, songs that mimicked a specific feature found in human (Japanese) language—the birds still only responded to songs that followed the rules.

在每一次实验里，研究人员对文雀们播放同一首歌，直到它们熟悉为止。然后，把歌的音符打乱编成一些新歌。结果发现，并不是每一首新歌都能引起文雀们的注意，它们只对有某种特定排序的音符给以更多的响应，这说明它们在“创作”那首歌曲时运用的是同一规则。研究人员又在新歌中加入一些更加复杂的人工元素——例如，模仿日本语的一些特征——文雀们还是只对符合特定规则的歌曲产生反应。

Because the birds responded strongly to tunes ordered with certain structure, even when this structure was artificially constructed, the research team determined that the finches were able to spontaneously learn new grammar. This ability, though, seemed to be dependent upon their social context.

小鸟们对具有某种结构的曲调做出了强烈响应，即使对人工编造的曲调也不例外。由此，该研究组确定，小鸟能够本能地学习新规则，不过，这种能力依赖于它们所处的环境。

Birds isolated as babies from other birds were still able to learn artificial rules of grammar, but they failed to respond to songs with modified syntax—that is, normal Bengalese finch songs with the notes shuffled. However, after being reintroduced to other birds, it took them only two weeks to learn to respond to the shuffled songs, indicating that the birds needed to hear other birds' songs to absorb the precise rules of Bengalese finch grammar.

从小就与其种群隔离开的白腰文雀还是能学习人工创作的曲调规则，但当把白腰文雀常用的天然鸣声打乱音符后，对于这样改变后的调子，它们却没有做出响应。然而，把它们放回种群以后，只要两周时间就可以学会打乱后的调子。这说明鸟儿需要通过听同类的鸣叫声来掌握其中精确的规则。

While birdsong has long been known to share similarities with human language, the ability to convey different bits of information by simply rearranging word order was thought to be exclusively human.

虽然长久以来鸟鸣声被认为与人类语言有相似之处，但人类一直认为只有自己才能单纯通过排列不同的词序来传递不同的信息。

This study revealed that Bengalese finches can learn grammar and, furthermore, that their grammatical abilities involve a specific part of the brain region distinct from other brain regions involved in singing. This is similar to what neuroscientists understand about human language processing.

这项研究表明，白腰文雀能够学习语法结构，而且，与它们的语法能力相关联的脑部区域和与鸣叫相关联的脑部区域截然不同。这和神经科学家所了解的人类处理语言的能力是相似的。

If the tweets of birds can be roughly likened to strings of human words, and if birdbrains process songs in a way similar to how human brains process language, future research may tackle whether these animals possess other cognitive abilities once thought to be singularly characteristic of human intelligence. The next time you hear a bird chirping outside your window, you might think twice about what's going on inside his little birdbrain.

如果鸟类的鸣叫能与人类的话语串相比，并且鸟类大脑处理曲调的方法和人类大脑处理语言相类似，那么进一步的研究可能就会是确定这些小家伙们是不是还具有其他认知能力——过去人类一直以为是自己的种群独一无二的能力。所以，下次当你听到一只鸟儿在窗外叽叽喳喳时，你可能就要留心它的小脑袋里到底在想些什么了。

Reading Comprehension 12

Why Are Some Feathers Blue?
为什么一些鸟的羽毛是蓝色的?

For decades, scientists have known how birds with yellow or red feathers usually get their color: It comes from pigments in foods the birds eat. Flamingoes, for instance, extract pink pigments from algae and crustaceans they filter out of the water. The challenge has been to figure out exactly how blue birds get their color. It can't be their diet: blue pigments, like those in blueberries, are destroyed when birds digest them. Scientists theorized that birds look blue for the same reason the sky looks blue: Red and yellow wavelengths

几十年来，科学家们已经探得鸟类的黄色或红色羽毛是怎么形成的：这些颜色来自鸟类所觅的食物，后者含有相应的色素。例如，火烈鸟，它们在水中筛选出藻类和甲壳类动物，并从中提取粉红色色素。目前的挑战是，弄清楚拥有蓝色羽毛的鸟类到底是怎么获取蓝色这种颜色的。它们不可能从食物中提取蓝色素，因为这些蓝色素，例如蓝莓中含有的蓝色素，会在鸟类消化的时候被破坏。科学家们认为，从理论上讲，鸟类之所以看上去是蓝色的

pass through the atmosphere, but shorter blue wavelengths bounce off of particles and scatter, emitting a blue glow in every direction.

原因和天空看上去是蓝色的原因是一样的：红色和黄色的波长能够穿过大气层，但是波长较短的蓝色被粒子反弹出并散播开来，向四面八方散发出蓝色的光弧。

Recently, an ornithologist Richard Prum discovered that birds make blue feathers in a different way. To find the origins of avian blue, Prum and his colleagues have analyzed hundreds of feathers from representatives of almost every group that evolved blue coloration. Prum discovered that as a blue feather grows, something amazing happens: inside each cell, stringy keratin molecules separate from water, like oil from vinegar. When the water dries away and is replaced by air, leaving a structure of keratin protein interspersed with air pockets. When white light strikes a blue feather, the keratin pattern causes red and yellow wavelengths to cancel each other out, while blue wavelengths of light reinforce and amplify one another and reflect back to the beholder's eye, and different shapes and sizes of these air pockets and keratin make different shades of blue.

近期，鸟类学家理查德·普吕姆发现鸟类形成蓝色羽毛另有途径。为了找出鸟类蓝色的起源，普吕姆和他的同事们对数百种羽毛进行了分析，而这些羽毛来自几组具有代表性的鸟类，几乎每一组都进化出蓝色羽毛。普吕姆发现，随着蓝色羽毛的生长，一些不可思议的事情也在发生：在每个细胞内部，纤维蛋白分子从水中分离，就像油从醋中分离一般。当其中的水干涸，并被空气取代，留下了角蛋白被气泡穿插的结构。当有白光照射到蓝色羽毛的时候，角蛋白结构引发红色和黄色的波长相互抵消，而同时蓝色波长增强并扩大，再反射到观察者的眼中。由于气泡和角蛋白的大小和形状不同，产生的蓝色也会深浅不同。

Building such precise nanostructures is an exceptional evolutionary feat of engineering, yet the color blue has popped up independently on many different branches of the bird family tree, especially in males. Which raises the question: Why? One theory is that a set of fine blue feathers signifies a healthy, well-fed male, advertising his good genes to potential mates. But there have been some biologists who have gone too far with the idea that male ornaments, such as antlers or wattles, are signals to females. That claim can be possibly true, but that could be to some extent hasty or improper for the reason that perhaps they are "merely beautiful."

建立这样一个精准的纳米模型是工程领域内的特殊壮举，到目前为止，蓝色已经在鸟类系统的许多鸟类分支中出现，特别是在雄性鸟类身上。这就引发了一个问题：为什么会这样？其中一个理论提到，拥有一身精致的蓝色羽毛标志着雄性鸟健康并具有出色的捕食能力，同时可以向潜在的雌性伴侣展示自己的优良基因。但是，有些生物学家的说法就有点过了，他们认为雄性动物的装饰物，如鹿角和（火鸡的）垂肉，就是给雌性动物的信号。这有可能，但显得有些草率且不合适，也许它们就是"仅仅为了漂亮"而已。

Reading Comprehension 13

Leonardo da Vinci's Formula Explains Why Trees Don't Splinter
树木为何不会断裂？达·芬奇公式有了新解释

The graceful taper of a tree trunk into branches, boughs, and twigs is so familiar that few people notice what Leonardo da Vinci observed: A tree almost always grows so that the total thickness of the branches at a particular height is equal to the thickness of the trunk. Until now, no one has been able to explain why trees obey this rule. But a new study may have the answer.

树干分叉为树枝、树杈、小枝椏，这种分叉交错的倒锥形颇具美感，但人们对此异常熟悉，因此极少有人像列奥纳多·达·芬奇那样，细心探究其中的规律所在。他发现，在同一高度处，所有树枝粗度的总和等于树干的粗度。直到今日，仍然没有人能够解释树遵守这一规律的原因。不过，最近的一项研究或许可以给出答案。

Leonardo's rule holds true for almost all species of trees, and graphic artists routinely use it to create realistic computer-generated trees. The rule says that when a tree's trunk splits into two branches, the total cross section of those secondary branches will equal the cross section of the trunk. If those two branches in turn each split into two branches, the area of the cross sections of the four additional branches together will equal the area of the cross section of the trunk. And so on.

达·芬奇发现的这条规律对绝大多数树种都是适用的，平面设计艺术家也常常用它来在电脑上制作仿真树木。这条规律可以简单描述为：如果一根树干分叉为两个树枝，那么两个树枝的横截面积之和等于树干的横截面积；如果树枝又分别分叉为两根小树枝，那么这四个次生分枝的横截面积总和仍等于树干的横截面积……依此类推。

Expressed mathematically, Leonardo's rule says that if a branch with diameter（D）splits into an arbitrary number（n）of secondary branches of diameters（d1, d2, et cetera), the sum of the secondary branches' diameters squared equals the square of the original branch's diameter. Or, in formula terms: D2 = $\sum$di2, where i = 1, 2, ... n. For real trees, the exponent in the equation that describes Leonardo's hypothesis is not always equal to 2 but rather varies between 1.8 and 2.3 depending on the geometry of the specific species of tree. But the general equation is still pretty close and holds for almost all trees.

达·芬奇法则也可以用数学公式来表述。一根树干分叉为若干根树枝，设树干直径为D，树枝总数为n，直径分别为d1, d2, ..., dn，那么所有次生树枝直径的平方和等于原生树干的直径的平方，即 $D^2 = \sum di^2$，其中 i = 1, 2, ..., n。对于自然界的树木来说，这一描述达·芬奇法假说的公式中，指数并不一定是2；根据不同树种几何形态的不同，其数值介于1.8至2.3之间。不过，对于大多数的树木来说，这一通用公式是相当接近事实的。

Botanists have hypothesized that Leonardo's observation has something to do with how a tree pumps water from its roots to leaves—that the tree needs the

一些植物学家猜测，达·芬奇的这一发现与树木从根部向树叶的泵水过程有关。树木将水分从根部输送至叶片的整个过程中，自下而

same total vein diameter from top to bottom to properly irrigate the leaves. But Eloy, a specialist in fluid mechanics, held that the equation had something to do with a tree's leaves, and the force of the wind caught by the leaves as it blew, contrast to how they took up water.

上的管脉直径总和应当是相同的。不过，在物理学家埃洛伊看来，达·芬奇公式并不与树干和树枝如何传递水分相关，而是和树叶以及风施加在树叶上的压力存在关系。

Eloy used some insightful mathematics to find the wind-force connection. He modeled a tree as cantilevered, that is, anchored at only one end, beams assembled to form a fractal—a shape that can be split into parts, each of which is a smaller, though sometimes not exact, copy of the larger structure—network. For Eloy's model, this meant that every time a larger branch split into smaller branches, it split into the same number of branches, at approximately the same angles and orientations.

为了探究这一问题与风力之间的关系，埃洛伊展开了较为深入的数学研究。他将树木当作悬臂结构来建模，并形成一个分形网络。这个悬臂结构只有一端固定；所谓分形，就是指能够分叉成多个部分的结构，每个子结构与母结构是大体近似的，但是会小一些。根据埃洛伊的模型，每个母树枝以相近的角度和方向分叉形成相同数量的小树枝。

Because the leaves on a tree branch all grow at the same end of the branch, Eloy modeled the force of wind blowing on a tree's leaves as a force pressing on the unanchored end of a cantilevered beam. When he plugged that wind-force equation into his model and assumed that the probability of a branch breaking due to wind stress is constant, he came up with Leonardo's rule. He then tested it with a numerical computer simulation that comes at the problem from a different direction, calculating forces on branches and then using those forces to figure out how thick the branches must be to resist breakage (see illustration). The numerical simulation accurately predicts the branch diameters and the 1.8-to-2.3 range of Leonardo's exponent.

由于同一根树枝上的叶子都长在树枝的同一侧，因此在埃洛伊的模型中，作用于树叶的风力都施加在这一悬臂结构的非固定端。他将风力公式应用到他的模型中，并假定树枝受到风力作用而断裂的概率是恒定不变的，据此他推导出了达·芬奇公式。随后，他从不同的角度对这一问题进行了计算机数值模拟，计算施加在树枝上的风力大小，并使用这一数值来得出树枝能够承受风力作用而不断裂的粗度值。数值模拟的结果精确地预测出了树枝的直径大小，并得出了达·芬奇公式中指数的范围是在 1.8 到 2.3 之间。

Reading Comprehension 14

Thanks to Plants, We Will Never Find a Planet Like Earth
感谢植物，让我们的地球与众不同

Astronomers are finding lots of exoplanets that are orbiting stars like the sun, significantly raising the odds that we will find a similar world. But if we do, the chance that the surface of that planet will look like ours is very small, thanks to an unlikely culprit: plants.

天文学家发现大量的系外行星，围绕着类似太阳的恒星运转，这大大提高了我们找到相似星球的可能性。但即使我们发现了，这个行星的地表也不大可能像我们的地球一样，原因出人意料：植物。

We all know that oceans and land masses formed, mountains rose, and precipitation washed over its surface; rivers weathered bare rock to create soil and plants took root. Well, new research indicates that the last stage of this scenario is not right. Vascular plants—those with structures such as xylem and phloem that can conduct water—are what created the rivers and muds that built the soils that led to forests and farmland.

我们都知道地表风貌是如何形成的：海洋和陆地大量形成，山脉突起，降水冲刷着地表，河流侵蚀裸露的岩石产生土壤，植物开始生根发芽。不过，新的研究表明，这种设想的最后阶段是错误的。维管植物——具有可以输送水分的木质部和韧皮部——形成河流和泥土，产生土壤，并最终有了森林和农田。

The evidence is laid out by Timothy Lenton, an Earth systems scientist. He presents data from the biogeochemical record showing that the evolution of vascular plants around 450 million years ago is what really began to soak up carbon dioxide from the atmosphere, much more than organisms in the oceans. As a result, global temperatures dropped, initiating a cycle of widespread glaciation and melting that, over millions more years, would significantly grind Earth's surface.

维管植物是塑造地表形态的主要力量这一观点的证据由地球系统科学家蒂莫西·兰顿提出。他通过生物地球化学记录的数据表明，维管植物的进化大约是在4.5亿年前，那时它们真正开始从大气中吸收二氧化碳，比海洋中的生物要多得多。结果导致全球气温骤降，大范围的冰河循环开始周而复始，在数百万年间有力地打磨着地表形态。

Perhaps even more surprisingly, vascular plants formed the kinds of rivers we see around us today, according to Martin Gibling of Dalhousie University in Nova Scotia and Neil Davies of the University of Ghent in Belgium, who analyzed sediment deposition going back hundreds of millions of years. Before the era of plants, water ran over Earth's landmasses in broad sheets, with no

在分析了数亿年以前的沉积物后，（加拿大）新斯科舍省达尔豪西大学的马丁·吉布林和比利时根特大学的尼尔·戴维斯提到，也许更让人吃惊的是，维管植物形成了今天我们所看到的所有形态的河流。在没有植物的年代，水漫山遍野地流淌在地球的广袤大地上，没有固定的河道。只有当地球上有了足够多的植

defined courses. Only when enough vegetation grew to break down rock into minerals and mud, and then hold that mud in place, did river banks form and begin to channel the water. The channeling led to periodic flooding that deposited sediment over broad areas, building up rich soil. The soil allowed trees to take root. Their woody debris fell into the rivers, creating logjams that rapidly created new channels and caused even more flooding, setting up a feedback loop that eventually supported forests and fertile plains.

被，将岩石粉碎成矿物质和泥土，然后将土壤固定，河道才得以形成。有了河道，河水就会定期泛滥，卷带着泥沙形成肥沃的土壤。有了土壤，树木才能生根。它们的枯枝落叶落入河中，使河道阻塞，并迅速形成新的河道，引发更多的洪水，这样循环的结果就是最终形成森林和平原。

"Sedimentary rocks, before plants, contained almost no mud," explains Gibling, a professor of Earth science at Dalhousie. "But after plants developed, the mud content increased dramatically. Muddy landscapes expanded greatly. A new kind of eco-space was created that wasn't there before."

"没有植物以前，沉积岩中几乎不含泥土，"达尔豪西大学的地球科学教授吉布林解释道。"但是植物生长以后，泥土含量开始显著增加，泥沙地貌面积急剧扩张。一种前所未有的新型生态空间产生了。"

"Plants are not passive passengers on the planet's surface system," Gibling says. "They create the surface system. Organisms tool the environment: the atmosphere, the landscapes, the oceans all develop incredible complexity once plant life grows." So as *Nature Geoscience*'s editors state in an editorial for their special edition, "Even if there are a number of planets that could support tectonics, running water and the chemical cycles that are essential for life as we know it, it seems unlikely that any of them would look like Earth." Because even if plants do sprout, they will evolve differently, crafting a different surface on the orb they call home.

"植物并不是地球表层系统的被动过客，"吉布林说。"他们是地表系统的缔造者。植物开始生长以后，生物体改变着周围的环境：大气，陆地，海洋，所有复杂的不可思议的环境。"就像《自然地球科学》的编辑在他们特别版的一篇评论中所说的，"即使有很多行星都具备地质构造、活水和化学循环这些众所周知的生命必不可少的元素，它们也不大可能看起来像我们的地球一样。"因为即使植物能够生根发芽，它们也会朝着不同的方向进化，将它们的星球精心打造成不同于地球的地表环境。

Reading Comprehension 15

Heart Disease May Be Treatable With Stem Cells
干细胞与医学：修补受损的心脏

Heart disease may be treatable with stem cells for the idea that worn-out organs might be repaired—or even replaced—by using stem cells, which spin off some offspring that remain as stem cells while others turn into functional tissue when they divides. Stem cells found in embryos can spin off a wide range of tissue types. Those found in adults are more limited: turning into blood cells, say, or muscle cells.

心脏病也许可以通过干细胞进行治疗，即设想可以用干细胞修复甚至替代受损器官。干细胞分裂后，一部分依旧成为干细胞，而另一部分则分化为功能组织细胞。胚胎干细胞可以生成多种类型的组织细胞。成年人体内的干细胞分化能力则大为有限：比如，分化为血细胞或肌细胞。

The bad news for those who have hopes of the field is that Geron, an American firm that was a pioneer of the therapeutic use of stem cells, is pulling out of the business for financial reason. It is ending a project that was testing embryonic stem cells as a treatment for people paralysed by injuries to their spinal cords. At a time when it is hard to raise new capital, the firm has decided to concentrate on anticancer therapies that, it hopes, are nearer to being commercial propositions than that of the stem-cell study .

对那些期待这一研究领域进展的人们来说，坏消息是干细胞治疗领域的先驱、美国的Geron公司由于经济原因即将退出这方面的研究。该公司正在结束一项对脊髓损伤导致瘫痪的病人试用干细胞疗法的研究课题。在目前这个难以筹措到新资金的时期，Geron公司决定集中力量进行抗癌疗法的研究，希望这项研究的商业前景比干细胞研究会好。

However, the good news for the field of stem-cell therapy comes from a paper published in this week's *Lancet* by Roberto Bolli of the University of Louisville and his colleagues. They have used more specialised stem cells—ones that spin off only cardiac cells—to repair the hearts of people with heart failure, but there are not enough spare thumpers around for all those who need them. Hence the idea of doing running repairs on a patient's existing organ.

不过，干细胞治疗领域的好消息来自本周《柳叶刀》杂志上发表的一篇论文，该论文由路易斯维尔大学的罗伯托·博利和其同事们共同撰写。他们利用更为特化的干细胞——只生成心脏细胞的干细胞——修复心力衰竭患者的心脏，但可供移植的心脏数量不足以满足所有患者的需要。于是，就产生了对患者现有的器官进行修复的想法。

The participants in Dr Bolli's study were 23 unfortunates who had each had at least one heart attack in the past, and were thus lined up for coronary-bypass

参与博利博士研究项目的是23名至少有过一次发病经历的心脏病人，他们因此被组织起来进行冠状动脉旁路手术（即俗称的“心脏

surgery, in which the furred-up blood supply to the heart is replaced with an alternative artery crafted from a blood vessel taken from elsewhere—usually the leg. Seven of the 23 acted as a control group, and received no intervention from Dr Bolli after the surgery. From the other 16, the researchers collected tissue samples during surgery. They broke these up, in order to extract cardiac stem cells from them (these cells can be identified by the presence on their surfaces of a particular protein), and then bred the stem cells in tissue cultures until they numbered millions.

搭桥手术”)，该手术是从患者身体其他部位——通常是从腿部——截取血管，再造成一条新的动脉，以取代堵塞的血管向心脏供血。23人中有7人作为对照组，在搭桥手术后不再接受博利博士的进一步治疗。而对于另外16人，研究者们在手术过程中收集了他们的组织样本，进行分离，从中提取心脏干细胞（这种细胞可以通过存在于其表面上的一种特殊蛋白质加以识别)，然后对这些干细胞进行组织培养，使它们的数量增长到数以百万。

About four months after each patient's original operation, when their hearts had stabilized, Dr Bolli used a catheter to deliver 1 million of the newly bred stem cells to their damaged heart muscle. The results were remarkable. Four months after the infusion their hearts were pumping an average of 38.5% of the optimal volume, and this had risen to 42.5% a year after the transfusion. No such improvement was seen in the hearts of the control patients.

在患者接受搭桥手术后约四个月、心脏状况稳定下来之后，博利博士使用一根导管向他们受损的心肌注入一百万个新培养出来的干细胞。实验结果非同凡响。输入干细胞四个月之后，他们的心脏平均供血量达到了最大供血量的38.5%，而在干细胞输入手术一年之后，这一数值又上升到42.5%。对照组患者的心脏则没有这种好转迹象。

Dr Bolli hopes soon to begin a bigger trial, based on the success of his small one. The day may not be far off, then, when a sick heart can be serviced in mid-life and made good for a few more years. That is no excuse for complacency: prevention will always remain a better course of action than cure. But for those for whom prevention has not succeeded, the work of Dr Bolli and his collaborators and rivals brings hope that a heart attack will, in the future, not be quite the fearful prospect it is today.

博利博士希望在已经获得成功的小规模实验的基础上，不久之后可以展开更大范围的实验。这样，患病的心脏可以在中年接受维修，并在接下来的一些年里保持健康，这一天可能不远了。我们不能因此而自满：预防永远比治疗有效。不过，对于那些未能成功预防疾病的人们来说，博利博士和他的同事以及竞争者们的研究成果带来了希望：心脏病发作在未来将不会像它在今天这样可怕。

Reading Comprehension 16

DNA Discovery May Boost Stem Cell Safety
基因，让干细胞疗法更安全

DNA discovery may boost stem cell safety.

基因，让干细胞疗法更安全。

A region of DNA that can boost the growth of stem cells has been found in the largest ever study of human embryonic stem cells.

迄今为止最大规模的人类胚胎干细胞研究发现了一段能促进干细胞生长的DNA片段。

The discovery could lead to safer cell therapies, says study co-author Dr Andrew Laslett from CSIRO Materials Science and Engineering.

作为论文的合著者，澳大利亚联邦科学与工业研究组织(CSIRO)材料科学和工程学实验室的安德鲁·拉斯利博士表示，这项发现能推动细胞疗法向更加安全的方向发展。

The research by the International Stem Cell Initiative involved 38 laboratories across the globe studying 125 ethnically diverse cell lines in parallel experiments whose findings uncover changes that arise from how cells are grown.

全球38所实验室通过研究125株不同人种的细胞系，共同完成了这项由国际干细胞研究院组织的实验，其结果揭示了细胞生长方式转变的奥秘。

Stem cell therapy, which is entering early-stage human trials, turns stem cells into other cell types to treat spinal cord injury, blindness and other ailments. The cells need to be grown in nutritious culture to produce enough amounts for therapy. But many stem cells die when they are initially moved to a new environment, resulting from natural selection and adaptation.

正在进行人体前期试验的干细胞疗法，可以通过干细胞替代的方式，治疗脊髓损伤、眼盲和其他疾病。只有外界环境营养充足，才能产生治疗所需的足量细胞。但当干细胞进入新的培养环境，自然选择和适应会导致大量的细胞死亡。

"However, it's the small fraction of cells that become abnormal that can be dangerous in a clinical situation," says Laslett. "If they find growth situations that suit them, they could grow into cancers." One in five cell-lines mutated a particular region of chromosome 20, gaining extra copies of the region seemed to give them a growth advantage. From the three genes in the region, it's likely the advantage is from BCL2L1. It's known to stop

"但是，应用于临床的细胞发生了突变是非常危险的，如果在体内有适宜的生长环境，它们将发育形成肿瘤"，拉斯利博士说。五分之一的培养细胞在20号染色体上的特定区域发生突变。有证据表明，突变导致的该区域延长会使细胞获得生长优势。在该区域的三个基因中，BCL2L1基因被认为是导致生长旺盛的原因所在。BCL2L1基因具有能够中止程序性

controlled cell death, or apoptosis. The same mutation is also found in some cancer cells.

细胞死亡(或凋亡)的功能，在一些肿瘤细胞中也能发现该基因的突变。

Scientists could use these tests to improve current techniques used to grow stem cells.

科学家应当利用这些试验结果来改进现有的干细胞培养技术。

Embryonic stem cells walk a tightrope with maintaining their normal genetic nature, it is necessary to culture them in the best possible way so they keep those genes normal.

胚胎干细胞遗传性状并不稳定，我们需要用尽可能好的培养方式来保持其遗传信息正常。

One of the interesting findings is that most of the embryonic stem cells are normal, even though they have been cultured for a long period. About two thirds were constant.

一个有趣的发现是，大约三分之二的胚胎干细胞，即使经过长时间的培养，也能保持遗传性状的稳定。

Reading Comprehension 17

Stopping the Brain from Hurting Itself
停止大脑的自我损害

One-third of stroke survivors never recover enough brain function to live on their own. Now scientists think they know why. Once a stroke kills a swath of brain cells, a neurotransmitter known as GABA impairs the surviving, apparently healthy, brain tissue. Targeting GABA could help a stroke-afflicted brain better overcome its damage, the researchers suggest.

三分之一的中风幸存者永远无法再恢复全部的脑功能并生活自理。现在，科学家们认为他们找到了原因。当中风杀死一个带状区域的脑细胞后，一种叫GABA(氨基丁酸)的神经传递素将破坏残存的、看起来还健康的脑组织。研究者建议，如果能抑制GABA，则可能帮助遭受中风的大脑更好地克服因此产生的损害。

When a stroke hits, physicians have few options. If they catch it early enough, they can administer the clot-busting drug tPA to keep even more brain cells from dying—but tPA is not appropriate for all types of stroke. Physicians can also prescribe physical therapy, which can occasionally help recover impaired motor function. Yet there are no approved drugs that help the brain heal.

发生中风时，医生通常无计可施。如果他们能够在早期发现中风征兆，那么可以通过给病人服用抗栓塞药物(tPA)以避免更多的脑细胞死亡，但这种药物不是对所有种类的中风都有效。医生也可以让病人进行物理治疗，这样有时可以帮助病人恢复受损的运动机能。但目前仍旧没有被人们认可的药物来治愈大脑。

For its part, the brain appears to try a sort of natural drug therapy to limit the spread of damage. It releases extra amounts of GABA, which reduces the firing of neurons. GABA initially prevents stroke-damaged brain tissue from becoming overexcited and dying. But University of California, Los Angeles (UCLA), investigators led by Thomas Carmichael, a specialist in stroke, and Istvan Mody, an expert in inhibition, wondered whether GABA might also interfere with the brain's plasticity, the ability of healthy regions to take over for injured ones.

大脑本身会试图对受损部分进行一种自然药物治疗，从而限制破坏的扩大化。它会释放多余的GABA，以降低中风对受损位置神经元的刺激。GABA最初会抑制中风破坏的大脑组织过分兴奋和死亡。但以中风研究专家托马斯·卡迈克尔和抑制作用专家伊斯特万·莫迪为代表的加州大学洛杉矶分校的研究员们考虑，GABA是否有可能同时抑制大脑的重塑性，也就是健康区域逐渐接管受损区域功能的能力。

Previous studies had tried to address this question, but they produced confusing results. The UCLA team hypothesized that others had failed to distinguish between two types of inhibition—phasic, in which GABA acts upon specific receptors at nerve cell sites called synapses, and tonic, in which the neurotransmitter acts on other receptors elsewhere on the nerve cell. "We looked at all the properties of neural transmission after stroke, and we found the most prominent change was an increase in the tonic form of inhibition in the cortical region next to the stroke damage," says graduate student and study co-author Ben Huang. So the group gave stroke-afflicted rodents a drug that could specifically block GABA-mediated tonic inhibition but left phasic inhibition intact. The mice had suffered damage in areas that control movement, yet they recovered about 50% more function in their limbs than similar rodents treated with a control therapy, the team reports online today in *Nature*.

过去的研究曾试图解决这个问题，但结果令人困惑。加州大学的研究组猜测其他人可能没有区分开两种抑制力：一种是短暂性抑制，GABA对神经细胞突触上的某些受体产生作用；另一种是持续性抑制，GABA作用于神经元细胞其他位置的其他受体。"我们观察了中风后神经传输的所有特性之后发现，最显著的变化是中风破坏处附近的皮层区的持续性抑制增加了。"著作共同撰稿人、研究生黄贲说。于是，研究小组给中风后的啮齿类动物服用可以单纯阻止GABA持续性抑制而不影响其短暂性抑制的药物。根据研究小组今天发布在《自然》杂志网上的报告，运动系统控制区域受损的老鼠四肢恢复了大约50%以上的功能，比其他只接受物理治疗的啮齿类动物要高得多。

The findings suggest a new, potentially therapeutic window for treating stroke, says Carmichael. Physicians might be able to give a GABA-blocking drug after stroke, for example. The key would be proper timing: after tonic inhibition had initially protected as many brain cells as possible but before it begins interfering with the brain's recovery attempts. The class of drugs used by the UCLA team to block GABA receptors is currently in clinical

卡迈克尔说，这项发现为中风治疗提供了一种新的、可能有疗效的方案。比如，医生们可以给中风患者服用GABA的抑制药物。问题的关键在于找到合适的用药时间：要在持续性抑制拯救了足够多的脑细胞之后，和它开始干涉脑恢复之前。这类GABA受体的抑制药物现正被加州大学的研究小组用于其他方面的临床研究，如失忆，并在一些小的研究上得到了

development for other conditions, such as memory loss, and has been well-tolerated in small studies. However, the drugs have not yet been tested on stroke patients. Clinical trials are a long way off, cautions Carmichael, because more animal studies by other labs must be performed first.

广泛的认同。但这种药物还没有在中风病人中进行实验。卡迈克尔谨慎提到，临床试验还有很长的路要走，必须有其他实验室做出更多的动物研究才行。

Nonetheless, other neuroscientists say the work offers a new direction for developing stroke drugs. "The result is very gratifying because for many, many years people have focused on excitatory synapses and excitatory connections in terms of brain plasticity," says Takao Hensch, a developmental plasticity researcher in the Molecular and Cellular Biology Department at Harvard University. "It's only in the recent past that we've started to appreciate that the balance of excitation to inhibition is what's important."

然而，其他神经科学家认为这项研究为研制中风药物提供了新的思路。"研究结果是很可喜的，因为很多很多年以来，人们的研究集中在大脑可塑性的兴奋性突触和兴奋性连接上，"高尾贵雄说，他是哈佛大学分子与细胞生物学系的一名发育可塑性研究员。"只是在前段时间，我们才开始意识到激发和抑制的平衡是多么重要。"

Reading Comprehension 18

Fish, Omegas, and Cholesterol
鱼、欧米伽和胆固醇

Americans kill and eat 18 billion marine animals every year. Some are genetically engineered on fish farms, while the rest are hooked by the mouth or netted by huge trawlers that catch and kill everything in their path.

美国人每年捕杀食用180亿的海洋动物。有些是养鱼场基因改造的鱼，其余的则是（被天然捕捞），嘴被钩住或是被巨大的拖网渔船网住，拖网渔船所过之处一路捕杀，生命所剩无几。

Here's an analogy to help you empathize with fish: imagine you are walking down a country road lined with apple trees. Hungry from the walk, you reach up to grab a piece of fruit. Suddenly, your hand becomes impaled with a large, metal hook that pulls you out of the air and into an atmosphere in which you cannot breathe. We drown fish and other aquatic animals in our atmosphere the same way we drown in theirs.

这里有一个比喻会让你同情鱼：想像一下，你正走在苹果树林立的乡间路上。走饿了，你伸手摘个果实。突然，你的手被一个大金属钩刺穿，把你拉起，把你拖入让你不能呼吸的环境中。我们把鱼类和其他水生动物放入我们的空气中淹死，与我们在它们的环境中淹死一样。

Contrary to the slick advertisements of the fish industry, or the misinformed American doctors who only

与鱼类加工业花言巧语的广告，或学医八年只听过大约三小时营养课而被误导的美国

receive around THREE HOURS of nutrition information during their eight-year medical programs, fish is not a health food. With mercury, dioxin and PCBs, fish meat is the most contaminated food product available. Additionally, a 3.5-ounce serving of fish meat has twice the amount of cholesterol as a single hot dog. Contrary to anyone who espouses otherwise, cholesterol produced by YOUR body is the only good cholesterol. If you bring it in from an outside source, it's bad cholesterol.

医生所说的相反，鱼不是一种健康食物。鱼肉中含有汞、二恶英和多氯联苯，是污染最严重的食品。此外，一份3.5盎司的鱼肉所含胆固醇量是一个热狗的两倍。和赞成鱼类胆固醇于人有益的观念相反，其实你身体产生的胆固醇才是唯一的好胆固醇。如果你是从外部摄取，那样的胆固醇就不好。

Claims about omega fatty acids being found solely in fish are absolute lies. Some fish have omegas because they've eaten algae/seaweed or consumed other fish who have already eaten algae/seaweed. Every vitamin, mineral and nutrient comes from the earth in the form of fruits, vegetables (sea or land), nuts, seeds, grains and legumes. Animal products only contain trace amounts of vitamins, minerals and nutrients because animals eat plants (sea or land). Meat is, at best, a secondary source of essential elements.

宣称欧米伽脂肪酸只在鱼中才有，这绝对是谎言。有些鱼含有欧米伽，是因为它们吃了海藻/海草或其他已经吃了海藻/海草的鱼类。地球上每种维生素、矿物质和营养素都来自水果、蔬菜（海洋或陆地）、坚果、种子、谷类和豆类。动物产品只含有微量的维生素、矿物质和营养素，因为动物吃（海洋或陆地）植物。肉类充其量不过是身体基本要素的次要来源。

Açaí (fruit), beans, black currant seed oil, blue-green algae, borage seed oil, cabbage, canola oil, flax (oil/seeds), chlorella, corn, green vegetables (leafy), hemp (oil/seed/powder/milk), pine nuts, pumpkin seeds, sesame seeds, soy, sprouts (all), squash, vegetable oils, walnuts and wheat all contain omega fatty acids WITHOUT cholesterol, WITHOUT enormous amounts of saturated fat, WITHOUT trans-fatty acids, WITHOUT animal protein and, most importantly, WITHOUT cruelty!

巴西莓、豆类、黑醋栗籽油、蓝绿藻、琉璃苣籽油、卷心菜、油菜、亚麻（油/种子）、绿球藻、玉米、绿叶菜、火麻（油/种子/粉/奶）、松子、南瓜子、芝麻、大豆、芽（所有种子的芽）、菜瓜、植物油、核桃和小麦所有这些都含有欧米伽脂肪酸，而不含胆固醇，没有大量的饱和脂肪，没有反式脂肪酸，没有动物蛋白，最重要的是：无残忍！

If someone told you to smoke cigarettes because they contained trace amounts of omegas or calcium (they do not), would you do it? Of course not. Yet every meat-eater engages in the same aforesaid analogy of putting deadly products into their body by eating meat, cheese, milk and eggs in order to obtain trace amounts of nutrients. As the great philosopher Pythagoras said, "Men dig their graves with their own teeth, and die more by those instruments than by all weapons of their enemies."

如果有人让你抽烟，因为烟含微量的欧米伽或钙（其实烟不含），你会抽吗？当然不会。然而，每一个肉食者都如上述比喻一样，通过进食肉类、奶酪、牛奶和鸡蛋以获得微量营养素，却同时也把致命的产物放入自己的体内。正如伟大的哲学家毕达哥拉斯所说的：“人们用自己的牙齿自掘坟墓，这样死的人比所有敌人用武器杀死的还多。”

Reading Comprehension 19

The End of Biofuels?
生物燃料的穷途末路?

Hartmut Michel makes his views clear: "The Nonsense of Biofuels". He essentially comes down hard on biofuel proponents of all stripes and not just the much hyped ethanol-from-corn lobby. Michel won the Nobel Prize for cracking open the structure of one of earth's most important proteins—the photosynthetic reaction center—so he certainly knows his photosynthesis.

哈特穆特·米歇尔已经言明了他的态度:"生物燃料就是胡扯"。他对所有生物燃料领域的研究者和支持者集体发难,而不仅仅是成为现今研究大热门的玉米制乙醇这一隅。米歇尔揭示了地球上最重要的蛋白质之一的结构——光合作用的中心,并因此获得了诺贝尔奖;他理所当然知道光合作用是怎么回事。

He starts by looking at the energy efficiency of the process. It's not always appreciated that for all its rightly deserved glory, photosynthesis is not as efficient as we think, which would indeed be the case for something that's been tuned by evolutionary fits and starts and historical contingency. For one thing, UV, IR and green light cannot be utilized by plants so that leaves out a pretty high-energy part of the spectrum. Then there's all the wonderful machinery of electron transfer and light-harvesting proteins involved in the dark and light processes. The light step essentially captures photon energy and generates NADPH and ATP, and the dark step uses this energy source and reducing potential to synthesize carbohydrates from CO2. Considering the inefficiencies inherent in using the energy of massless, transient photons, only about 12% of energy from sunlight is stored as NADPH.

(在评论中)他先讲述了光合作用这一过程的能量效率。遗憾的是,在一片应得的鲜花和掌声中,光合作用并不如我们想的那么高效。从生物进化的起起伏伏和历史的偶然性上看,确实是这样的。一个原因是,植物因无法利用紫外、红外和绿色光而浪费了光谱中很大一部分能量。而在接下来的光反应和暗反应中,电子转移及蛋白质捕获光的机制很完美。光反应主要获取光能并产生还原型辅酶II(NADPH)和三磷酸腺苷(ATP);然后,暗反应利用这部分能源和降低的电势用二氧化碳合成碳水化合物。由于无质量的瞬时光子的能量的利用率本身比较低,因此只有12%的光能被储存在NADPH中。

But try to improve the efficiency by bumping up the intensity and you will get photodamage. To avoid this photodamage, plants have to recycle one of the key proteins called RuBisCO, which has a hard time distinguishing between CO2 and O2. A significant amount of energy has to be spent in getting rid of the product formed from O2 insertion.

然而,如果我们试图通过增加光强提高效率,又会造成光损失。如果想要避免这种光损失,植物需要收集一种关键蛋白——二磷酸核酮糖氧合酶/羧化酶,而这种酶却很难区分二氧化碳和氧气。要去掉有氧气参与生成的产物,需要消耗很大的能量。

All these hurdles lead to a rather drastic lowering of photosynthetic efficiency which gets watered down to a rather measly 4% or so. It's pretty clear from this description that any kind of efforts to get better efficiency from biofuels will have to overcome enormous protein engineering hurdles. This does not bode well for current studies aimed at such goals.

这些困难都导致光合作用的效率严重低下——降到小之又小的4%。以上种种显示，想要提高生物燃料效率的任何尝试都需要克服蛋白质工程的无数障碍。这对于旨在达成这些目标的当前研究来说可不是什么好兆头。

Personally I am a proponent of context-specific energy use. I think that considering the vast variation of resource distribution, geography, energy requirements, paying capacity and economics, it doesn't make much sense to search for any one-size-fits-all solution. But that seems to usually be the case every time someone touts a single, seemingly miraculous solution as being universally applicable around the world. I have similar thoughts about solar energy. The solutions currently available don't seem to solve the problem of transmission and availability in regions where the sun doesn't shine that ·much. Part of Michel's "vision" is the widespread deployment of superconducting cables which even now (more than 25 years after the discovery of "high-temperature" superconductors) seems like a minor fantasy. Notwithstanding these issues though, solar power certainly seems to have a much larger role to play in our economy than it currently does, especially in regions which get plenty of sunlight.

在能量利用上，我个人是赞成具体问题具体分析的。由于能源分布、地理情况、能源需求、购买力和经济的极度不均衡，想找到一劳永逸的统一解决方案不太现实。不过往往总是有人站出来推行一个似乎很神奇的、全世界普遍适用的单一方案。对于太阳能的利用，我也秉持类似观点。现有的解决方案好像无法解决阳光不充足地区的太阳能传送和利用率问题。米歇尔的关注点一部分落在了超导电缆的广泛使用上，然而即使(在“高温”超导体发现后超过25年的）今天，这也仅是黄粱美梦罢了。尽管还有上述这些问题，但太阳能在我们的经济中还会起到更大的作用，特别是在那些阳光充足的地区。

But biofuels? The problems there seem much more grounded in fundamental biological constraints rather than technological ones. And it's hard to overturn 3.5 billion years of evolution so I am not sure I should hold my breath. Time will tell.

而生物燃料呢？其问题存在于，与其说是技术层面，不如说是生物学本身的限制。要一下子颠覆35亿年的进化过程是很困难的，我不知道我是否应该保持冷静。时间会证明一切。

Reading Comprehension 20

The Incredible Secret Language of Plants
植物的奇妙私语

We've all heard about the benefits of talking or playing music to your plants. Plants even have musical preferences—they apparently love Mozart but hate Jimi Hendrix. Although this is yet to be confirmed by the scientific community, at least one plant biologist concedes it may be due to the effects of sound vibrations on the plants.

相信很多人听说过，和盆栽植物聊聊天，为它们播放一些音乐，对植物的生长是很有益处的。有些植物甚至有自己偏好的音乐风格——它们显然更喜爱莫扎特(舒缓优雅的古典音乐)，而对吉米·亨德里克斯（澎湃激情的流行音乐）则嗤之以鼻。此说法虽尚未在科学界得到证实，但至少有植物学家提出，这可能归因于声音振动对植物产生的不同影响。

Whether or not this turns out to be true, two new studies have proven that plants do at least communicate with each other in ways not previously understood by us. In the most recent study, conducted by a team at the Ben-Gurion University in Israel, pea plants have been found to alert each other to stressful situations. In the experiment, the plants were placed close to each other, but not touching in any way. Some plants shared soil with those next to them, while others were completely separated. Next, a few of the plants were given drought-like situations, while others were kept healthy and watered.

不管这个说法是真是假，两项新的研究已经证明，植物间确实有交流，但其方式与人类先前所认知的不一样。最近一项由以色列本—古里安大学的一个团队进行的研究表明，豌豆类植物具有在恶劣环境下互相警戒的能力。在这项实验里，植物被种植在一起，但相互之间没有任何接触。有些植物与旁边的植物一起共享土壤，有些则是完全隔离的。同时，一些植物被放置在类似干旱的环境中，而另一些植物则给予充足养分。

The plants kept in dry conditions responded to the situation by closing the pores on their leaves (which are called stoma) a normal reaction for plants in drought. What was unexpected was that plants nearby (not kept in drought conditions but sharing the same soil) did the same thing! Not only that, but they seemed to pass the message on to un-stressed plants even further away, which responded with stomatal closure as well. The plants that did not share any soil did not respond at all, meaning that the communication between the plants was done through root systems rather than the leaves.

干旱时，植物叶片闭合气孔以减少水分蒸发，这是植物适应干旱环境的正常反应。可是出人意料的是，邻近的植物（只是共享土壤而不处于干旱环境）出现相似的情形。不仅如此，植物们似乎将这一干旱信息传播得更远，更多处于良好生长环境的植物也受其影响关闭了气孔。可是，没有与它们共享土壤的植物则不受影响，这意味着植物间是通过根部系统而不是叶子传递信号的。

According to Professor Ariel Novoplansky who oversaw the research. The results demonstrate that unstressed plants are able to perceive and respond to stress cues emitted by the roots of their drought-stressed neighbors and, via "relay cuing", elicit stress responses in further unstressed plants. Further work is underway to study the underlying mechanisms of this new mode of plant communication and its possible adaptive implications for the anticipation of forth coming abiotic stresses by plants.

这项研究的监管负责人，阿里埃勒·诺沃普朗斯基教授说，实验结果表明：生长环境良好的植物(即无压植物)能感知并回应来自邻近生长于干旱环境的植物(有压植物)通过根部系统传达的压力信息。并且，通过“中继信号”，压力信息又会传给更远的无压植物。进一步的研究正在进行中，目的在于探究植物的这种新式交流方式是如何实现的，以及通过植物对其逼近的非生物性压力的感应，发现其可能存在的适应性机制。

Previous research by Exeter University in Britain also turned up evidence of plant communication. In that study, cabbages were used rather than pea plants and the form of communication was quite different. In this case, the cabbages were also placed close to each other. Certain cabbages had their leaves snipped with scissors. This caused the damaged plants to emit a gas, made visible through genetic mutation, which alerted their neighbors. The nearby cabbages reacted to this gas by producing a toxin in their leaves making them less palatable to predators such as caterpillars.

英国埃克塞特大学过去也做过相关研究，提出了植物间交流的证据。他们用卷心菜而非豌豆类植物作为研究对象，卷心菜的交流方式则非常不同。在这项研究里，同样将卷心菜相互靠近栽种。其中一些卷心菜的叶子被剪去，这样的破坏会让植物排出一种气体，并且通过基因变异这种气体变得可见。这些变化是给邻近卷心菜以警示。感受到这种气体后，邻近的卷心菜在叶片上产生毒素，这样一来，卷心菜的口味变差了，像毛虫这种捕食者就不吃它们了。

Reading Comprehension 21

Aspirin's Fat Burning Mechanism Found
阿司匹林燃烧脂肪的机制已被发现

It may be great for curing a splitting headache, but scientists have now discovered that aspirin also activates an enzyme that burns fat, a finding that could unlock its cancer fighting properties, according to a new study.

人们早已发现，阿司匹林对治疗剧烈的头痛有效。目前，一项新的研究显示，科学家又发现阿司匹林还能激活一种燃烧脂肪的酶，这一发现可能会开启阿司匹林的抗癌功能。

Previous research has shown that once ingested, aspirin breaks down into salicylate—a compound derived from plants such as willow bark, and used as a drug for

早期的研究显示，阿司匹林一旦被摄入体内就会分解成为水杨酸盐。水杨酸盐是一种从植物(如柳树皮)中提取的化合物，已经作为药

thousands of years. Now Professor Grahame Hardie, a cell biologist at the University of Dundee in Scotland, has discovered how salicylate affects metabolism. Hardie suspected that salicylate affected an enzyme known as AMPK, which is a key regulator of cell metabolism.

物使用多年。目前，由来自苏格兰邓迪大学的细胞生物学家格雷厄姆·哈迪已经发现了水杨酸盐作用于代谢的机制。哈迪猜测，水杨酸盐会影响到一种酶——腺苷酸活化蛋白激酶（AMPK），这种酶是细胞代谢的主要调节者。

To test this, researchers compared a control group of mice, with another group that lacked a sub-unit of the AMPK enzyme. They injected both groups of mice with salicylate and measured the rate at which they utilised fat. They found that the mice with AMPK were able to burn fat at a faster rate. This indicated that salicylate switches on AMPK, increasing the breakdown of fat.

为了验证这种猜测，研究者比较了对照组小鼠和缺乏AMPK组小鼠的试验。研究者对两组小鼠都注射了水杨酸盐，然后测量两组小鼠对脂肪的利用率。他们发现，有AMPK的小鼠组能够快速地燃烧脂肪。这表明水杨酸盐激活了AMPK，进而加速脂肪分解。

It’s exciting that researchers worked out a new and different way to deal with cancer. Hardie says recent studies have shown that people who take aspirin over long time periods appear to have a lower incidence of cancer. But doctors warn against prolonged aspirin use, which can cause stomach bleeding. “I’m particularly interested in these protective effects against cancer,” says Hardie. “Further research may help us discover another way of taking salicylate, other than aspirin, which has fewer side-effects.”

这非常令人兴奋，因为研究者们发现了一条治疗癌症的全新道路。哈迪说，近期的研究显示，长期服用阿司匹林的人患癌症的概率较低。但是医生警告患者不要一直使用阿司匹林，这会导致胃出血。“我对阿司匹林抗癌的机制非常感兴趣，”哈迪说。“今后的研究可能帮助我们找到不是以服用阿司匹林的形式摄入水杨酸盐的方法，这就会减少副作用”。

He explains that anti-cancer effects may be due to the activity of AMPK, as diabetic drugs that target AMPK in cells are also associated with a reduced incidence of cancer. “The surprising finding that salicylate promotes AMPK activity also opens up exciting avenues for diabetes prevention and treatment.”

他解释道，其抗癌的效果可能与AMPK的活性有关，因为作用于AMPK的糖尿病药物与癌症发生率降低相关。“这一关于水杨酸盐激活AMPK的发现相当令人惊异，这也为糖尿病的预防和治疗找到了非常好的途径。

生命科学类题源单词补充

分类	编码	真题原词	真题背景精确注释
生物	001	aerobic	需氧微生物的
生物	002	anaerobe	厌氧微生物
生物	003	archaebacteria	原始细菌
生物	004	bacillus	杆菌
生物	005	bacteria	细菌
生物	006	capsid	蛋白壳
生物	007	chimpanzee	黑猩猩
生物	008	Ebola	伊波拉病毒
生物	009	fungus	真菌
生物	010	microbe	微生物
生物	011	microbial	微生物的
生物	012	microinjection	显微注射
生物	013	microorganism	微生物
生物	014	microscope	显微镜
生物	015	microscopic	微观的
生物	016	microstructure	微观结构
生物	017	miniature	极小的
生物	018	organism	有机体
生物	019	puromycin	嘌呤霉素
生物	020	retrovirus	逆转录酶病毒
生物	021	salmonella	沙门氏菌
生物	022	strain	菌株
生物	023	streptomycin	链霉素
生物	024	virus	病原体
动物	001	adipose	动物脂肪
动物	002	aedes albopicta	白纹伊蚊
动物	003	aestivation	夏蛰
动物	004	amphibian	两栖动物
动物	005	androgenous	雄性单性生殖的
动物	006	annelid	环节动物
动物	007	anopheles	疟疾按蚊
动物	008	anteater	食蚁动物
动物	009	antelope	羚羊
动物	010	aquatic	水栖的
动物	011	avian	鸟的
动物	012	barnacle	藤壶
动物	013	beaver	河狸

分类	编码	真题原词	真题背景精确注释
动物	014	beekeeping	养蜂业
动物	015	bilateral symmetry	双侧对称性
动物	016	bill	喙
动物	017	bison	北美野牛
动物	018	blotchy	有斑点的
动物	019	bobcat	美洲山猫
动物	020	bovine	牛
动物	021	brachiopod	腕足动物
动物	022	bristle	鬃毛
动物	023	brood	幼虫群落
动物	024	bryozoan	苔藓虫类
动物	025	budworm	蚜虫
动物	026	buffalo runner	套牛马
动物	027	bull	未阉公牛
动物	028	bumblebee	大黄蜂
动物	029	carnivore	食肉动物
动物	030	carnivorous	食肉的
动物	031	castor	海狸
动物	032	catbird	北美猫鸟
动物	033	caterpillar	毛毛虫
动物	034	cell wall	蜂巢壁
动物	035	cephalopod	头足纲动物
动物	036	cetacean	鲸
动物	037	chameleon	美洲变色蜥蜴
动物	038	chimpanzee	黑猩猩
动物	039	cladoceran	水蚤
动物	040	claw	螯
动物	041	coelenterate	腔肠动物
动物	042	copepod	桡足动物
动物	043	cormorant	鸬鹚
动物	044	crab	蟹
动物	045	crest	鸟冠
动物	046	cricket	蟋蟀
动物	047	crustacean	甲壳纲
动物	048	cuttlefish	乌贼
动物	049	dealate	脱翅昆虫
动物	050	dinosaur	恐龙
动物	051	dolphin	海豚
动物	052	dormouse	冬眠鼠
动物	053	down	软毛

分类	编码	真题原词	真题背景精确注释
动物	054	drone	雄蜂
动物	055	dugong	儒艮
动物	056	egg	卵
动物	057	emergence	羽化
动物	058	endogamy	同系交配
动物	059	entomologist	昆虫学家
动物	060	entomology	昆虫学
动物	061	exogamy	异系交配
动物	062	exoskeleton	外骨骼
动物	063	fecundity	繁殖力
动物	064	fin	鳍
动物	065	flatfish	比目鱼
动物	066	fledgling	雏鸟
动物	067	flounder	鲽形比目鱼
动物	068	foal	驹
动物	069	furry	毛皮的
动物	070	gopher	衣囊鼠
动物	071	gosling	幼鹅
动物	072	grazing rate	捕食速率
动物	073	green turtle	绿甲海龟
动物	074	gregarious	群居的
动物	075	grizzly	灰熊
动物	076	gull	鸥
动物	077	hamster	仓鼠
动物	078	helix	蜗牛耳轮
动物	079	heron	鹭
动物	080	herring	鲱
动物	081	hippopotamus	河马
动物	082	hive	蜂群
动物	083	hog	猪
动物	084	honeycomb	蜂巢
动物	085	horny	角状的
动物	086	hummingbird	蜂鸟
动物	087	humpback	驼背鲸
动物	088	ichthyosaur	鱼龙
动物	089	iguana	鬣蜥
动物	090	incubate	孵卵
动物	091	indigo bunting	雀科小鸣鸟
动物	092	infest	昆虫泛滥
动物	093	invertebrate	无脊椎动物

分类	编码	真题原词	真题背景精确注释
动物	094	lazuli bunting	天青石鸟
动物	095	livestock	牲畜
动物	096	lizard	蜥蜴
动物	097	lobster	龙虾
动物	098	macaque	猕猴
动物	099	mammalian	哺乳动物的
动物	100	mammoth	猛犸象
动物	101	mare	母马
动物	102	marlin	枪鱼
动物	103	mastodon	乳齿象
动物	104	maternal	母系的
动物	105	medfly	地中海果蝇
动物	106	migration	定期迁徙
动物	107	mite	螨
动物	108	mole	鼹鼠
动物	109	mollusc	软体动物
动物	110	monogamous	单配的
动物	111	mosquito	蚊
动物	112	moth	蛾
动物	113	muskrat	麝鼠
动物	114	nesting chamber	巢穴
动物	115	ornithology	鸟类学
动物	116	otter	水獭
动物	117	owl	猫头鹰
动物	118	oyster	牡蛎
动物	119	paleontologist	古生物学家
动物	120	paleontology	古生物学
动物	121	piglet	猪崽
动物	122	planktonic algae	浮游生物水藻
动物	123	plasmodium	疟原虫
动物	124	pluck	鞭毛
动物	125	polyp	珊瑚虫
动物	126	poultry	家禽
动物	127	predation	捕食行为
动物	128	predator	捕食者
动物	129	predatory	食肉的
动物	130	pteropod	翼足目动物
动物	131	pterosaur	翼龙
动物	132	pupa	蛹
动物	133	red herring	熏鲱鱼

分类	编码	真题原词	真题背景精确注释
动物	134	salmon	鲑
动物	135	scale	鳞
动物	136	scavenge	腐食者
动物	137	seal	海豹
动物	138	shellfish	贝壳类
动物	139	shrew	鼩鼱
动物	140	sloth	树懒
动物	141	spawn	卵
动物	142	sperm whale	抹香鲸
动物	143	spiny anteater	针鼹
动物	144	squid	鱿鱼
动物	145	stallion	牡马(尤指种马)
动物	146	suctorial	有吸盘的
动物	147	talon	猛禽的爪
动物	148	tapeworm	绦虫
动物	149	termite	白蚁
动物	150	tern	燕鸥
动物	151	tick	壁虱蜱
动物	152	tuna	金枪鱼
动物	153	urchin	海胆
动物	154	venom	毒液
动物	155	warbler	鸣鸟
动物	156	wasp	黄蜂
动物	157	weasel	鼬鼠
动物	158	weevil	象鼻虫
动物	159	woodpecker	啄木鸟
动物	160	zooplankton	浮游生物
生化	001	aberrant	异常的
生化	002	aberration	变形
生化	003	abscisic acid	脱落酸
生化	004	abundance	个体密度
生化	005	acetone	丙酮
生化	006	acid	酸
生化	007	acidity	酸性
生化	008	actin	肌动蛋白
生化	009	activation	活化作用
生化	010	adenine	腺嘌呤
生化	011	adenosine	腺苷
生化	012	adenylate cyclase	腺苷酸环化酶
生化	013	adrenal cortex	肾上皮质

分类	编码	真题原词	真题背景精确注释
生化	014	adrenal gland	肾上腺
生化	015	adrenaline	肾上腺素
生化	016	adrenergic	肾上腺素的
生化	017	aerobic	需氧生物的
生化	018	agarose	琼酯糖
生化	019	agent	剂
生化	020	aldehyde	醛,乙醛
生化	021	aldosterone	醛固酮
生化	022	alkaloid	生物碱
生化	023	amino	氨基的
生化	024	amino acid	氨基酸
生化	025	ammonia	氨
生化	026	analogous	同功的
生化	027	anneal	核酸分解
生化	028	autonomous	独立存在的
生化	029	bioactive	生物活性的
生化	030	biocatalyst	生物催化剂
生化	031	biodegradable	可生物降解的
生化	032	bioluminescence	生物发光
生化	033	biomass	生物团
生化	034	caffeine	咖啡因
生化	035	carbohydrate	碳水化合物
生化	036	catalyst	催化剂
生化	037	cell	细胞
生化	038	cellulase	纤维素酶
生化	039	cellulose	纤维素
生化	040	centriole	细胞中心粒
生化	041	chelate	螯合物
生化	042	chimaeric	嵌合体
生化	043	cholesterol	胆固醇
生化	044	cline	地域变异
生化	045	collagen	胶原蛋白
生化	046	colony	集群
生化	047	complex	染色体组
生化	048	compound	化合物
生化	049	conduction	传导
生化	050	conjugation	共轭效应
生化	051	couple	偶联
生化	052	crystalize	结晶
生化	053	cytokinin	细胞分裂素

分类	编码	真题原词	真题背景精确注释
生化	054	cytoplasm	细胞质
生化	055	cytosine	胞核嘧啶
生化	056	decompose	分解
生化	057	degradation	降解
生化	058	degrade	使降解
生化	059	determinant	因子
生化	060	diastase	淀粉酵素
生化	061	DNA	脱氧核糖核酸
生化	062	ecosystem	生态系统
生化	063	ectoderm	外胚层
生化	064	elastin	弹性蛋白
生化	065	electrophoresis	电泳
生化	066	endocrine	激素
生化	067	endorphin	内啡肽
生化	068	enzymatic	酶的
生化	069	enzyme	酶
生化	070	enzymology	酶学
生化	071	epitope	抗原决定基
生化	072	erythropoietin	生成素
生化	073	esterase	酯酶
生化	074	ethanol	乙醇
生化	075	ethylene	乙烯
生化	076	fibrosis	纤维化
生化	077	fluoridation	氟化物
生化	078	gel	凝胶
生化	079	gelatinous	凝胶状的
生化	080	gene	基因
生化	081	genetic	基因的
生化	082	genetic engineering	遗传工程
生化	083	genome	基因组
生化	084	gibberellin	赤霉素
生化	085	glucose	葡萄糖
生化	086	glycerol	甘油
生化	087	glycogen	肝糖
生化	088	glycolysis	酵解作用
生化	089	glycosylation	糖基化
生化	090	growth stimulant	助长剂
生化	091	guanine	鸟嘌呤
生化	092	helix	螺旋结构
生化	093	hemoglobin	血红蛋白

分类	编码	真题原词	真题背景精确注释
生化	094	hemolymph	血淋巴
生化	095	heterozygote	杂合体
生化	096	heterozygous	杂合的
生化	097	histidine	组氨酸
生化	098	histocompatibility	组织相容性
生化	099	histone	组蛋白
生化	100	homeostatic	体内平衡的
生化	101	homogeneous	同种类的
生化	102	homozygote	纯合体
生化	103	hormonal	荷尔蒙的
生化	104	hormone	荷尔蒙
生化	105	hybrid	杂交种
生化	106	hybridoma	杂种细胞
生化	107	hydrogenase	氢化酶
生化	108	hydrolyze	水解
生化	109	hypoblast	内胚层
生化	110	incompatibility	不亲和性
生化	111	innate	遗传的
生化	112	insulin	胰岛素
生化	113	interbreed	使品种间杂交
生化	114	interferon	干扰素的总称
生化	115	intraspecies	种内的
生化	116	invertase	蔗糖酶
生化	117	isogenic	同基因的
生化	118	keratin	角蛋白
生化	119	lactic	乳的，乳汁的
生化	120	lactic acid	乳酸
生化	121	leucine	亮氨酸
生化	122	level	物质浓度
生化	123	lignin	木质素
生化	124	lipase	脂肪酶
生化	125	lipid	脂质
生化	126	liquefied	溶解的
生化	127	liqueur	液，汁
生化	128	living tissue	活组织
生化	129	low calorie	低热能
生化	130	low carbohydrate	低碳水化合物
生化	131	lysate	溶解产物
生化	132	lysine	赖氨酸
生化	133	lysis	细胞溶解

分类	编码	真题原词	真题背景精确注释
生化	134	machanism	机制
生化	135	macrophage	巨噬细胞
生化	136	meiosis	减数分裂
生化	137	membrane	细胞膜
生化	138	messenger	信使
生化	139	methylene	亚甲基
生化	140	methylmercury	甲基水银
生化	141	mitochondrial	线粒体的
生化	142	mitochondrion	线粒体
生化	143	mitosis	有丝分裂
生化	144	molecular	分子构成的
生化	145	molecular biology	分子生物学
生化	146	molecular probe	分子探针
生化	147	molecule	分子
生化	148	monoclonal	单细胞系的
生化	149	mutant	突变异种
生化	150	mutated	突变的
生化	151	mutation	变异
生化	152	neurotransmitter	神经传递素
生化	153	nitrogen	氮
生化	154	nitrogen fixation	固氮法
生化	155	nitrogenase	固氮酶
生化	156	nitrogen fixer	固氮菌
生化	157	nucleic	核素的
生化	158	nucleotide	核苷酸
生化	159	nylon	尼龙
生化	160	organism	细胞器
生化	161	osmotic	渗透的
生化	162	oxidase	氧化酶
生化	163	oxidative	氧化的
生化	164	phenol	苯酚
生化	165	phenylalanine	苯基丙氨酸
生化	166	phosphate uptake	磷酸盐摄入
生化	167	phosphodiesterase	磷酸二酯酶
生化	168	phosphorous	磷的
生化	169	phthalate	酞酸盐
生化	170	pigment	色素
生化	171	pigmentation	色素沉着
生化	172	plasma	原生质
生化	173	plasma cell	浆细胞

分类	编码	真题原词	真题背景精确注释
生化	174	plasmid	质粒
生化	175	pleiotropic	多向性的
生化	176	pleiotropy	基因多效性
生化	177	polyclonal	多细胞系的
生化	178	polymerase	聚合酶
生化	179	polymorph	多晶形物
生化	180	polymorphism	多态性
生化	181	polypeptide	多肽
生化	182	potassium	钾
生化	183	precursor	产物母体
生化	184	preservative	防腐剂
生化	185	prick	尖形物
生化	186	projection	突出
生化	187	prokaryotic	原核的
生化	188	proliferate	增生
生化	189	protein	蛋白质
生化	190	protein coat	蛋白外壳
生化	191	protoplast	原生质体
生化	192	psychrophilic	嗜冷性的
生化	193	puromycin	嘌呤霉素
生化	194	qualitative	定性的
生化	195	receptor	感受器
生化	196	recession	退化
生化	197	recessive	隐性的
生化	198	recombinant	重组细胞
生化	199	red blood cell	红细胞
生化	200	reflex	反射的
生化	201	regulate	调整
生化	202	regulatory	调整的
生化	203	renin	高血压蛋白原酶
生化	204	resistor	电阻
生化	205	respiration	呼吸作用
生化	206	reticular	网状的
生化	207	ribosome	核糖体
生化	208	RNA	核糖核酸
生化	209	sebum	皮脂
生化	210	secrete	分泌
生化	211	sediment	沉淀物
生化	212	sequence	序列
生化	213	serotonin	血清素

分类	编码	真题原词	真题背景精确注释
生化	214	serum	血液
生化	215	sickle cell	镰形血球
生化	216	solution	溶液
生化	217	somatic	体细胞的
生化	218	somatotropin	生长激素
生化	219	stain	染色
生化	220	subcellular	亚细胞的
生化	221	substrate	酶作用物
生化	222	sucrose	蔗糖
生化	223	sulfide	硫化物
生化	224	sulfur	硫磺
生化	225	symbiont	共生有机体
生化	226	symbiotic	共生的
生化	227	synthesis	合成体
生化	228	synthesize	使合成
生化	229	tannin	单宁酸
生化	230	testosterone	睾丸素
生化	231	thermophilic	嗜热的
生化	232	thymine	胸腺嘧啶
生化	233	thyroid	甲状腺
生化	234	transcript	转录
生化	235	triglyceride	甘油三酸酯
生化	236	triphosphate	三磷酸盐
生化	237	tryptophan	色氨酸
生化	238	tyrosine	酪氨酸
生化	239	unicellular	单细胞的
生化	240	vacuole	液泡
生化	241	variable	变异的
生化	242	variant	变体
生化	243	variation	变异
生化	244	wall	细胞壁
生化	245	yogurt	酸乳酪
医学	001	abscission	切除
医学	002	acrophobia	恐高症
医学	003	ail	生病
医学	004	ailment	疾病
医学	005	albino	白化变种
医学	006	alimentary	营养的
医学	007	allergic	过敏的
医学	008	amnesia	健忘症

分类	编码	真题原词	真题背景精确注释
医学	009	amputate	截肢
医学	010	analgesic	镇痛剂
医学	011	anatomical	解剖学的
医学	012	anemia	贫血症
医学	013	anemic	贫血的
医学	014	anodyne	止痛药
医学	015	anorexia	厌食症
医学	016	antibiotic	抗生素
医学	017	antibody	抗体
医学	018	antidote	解毒药
医学	019	antihistamine	抗组胺剂
医学	020	apoplectic	中风的
医学	021	arthritis	关节炎
医学	022	asphyxiate	窒息而死
医学	023	asthma	哮喘症
医学	024	astringent	止血的
医学	025	balm	药膏
医学	026	blotch	红斑点
医学	027	canker	溃疡病
医学	028	carcinogen	致癌物
医学	029	cauterize	烧灼消毒
医学	030	clinical	临床的
医学	031	collapse	晕倒
医学	032	coma	昏迷状态
医学	033	comatose	昏迷的
医学	034	concussion	脑震荡
医学	035	contagious	传染的
医学	036	contagiousness	接触传染
医学	037	convalesce	康复
医学	038	convalescent	康复中的
医学	039	corpuscle	血球
医学	040	depressant	镇静剂
医学	041	derangement	精神错乱
医学	042	diabetes	糖尿病
医学	043	diagnose	诊断
医学	044	dietetics	营养学
医学	045	dipsomania	嗜酒症
医学	046	dissect	解剖
医学	047	dissection	解剖
医学	048	dose	剂量

分类	编码	真题原词	真题背景精确注释
医学	049	dyslexia	阅读障碍
医学	050	dyspeptic	消化不良的
医学	051	elixir	长生不老药
医学	052	epidemic	传染性的
医学	053	eviscerate	取出内脏
医学	054	febrile	发烧的
医学	055	fester	溃烂
医学	056	fracture	骨折
医学	057	frantic	狂乱的
医学	058	frenetic	发狂的
医学	059	fumigate	以烟熏消毒
医学	060	fungicide	杀真菌剂
医学	061	gastritis	胃炎
医学	062	geriatrics	老年病学
医学	063	gerontology	老人病学
医学	064	hamstring	使残废
医学	065	heal	治愈
医学	066	hemophilia	血友病
医学	067	hemorrhage	出血
医学	068	hemostat	止血剂
医学	069	hepatitis	肝炎
医学	070	hydrophobia	恐水病
医学	071	hygiene	卫生学
医学	072	hypertension	高血压
医学	073	hypnotic	催眠药
医学	074	hypodermic	皮下注射的
医学	075	hysteria	歇斯底里症
医学	076	immune	免疫的
医学	077	immunity	免疫
医学	078	immunize	使免疫
医学	079	infection	感染
医学	080	infectious	感染的
医学	081	inflamed	发炎的
医学	082	injection	注射
医学	083	inoculate	预防注射
医学	084	insane	疯狂的
医学	085	insanity	精神错乱
医学	086	insomnia	失眠症
医学	087	irremediable	无法治愈的
医学	088	lancet	手术刀

分类	编码	真题原词	真题背景精确注释
医学	089	laxative	轻泻药
医学	090	lesion	伤口
医学	091	ligature	止血线
医学	092	mania	癫狂
医学	093	measly	患麻疹的
医学	094	medicate	用药医治
医学	095	mesmerism	催眠术
医学	096	monomania	偏狂症
医学	097	morbid	病态的
医学	098	myopia	近视
医学	099	myopic	近视眼的
医学	100	narcotic	催眠药
医学	101	nephritis	肾炎
医学	102	neurology	神经学
医学	103	nostrum	万灵丹
医学	104	nurture	营养物
医学	105	nutrient	滋养物质
医学	106	opiate	鸦片制剂
医学	107	opium	鸦片
医学	108	orthodontics	畸齿矫正学
医学	109	overdose	过度剂量
医学	110	painkiller	止痛药
医学	111	palliative	缓释剂
医学	112	pallid	没血色的
医学	113	palpate	接触
医学	114	palpitation	心悸
医学	115	panacea	万灵药
医学	116	paranoia	偏执狂
医学	117	paranoid	偏执狂的
医学	118	parturition	分娩
医学	119	pasteurize	以高热杀菌
医学	120	pathogen	病原体
医学	121	pathology	病理学
医学	122	pediatrics	小儿科
医学	123	penicillin	青霉素
医学	124	pharmaceutical	制药的
医学	125	phobia	恐惧症
医学	126	placebo	安慰剂
医学	127	plague	瘟疫
医学	128	podiatrist	足医

分类	编码	真题原词	真题背景精确注释
医学	129	poultice	膏状药
医学	130	prescribe	开处方
医学	131	prescription	处方
医学	132	purgative	泻药
医学	133	quarantine	隔离检疫期
医学	134	rabid	患狂犬病的
医学	135	rabies	狂犬病
医学	136	reagent	试剂
医学	137	recuperate	恢复
医学	138	relapse	旧病复发
医学	139	salubrious	有益健康的
医学	140	salutary	有益的
医学	141	salve	药膏
医学	142	sanatorium	疗养院
医学	143	scalpel	解剖刀
医学	144	sedative	镇静的
医学	145	septic	受感染的
医学	146	soporific	安眠药
医学	147	spasmodic	痉挛的
医学	148	sterilization	消毒
医学	149	sterilize	杀菌
医学	150	stethoscope	听诊器
医学	151	stutter	口吃
医学	152	suffocate	窒息而死
医学	153	syndrome	综合症状
医学	154	syringe	注射器
医学	155	therapeutic	治病的
医学	156	tourniquet	止血带
医学	157	transfuse	输血
医学	158	ulcer	溃疡
医学	159	ulcerate	溃烂
医学	160	unguent	药膏
医学	161	vaccinate	接种疫苗
医学	162	vaccination	接种疫苗
医学	163	vaccine	疫苗
医学	164	vivisection	活体解剖
医学	165	vomit	呕吐
医学	166	wan	病态的
医学	167	wanderlust	漫游癖
医学	168	wholesome	促进健康的

分类	编码	真题原词	真题背景精确注释
植物	001	acarpous	不结果实的
植物	002	acorn	橡实
植物	003	agrarian	土地的
植物	004	agronomy	农艺学
植物	005	almond	杏树
植物	006	arboreal	树木的
植物	007	arboretum	植物园
植物	008	aspen	白杨
植物	009	atrophy	萎缩
植物	010	bark	树皮
植物	011	barren	贫瘠的
植物	012	beet	甜菜
植物	013	blight	枯萎
植物	014	blossom	树木开花
植物	015	botany	植物学
植物	016	bough	树干
植物	017	bouquet	花束
植物	018	bud	芽
植物	019	bulb	球茎
植物	020	cactus	仙人掌
植物	021	capsule	荚
植物	022	cereal	谷类食品
植物	023	chaff	谷物的皮壳
植物	024	chrysanthemum	菊
植物	025	cob	玉米棒子
植物	026	cone	松果
植物	027	conifer	针叶树
植物	028	core	果心
植物	029	cultivate	种植
植物	030	cultivated	耕种的
植物	031	cypress	柏树
植物	032	defoliate	落叶
植物	033	fallow	闲置土地
植物	034	fatten	施肥
植物	035	fern	蕨
植物	036	fertile	肥沃的
植物	037	fertilize	施肥
植物	038	fertilizer	肥料
植物	039	fig	无花果
植物	040	flaggy	枯萎的

分类	编码	真题原词	真题背景精确注释
植物	041	flax	亚麻
植物	042	flora	植物群
植物	043	florescence	繁花时期
植物	044	fodder	草料
植物	045	foliage	叶子
植物	046	forage	粮草
植物	047	forestry	森林学
植物	048	frond	棕榈复叶
植物	049	fungi	菌类
植物	050	gardenia	栀子花
植物	051	genus	(动植物的)属
植物	052	germinate	发芽
植物	053	ginger	姜
植物	054	graft	嫁接
植物	055	grain	谷类植物
植物	056	granary	粮仓
植物	057	graze	放牧
植物	058	greenhouse	花房；温室
植物	059	grove	小树林
植物	060	gum	树胶
植物	061	heliotrope	向阳植物
植物	062	herbaceous	草本植物的
植物	063	horticulture	园艺学
植物	064	hull	荚
植物	065	humus	腐殖质
植物	066	husbandry	耕种
植物	067	husk	外壳
植物	068	irrigate	灌溉
植物	069	kernel	果仁
植物	070	loam	沃土
植物	071	maize	玉米
植物	072	manure	粪肥
植物	073	maple	枫树
植物	074	melon	甜瓜
植物	075	menthol	薄荷醇
植物	076	mushroom	蘑菇
植物	077	needle	松针
植物	078	nutrient	营养物质
植物	079	oak	橡树
植物	080	oatmeal	燕麦片

分类	编码	真题原词	真题背景精确注释
植物	081	orchard	果园
植物	082	pecan	山核桃
植物	083	petal	花瓣
植物	084	pine	松树
植物	085	plough	犁耕
植物	086	pod	豆荚
植物	087	pollen	花粉
植物	088	pollinate	授粉
植物	089	prairie	草地
植物	090	provender	粮秣
植物	091	raisin	葡萄干
植物	092	reap	收获
植物	093	reed	芦苇
植物	094	rhubarb	黄芪
植物	095	sap	树液
植物	096	sapling	树苗
植物	097	scion	嫩芽
植物	098	scrub	矮树丛
植物	099	scythe	大镰刀
植物	100	seaweed	海藻
植物	101	seedling	幼苗
植物	102	sere	凋萎的
植物	103	shrivel	枯萎
植物	104	shrub	灌木
植物	105	sod	草地
植物	106	spackle	填泥料
植物	107	spear	嫩叶
植物	108	sprig	嫩枝
植物	109	sprout	萌芽
植物	110	spruce	云杉
植物	111	stem	叶柄
植物	112	sterile	无细菌的
植物	113	tare	莠草
植物	114	terrace	梯田
植物	115	thicket	灌木丛
植物	116	thresh	脱粒
植物	117	tiller	耕种
植物	118	timber	木材
植物	119	trunk	树干
植物	120	tuber	球根

分类	编码	真题原词	真题背景精确注释
植物	121	twig	小枝
植物	122	vanilla	香草
植物	123	violet	紫罗兰
植物	124	weed	野草
植物	125	whorl	轮生体
植物	126	willow	柳树
植物	127	wilt	凋谢
植物	128	windfall	风吹落的果实
植物	129	wither	凋零
植物	130	wizen	凋谢的
植物	131	xerophyte	旱生植物

Note

第三节 人文艺术类

人文艺术类的文章历来是GRE阅读的压轴大戏，也是考生们最害怕的文章类型之一。我们在之前的章节中论述过，英文阅读的方向分为文艺型文章和学术型文章：学术型文章讲究论述性、逻辑性，而文艺类文章强调通过语言的修饰给读者呈递一幅美好的画面。在GRE的人文艺术类文章中，可谓是二者特点兼而有之：段落细节中晦涩复杂而又优雅曼妙的语句、文章行文结构上规范严谨的思维模式和逻辑关系，二者交织错落形成了GRE文章中一朵又一朵的"奇葩"。

在人文艺术类的文章中，尤其是对于某著名小说的评价文章中，最容易出现的题目就是细节题，而细节题考查的内容定位往往让人头晕眼花。究其原因，在于考生在阅读的过程中没有搞清楚文中出现过的人物和事件到底是小说中的人物事件，还是评论中的人物。所以，在解决人文类型的文章时，考生一定要注意"读关系、审细节、定准位"，所谓"关系"既包括人物与人物间的关系、事件与事件间的关系，也包括作者与人物间的关系，要注重分清楚层面，才好真正做到"定准位"。比如在GRE考试中曾经有一篇"倾国倾城"的难文《普鲁斯特·追忆我的似水流年》就完美地把各种人物及事件之间的关系复杂地呈现在考生眼前，该文的作者就是一位研究普鲁斯特的学者，更何况又在文中增加了大量的插叙，还有角色转换的写法，令考生读起来如云里雾里。

话说回来，不管人文艺术类的文章到底多么令人眼花缭乱，其根本的症结在于中国同学的英文硬实力。相较于之前的两种"物理科学类"和"生命科学类"来说，人文艺术类的GRE文章中最容易出现诸多令考生瞠目不识的英文单词。如果说前面两类的难点在于：句子意思晦涩，即使翻译成中文也很难理解；那么人文艺术类的难点就在于：眼睁睁看着的句子就是读不懂。这种难点不光体现在GRE阅读里人文艺术类的文章中，在填空里也有浩如烟波的晦涩难懂的长句子，像填空中非常经典的一句话：

"十七世纪的东方园林并非那么令人心旷神怡，它们设计的初衷其实是为了唤起人们心中那一丝令人愉悦的忧伤，这种感觉来源于自然之美与人间荣耀如白驹过隙般的短暂。"

抑或像阅读中曾经出现过这样的句子：**"种族和宗教此二者构成了一种共生共栖的状态：宗教情感往往应用在种族问题之中；种族问题也经常被投射到形而上的玄学层面上讨论。瓦格纳发现这一特性在黑人圣歌当中表现得最为明显：对于今生自由的渴望和对于来世的涅槃重生的希望，二者交织缠绕、不可分割。"**

至此，诸如像"GRE只靠考试技巧即可"、"GRE文章都是靠提示词就能读懂"等等这样令人贻笑大方的说法可以休矣。没有足够深厚的英文功底的同学是不可能在GRE考试中取得好成绩的，这也是为何GRE作为美国研究生院入学最重要的测试这杆大旗屹立70余年不倒的根本原因所在。

那么，面对这种类型的文章，我们首先要搞清楚自己的优势和劣势分别是什么。相对来说我们的优势在于分析信息的能力：因为文艺类的文章(尤其是短文章)不可能每句话之间都存在着那么精炼的逻辑关系，它往往连着两三句话都在做叙述，于是对于我们来说文章就很容易地被分成了若干个组成部分，这样对于分析过程也能有帮助。当然我们的劣势也很明显，就是语言层面的问题，能否顺利地把句子意思读懂、能否正确地理解某些单句甚至是段落的意思，都将决定着我们是否能把文章搞定。对于这种文艺型文章的题目，一般来说倒不会太难，而且为了追求整体文章的平衡性，文艺型文章的题目大都比较容易找到原文中的对应点，以帮助我们解题。

Exercise 5

《玛丽·巴顿》书评

Mary Barton, particularly in its early chapters, is a moving response to the suffering of the industrial worker in the England of the 1840's. What is most impressive about the book is the intense and painstaking effort made by the author, Elizabeth Gaskell, to convey the experience of everyday life in working-class homes. Her method is partly documentary in nature: the novel includes such features as a carefully annotated reproduction of dialect, the exact details of food prices in an account of a tea party, an itemized description of the furniture of the Bartons' living room, and a transcription （a recording（as on magnetic tape）made especially for use in radio broadcasting）（again annotated）of the ballad "The Oldham Weaver." The interest of this record is considerable, even though the method has a slightly distancing effect.

As a member of the middle class, Gaskell could hardly help approaching working-class life as an outside observer and a reporter, and the reader of the novel is always conscious of this fact. But there is genuine imaginative re-creation in her accounts of the walk in Green Heys Fields, of tea at the Bartons' house, and of John Barton and his friend's discovery of the starving family in the cellar in the chapter "Poverty and Death." Indeed, for a similarly convincing re-creation of such families' emotions and responses (which are more crucial than the material details on which the mere reporter is apt to concentrate), the English novel had to wait 60 years for the early writing of D. H. Lawrence. If Gaskell never quite conveys the sense of full participation that would completely authenticate this aspect of *Mary Barton*, she still brings to these scenes an intuitive recognition of feelings that has its own sufficient conviction.

The chapter "Old Alice's History" brilliantly dramatizes the situation of that early generation of workers brought from the villages and the countryside to the urban industrial centers. The account of Job Legh, the weaver and naturalist who is devoted to the study of biology, vividly embodies one kind of response to an urban industrial environment: an affinity for living things that hardens, by its very contrast with its environment, into a kind of crankiness. The early chapters—about factory workers walking out in spring into Green Heys Fields; about Alice Wilson, remembering in her cellar the twig-gathering for brooms in the native village that she will never again see; about Job Legh, intent on his impaled insects—capture the characteristic responses of a generation to the new and crushing experience of industrialism. The other early chapters eloquently portray the development of the instinctive cooperation with each other that was already becoming an important tradition among workers.

Sample Multiple-choice Questions — Select One Answer Choice

1. Which of the following best describes the author's attitude toward Gaskell's use of the method of documentary record in *Mary Barton*?

   (A) Uncritical enthusiasm

   (B) Unresolved ambivalence

   (C) Qualified approval

   (D) Resigned acceptance

   (E) Mild irritation

Sample Multiple-choice Questions — Select One Answer Choice

2. According to the passage, *Mary Barton* and the early novels of D. H. Lawrence share which of the following?

   (A) Depiction of the feelings of working-class families

   (B) Documentary objectivity about working-class circumstances

   (C) Richly detailed description of working-class adjustment to urban life

   (D) Imaginatively structured plots about working-class characters

   (E) Experimental prose style based on working-class dialect

Sample Multiple-choice Questions — Select One Answer Choice

3. Which of the following is most closely analogous to Job Legh in *Mary Barton*, as that character is described in the passage?

   (A) An entomologist who collected butterflies as a child

   (B) A small-town attorney whose hobby is nature photography

   (C) A young man who leaves his family's dairy farm to start his own business

   (D) A city dweller who raises exotic plants on the roof of his apartment building

   (E) A union organizer who works in a textile mill under dangerous conditions

Sample Multiple-choice Questions — Select One Answer Choice

4. It can be inferred from examples given in the last paragraph of the passage that which of the following was part of "the new and crushing experience of industrialism" (line 26) for many members of the English working class in the nineteenth century?

   (A) Extortionate food prices

   (B) Geographical displacement

(C) Hazardous working conditions

(D) Alienation from fellow workers

(E) Dissolution of family ties

Sample Multiple-choice Questions — Select One Answer Choice

5. It can be inferred that the author of the passage believes that *Mary Barton* might have been an even better novel if Gaskell had

(A) concentrated on the emotions of a single character

(B) made no attempt to re-create experiences of which she had no firsthand knowledge

(C) made no attempt to reproduce working-class dialects

(D) grown up in an industrial city

(E) managed to transcend her position as an outsider

Sample Multiple-choice Questions — Select One Answer Choice

6. Which of the following phrases could best be substituted for the phrase "this aspect of *Mary Barton*" in line 17 without changing the meaning of the passage as a whole?

(A) the material details in an urban working-class environment

(B) the influence of *Mary Barton* on lawrence's early work

(C) the place of *Mary Barton* in the development of the English novel

(D) the extent of the poverty and physical suffering among England's industrial workers in the 1840's

(E) the portrayal of the particular feelings and responses of working-class characters

Sample Multiple-choice Questions — Select One Answer Choice

7. The author of the passage describes *Mary Barton* as each of the following EXCEPT:

(A) insightful

(B) meticulous

(C) vivid

(D) poignant

(E) lyrical

译文及解析

第一段

第一句：《玛丽·巴顿》这本书——尤其在前几章中——可以说是对19世纪40年代英格兰产业工人悲惨经历的一种动人的反映。

（第一句话是作者发表的评价，作为结论。）

第二句：此书中令人印象最深刻的就是，作者伊丽莎白·盖斯凯尔颇费苦心地为读者描绘出工人阶级家庭的日常生活经历。

第三句：其写作中带有一定的写实手法：仔细注音的方言、一个对茶会的描述当中精确的食品价格、对巴顿卧室中家具的分类描述，以及对民歌“The Oldham Weaver”的注音文字记录。

第四句：即使作者这样的写作手法会有一种疏远感，但这些记录仍十分有趣。

（第二句到第四句都是对于第一句结论的具体描述，是细节。）

第二段

第一句：作为中产阶级，盖斯凯尔很难不以一个局外人的角度来看工人阶级。对于这一点，小说的读者也明显感觉到了。

第二句：但是书中也的确有一些奇思妙想的再塑造，比如：在Green Heys田野间漫步、在巴顿家中的茶会，以及在“贫困与死亡”章节中约翰·巴顿和他朋友在一个地下室中发现了饥寒交迫的一家人，等等。

（第二句与第一句形成对比，其目的在于突出第二句的内容，说明小说有构思奇妙的神来之笔，60年内无人能出其右。）

第三句：的确，英国小说界苦盼了60年之久才等到了劳伦斯的早期作品——其关于家庭情感与反应的再塑造的影响力堪比《玛丽·巴顿》(这些塑造比一个纯粹的观察者醉心其中的物质细节描写要更重要)。

（第三句是对第二句的补充描述，目的在于突出小说的重要意义。）

第四句：哪怕说盖斯凯尔从未以真正地传达出一种全身心的参与感的方式使得《玛丽·巴顿》在“再塑造”方面得以真实化的话，那么她仍然在这些“再塑造”的场景中注入了情感的直觉性认知，并有自身充分的说服力。

（第四句是对第二句中“再塑造”评价颇高的一个原因。）

第三段

第一句：“老爱丽丝的故事”那章活灵活现地描绘了第一代从乡村移往城市的工人们的境遇。

第二句：乔布·利，一个纺织工人，同时也是一个致力于研究生物的自然主义者，文中对于这个人物的生动描写表达了作者对于城市工业化的回应：对生活的热望与环境反差甚大，结果(他的爱好)发展成了一种怪癖。

（第二句是第一句的细节。）

第三句：书的前几个章节抓住了这一代人对于工业化的全新的、毁灭性的感受和反应：工人们在春天里漫步于Green Heys田野；爱丽丝在地下室中回想在故乡收集树枝编扫帚的情景，而故乡却是再也回不去的家；还有乔布·利，一心想着他的那些孤苦无援的昆虫。

（第三句是对第一、二句的总结。）

第四句：在其他较前的章节中，作者描绘了现在已经成为工人之间重要传统的、发乎于本能的互相合作的发展过程。

（第四句的内容和前三句是平行关系，作为第二段最后一句话的细节说明。）

逻辑图

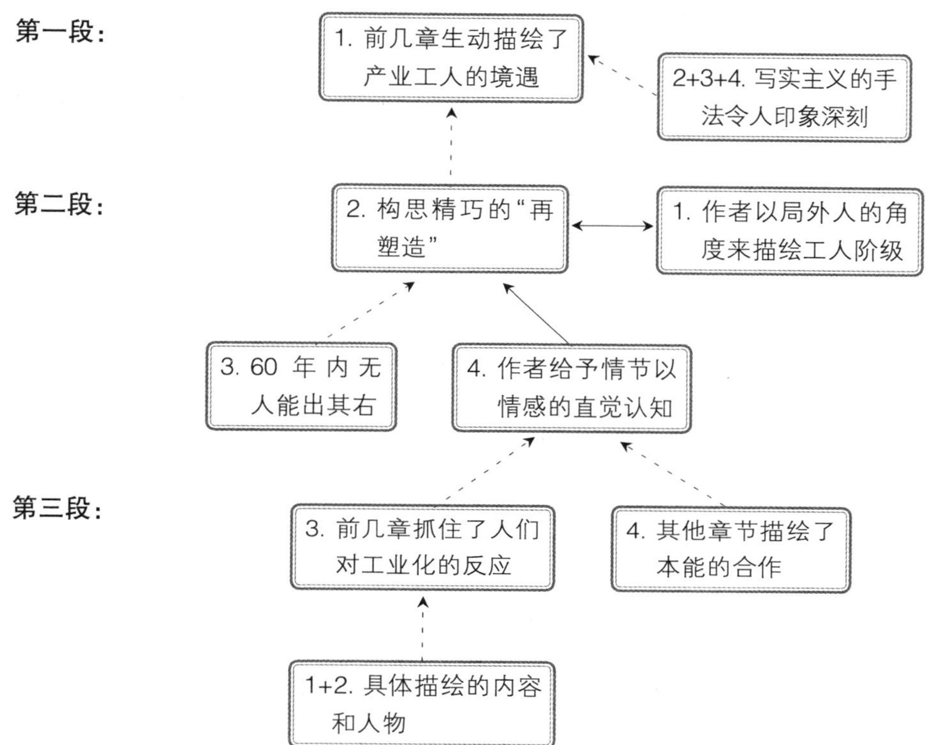
第一段：
1. 前几章生动描绘了产业工人的境遇
2+3+4. 写实主义的手法令人印象深刻
第二段：
2. 构思精巧的“再塑造”
1. 作者以局外人的角度来描绘工人阶级
3. 60 年内无人能出其右
4. 作者给予情节以情感的直觉认知
第三段：
3. 前几章抓住了人们对工业化的反应
4. 其他章节描绘了本能的合作
1+2. 具体描绘的内容和人物

题目及解析

1. Which of the following best describes the author's attitude toward Gaskell's use of the method of documentary record in *Mary Barton*?

   (A) Uncritical enthusiasm

   (B) Unresolved ambivalence

   (C) Qualified approval

   (D) Resigned acceptance

   (E) Mild irritation

解析

这是一道态度题，问“作者对于盖斯凯尔在小说中运用的纪实写作手法是什么态度？”这道题自然定位到第一段的第四句，作者在原文中采取的是混合态度，认为这样的写作手法“尽管疏远了读者与情节的距离，但还是十分有趣的”，因此是个“大正小负”的态度。

（A）热情称赞毫无批评

（B）模棱两可难以解决

（C）有保留的赞同

（D）无可奈何的接受

（E）愠怒

本题正确答案应该是选项C，其他几个都不合适。

2. According to the passage, *Mary Barton* and the early novels of D. H. Lawrence share which of the following?

（A）Depiction of the feelings of working-class families

（B）Documentary objectivity about working-class circumstances

（C）Richly detailed description of working-class adjustment to urban life

（D）Imaginatively structured plots about working-class characters

（E）Experimental prose style based on working-class dialect

解析

本题题干不难，问"《玛丽·巴顿》和劳伦斯早期作品都有什么样的特征？"这道题肯定是利用劳伦斯去定位，即第二段的第三句。文中明确说到"for a similarly convincing re-creation of such families' emotions and responses"，在对于家庭情感与反应的再塑造上，只有劳伦斯的早期作品堪与《玛丽·巴顿》匹敌，说明此二者一定是在"情感的再塑造"上具有相同点。

（A）对于工人阶级家庭情感的描绘

（B）关于工人阶级境况的客观纪实

（C）关于工人阶级适应城市生活的大量细节描述

（D）关于工人阶级性格的异想天开的情节结构

（E）基于工人阶级方言的试验性散文结构

很明显，这道题考查的相似点应该是"情感"，其他都不对，正确答案选A。

3. Which of the following is most closely analogous to Job Legh in *Mary Barton*, as that character is described in the passage?

（A）An entomologist who collected butterflies as a child

（B）A small-town attorney whose hobby is nature photography

（C）A young man who leaves his family's dairy farm to start his own business

（D）A city dweller who raises exotic plants on the roof of his apartment building

（E）A union organizer who works in a textile mill under dangerous conditions

解析

这是一道类比关系题，属于GRE阅读当中比较难做的题目类型，但是本题好在定位容易，而且Job Legh出场的次数也很少，故而不难总结他的特点。在第三段的第二句和第三句能够找到对于Job Legh的描述：由于环境反差太大，在城市中没有他想要的大自然环境，故而他对于生物的痴迷最终变成了怪癖。我们不妨总结为“由于环境反差大造成的走火入魔”。

（A）一个昆虫学家从小就收集蝴蝶

（B）一个小镇上的律师喜好自然类摄影

（C）一个年轻人离开自家的乳制品农场去开拓自己的事业

（D）一个城市居民在自己公寓的楼顶上种植珍奇植物

（E）一个联盟组织者在条件相对危险的纺织厂工作

本题答案应该选D。由于那个居民没有办法在应该欣赏植物的大自然环境里去欣赏那些珍奇植物，所以只得将这些植物移到本不该属于它们的地方，这是一种“不正常的现象”。

4. It can be inferred from examples given in the last paragraph of the passage that which of the following was part of “the new and crushing experience of industrialism”（line 26）for many members of the English working class in the nineteenth century?

（A）Extortionate food prices

（B）Geographical displacement

（C）Hazardous working conditions

（D）Alienation from fellow workers

（E）Dissolution of family ties

解析

本题问到以下哪个选项能够作为“工人对于工业化的全新的、毁灭性的反应”的表现之一？本题可定位到第三段的第三句话。而本题的正确答案，只要符合第三句话中插入语部分的例子就可以了。

（A）食物价格高得离谱

（B）背井离乡

（C）危险的工作条件

（D）与其他工人的疏离

（E）家庭关系的破碎

第三段的第三句话当中有三个例子，其中第二个“爱丽丝的背井离乡”就正好符合B选项的内容。而其他几个选项在原句中没有得到体现，也无法推断出来。

5. It can be inferred that the author of the passage believes that *Mary Barton* might have been an even better novel if Gaskell had

(A) concentrated on the emotions of a single character

(B) made no attempt to re-create experiences of which she had no firsthand knowledge

(C) made no attempt to reproduce working-class dialects

(D) grown up in an industrial city

(E) managed to transcend her position as an outsider

解析

这又是一道推断题，我们把它称之为正改善题目，问"盖斯凯尔如何做就可以让《玛丽·巴顿》这部小说变得更好?"这种正改善题目的解决方案就是把作者对盖斯凯尔负评价的地方找出来，再予以取反。本文对盖斯凯尔负评价的地方只有一处，就是第二段的第一句话："作为中产阶级，盖斯凯尔很难不以一个局外人的角度来看工人阶级"。因此，本题的答案应该围绕盖斯凯尔的阶级身份展开，而不是其他的因素。

(A) 只着力描述一个人物角色的情感
(A错。这个和盖斯凯尔描绘了几个角色没有关系。)

(B) 对于那些没有第一手信息的事物不做"再塑造"的尝试
(B也不对。如果这样的话，这个小说的长处就没有了。)

(C) 不对工人阶级的方言进行再塑造
(C也错。本题和方言没关系。)

(D) 成长于工业化的城市
(D是迷惑选项。盖斯凯尔的身份问题并未得到解决。)

(E) 能够改变她作为一个局外人的身份
(E是本题的正确答案。只要她不以一个"outside observer and a reporter"的角色进行创作。)

6. Which of the following phrases could best be substituted for the phrase "this aspect of *Mary Barton*" in line 17 without changing the meaning of the passage as a whole?

(A) the material details in an urban working-class environment

(B) the influence of *Mary Barton* on lawrence's early work

(C) the place of *Mary Barton* in the development of the English novel

(D) the extent of the poverty and physical suffering among England's industrial workers in the 1840's

(E) the portrayal of the particular feelings and responses of working-class characters

解析

本题问"以下哪个选项能够在不改变原文意思的情况下替换 'this aspect of *Mary Barton*'?"很明显这道题的考点在于准确理解"this aspect"指代的内容是什么。这句话可定位在第二段的第四句话，既然原文用"this aspect"进行指代，说明这个内容在上一句话中已经有所体现，即让盖斯凯尔和劳伦斯相提并论的他们关于“工人阶级对于工业化的情感以及反应”的表现。

（A）工人阶级在城市环境中的物质细节

（B）《玛丽·巴顿》对于劳伦斯早期作品的影响力

（C）《玛丽·巴顿》在英国小说发展史上的地位

（D）19世纪40年代英格兰工人阶级受穷受苦的程度

（E）关于工人阶级角色感受和反应的描写

本题的正确答案是E选项。

7. The author of the passage describes *Mary Barton* as each of the following EXCEPT:

（A）insightful

（B）meticulous

（C）vivid

（D）poignant

（E）lyrical

解析

这是一道态度题，问“作者对于《玛丽·巴顿》的描述中，没有下面哪种评价？”

（A）有见地的。

（这一点体现在作者从第一句话开始的行文过程中。）

（B）注重细节。

（这一点体现在第一段描写的“写实主义”中。）

（C）活灵活现。

（这一点体现在第三段中小说前几个章节的描写中。）

（D）深刻的。

（这一点也体现在第三段中小说前几个章节的描写中。）

（E）抒情的田园风格。

（这一点恰恰没有体现，《玛丽·巴顿》描述的是脱离了田园清新的尘世，工业化的滚滚浪潮淹没了风飘飘而吹衣的惬意。）

Exercise 6

威尔逊的《刘易斯传》

The sweep of narrative in A. N. Wilson's biography of C. S. Lewis is impressive and there is much that is acute and well argued. But much in this work is careless and unworthy of its author. Wilson, a novelist and an accomplished biographer, has failed to do what any writer on such a subject as Lewis ought to do, namely work out a coherent view of how the various literary works by the subject are to be described and commented on. Decisions have to be made on what to look at in detail and what to pass by with just a mention. Wilson has not thought this problem out. For instance, *Till We Have Faces*, Lewis' treatment of the Eros and Psyche story and one of his best-executed and most moving works, is merely mentioned by Wilson, though it illuminates Lewis' spiritual development, whereas Lewis' minor work *Pilgrim's Regress* is looked at in considerable detail.

Sample Multiple-choice Questions — Select One Answer Choice

1. The author of the passage implies that Wilson's examination of *Pilgrim's Regress*

   (A) is not as coherent as his treatment of *Till We Have Faces*

   (B) would have been more appropriate in a separate treatise because of the scope of *Pilgrim's Regress*

   (C) demonstrates how Wilson's narrow focus ignores the general themes of Lewis' works

   (D) was more extensive than warranted because of the relative unimportance of *Pilgrim's Regress*

   (E) was disproportionately long relative to the amount of effort Lewis devoted to writing *Pilgrim's Regress*

Sample Multiple-choice Questions — Select One Answer Choice

2. Which of the following best describes the organization of the passage?

   (A) An evaluation is made, and aspects of the evaluation are expanded on with supporting evidence.

   (B) A theory is proposed, and supporting examples are provided.

   (C) A position is examined, analyzed, and rejected.

   (D) A contradiction is described, then the points of contention are evaluated and reconciled.

   (E) Opposing views are presented and evaluated, then modifications are advocated.

Sample Multiple-choice Questions — Select One Answer Choice

3. Which of the following best describes the content of the passage?

   (A) A critique of A. N. Wilson as a biographer

   (B) An evaluation of the significance of several works by C. S. Lewis

   (C) An appraisal of a biography by A. N. Wilson

(D) A ranking of the elements necessary for a well-structured biography

(E) A proposal for evaluating the literary merits of the works of C. S. Lewis

译文及解析

第一句： 威尔逊在刘易斯传记中的情节叙述令人印象深刻，其中有很多内容是尖锐且论述有力的。
(第一句话表达了作者对于威尔逊作品的一个正评价。)

第二句： 但是，在此作品当中有很多的内容是漫不经心的，与作者的地位极不相称。
(第二句和第一句形成对比，对于威尔逊的作品给出负评价。)

第三句： 威尔逊，一个小说家与颇有造诣的传记作家，对于像刘易斯这样的题材却忽视了别的作家都该做的事情——即对于刘易斯的各种文学作品应该如何描述以及评价给出一个始终如一的意见。
(第三句论述为何对此作品有负评价，这是分论点，处于第二句的逻辑下一层。)

第四句： 作家必须要确定哪些内容是要详细说的，哪些只需一笔带过。
(第四句和第三句是平行并列关系，是第二句的另外一个分论点。)

第五句： 威尔逊就没有把这个问题想清楚。

第六句： 比如，刘易斯的*Till We Have Faces*中对于厄洛斯和塞姬之间爱情故事的处理使其成为刘易斯最为妙笔生花、触动人心的作品，阐明了刘易斯的精神发展过程，而(如此重要的作品)却被威尔逊简单一笔带过。但对于刘易斯的一个不起眼的作品*Pilgrim's Regress*，威尔逊却进行了详尽的细节分析。
(第五、六两句是第四句的例子，处于逻辑下一层。)

逻辑图

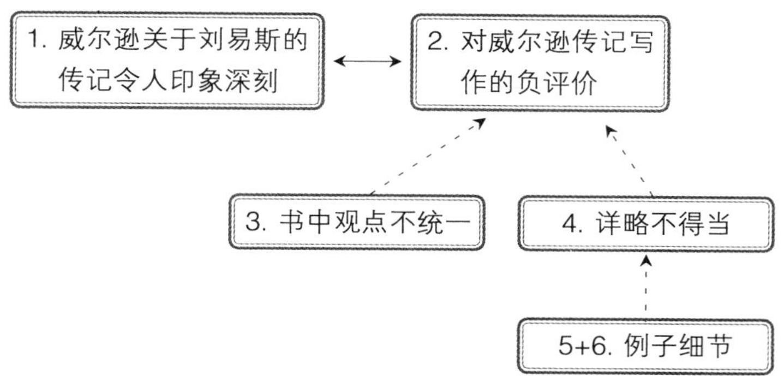

题目及解析

1. The author of the passage implies that Wilson's examination of *Pilgrim's Regress*

(A) is not as coherent as his treatment of *Till We Have Faces*

(B) would have been more appropriate in a separate treatise because of the scope of *Pilgrim's Regress*

(C) demonstrates how Wilson's narrow focus ignores the general themes of Lewis' works

(D) was more extensive than warranted because of the relative unimportance of *Pilgrim's Regress*

(E) was disproportionately long relative to the amount of effort Lewis devoted to writing *Pilgrim's Regress*

解析

这是一道推断题，问“关于威尔逊对*Pilgrim's Regress*的研究，作者暗示了什么？”本题首先定位到本文的最后一句话中，第六句话作为第四句话的逻辑下一层，为了说明威尔逊在做传记的时候没有注意好详略轻重的问题。原句中说“Lewis' minor work *Pilgrim's Regress* is looked at in considerable detail”（对于刘易斯的一个不起眼的作品*Pilgrim's Regress*，威尔逊却进行了详尽的细节分析），这说明作者认为这个作品本应该简略描述。

（A）其思路与对*Till We Have Faces*的处理不一致
（A错误。这里不牵涉思路是否一致的问题，而是哪个详哪个略的问题。）

（B）由于*Pilgrim's Regress*涉及的范围，适合单独进行专题论述
（这是文中没有出现的信息，没有证据不能选。）

（C）证明了威尔逊由于关注点狭窄而忽视了刘易斯作品的主题
（C也不正确。这个例子说的是详略问题，而非主题问题。）

（D）由于该作品相对次要所以该叙述显得冗长
（D是本题的正确答案。）

（E）相对于刘易斯为这部作品倾注的心力来说，威尔逊对它的冗长叙述显得不成比例
（E是一个迷惑性选项。大体来说和D有相近之处，但关于刘易斯对作品付出的effort，文中是没有提供给我们任何证据的。我们只知道这是个次要作品，并不知道这个作品是否包含了刘易斯的大量心血。）

2. Which of the following best describes the organization of the passage?

（A）An evaluation is made, and aspects of the evaluation are expanded on with supporting evidence.

（B）A theory is proposed, and supporting examples are provided.

（C）A position is examined, analyzed, and rejected.

（D）A contradiction is described, then the points of contention are evaluated and reconciled.

（E）Opposing views are presented and evaluated, then modifications are advocated.

解析

本题问“以下哪个选项最恰当地描述了本文的结构？”通过逻辑关系图我们不难看出，本文是在第二句中提出了论点，然后在后文进行两个方面的论述。

（A）作出一个评价，并给出例子来扩展该评价的各方面。
（A是本题的正确答案。这里的“evaluation”就是第二句话，“aspects of evaluation”就是第三句和第四句的内容。）

（B）提出一个理论，并对这个理论予以细节支持。
（B是一个迷惑选项。在本文中并没有出现所谓的“理论”。）

（C）某个观点被考察、分析，然后被推翻。
（C也错误。没有推翻观点的过程。）

（D）描述了一种矛盾，评价争论点并进行调解。
（D错在了调解争论点上，没有调解的过程。）

（E）表明并评价对立的观点，并提出改进意见。
（E不正确。作者没有改变自己的立场。）

3. Which of the following best describes the content of the passage?

（A）A critique of A. N. Wilson as a biographer

（B）An evaluation of the significance of several works by C. S. Lewis

（C）An appraisal of a biography by A. N. Wilson

（D）A ranking of the elements necessary for a well-structured biography

（E）A proposal for evaluating the literary merits of the works of C. S. Lewis

解析

本题问"以下哪个选项最好地概括了本文的内容？"

（A）对威尔逊作为一位传记作家的评价

（B）评价刘易斯的几部作品的重要性

（C）评价威尔逊写的一部他人传记

（D）把一部优秀传记的要素进行排序

（E）为评价刘易斯文学作品的价值提出建议

本文讨论的内容并不是刘易斯的作品，而是借助刘易斯的作品来评述威尔逊为其所著传记的功过是非，因而本题应该选C。

Reading Comprehension 22

Book review: *Van Gogh: The Life*
书评：《梵高的人生》

Vincent Van Gogh is an extraordinary artist about whom everything including brilliant work and tragic life seems to be an irresistible subject for art historians, biographers, and psychologists since his death from a gunshot wound in 1890. The Dutch painter of dazzling landscapes and searing portraits may be permanently engraved in the public imagination as a mad, self-destructive genius, but scholars continue to probe every last detail of his 37 years on Earth. And now, drawing heavily on the letters and the museum's resources, Steven Naifeh and Gregory White Smith have written the most extensive biography of Van Gogh. Reading his life story is like riding an endless roller coaster of delusional highs and lows.

文森特·梵高是位非凡的画家，自从1890年不幸去世以来，他的杰出画作、凄惨生平，一直都是众多艺术史家、传记作家乃至心理学家常常谈及的话题。或许，在世人眼里，这个擅长绚烂风景画和深刻肖像画的荷兰画家只不过是个疯狂的、自我毁灭的天才。但是，对专家学者而言，他这短短37年的一生，每一点蛛丝马迹都值得仔细探究。于是，主要通过参考书信以及博物馆的其他资料，史蒂文·奈非和格雷戈里·怀特·史密斯撰写了史上内容最为详实的梵高传记。品读梵高的人生，恰似坐上一辆无止境的过山车，充满了迷幻的跌宕起伏。

Desperate for the comfort of family and community, the rewards of an honorable career and, finally, a way of making art that would fulfill a sort of religious quest, he was so needy, demanding and unstable that he repeatedly crashed and burned. His journey from youthful sketches to the evanescent, almost electrically charged body of work produced in his final years is equally fraught with impossible dreams and self-doubt. But Naifeh and Smith reveal a keen intellect, an avid reader and a passionate observer of other artists' work who progressed from labored figure studies to inspired outbursts of creative energy. Far from an artistic flash in the pan, he pursued his calling with dogged determination against nearly insurmountable odds.

由于迫切渴求家庭和社会的温暖，渴求事业的成功，并希望将自己的宗教信仰完美地融合到艺术作品中去，梵高变得异常困窘动荡，总是周而复始地陷入崩溃状态。梵高早期的画作生机勃勃，但随着对梦想的狂溺和不断的自我怀疑，他最后几年的作品都如闪电般一挥而就。但是，在奈非和史密斯的传记里，梵高是一位热情的智者，他博览群书，不断汲取其他艺术家的精华，逐渐摆脱了辛苦的人体素描，迸发出惊人的创造力。他反对稍纵即逝的肤浅艺术，也强烈抵制那种无法逾越的境界。

No one knows what happened, either, on the afternoon when Van Gogh went out to paint near the town of Auvers, about 20 miles north of Paris, and was fatally

当然，也没人确切知道，当时梵高在距离巴黎北部大约20英里的奥弗小镇写生时，又是怎么一命呜呼的。按照一般的传言来说，梵高

wounded. The standard account is that he shot himself and staggered back to his lodgings, where he died two days later. But no weapon was found and a doctor's report suggests that the gun was fired from a distance. Picking up on a rumor that the artist was accidentally shot by young boys — told to art historian John Rewald by villagers in the 1930s — Naifeh and Smith theorize that Rene Secretan, a teenager who had harassed the artist, was the culprit. Although the authors argue their case in an appendix, admitting that they have no evidence, their treatment of the mystery seems to be as concerned with selling books as with getting at the truth.

是持枪自杀，然后一步一步捱回了住所，两天后断了气。但是，当时根本就没发现自杀的手枪；而医生的报告也显示子弹是从较远的距离射击的。20世纪30年代，附近的村民告诉艺术史家约翰·里瓦尔德说，是一帮小年青射杀了梵高。据此推论，奈非和史密斯认为凶手可能是勒内·塞克雷坦——这个少年以前骚扰过梵高。当然，作者也表明他们的推论并无真凭实据，但这种假设毋庸置疑会让这本著作大为畅销。

All their work considered, though, these are minor flaws in a sweepingly authoritative, astonishingly textured book.

如此而论，此书虽有微小瑕疵，仍不失为一部权威的、内容结构新颖的杰作。

Reading Comprehension 23

A History of Protest Songs
反抗音乐历史

What is protest music? In April 1966, Bob Dylan arrived in Stockholm as part of his controversial "electric" world tour, and called one of his new rock "n" roll compositions as the very height of protest music: "Very, very protesty. And, uh, one of the protestiest of all things I ever protested against in my protest years."

什么是反抗音乐？1966年4月，鲍勃·迪伦来到斯德哥尔摩举办他的颇有争议的"电吉它音乐"演唱会时，他说他新创作的一首摇滚乐是反抗音乐的高峰："我的音乐非常非常地反抗，是我的反抗音乐生涯中最具反抗精神的音乐。"

In "33 Revolutions Per Minute," its author Dorian Lynskey works with a more traditional definition: a protest song, he writes, is a song that "addresses a political issue in a way which aligns itself with the underdog." Specifically, Lynskey is concerned with the long tradition of radical songwriting and performance—mainly in folk music but also in jazz—that emerged

作家多里安·林斯基的新书《每分钟33次革命》定义"反抗音乐"时更加传统一些，他写道："反抗歌曲在解决政治问题时，会站在弱者的一边。"具体地说，他更加关心具有悠久传统、曲风激进的歌曲创作和表演。这些歌曲主要是民谣，也可以是爵士乐，大多来自20世纪30年代末和40年代期间美国共产主义

forcefully in the United States out of the Communist-affiliated Popular Front left during the late 1930s and the 1940s. Artists sympathetic to the civil rights and anti-Vietnam War movements revised the tradition in the 1950s and '60s, and thereafter it splintered into a plethora of angry anthemic styles, ranging from the black power hip-hop to the neo-punk. In 33 chapters, each one centered on a particular song and not only explored the gamut of this protest tradition, but also explicated the shifting historical context from the Great Depression until today, and bringing in dozens of other lesser-known artists and songs.

左翼的前沿音乐界。然后到了50或60年代艺术家们开始同情民权、反越战等运动，这对反抗歌曲的意义又有了重新修订。最后，这种歌曲又分裂成为大量具有现代流行音乐节奏、情绪暴躁的音乐，从动感的hip-hop黑人音乐到新朋克流派。本书共有33章，每一章关注一首歌曲，并探讨了这种颇具传统的反抗音乐的方方面面。不止这些，作者还介绍了反抗音乐从大萧条到现在的一系列历史背景的转换，并且提到了几十首不那么出名的音乐以及一些音乐家。

A British music critic and journalist, Lynskey ranges far as well as wide. Unlike most treatments of protest music, the book discusses songs and singers from outside the United States. If, as the political left claims, Western and especially American imperialism is largely responsible for the world's woes, the empire's cultural styles have powerfully shaped anti-imperial protest songs.

作者林斯基来自英伦三岛，是一位音乐评论人和记者，他涉猎繁杂，范围广。和其他评述反抗音乐的书籍不同的是，此书中还讨论了美国以外的反抗歌曲和演唱者。就像左翼政治人物宣称的那样，西方国家特别是"美帝国主义"要为这个"悲惨世界"负责，这个帝国的文化特质造就了反对它的反抗歌曲。

And his judgments about the music can be sharp and convincing. He persuasively discusses Neil Young's response to the Kent State killings in 1970, "Ohio," as a musical as well as a lyrical "masterpiece" of "fury, grief and topical precision." He then just as persuasively describes John Lennon and the Plastic Ono Band's excursion into left-wing topical song two years later, "Some Time in New York City," as the album "where the heyday of the 1960s protest song came to die."

林斯基对音乐的判断力还是非常精准独到和令人信服的。在书中，林斯基探讨了歌曲《俄亥俄州》，这首歌曲源于词曲创作者尼尔·扬对肯特州立大学枪击事件的有感而发，它不仅仅是音乐，还是一首"愤怒、悲痛、主题鲜明"的具有诗歌特质的优秀音乐作品。然后作者又讲述了约翰·伦农及其塑胶洋子乐队在涉足创作左翼主题歌曲两年后的一张专辑《有时在纽约城》，断送了60年代反抗歌曲的黄金时代。

But what does the difference derive from? The key point is that the former artist could write a political song as powerful as "Ohio" remains hard to fathom, and it does support the idea that, in art, simple outrage surpasses ideology. Lennon's failure, shows that attempting to compose political music can defeat even a supremely gifted songwriter. What explains his failure? According to

为什么这两个音乐人创作的反抗歌曲会有不同的结果呢？其原因在于，前者能写出像《俄亥俄州》这样力量强大的政治歌曲，至今为止还是让人有些难以理解，而且其在艺术创作上认为单纯的愤怒要好过抽象的思考。伦农的失败证明，即使再有才华的创作人试图创作政治歌曲也可能面临失败的危险。如何解释他的

Lynskey, Lennon's puzzling, half-baked politics, along with a more general political bewilderment after 1970, were at fault. Another simpler explanation is that as Lennon became more of a doctrinaire "smash the state" radical, his writing turned into puerile propaganda.

失败呢？作者林斯基解释道，伦农对政治的迷茫和不成熟心态，再加上1970年后整个社会政治环境的混乱状态是他失败的原因。另一个简单的理由是他变得太过激进、不切实际地空谈要“毁掉这个国家”，他的创作也成为了幼稚的宣传。

Reading Comprehension 24

Heirs to the Throne
《圣经》与美国的文学传承

Historically speaking, America and the Bible are almost twins. The first English colony in North America was established at Jamestown, Virginia in 1607; four years later, the Church of England completed its translation of the Authorized Version of the Bible, which, like the colony, bore the name of the reigning monarch. And it is safe to say that, for the next three hundred years at least, just about every English-speaking American grew up knowing the Bible better than any other book.

从历史角度分析，美国和《圣经》几乎是一对双胞胎。北美大陆的第一个英国殖民地于1607年在弗吉尼亚州詹姆斯敦建立。四年后，英国教会完成了（英国国王詹姆斯一世）钦定本《圣经》的翻译。和在美国的殖民地一样，这个版本的《圣经》同样以当时统治君王的名字命名。可以说，之后的300年间在每一个讲英语的美国人的成长过程中，没有哪一本书比钦定英译本《圣经》对他们的影响更深远。

The English settlers were Christians, of course, but it was the Old Testament, much more than the New, that spoke to them and their experience. The Bible, then, was not just the matrix of the American language, but the means of transmitting Jewish history, and the morality of the Hebrew Bible, to the American people.

讲英语的英国定居者当然是基督徒，但是《旧约》比《新约》更能让他们愿意阅读，更能让他们在经历上与书中内容感同身受。钦定英译本《圣经》不仅是美国语言文化的基石，它还把犹太人的历史和希伯来文《圣经》中的道德准则传递给美国人民。

As a leading scholar and translator of the Bible, who is also deeply knowledgeable about American literature, Robert Alter is ideally suited to study this complicated inheritance from the Bible. Alter's own translations of Scripture have inevitably been measured against the familiar cadences of the Bible. But in literary terms, Alter recognizes, the Bible—though it may be "often inaccurate"—is canonical and irreplaceable. In a sense, the

作为著名的《圣经》翻译和研究学者，罗伯特·奥尔特还精通美国文学，因此关于美国文学如何继承《圣经》传统的这个复杂课题的研究，由他来研究是非常适合的。奥尔特自己的《圣经》翻译版本免不了被拿来和人们所熟悉的经典《圣经》版本相比较。而奥尔特承认，钦定本《圣经》也许有一些“不太准确”的地方，但是在文学领域它却是最标准的，是不可替代

Bible has ceased to be a translation and become a second original. If you were more mystically inclined than Alter, you could consider it an example of Walter Benjamin's theory of translation, which holds that every true translation completes the meaning of a text as it appears in the mind of God.

的。从某种意义上说，钦定本《圣经》已经不再是翻译本，而是成为了另外一个原版。如果你比奥尔特更加笃信神秘主义，那么你也会像沃尔特·本杰明一样坚持这个翻译理论：真正的翻译是完整诠释每一个文本的内在含义，就像上帝脑中所想的那样。

At the core of *Pen of Iron*, Alter analzed the Bible's influence on three great American novels: *Moby-Dick*, *Absalom, Absalom!* and *Seize the Day*. In discussing these books, Alter shows that that influence cannot be measured strictly in allusions or verbal echoes. Three authors Melville, Faulkner, and Bellow do not simply use Biblical language, they think in Biblical categories—especially, Alter argues, when they are challenging the faith and morality that the Bible teaches.

在《铁笔》(*Pen of Iron*)一书的核心部分，作者罗伯特·奥尔特分析了《圣经》对美国三大著名小说的影响：《白鲸》(*Moby-Dick*)，《押沙龙，押沙龙！》(*Absalom, Absalom!*)和《勿失良辰》(*Seize the Day*)。奥尔特对这三本书分析道，《圣经》对这些文学作品的影响不能只用如何引用典故或词语来衡量。这三部作品的作者梅尔维尔、福克纳和贝洛不仅仅是简单使用圣经中的语言；他们的思想都浸润在《圣经》当中，有时甚至会挑战《圣经》当中所宣扬的信仰和道德规范。

Moby-Dick is a perfect case in point: Melville's novel is a riot of language, whose lavish rhetoric owes a great deal to Shakespeare and other seventeenth-century writers. But the elemental power and metaphysical scope of the novel are rooted in its complex response to the Bible. The irony is that Melville uses these Biblical tropes in constructing a book that is a kind of anti-Bible—a long refutation of the existence of God and the goodness of Creation. Alter's another subject, Faulkner, is also powerful prose stylists, but he is less directly indebted to the Bible. The style of *Absalom, Absalom!* with its nonce words, Latinisms, involved syntax, and general fanciness, is as unlike the plainness of the Bible as English can well be. Yet as Faulkner's title announces, the novel's plot is based on events from the life of King David. More, Faulkner builds the book around certain primal words that come straight from the King James Bible.

《白鲸》(*Moby-Dick*) 就是一个很好的例子：梅尔维尔小说的语言很繁复，其华丽修辞深受莎士比亚和十七世纪其他作家的影响。但是，小说中强大的力量和形而上学的视角来源于作家对《圣经》的复杂回应。具有讽刺意味的是，梅尔维尔使用圣经中的比喻来组织小说的结构，但小说的中心主题却和《圣经》相反：驳斥上帝的存在，反对创世纪的说法。奥尔特还分析了福克纳的作品。福克纳是出色的散文家，受《圣经》的影响没有那么直接。《押沙龙，押沙龙！》(*Absalom, Absalom!*)的语言风格非常丰富，既有杜撰词、拉丁词、复杂的句法结构，还有荒诞情节。这和《圣经》简单平实的风格完全不同。但是，就像这本书的书名一样，这部小说的情节是基于国王戴维生活中的一些事件。另外，这本书叙述中围绕的几个核心词汇都直接来源于钦定本《圣经》。

Pen of Iron makes a convincing case that it is impossible to fully appreciate American literature without knowing the Bible—indeed, without knowing it almost instinctively, the way generations of Americans used to know it. The problem is that, over the course of the last century, Biblical literacy has plummeted, even as translations and editions of the Bible have proliferated.

《铁笔》(*Pen of Iron*) 证明了，只有熟悉《圣经》才能真正欣赏美国的文学，用几代美国人熟悉《圣经》的方式，而这种方式几乎是出于本能的。但现在的问题是，自从上世纪以来，虽然《圣经》的翻译版本和再版大量增加，而和《圣经》有关的文学作品却走向了衰落。

Reading Comprehension 25

Translating in the Dark
在黑暗中翻译

"We must believe in poetry translation, if we want to believe in World Literature." Thus Thomas Tranströmer, the Swedish poet and winner of this year's Nobel Prize in Literature, quoted in a recent essay by Robert Robertson, one of his translators. Robertson goes on to describe the difficulties of capturing Tranströmer's spare voice and masterful evocation of Swedish landscape in English. Nevertheless, Robertson feels the need to call on various authorities to sanction a translation process that assumes that poetry is made up of a literal semantic sense, which can easily be transmitted separately from the verse, and a tone, or music, which only a poet is sufficiently sensitive to reconstruct.

"若要信奉世界文学，就必须信任诗歌翻译。"今年(这里指2011年)诺贝尔文学奖获得者瑞典诗人托马斯·特兰斯特勒默的这句话，被他的诗歌译者之一罗伯特·罗伯特森用到了其近日发表的一篇随笔中。罗伯特森在随笔中写道，特兰斯特勒默简朴的用语以及对瑞典风光极为传神的刻画，很难用英语来精确传达。不过，罗伯特森认为有必要号召各方权威人士一起认可这样一种翻译过程：认为诗歌由文字的语义层面和语气语调(或音乐性)组成，单独传达出前者很容易，而要想重现后者，却只有诗人才具备足够的敏感性。

Robertson also calls on the British poet Jamie McKendrick who, he feels, is "surely right" when he says "The translator's knowledge of language is more important than their knowledge of languages." How vague this remark is! Does it mean that the translator has one kind of knowledge of how language in general achieves its effects, and another of the nuts and bolts of the different languages he knows, the first kind being "more important"

罗伯特森还拉来英国诗人杰米·麦肯德里克为自己引证，认为麦克肯德里克下面这句话"无疑是正确的"："译者对语言这一形式本身的了解，比他们对具体语言的了解更为重要。"这种说法未免太玄妙了吧！这是不是在说，译者既要了解广义的语言如何实现表达效果，也要掌握各种不同语言的细枝末节，而前者比后者"更为重要"？如果是这样的话，又重要到哪

than the second? If that is the case, then to what degree more important? Wouldn't the two, rather, be interdependent and mutually sustaining?

种程度呢？难道这两者不是互相依赖、相辅相成的吗？

These perplexities apart, the thrust of McKendrick's argument is clear enough: we are sweeping aside the objection that a profound knowledge of a foreign language might be required to translate its poetry, or prose for that matter, thus clearing the path for a translation by someone who is an expert in the area that counts: our own language.

尽管有诸多令人困惑之处，麦肯德里克这句话的重点还是非常突出的：翻译诗歌或散文需要克服一个障碍，那便是需要掌握写就诗歌或散文的那门外语的深入知识；而我们所做的，就是为母语这个更重要领域里的专家扫除障碍，担当他们在翻译路上的清道夫。

Why do those "usual reliable translators" often give us work that we feel is wooden or lackluster, thus inviting the poets to get involved? Teaching translation, I frequently deal with students who write well in their mother tongue, but whose translations into that tongue lack fluency. This brings us to a paradox at the heart of translation: the text we take as inspiration is also the greatest obstacle to expression. Our own language prompts us in one direction, but the text we are trying to respect says something else, or says the same thing in a way that feels very different. We have come to what Paul Celan meant when, despairing of translating Baudelaire, he remarked that "poetry is the fatal uniqueness of language." All the same, what often frees the student to offer better translations is a deeper knowledge of the language he is working from: a better grasp of the original allows the translator to detach from formal structures and find a new expression for the tone he is learning to feel: in this case, however, every departure from strict transposition is inspired by an intimate and direct experience of the original.

那些所谓的"一般可靠的译者"翻译的作品，常常让人觉得呆板、乏味，因此便让诗人们掺和进来，为什么？在教翻译课的时候，我经常跟这样一些学生打交道：他们母语写作很好，但把外语作品翻译成母语时，却很不流畅。自此，我们可以看到翻译本质上的一个悖论：我们用来获取灵感的语言，也是我们在表达上的最大障碍。母语从某个方面给我们以提示，然而我们想遵循的原文，说的却是别的事情，或者，说的是同一件事情，却在某程度上让人有不同的感觉。这不由让人想起保罗·策兰，他在翻译波德莱尔（Baudelaire）时感到万分绝望，他认为"诗歌就是语言中那种绝对的唯一性"。话虽如此，对原文语言更深入的了解，常常能让学生们在改进翻译的时候拥有更多的自由：更好地理解原文，可以帮助译者摆脱形式上的语言结构，试着去感受原文的基调，从而寻找新的表达方式——不过，在这种情况下，不管用哪种方法挣脱"拘谨的翻译模式"，都要依赖于对原文精准而直接的体验。

All this to arrive at the obvious conclusion that while expression and creativity in one's own language is crucial, a long experience in the language we are working from can only improve the translations we make. But having hit that rather easy nail on the head, we can now ask the

所有这些可得出一个明显的结论：母语的表达和创新很关键，同时，长期浸润于原文语言中，也会有利于我们改善翻译质量。既然这么容易就能一针见血得出结果，我们不妨来提一个非常有趣的问题：为何聪明如艾略特、洛

really interesting question: why are such intelligent writers as Eliot, Lowell, Pasternak, Robertson, and McKendrick unwilling to consider the question more carefully. Is it because, to return to Tranströmer, "We must believe in poetry translation, if we want to believe in World Literature." There is no point, that is, in examining what we do too closely if we've already decided what we want our conclusion to be.

厄尔、帕斯特纳克、罗伯特森和麦肯德里克这样的作家，却不愿更认真地思考这个问题呢？难道是因为——再回到特兰斯特勒默所提的那句话上吧——"若要信奉世界文学，就必须信任诗歌翻译。"如果已经决定了我们想要什么样的结论，再去纠缠于具体的细节，就没什么意义了。

So why is it imperative that we believe in World Literature? It seems we must imagine that no literary expression or experience is ultimately unavailable to us; the single individual is not so conditioned by his own language, culture and literature as not to be able to experience all other literatures; and the individual author likewise can be appreciated all over the globe. It is on this premise that all international literary prizes, of which there are now so many, depend. The zeitgeist demands that we gloss over everything that makes a local or national culture rich and deep, in order to believe in global transmission. There must be no limitation.

那么，为何信奉世界文学就那么必要？看起来，我们一定要作如此设想：没有哪种文学表达和体验是彻底不可得的；个体的人会受到语言、文化和文学方面的限制，并不代表无法体验到其他文学作品；而同样，个体的作家也可以被全球的读者欣赏。正是在这样一个前提下，才有了各种世界性的文学奖项——如今已有了许多类别。这种时代精神要求我们把一切能让地方或民族文化博大精深的东西都抹掉，就只为了信奉全球性的传播。一定不能存在界限。

I have no quarrel with the aspiration, or all the intriguing translation/imitation processes it encourages. My sole objection would be that it is unwise to lose sight of the reality that cultures are immensely complex and different and that this belief in World Literature could actually create a situation where we become more parochial and bound in our own culture, bringing other work into it in a process of mere assimilation and deluding ourselves that, because it sounds attractive in our own language, we are close to the foreign experience.

我对这种抱负及其所激励的一切翻译/模仿过程并无不满。我唯一的异议便是，忽视这一事实是不明智的：文化是非常复杂、各不相同的，信奉世界文学实际上会让我们变得越来越狭隘，束缚于我们自己的文化中；我们不能把其他文化作品纳入简单的同化进程里，只因作品在我们的母语中很有吸引力，便自欺欺人地相信，我们已经接近了国外的体验。

Reading Comprehension 26

Hegel's God
黑格尔的上帝观

In the debate about God that has been stirred up by Richard Dawkins, Sam Harris, Christopher Hitchens and Daniel Dennett, writers regularly refer to certain famous philosophers. We hear about St Thomas Aquinas's "five ways" of proving God's existence. Sometimes we hear about Benedict Spinoza's unorthodox doctrine that God is Nature. Of course we are told about David Hume's critique of the idea of miracles; about Immanuel Kant's critique of the "ontological argument" for God; and about Friedrich Nietzsche's famous announcement that "God is dead." There is one major modern philosopher who deals extensively with the issue of God and who should have been taken into account in these recent discussions, but hasn't been. This is Georg Wilhelm Friedrich Hegel.

在由理查德·道金斯、萨姆·哈里斯、克里斯多夫·息钦斯和丹尼尔·丹尼特等人发起的关于"上帝"的讨论中，他们经常提到一些著名的哲学家。也许我们听说过圣·托马斯·阿奎纳斯证明上帝存在的五种方法；也许还听说过贝内迪克特·斯宾诺莎"上帝就是自然"的非主流学说。当然我们还听过戴维·休姆对"神迹"这一概念的批判，伊曼努尔·康德(Immanuel Kant)对上帝"本体论论证"的批判，还有弗里德里克·尼采那句"上帝死了"的著名宣言。其实，还有一位现代重要的哲学家就上帝这一问题进行过详细的分析和讨论，但他似乎在近年的讨论中被遗忘了，这就是黑格尔。

It's well known that various liberal theologians during the last century and a half have wanted to produce a conception of God that could satisfy people's spiritual longings without conflicting with Darwinian evolution and other well-established scientific discoveries. What's not well known is that Hegel already did this, with remarkable power and subtlety, in response to the great modern skeptics, Hume and Kant.

众所周知，在过去的一个半世纪中，众多自由主义神学家一直想找出一个可以满足人们精神需求的"上帝观"，使其不与达尔文进化论及其他现有的科学发现相抵触。其实这一点黑格尔已经做到了，只是不为人知罢了。他十分有力而且精妙地回应了现代杰出的怀疑论者：休姆和康德。

Hegel's philosophy is difficult to access because of his intricate manner of writing, and because of various misleading rumors that have become attached to his name. Karl Marx claimed that Hegel was an important influence on Marx's own thinking, and since Marx was an atheist, many believers have wanted nothing to do with his supposed teacher, Hegel. So Hegel's philosophical theology has been caught between the battle-lines of atheists who reject it or try to soft-pedal it and believers to

其晦涩的写作风格，以及各种关于他名声的误导性谣言，使黑格尔的哲学很难被人理解。卡尔·马克思称自己的思想深受黑格尔的影响，但他是一个无神论者，因此很多信徒一点儿也不指望从马克思自认的老师黑格尔那里得到什么(有关神的东西)。黑格尔的哲学神学体系也因此被夹在了无神论者和信徒中间，无神论者将其拒之门外或者极力淡化其重要性，信徒们亦觉得黑格尔的异端理论让他们觉

whom its terminology is foreign and off-putting. As a result, there have been few commentators who've had enough sympathy for it to lay it out in a way that makes it seem attractive.

得很难接受。结果就是，很少有人给予其肯定和赞同的评论，哪怕使其看起来有那么一点点吸引力。

However, I think Hegel's time should be now: large numbers of people both within traditional religions and outside them are looking for non-dogmatic ways of thinking about transcendent reality. Hegel begins with a radical critique of conventional ways of thinking about God. God is commonly described as a being who is omniscient, omnipotent, and so forth. Hegel says this is already a mistake. If God is to be truly infinite, truly unlimited, then God cannot be "a being", because "a being", that is, one being (however powerful) among others, is already limited by its relations to the others.

但我认为现在黑格尔的时机来了。传统宗教内外的大量人士都在寻求一种非教条的思维方式，去理解超现实。首先，黑格尔对理解上帝的传统方式进行了彻底的批判。上帝通常被描述为一个无所不知、无所不能的存在体。黑格尔认为这种想法已经错了。如果上帝是真正无穷、无限的话，那他（她/它）就不能是一个存在体，因为一个存在于其他存在体之中的存在体，无论他有多强大，始终还是会受限于他和其他存在体之间的关系。

But if God isn't "a being", what is God? Here Hegel makes two main points. The first is that there's a sense in which finite things like you and me fail to be as real as we could be, because what we are depends to a large extent on our relations to other finite things. If there were something that depended only on itself to make it what it is, then that something would evidently be more fully itself than we are, and more fully real, as itself. This is why it's important for God to be infinite: because this makes God more himself (herself, itself) and more fully real, as himself (herself, itself), than anything else is.

但如果上帝不是一个存在体，那他又是什么呢？关于这个问题，黑格尔提出了两个要点。首先，我们应该能感觉到，像你我这样的有限体是无法让自己尽可能真实地做自己的，因为我们很大程度上要依赖与其他有限体之间的关系。如果存在一个东西，只依赖于自己就可以真实做自己，那么这个东西显然比我们更具有完全自我和完全真实的特性。上帝是无限体这一点尤为关键，因为这一点可以使上帝，作为他自己，比任何其他事物都更加自我和真实。

Hegel's second main point is that this something that's more fully real than we are isn't just a hypothetical possibility, because we ourselves have the experience of being more fully real, as ourselves, at some times than we are at other times. We have this experience when we step back from our current desires and projects and ask ourselves, what would make the most sense, what would be best overall, in these circumstances? When we ask a question like this, we make ourselves less dependent on

黑格尔所提的第二个要点是，这样一个比我们更具备完全真实特性的东西，不是一个假设的可能存在物，因为我们自己有时也能体验到比平时更完全真实的那种感觉。有时我们会从当前的欲望和事务中退一步出来，然后自问：此时什么才是最重要的，什么才是最好的。这个时候所体会到的就是那种感觉。当我们问自己这类问题的时候，不论引发我们当时怀有那种欲望和想做某事的原因是什么，我们

whatever it was that caused us to feel the desire or to have the project. We experience instead the possibility of being self-determining, through our thinking about what would be best. But something that can conceive of being self-determining in this way, seems already to be more "itself", more real as itself, than something that's simply a product of its circumstances.

可以让自己更少地依赖于这些原因。通过思考何为最佳，我们体会到了自主的可能性。但可以这样主动设想或持有这种自主性，似乎已经比那些仅仅是特定情况下的产物更自我、更真实。

Putting these two points together, Hegel arrives at a substitute for the conventional conception of God that he criticized. If there is a higher degree of reality that goes with being self-determining (and thus real as oneself), and if we ourselves do in fact achieve greater self-determination at some times than we achieve at other times, then it seems that we're familiar in our own experience with some of the higher degree of reality that we associate with God. Perhaps we aren't often aware of the highest degree of this reality, or the sum of all of this reality, which would be God himself.

将这两点综合起来，黑格尔就得出了一个新的上帝观，这个上帝观可以取代他所批判的传统上帝观。如果确实存在拥有自主能力(亦即真实自我）的更高等的实体，如果我们在某些时候确实可以做到比平时更自主一些，那么根据我们自己的经验，我们似乎对更高等的真实是熟悉的，而这与上帝是相联系的。也许我们不是常常能意识到，但最高等的真实，或者所有这类真实存在的总和，就是上帝本身。

What is God, then? God is the fullest reality, achieved through the self-determination of everything that's capable of any kind or degree of self-determination. Thus God emerges out of beings of limited reality, including ourselves. Though Hegel's conception doesn't reduce God to us or to the world, it does avoid the mistake that Hegel identified in conventional conceptions of God as a separate being.

现在，我们再来讨论什么是上帝。上帝是一个最完全的真实体，对所有事物都具有任意种类、任意程度的自主能力。因此，上帝是来源于但凌驾于包括我们自己在内的有限体之上的。黑格尔并没有将上帝这个概念拉低、弱化到我们人类或现实世界这个层次，同时还避开了他指出的传统上帝观所犯下的错误：将上帝视为一个“独立的存在”。

Many critics have pored over a great puzzle concerning Hegel's profound conception of "God": that "God" can be seen as the being emerging out of beings of limited reality, and then "God" finally transcend those. The key to such a perplexing conception is that what we're talking about isn't a "thing" at all, because if he (or she or it) were a "thing", he would be limited, as we are, and wouldn't be God. So we need to stretch the limits of our ordinary language, which is pretty much designed for

很多文学评论者仔细思考并深深地困惑于黑格尔关于“上帝”的高深定义：上帝源于并最终超越有限真实的存在。若想解决这个难题，我们的取胜之匙在于：我们讨论的“上帝”根本就不是现实存在的。如果他是，那他就像我们一样，是有限的，就不是上帝了。因此我们要将日常语言的界限进行扩展，因为日常语言只是为谈论像我们一样的物体所设计的。首先，我们需要适应黑格尔的这种思维。像“真

talking about limited "things" like ourselves. Above all, we need to get used to the idea that for Hegel a word like "real" doesn't necessarily refer simply to material objects that we can measure, weigh, and kick, nor need it refer to an additional category of objects, such as "souls", that aren't material objects but somehow get connected with material objects. Instead, "reality" can be a matter of degree, proportional to the object's degree of success in being self-governing, self-determining, and "itself". Without an understanding of this dimension of increasing reality, the notion of "God" is almost inevitably doomed to the sort of another conception that Hegel criticized, in which God is pictured as "a being", a quasi-object, like us.

实”这个词，不一定非指那些我们看得见、摸得着的物质对象，或者另一种不以物质为对象，但多少也和物质有关的对象，如“灵魂”。相反，“真实”也可以指一种程度，描述所谈对象在多大程度上可以实现自治、自主、或做自己。如果不能从这个意义上理解“真实”程度的增加范畴，那么上帝这一概念几乎不可避免地会沦为另一种概念，即将上帝描述为一个跟我们类似的存在体，而这正是黑格尔所批判的。

Note

人文艺术类题源单词补充

分类	编码	真题原词	真题背景精确注释
美术	001	abstract expressionist	抽象表现主义者
美术	002	caricature	漫画
美术	003	cherubim	小天使
美术	004	chiaroscuro	明暗对比
美术	005	collage	抽象拼贴画
美术	006	cubist	立体雕塑家
美术	007	ensemble	镌刻艺术
美术	008	foreground	前景
美术	009	fresco	壁画
美术	010	halo	光环
美术	011	hue	色彩
美术	012	iconography	肖像学
美术	013	portraiture	肖像特写
美术	014	sculptor	雕塑家
美术	015	stock	绘画颜料
文学	001	abstract terms	抽象词语
文学	002	acronym	首字母缩略词
文学	003	action	情节
文学	004	allegory	讽喻
文学	005	antihero	反派
文学	006	antithesis	对偶
文学	007	authoress	女作家
文学	008	bestiary	动物寓言集
文学	009	characterization	(人物)性格塑造
文学	010	coinage	新造词语
文学	011	critique	评论文章
文学	012	diction	措辞
文学	013	dome	穹顶
文学	014	drama	戏剧艺术
文学	015	epic	史诗
文学	016	fiction	杜撰
文学	017	flashback	倒叙
文学	018	folklore	民谣
文学	019	hymn	赞美诗
文学	020	hymnal	赞美诗集
文学	021	interlude	插曲

分类	编码	真题原词	真题背景精确注释
文学	022	legitimate stage	正剧
文学	023	madrigal	抒情短诗
文学	024	melodrama	情节剧
文学	025	memoir	回忆录
文学	026	message	寓意
文学	027	metaphor	隐喻
文学	028	monologue	独角戏
文学	029	motet	圣歌
文学	030	myth	神话，虚构情节
文学	031	mythology	神话集
文学	032	pantomime	哑剧
文学	033	personification	人格化，拟人
文学	034	picture	特写
文学	035	playwright	剧作家
文学	036	pot-boiler	商业作品
文学	037	prose	散文
文学	038	protagonist	主角
文学	039	psalm	颂歌
文学	040	Pulitzer Prize	普利策奖
文学	041	reel	（电影胶片等的）一盘
文学	042	rhetoric	修辞
文学	043	rhythm	韵律
文学	044	satire	讽刺文学
文学	045	screenplay	电影剧本
文学	046	skit	滑稽短剧
文学	047	spiritual	灵歌，圣歌
文学	048	spoof	讽刺诗文
文学	049	support	配角
文学	050	synonym	同义词
文学	051	syntax	句法
文学	052	thesis	命题
文学	053	thespian	悲剧演员
文学	054	thriller	惊悚小说
文学	055	verse	韵文
文学	056	vignette	小品文
文学	057	villain	反面人物
音乐	001	accompaniment	伴奏
音乐	002	aria	咏叹调
音乐	003	arpeggio	琶音
音乐	004	bar	乐谱小节

分类	编码	真题原词	真题背景精确注释
音乐	005	bass	低音部
音乐	006	bebop	比博普爵士风
音乐	007	cantata	清唱剧
音乐	008	choir	唱诗班
音乐	009	chorus	合唱团
音乐	010	counterpoint	和弦
音乐	011	dirge	挽歌
音乐	012	downbeat	强拍，下拍
音乐	013	flat	降半音
音乐	014	fugue	赋格曲
音乐	015	impresario	制作人
音乐	016	madrigal	牧歌
音乐	017	measure	节拍
音乐	018	melody	旋律
音乐	019	motif	基调
音乐	020	musical	音乐电影
音乐	021	notation	乐谱标注
音乐	022	note	音符
音乐	023	ornament	装饰音
音乐	024	orthodoxy	正统艺术
音乐	025	overture	序曲
音乐	026	rhythm	节奏
音乐	027	rock	摇滚乐
音乐	028	saxophonist	萨克斯吹奏者
音乐	029	scale	音阶
音乐	030	score	乐谱
音乐	031	sharp	升调
音乐	032	shawm	肖姆双簧管
音乐	033	sonata	奏鸣曲
音乐	034	soprano	女高音
音乐	035	strain	曲调
音乐	036	suite	组曲
音乐	037	symphony	交响乐
音乐	038	syncopate	切分音
音乐	039	syncopation	切分省略
音乐	040	tenor	男高音
音乐	041	theme	主旋律
音乐	042	trio	三重奏
音乐	043	tune	乐曲曲调
综合	001	acculturation	文化移入

分类	编码	真题原词	真题背景精确注释
综合	002	address	演说
综合	003	aestheticism	唯美主义
综合	004	affinity	共鸣
综合	005	afterlife	轮回
综合	006	agitprop	宣传
综合	007	amateur	业余爱好者
综合	008	animation	动画片
综合	009	anomie	颓唐艺术
综合	010	anthology	绘画选集
综合	011	artisan	手艺工匠
综合	012	asceticism	禁欲主义
综合	013	barbarian	粗鄙之人
综合	014	bluestocking	女学者
综合	015	cast	演员班底
综合	016	catharsis	情绪宣泄
综合	017	close-up	特写镜头
综合	018	clown	乡巴佬；丑角
综合	019	collaboration	合著作品
综合	020	colloquium	学术讨论会
综合	021	composer	创作型艺术家
综合	022	composition	艺术创作
综合	023	connoisseur	行家里手
综合	024	contemporary	当代作品
综合	025	contrary	对立面
综合	026	cornerstone	奠基石
综合	027	craft	手艺
综合	028	credo	信条
综合	029	culmination	顶点
综合	030	cynicism	犬儒主义
综合	031	demon	魔鬼
综合	032	derision	嘲笑
综合	033	detachment	超然态度
综合	034	device	艺术手法
综合	035	dichotomy	二分法
综合	036	doctrinaire	教条主义者
综合	037	doctrine	教条
综合	038	dogma	宗教信条
综合	039	elite	精英
综合	040	empathy	共情
综合	041	empiricism	经验主义

分类	编码	真题原词	真题背景精确注释
综合	042	entity	实体
综合	043	ethics	道德标准
综合	044	ethos	精神特质
综合	045	etiquette	礼仪
综合	046	expressionism	表现主义
综合	047	fantasy	幻想
综合	048	farce	闹剧
综合	049	feat	技艺
综合	050	figure	舞步
综合	051	fin de siecle	19 世纪末艺术风格
综合	052	fine art	高雅艺术
综合	053	forerunner	先驱
综合	054	frenzy	狂乱
综合	055	frequency	主题复现
综合	056	genre	流派
综合	057	genus	种类
综合	058	grandeur	富丽豪华
综合	059	heresy	异端邪说
综合	060	heritage	传统
综合	061	hireling	雇员
综合	062	historicism	历史决定论
综合	063	hive	熙攘拥挤
综合	064	humanity	人性
综合	065	ideal image	理想的形象
综合	066	ideology	意识形态
综合	067	improvisation	即兴创作
综合	068	inspiration	灵感
综合	069	isolationist	孤立主义者
综合	070	juxtaposition	并列放置
综合	071	kaleidoscope	万花筒
综合	072	lament	哀歌
综合	073	landmark	里程碑
综合	074	legend	传奇
综合	075	liberalism	自由主义
综合	076	magpie	话痨
综合	077	majesty	庄严威仪
综合	078	mason	泥瓦匠
综合	079	masterpiece	杰作
综合	080	maxim	格言
综合	081	metaphorical meaning	象征意义

分类	编码	真题原词	真题背景精确注释
综合	082	milieu	社会环境
综合	083	mystique	神秘气氛
综合	084	naturalistic mode	自然主义手法
综合	085	nonconformist	非正统主义者
综合	086	nostalgia	怀旧情绪
综合	087	nuance	细微差别
综合	088	Op Art	幻视艺术
综合	089	oyster	谨慎的人
综合	090	pamphleteer	小册子作者
综合	091	pathos	伤感情绪
综合	092	pedant	迂腐的人
综合	093	pessimism	悲观主义
综合	094	pioneer	先驱
综合	095	polemic	辩论
综合	096	pose	姿态
综合	097	prelude	序幕
综合	098	prop	后盾
综合	099	propensity	性格特质
综合	100	radical	激进分子
综合	101	rancher	大农场主
综合	102	renaissance	文艺复兴
综合	103	repertoire	作品全集
综合	104	resurgence	复活
综合	105	reverie	沉思
综合	106	ruffian	下流的人
综合	107	scenario	情节
综合	108	sentimentalism	忧郁风格
综合	109	sentimentality	伤感
综合	110	shot	镜头
综合	111	show business	娱乐圈
综合	112	solidarity	步调一致
综合	113	spectacle	奇观
综合	114	stream of consciousness	意识流
综合	115	surrealism	超现实主义
综合	116	sweep	磅礴之势
综合	117	symposium	讨论会
综合	118	taboo	禁忌
综合	119	temperament	气质
综合	120	tempo	音乐拍子
综合	121	terminology	术语

分类	编码	真题原词	真题背景精确注释
综合	122	troupe	剧团
综合	123	undertone	低调表现
综合	124	Utopian	乌托邦
综合	125	vestige	遗迹
综合	126	virtuosity	艺术鉴赏力
综合	127	vision	洞察力
综合	128	visionary	梦想家
综合	129	vista	远景
综合	130	vogue	时尚

Note

第四节 社会科学类

社会科学类文章是除了刚才我们论述过的三种文章之外最后一种文章题材，这种题材的难度不高，也是中国考生信心最足的一种文章。在这种社会科学类的文章之中，GRE考试本身最喜欢考查的，是考生能否对文中已给的论点及其论据做出准确的判断。在社会科学类的文章中，GRE考试比较青睐的题材有：公共政策、妇女权利保护、黑人问题研究、立法问题等等。文章本身的英语语言难度不如人文科学类文章，但是其题目的难度很高，而且选项的辨析度较低，造成考生会有这样的感觉：读文章时能明白文章大意，但是做题的时候却不知道应该选哪个答案。

鉴于这种情况，考生们在考场上和日常训练中应对这种类型的文章时一定要注意对结构化阅读法的使用，准确而快速地判断句间逻辑关系，把文章简化成逻辑条理清晰、论证过程严密的框架，而不是一堆没有生命力堆在眼前的文字。找出作者运用过的例子、使用过的理论，分清楚总论点和分论点，这样考生会更容易理解全文。

在文后选项的处理上，也需要格外小心，常见的错误选项特征有如下几种：

1. 选项中贸然出现比较级或者最高级

如果在GRE的原文中没有出现比较级或者最高级的字眼，在选项中出现往往是错误的。原因很简单，GRE阅读强调“言之有据”，如果原文中只是对某事物A进行了正评价，认为“A很好”，而在选项中却出现了“A比B更好”，这显然是错误的，原因在于没有证据。

2. 选项中出现与文中态度不符的态度词

这一点相对来说容易理解，但关键在于考生需要学会准确定位：利用句间逻辑关系定位是最佳的方法。态度词不光是形容词，很多副词甚至是动词都会体现作者的态度，在做题时需要格外注意。

3. 选项中贸然推断某事物发生的原因

这一种错误也是很常见的，GRE文章篇幅有限，不可能把所有事情和细节的来龙去脉交代得完全清楚。比如在某一篇研究荷尔蒙与记忆力的关系的文章中，作者提到了“葡萄糖能够影响记忆力”，而选项中出现了“葡萄糖影响记忆力的机理”，这显然是错误的。在判断选项过程中要保持清醒的头脑，对于某事物要做到“知其然，亦知其所以然”。

Exercise 7

公共事务的决定

Although the development of new infrastructure (such public facilities as power plants, schools, and bridges) is usually determined by governmental planning, sometimes this development can be planned more flexibly and realistically by private investors who anticipate profit from the collection of user fees. Such profits can contribute to the financing of more infrastructure if demand proves great enough, whereas the reluctance of developers to invest in such projects can signal that additional infrastructure is not needed. During the economic boom of the 1980's, for example, the state of Virginia authorized private developers to build a $300 million toll road. These developers obtained the needed right-of-way from property owners, but by 1993 they still had not raised the necessary financing. The unwillingness of investors to finance this project does not negate the viability of privately financed roads; rather, it illustrates a virtue of private financing. If a road appears unlikely to attract enough future traffic to pay for the road, then it should not be built.

Sample Multiple-choice Questions — Select One Answer Choice

1. The primary purpose of the passage is to

(A) build a case for increasing the development of new infrastructure

(B) advocate an alternative to government financing of infrastructure

(C) explain the failure of a privately financed venture

(D) suggest the types of infrastructure most appropriate for private financing

(E) argue against government restrictions on developing new infrastructure

Sample Multiple-choice Questions — Select One Answer Choice

2. The passage implies that the "governmental planning" mentioned in line 2 may lead to which of the following problems?

(A) Improper use of profits derived from user fees

(B) Unduly slow development of necessary new infrastructure

(C) Unrealistic decisions about developing new infrastructure

(D) Incorrect predictions about profits to be gained from user fees

(E) Obstruction of private financing for the development of new infrastructure

Sample Multiple-choice Questions — Select One Answer Choice

3. According to the passage, which of the following is true of the toll road mentioned in line 7?

(A) After it was built, it attracted too little traffic to pay for its construction.

(B) It was partially financed by the state of Virginia.

(C) Its development was authorized during an economic boom.

(D) Its construction was controversial among local residents.

(E) Its developers were discouraged by governmental restrictions on acquiring the necessary land.

译文及解析

第一句： 尽管基础设施(如发电厂、学校和桥梁)通常由政府规划，但是有时候私人投资的建设模式更为灵活并且切合实际，同时私人投资者会从设施使用者的集资中获取一些利润。

第二句： 若对基础设施的需求足够多，这些利润可有助于以后更多的建造；同样，如果投资者不愿意给钱，则说明没必要再建造了。

(第一句和第二句的关系：第二句处于逻辑下一层，是对第一句话的顺承连接。因为第二句所说的关于利润的再次使用和是否兴建基础设施的问题，正迎合了第一句的副词"flexibly and realistically"，写第二句话是为第一句话而服务的。)

第三句： 比如，在80年代的经济繁荣期弗吉尼亚州(政府)授权私人投资者建造一条市值三亿的收费公路。

第四句： 这些开发商们从地产拥有者手里获得了足够的建筑用地，但是直到1993年他们都没有筹到足够的资金。

(第三、四句都是对第二句的具体举例，是逻辑下一层，说明的问题是"如果人们不给钱则表明没必要修"。)

第五句： 人们不乐意给钱并非否定私人投资公路(修建)这种模式的可行性；恰恰相反，这样一个例子却印证出了私人投资的一个优点。

第六句： (优点就是，)如果这条公路难以吸引足够的交通流量来为其付款，那就不应该建它。

(第五、六句可以看做一个整体，是对第三、四句的例子的补充说明，处于第三、四句的逻辑下一层，都是对第二句话的具体说明。)

逻辑图

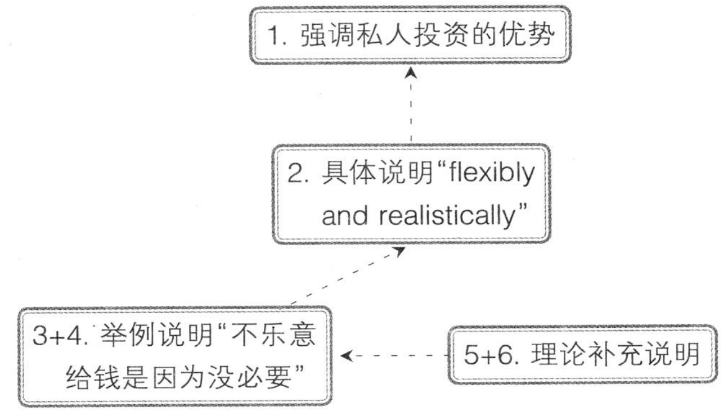

题目及解析

1. The primary purpose of the passage is to

(A) build a case for increasing the development of new infrastructure

(B) advocate an alternative to government financing of infrastructure

(C) explain the failure of a privately financed venture

(D) suggest the types of infrastructure most appropriate for private financing

(E) argue against government restrictions on developing new infrastructure

解析

这是一道主题作用题，问"本文的写作目的是什么？" 通过分析文章中的句间逻辑关系，我们很容易了解到本文其他五句话都是为了围绕第一句来展开的，所以第一句是全文的逻辑最高层，即：在基础设施建设中，私人投资更具灵活性并切合实际。那么本文的写作目的就在于支持私人投资的建设模式。

(A) 为了建造更多新的基础设施而塑造的例子

(B) 宣扬能够替代政府投资建设基础设施的模式

(C) 解释私人投资失败的原因

(D) 推荐最适合私人投资建设的基础设施类型

(E) 反对政府对于新建基础设施的限制

本题的答案一目了然，选B。本文行文中出现最多的关键词就是 "infrastructure"(基础设施)，但是本文一直在借用基础设施作为媒介，通过它来说明私人投资的优势所在，所以核心词是 "private investor"（私人投资者）。

2. The passage implies that the "governmental planning" mentioned in line 2 may lead to which of the following problems?

(A) Improper use of profits derived from user fees

(B) Unduly slow development of necessary new infrastructure

(C) Unrealistic decisions about developing new infrastructure

(D) Incorrect predictions about profits to be gained from user fees

(E) Obstruction of private financing for the development of new infrastructure

解析

这是一道推断题，提示词是"imply"（暗示），问"原文暗示在第二行提到的'政府规划'可能会引发什么样的问题？"这种推断题的解决办法就是回文定位以后进行逻辑转化，原文当中说到有两种建设方式：私人投资和政府规划，那么此二者的区别就在于"more flexibly and realistically by private investors"（私人投资更灵活且更切合实际）。那么，基于此政府规划可能会出现的问题就是 "不够灵活" 和"不够实际"。

（A）对于集资所获得之利润使用不当

（B）必要的基础设施发展速度过慢

（C）建设基础设施时有些不切实际的想法

（D）对从集资中所获得的利润估计不当

（E）阻碍私人投资基础设施的发展

本题正确答案应该是选项C。"不切实际"才是文章"imply"（暗示）的信息；其他几个选项看起来合情合理，带入题干貌似也并不矛盾。但是推断题的一个非常重要的原则就是要言之有据，选项答案在文章中一定要有据可查。而这几个选项在文章中均没有证据证明。

3. According to the passage, which of the following is true of the toll road mentioned in line 7?

（A）After it was built, it attracted too little traffic to pay for its construction.

（B）It was partially financed by the state of Virginia.

（C）Its development was authorized during an economic boom.

（D）Its construction was controversial among local residents.

（E）Its developers were discouraged by governmental restrictions on acquiring the necessary land.

解析

这是一道信息题，关键词在于"toll road"（收费公路），问"以下哪个关于文中收费公路的选项是正确的？" 做这种信息定位相对明确的题目时，需要阅读文中关于"收费公路"这个逻辑层面的信息，然后根据选项内容做出选择。

（A）完工之后该公路的车流量太小，所收路费还不及建筑费用多。
（这个选项错在了信息上，由于建造工路的资金没有筹齐，所以根本就没建起来，何来"after it was built"？）

（B）弗吉尼亚州政府为其建设出资一部分。
（这个选项也错误，原文中说的是弗吉尼亚州政府授权私人投资者建工路，只是授权，并未提到给他们资金。）

（C）这个工程的建设是在经济繁荣期授权的。
（C选项是本题的正确答案。可定位原文的年代数字"the 1980s"，可知在此经济繁荣期，政府授权私人投资者来建造公路。）

（D）建设此公路在当地居民中颇有争议。
（本文没有提到建设公路时居民们对其有争议。）

（E）工程建设者受制于政府对其获取用地的限制。
（这里，政府授权私人投资者建造公路，没有给他们任何限制。）

本题属于GRE阅读文章当中相对简单的细节题，正确答案选C，其他错误选项的干扰性较弱，也较容易识别。

Exercise 8

黑人民间故事的意义和作用

Extended debate concerning the exact point of origin of individual folktales told by Afro-American slaves has unfortunately taken precedence over analysis of the tales' meaning and function. Cultural continuities with Africa were not dependent on importation and perpetuation of specific folktales in their pristine form. It is in the place that tales occupied in the lives of the slaves and in the meaning slaves derived from them that the clearest resemblances to African tradition can be found. Afro-American slaves did not borrow tales indiscriminately from the Whites among whom they lived. Black people were most influenced by those Euro-American tales whose functional meaning and aesthetic appeal had the greatest similarity to the tales with deep roots in their ancestral homeland. Regardless of where slave tales came from, the essential point is that, with respect to language, delivery, details of characterization, and plot, slaves quickly made them their own.

Sample Multiple-choice Questions — Select One Answer Choice

1. The author's main purpose is to

   (A) create a new field of study

   (B) discredit an existing field of study

   (C) change the focus of a field of study

   (D) transplant scholarly techniques from one field of study to another

   (E) restrict the scope of a burgeoning new field of study

Sample Multiple-choice Questions — Select One Answer Choice

2. The passage suggests that the author would regard which of the following areas of inquiry as most likely to reveal the slaves' cultural continuities with Africa?

   (A) The means by which Blacks disseminated their folktales in nineteenth-century America

   (B) Specific regional differences in the styles of delivery used by the slaves in telling folktales

   (C) The functional meaning of Black folktales in the lives of White children raised by slave

   (D). The specific way the slaves used folktales to impart moral teaching to their children

   (E) The complexities of plot that appear most frequently in the slaves' tales

Sample Multiple-choice Questions — Select One Answer Choice

3. Which of the following techniques is used by the author in developing the argument in the passage?

(A) Giving a cliché a new meaning

(B) Pointedly refusing to define key terms

(C) Alternately presenting generalities and concrete details

(D) Concluding the passage with a restatement of the first point made in the passage

(E) Juxtaposing statements of what is not the case and statements of what is the case

译文及解析

第一句： 不幸的是，目前关于黑人民间故事精确起源的问题的争论已然超过了对于这些故事意义和作用的分析。

（第一句话是作者表述的一个观点，作者对这件事情持负评价。）

第二句： 非洲文化的传承并非依靠引入故事并维持其原始面貌来实现的。

（第二句是第一句话中作者发表观点的原因。）

第三句： 只有在充满了故事的生活中、只有在黑人们从故事里总结出的道理中，人们才能寻觅到非洲文化传统中最纯真的体现。

（第三句是第二句的论据，用来说明"重要的不是原始面貌"。）

第四句： 美国的黑人们并非不加辨别地借用白人社会的民间故事。

（从第四句开始的内容和第三句是一种平行并列的关系，共同作为支持第二句的论据。）

第五句： 对黑人影响最深的欧美故事，其作用、意义和美感对人的吸引与那些深深根植于黑人祖先们生活之地的故事极为相似。

第六句： 无论这些黑人民间故事源从何来，关键在于黑人们能够很快地把故事从语言、传递的信息、人物塑造的细节以及情节这些方面变成属于自己的东西。

（第四、五句作为一个整体是第六句的细节，属于逻辑下一层。第六句和第三句是平行关系。）

逻辑图

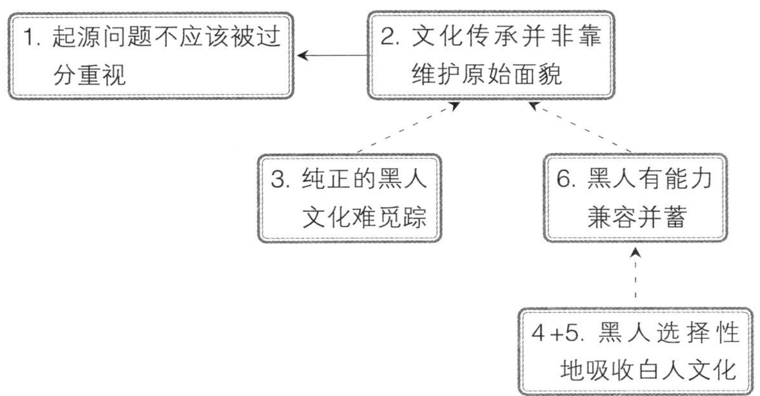

题目及解析

1. The author's main purpose is to

(A) create a new field of study

(B) discredit an existing field of study

(C) change the focus of a field of study

(D) transplant scholarly techniques from one field of study to another

(E) restrict the scope of a burgeoning new field of study

解析

这是一道非常典型的主题作用题，做这种题目不在于考生能够把文章内容总结得多么清楚，而在于能够弄明白作者为何要写这篇文章，或者说这篇GRE文章在整个学术论文中所起到的作用是什么。从本文中我们不难看出，作者的主要写作内容是第二句开始之后的内容，即强调"非洲文化是动态变化，并不是原封不动的"。那么作者为何要写本文就需要看第一句话了，第一句话中作者对于"钻研起源"的问题持负态度，说明在这篇GRE阅读所取材的论文中，本文之前的内容一定是涉及"探寻黑人民间故事精确起源"的问题。这样一来，作者写这篇文章的目的就比较明确了：为了把学术研究点从"起源"的问题上转移。

(A) 创造某一新的研究领域

(B) 否认现存的某种研究领域

(C) 把研究重点从某一领域上转移

(D) 把某领域的研究方法移植到另一个领域

(E) 对某一热门研究领域的范围进行限制

根据以上的分析，不难得出本题正确答案为选项C。

2. The passage suggests that the author would regard which of the following areas of inquiry as most likely to reveal the slaves' cultural continuities with Africa?

(A) The means by which Blacks disseminated their folktales in nineteenth-century America

(B) Specific regional differences in the styles of delivery used by the slaves in telling folktales

(C) The functional meaning of Black folktales in the lives of White children raised by slave

(D) The specific way the slaves used folktales to impart moral teaching to their children

(E) The complexities of plot that appear most frequently in the slaves' tales

解析

本题中"suggest"是标志词，题目主干部分为"passage suggests that the author would regard which of the following..."(文章暗示，作者将会得出以下哪个信息？)，这实际上是把文中出现过的作者的态度进行一次逻辑转化。题干中问道"关于以下哪个领域的调查能够展现出非洲黑人们的文化继承?"在文中第三句话中能够找到答案："...and in the meaning slaves derived from them that the clearest resemblances to African tradition can be found.” 这几乎明确地告诉我们“在黑人们从故事里总结的道理中才能找到清晰的非洲文化原貌”，也就是说，这个“总结道理”的过程就代表了“文化的延续性”。

（A）19世纪美国黑人们传播故事的方式

（B）在讲述故事过程中不同区域的黑人传递信息的风格之间存在差异

（C）黑人民间故事对于由黑人抚养长大的白人孩子生活的意义

（D）黑人们利用民间故事向孩子们灌输道德知识的方式

（E）在黑人的故事当中出现频率最高的情节的复杂性

本题的正确答案应该为选项D。

3. Which of the following techniques is used by the author in developing the argument in the passage?

（A）Giving a cliché a new meaning

（B）Pointedly refusing to define key terms

（C）Alternately presenting generalities and concrete details

（D）Concluding the passage with a restatement of the first point made in the passage

（E）Juxtaposing statements of what is not the case and statements of what is the case

解析

这道题的题型并不常见，问“作者是运用了何种方法展开本文论述的?”解决这种题目最好的方法就是从句子关系入手，掌握全文最主要的行文结构，然后选择一个最合适的答案。这种题的题干中虽然没有出现“most”这种极端词汇，但是我们也需要选择最合适的答案，因为这种问法相对具有开放性。

（A）给某一个陈腐的理念赋予全新的含义

（A不合适。文中没有出现哪个观念是陈腐的。）

（B）直截了当地拒绝定义某种名目

（B也不对。文章没有拒绝定义任何东西。）

（C）轮番呈递概念和具体细节

（C是本题的迷惑性选项。从本文的行文结构能够看出，对于第一句的内容作者并没有给出细节。C不是完全不对，而是作为本题的答案不合适。）

（D）通过重述第一个论点来结束行文过程

（D错误。第一个论点是关于“探寻黑人故事起源”的问题。）

（E）将“是”与“非”平行地放在一起

（E是本题最合适的答案。所谓的“what is not the case”就是指“故事的起源”；“what is the case”就是指“故事是发展的、兼容并蓄的”。）

Reading Comprehension 27

Risk and Recklessness in Public Affairs
公共事务中的风险与草率

Ross Douthat offers the provocative thesis that many of this nation's (and some other's) biggest blunders and troubles are due in large part to meritocracy in which intelligent and talented people rise to positions of influence, for that such people are prone to a form of hubris in which they overestimate their ability to understand and manipulate the world. Douthat centers his piece on the story of Jon Corzine, the former head of Goldman Sachs, whose most recent Wall Street firm, MF Global, has filed for bankruptcy after apparently taking some bad risks with $600 million of customers' money. But Douthat says the same sort of phenomenon has cropped up in the realm of public policy with such endeavors as the wars in Vietnam and Iraq, or the European Union's creation of a common currency.

罗斯·杜塔特提出了一个挑衅的观点，他认为美国(以及他国)很多严重的错误和问题在很大程度上都可归咎于精英阶层，他们当中的“天才牛人”把持着有影响力的重要位置。杜塔特称，问题就在于，这类人容易骄傲自大，他们高估了自己理解和掌控世界的能力。杜塔特此文围绕高盛前首席执行官乔恩·科塞的故事展开，乔恩·科塞的华尔街公司明富环球（MF Global）在用6亿美元的客户资金进行风险投资失败后申请破产。但杜塔特认为，同样的现象也出现在公共政策领域，比如越战和伊战，以及欧盟创造统一货币。

There is a lot of validity to this argument, and this type of hubris frequently appears in both public and private sector decision-making. But some indications that there is more to the blunders than Douthat describes can be seen in one of his examples: the Iraq War. Ideology was a big part of what drove the war. You don't need a one-party state for ideology to play such a role—just control for a time by one party of some of the functions of the state. And although the war-makers certainly had excessive confidence that they knew what they were doing, the launching of the war involved the rejection of much relevant expertise. The excessive and misguided risk-taking that was involved was due less to meritocracy than to some people getting in a position—through whatever means, not necessarily merit—in which they could place big bets with other people's money, and in this case with other people's lives.

这个观点从很大程度上讲是正确的，这种过分自信在公共和私人领域的决策中经常出现。但是，对于杜塔特所描述的错误，还有更多的原因，这在他所举的一个例子当中可以看到，那就是伊拉克战争。意识形态在很大程度上成为了战争的推手。意识形态扮演这个角色时无需一党制——只要某一政党对国家机构控制一段时间即可。尽管战争制造者有充分的信心，也知道自己的所作所为，然而，相关专家并不支持发动战争。相较于精英阶层，过分的和被误导的冒险行为应该更多地归咎于那些身处高位之人——不管通过什么手段，并一定是奖赏——这种地位使他们可以用别人的钱来打赌，在伊战的例子中，是用别人的生命来打赌。

That is the biggest common thread involving the reckless risk-taking of masters of the universe on Wall Street and that of makers of public policy in Washington: the ability to place big bets in which it is someone else's resources that are at stake. This is true of investment bankers who can operate on a "heads I win, tails the taxpayers lose" basis. It also is true of policy-makers who get to claim a win if things work out but who do not suffer the way that taxpayers or soldiers suffer if things do not work out. The fact that those who are in temporary control of the government at any one moment are playing with other people's money and lives is a further reason they should be cautions in placing any bets at all—in addition to Douthat's sensible reason that decision-makers need enough humility to realize that they don't really know enough to be confident that their gambles will work out.

这就是整个华尔街的投资大师们和华盛顿的政策制定者们轻率的冒险行为背后共同的大思路：能在别人岌岌可危的资产上下赌注。对于投资银行家来说是如此，他们的操作原则是"无论怎样，我都会赢"。对于政策制定者来说也是如此，如果事情做成了，他们就宣称自己赢了，如果做不成，他们却不用像纳税人或者士兵那样承受损失。任何时候，那些暂时控制着政府的人们都在用别人的钱做事和生活，这个事实是他们在下赌注时应该小心谨慎的另一个原因——除了杜塔特的合理原因之外，即政策制定者需要足够谦虚地意识到他们并不能真正知道他们的赌博是否会赢。

In foreign policy there are a couple of additional reasons for caution that do not apply similarly on Wall Street. One is that the policy-maker usually is dealing more with incalculable uncertainties and less with calculable risks than the gamblers on Wall Street are. The other reason is that with any public policy the inconsistent and selective nature of political attention means that some risks get paid far more attention than others, regardless of the actual magnitude of the risks involved. Something like the risks from a disliked regime owning powerful weapons tends to get plenty of attention; the risks of using military force to try to do something about such a regime get far less.

在外交政策上需要谨慎，这还有不同于华尔街的其他几个原因。其中一个就是政策制定者通常要比华尔街的赌徒们要更多地应对不可计算的不确定性，而要应对的可计算的风险与其相比较少。另一个原因则是，任何公共政策的政治关注度都具有多变性和选择性的本质，这意味着不管相关风险的真正重要性怎样，有些风险得到的关注远远多于另外一些。来自拥有强大武器的敌对政权的风险往往会获得众多关注，而使用军事力量对付这种政权的风险得到的关注就少很多了。

Reading Comprehension 28

The Mellon Doctrine
梅隆信条

It is justifiable to claim that the Mellon Doctrine whose liquidationism about liquidating labor, stocks and real estate especially under the depression is held as official doctrine of the G.O.P (one of the major parties in U.S. political area), though the existence of which is still theoretical for that the only evidence is the remembrance of President Hoover. Two weeks ago, Republican staff released a report about slashing government spending and employment in the face of a deeply depressed economy by claiming that a smaller government work force increases the available supply of educated, skilled workers for private firms, thus lowering labor costs. Specifically, that is the releasing of a great deal of educated, skilled employees would help to drop down the wage, thus instigate the demand for hiring.

我们可以肯定的是：梅隆式的清算主义现在成了共和党(Grand Old Party，大佬党，美国共和党的别称，是美国的一个主要政治党派)官方信奉的教条——清算劳工，清算股票，清算房地产；但梅隆到底有过没有这样的建议仍存在疑问，我们只是从胡佛多年后写的东西中得知的。两周以前，共和党人发布了一项报告说："面对严重的经济不景气形势，削减政府开支，裁减政府雇员，实际上就会创造就业。"报告是这样解释裁员创造就业的："政府雇员减少会增加对私营企业受教育和熟练工作人员的有效供应，从而减少劳工成本。"具体来说就是，通过提高失业，特别是受过教育和熟练工作人员的失业，来降低工资水平，这样反过来又会鼓励就业。

However, there is an immediate logical problem of the causal relationships above: is it unquestionable that decreasing employment would result in lower wage? And how could one exclude the possibility that such condition would lead to a higher wage from which the theoretically possible work dissolution could derived? Beyond that, why would lower wage promote higher employment? There's a fallacy of composition here: since workers at any individual company may be able to save their jobs by accepting a pay cut, you might think that we can increase overall employment by cutting everyone's wages. In fact, across-the-board wage cuts would almost certainly reduce, not increase, employment because debts would not fall while earnings would. So a general fall in wages would worsen the debt problems that are, at this point, the principal obstacle to recovery.

仔细想想，上述因果关系存在直接的逻辑问题：共和党人说削减就业可引起工资下降，从而导致创造就业。这完全没有疑问吗？这种创造就业难道就不可能引起工资增加，进而又导致劳工合约破裂吗？此外，为什么降低工资就能促进就业呢？这里存在一种合成谬误：既然在任何一家公司里，员工也许能够接受降薪以保住工作岗位，所以依据此就可以认为削减每个人的薪水就能提高整体就业水平。事实上，几乎可以肯定的是，全面减薪会减少而不是增加就业。为什么？因为赚的工资减少了，但债务却不会减少，因此整个工资的下降会使债务问题更加恶化，而当前来说，债务问题正是经济复苏的主要障碍。

Reading Comprehension 29

Runaway Capitalism
失控的资本主义

In evolutionary biology, the classic example of a runaway is the peacock's tail: Because females show a preference for flamboyant plumage, the tail continues to grow even to the point that it makes the birds more susceptible to predation and compromises the sustainability of the species.

在生物进化论中有一个关于失控的经典例子，即孔雀的尾巴：由于雌孔雀对艳丽的羽毛青睐有加，雄孔雀尾巴就不断地进化得更加长，而其长度竟然达到了危及其个体安危和种群延续的地步。

Capitalism's equivalents are its obsessive pursuit of return on equity and its determination to preserve competition. Both began as valid proxies for healthy trade, but conditions have changed to the extent that those proxies now misdirect our priorities.

而资本主义也存在类似的问题，即对资产回报的过度追求和维持竞争的坚强决心。这两点在初始阶段都是有利于商业的健康因素，但随着环境的变化，如今它们却与我们的初衷相违背。

Capitalism has the opportunity to adapt and develop in the green fields of emerging economies new rules that are more suited to today's environment. Those rules will take hold globally, to the benefit of us all.

新兴市场国家的新规则更好地适应了当今的环境，而资本主义也获得机会在这片新天地中得到适应和发展。这些新规则将主宰全球，它符合所有人的利益。

Capitalism, as it is practiced in rich countries, has taken two brilliant ideas too far. The first is return on equity (ROE), one way of measuring value creation that has managed to eclipse many other, and broader, ones. The second is competition, which has come to be seen as an end in itself rather than as a tool for promoting growth and innovation.

资本主义把两件绝妙的事情做得太过，这种情况发生在许多富裕国家。第一个是资产收益率，这是一种计算创造价值的方法，但不幸的是它已经产生了严重的排他性。第二个是竞争，它已经演变成“为了竞争而竞争”，而不再是促进增长和创新的工具。

Both ideas began as effective solutions to a pressing problem—how to allocate resources to produce, as Jeremy Bentham would have it, "the greatest good for the greatest number." Centuries on, the advanced economies cling tightly to these approaches, but the problem has changed. The mismatch has caused difficulties of such urgency that many people are now declaring capitalism a failure. The

对于“如何配置资源进行生产”这一紧要问题，资产回报率和竞争在初期的确是两个有效的手段，英国哲学家杰里米·本瑟姆曾把这一问题描述为“最大数目的最大好处”。历经数个世纪，不断进步的经济一直将这两者牢牢抓在手中，但是问题本身却已经有所改变。问题与方法的错误搭配导致了极其严重的后果，现

whole system has been indicted, not only because of the financial crisis but particularly since that event, as inherently unworkable.

在有许多人开始认为资本主义是个失败。随着经济危机的爆发，整个资本主义系统被认为从本质上就是不可行的，虽然危机并非这种看法的唯一起因，但也在很大程度对其产生了促进作用。

It isn’t true. Capitalism—broadly, private ownership and resources allocated by markets—remains the most powerful, flexible, and robust system for driving society’s prosperity and enhancing quality of life. But keeping it on track will depend on our ability to rethink the priorities that guide everyone in the system, from entrepreneurs to regulators to investors. Together the practitioners of capitalism will need to throttle back the headlong pursuits of ROE and competition, and that process begins with recognizing those ideas for what they are. They are runaways.

而事实并非如此。资本主义，概括地讲就是私有制和由市场配置各种资源，仍然是促进社会繁荣和提高生活品质最有力、最灵活和最坚强的经济体系。但如何让其重回正轨，需要我们重新思考资本主义的首要任务，从企业家、监管者到投资者无一例外。所有资本主义的实践者们都需要遏制住追求资产回报率和竞争的轻率举动，而首先要做的是认清它们的现状：它们确实已经失控了。

Reading Comprehension 30

Natural Selection Explains More About Economics than Adam Smith’s Invisible Hand
自然选择论比亚当·斯密之“看不见的手”更能解释诸多经济现象

With good reason, most contemporary economists regard Adam Smith as the founder of their discipline. But I would instead accord that honor to Charles Darwin, the pioneering naturalist.

大多数当代经济学家有充分的理由将亚当·斯密视为西方经济学的创始人。但笔者认为，这一殊荣应归于博物学先驱查尔斯·达尔文(Charles Darwin)。

Although the lack of access to formal training in economics initially limited Darwin’s opportunity for succeeding in the field, he studied the works of early economists carefully, and the plants and animals that were his focus were embroiled in competitive struggles much like the ones we see in the marketplace. His observations forged an understanding of competition that is subtly but profoundly different from Smith’s. The celebrated invisible

尽管从未接受过正式的经济学教育起初限制了达尔文在经济领域建功立业，但他细心研究了早期经济学家们的著作，他关注的动植物所参与的自然竞争并不亚于我们目前在市场中目睹的那种竞争。他在观察后得出的有关竞争的观点较为微妙，与斯密的观点截然不同。斯密所提出的著名的“看不见的手”这一理论认为，完全自由的市场最终将引导利己主义

hand theory that Smith developed holds that unfettered markets will ultimately channel self-interest to serve the common good, but this idea is really just an interesting special case of Darwin's more general theory.

为公共利益服务。但这一思想却只是达尔文更为普遍的理论中一个有趣的特例而已。

Smith held that the entrepreneurs who introduce them hope to steal sales from rivals often succeeded spectacularly in the short term based on the condition that pressures rivals to mimic the innovations. The ultimate beneficiaries of this competition, he explained, are not businesses but consumers, who enjoy ever better products at ever lower prices. In Darwin's theory, natural selection favors traits and behaviors that promote individual reproductive success that were closely analogous to Smith's account of former model. But Darwin also recognized that individual and group interests often conflict sharply and that, in those cases, individual interests generally trump group interests.

斯密认为，企业家希望从其竞争对手那里夺取市场份额，他们在短期内往往能够取得巨大成功，从而迫使其竞争对手对他们的创新进行模仿。斯密解释说，这种竞争的最终受益者并非企业，而是以较低价格购买到较好产品的消费者。达尔文的理论认为，自然选择倾向于能够促进个体繁殖成效的特性和行为，这与斯密之前的理论解释十分相似。不过达尔文还认识到，个体利益和群体利益经常会发生激烈的冲突，而在大多数情形下，个体利益都会战胜群体利益。

The evolution of keen eyesight among hawks is an example of the former type. A mutation that led to slightly improved vision benefited the individual in which it first occurred. By enabling that individual to catch more prey and feed more offspring, it spread quickly. Similar mutations accreted, with the result that virtually all modern hawks have astonishingly acute vision by human standards. Like Smith's product design improvements, these mutations no longer confer relative advantage to individual hawks, but their ultimate effect was to make hawks more effective as a species.

老鹰的敏锐视力的进化就是例证之一。导致视力稍微提高的进化突变给第一个经历这种突变的个体带来了好处。由于这种进化，该个体能够捕食到更多猎物并养活更多后代，因此这种突变迅速扩散。类似的进化不断继续，其结果是，几乎所有的现代老鹰都具有令人惊讶的、胜于人类的敏锐视力。像斯密的改善产品设计论一样，这些进化已经不再仅仅使单个的老鹰具有相对优势，最终结果是老鹰这整个物种变得更有生命力。

In many other cases, however, mutations that promote individual reproductive success prove costly to the larger group. A vivid case in point is the prodigious antlers of the bull elk. Like males of most other vertebrate species, these animals take more than one mate if they can. But if some succeed, others are left with none, making them the ultimate losers in Darwinian terms. It was thus inevitable that bulls would fight bitterly for access to females, and

然而，在许多其他情况下，促进个体繁衍成效的进化对于较大群体而言却是要付出巨大代价的。一个鲜明的例子就是公麋鹿的角的进化。像许多其他雄性脊椎动物一样，如有可能，它们会拥有不止一个配偶。根据达尔文的观点，其中一些麋鹿成功了，另一些则败阵而去，成为最终的失败者。因此，不可避免的，公麋鹿会为了争夺母鹿而进行残酷的搏斗，自

also inevitable that natural selection would spawn an arms race in the antlers that promoted success in those battles. But while the massive antlers of surviving bulls, which often span more than 4 feet and weigh more than 40 pounds, help them prevail in battles for mates, they are a serious handicap when bulls are chased into densely wooded areas by predators.

然选择势必导致公麋鹿的"军备竞赛"——通过角的进化以获得战斗的胜利。但是，当这些幸存下来的公麋鹿拥有大而重的鹿角——许多鹿角经常长逾4英尺、重逾40磅——使它们在争夺配偶中占据优势的同时，一旦其他掠食者发动袭击，这些鹿角又成为它们躲进繁密的林木中的严重障碍。

Because it is relative antler size that matters in battle, bulls would have good reasons to favor a proposal to trim each animal's antlers by half. The outcome of every fight would be the same as before, and each bull would be far better able to escape from wolves. Yet bulls are stuck with their handicap because any individual bull with smaller antlers would never win a mate.

因为鹿角的相对尺寸关乎求偶战斗的结果，公麋鹿有理由为了母鹿而折断其他公麋鹿的鹿角。每场战斗的结果一如从前，公麋鹿们能更好地逃离狼群(即它们的鹿角在搏斗中被折断了)。然而这些公麋鹿却因其（折断的)鹿角遭遇了麻烦，因为任何有着短小鹿角的公麋鹿将无法获得配偶。

In short, Darwin's understanding of competition makes clear that there can be no presumption that the process promotes the common good. Often it does. But success in Darwinian terms typically depends heavily on relative performance, and attempts to occupy scarce slots atop any hierarchy inevitably provoke wasteful, mutually offsetting arms races.

简而言之，达尔文有关竞争的观点明确表示，可能不存在竞争会促进公共利益这样的假设。大多数情况下都是这样。但是达尔文理论的成功完全取决于相对性能，试图在任何等级体系里占据稀缺的位置，势必导致浪费的、相互消耗的"军备竞赛"。

It's an important point, since the modern conservative's case for minimal government rests on the presumption that competition always promotes society's welfare. But our best understanding of how competition actually functions, as Darwin's work makes clear, supports no such presumption.

需要重点指出的一点是，追求最小政府（即最少管制）的现代保守观点以这一假设为基础——竞争会提升社会福利。但是，正如达尔文的研究所表明的，对于竞争实际上是如何起作用的最佳理解，并不支持这一假设。

Reading Comprehension 31

Justice: What's the Right Thing to Do?
正义：如何做正确的事

Hard cases may make bad law, but in Michael Sandel's hands they produce some cool philosophy. The course on justice that he's been teaching at Harvard for the past 30 years has made him one of the most popular teachers in the world. But he does not go with the flow of fashion or common opinion. As a self-styled "communitarian", he sets himself at odds with one of the reigning assumptions of modern public life—that moral and religious notions are private matters that should be kept out of public political debate.

有争议的案件可能使法律无能为力，但在迈克·桑德尔那里，它们则引发一些有趣的哲学思考。过去30年里在哈佛大学教授法律课程的桑德尔已成为全世界最有名的教师之一。但是，他并没有与流行的、普遍的理论和观点保持一致。作为一名自成风格的"社群主义者"，他对现代公共生活中占据主流地位的假设——道德和宗教观念是个人事务，因此应该置于公共政治事务之外——提出了挑战。

His communitarianism is too collectivist for kneejerk conservatives and too paternalistic for kneejerk radicals, but he matches his sharp and combative mind with a gentle and likable manner. If you heard his Reith Lectures earlier this year, you may have bridled at his appeals for "a new citizenship" founded on a "politics of the common good", but you can hardly have failed to be charmed by his patience, openness and intellectual generosity.

他的社群主义对保守主义者而言过于集体主义，在激进自由派眼中家长制倾向太严重，但他用温和、讨人喜欢的方式讲述着那些犀利而极具挑战性的理论。如果你在今年早些时候听了他的里斯讲座，你可能会对他基于"共同利益政治"的"新公民"的呼吁不以为然，但是你很难不被他的耐心、坦率和机智豁达所吸引。

Life is, you might say, one damned dilemma after another. We are constantly trying to work out what to do for the best: to marry or not to marry, to persevere in a boring career or try something new, to save fools from their folly or let them learn from mistakes. Sandel's routine is to present us with a problem, help us identify the principles we appeal to in assessing our options and then show us how hard it can be to get them to line up and point in the same direction.

你可能会说，所谓生活就是一个接一个该死的困境。我们总是在不断地思考做出最好的决定：结婚还是不结婚，坚持这份无聊的工作还是尝试改变一下、告诉别人所做的蠢事还是听之任之使其得到一点教训。桑德尔的解决方式就是，在我们面前呈现一个问题，在评价我们所作的选择的同时帮助我们确定原则，然后告诉我们将所有的事情捋顺并找到正确方向是多么困难。

Affirmative action is his hard cases. Poor, white Americans are understandably indignant if they are refused a university place when black applicants with worse

他给出的一个争议案例是平权法案。当贫穷的美国白人被一所大学拒绝，而分数比他们低的黑人申请者却被这所大学录取，他们为此

grades are admitted. But it all depends, Sandel says, on what the purpose of higher education is. If it is about offering prizes for merit, then favouring members of disadvantaged groups is unacceptable. But universities are also social devices that funnel new workers into the professions and it may be irresponsible for them to turn a blind eye to the impact of their policies on the future profile of professional employment. Again, the attempt to discuss the options in terms of abstract principles rather than concrete conceptions of public good begins to look ambivalent.

而产生的愤怒情绪是可以理解的。但是这也要视情况而定，桑德尔说，要看高等教育的目的为何。如果其目的是奖励优秀，那么有利于弱势群体的政策是不可接受的。但是大学还有其社会功能——为社会提供专业工作者，那么对于学校政策对未来职业领域的影响视而不见显然是不负责任的。此外，我们讨论这一问题时应该依据有利于公共福利的具体情况，而不是那些抽象的概念。

The past few months have seen a revival of moralism in political debate and there has been good sport in calling for bankers to have their bonuses cut off, or politicians and BBC executives to come clean about their claims for expenses. But, whether you regard it as bold and refreshing or dangerously self-indulgent, the new moralism is not Sandel's line. He is not asking us to give politics an infusion of saintly moral rectitude; he just wants us to recognise that it has had morality in its bloodstream all along.

过去几个月中道德主义在政治讨论中重新抬头：例如要求银行家削减其奖金，政治家和BBC高管公开其开支等。但是，不论你认为这是大胆的、令人振奋的，还是危险任性的，新道德主义都与桑德尔所倡导的理念不同。他不是要求我们灌注政治以崇高的道德公正性，他只是想让我们认识到政治的血液中自始至终都流淌着道德规范。

Reading Comprehension 32

The Rorschach Test
罗夏墨迹测试

The Rorschach test, in which elements of someone's personality can be deduced, its proponents claim, by his description of what he sees in a series of inkblots, has been used for 90 years, and is still going strong.

罗夏墨迹测试已经被运用了90年，并将依旧盛行。据它的支持者称，在这个测试中，一个人的性格要素能从他/她对一系列的墨迹的描述中推断出来。

The original test was devised by Hermann Rorschach, a Swiss psychiatrist, in 1921. It involved someone asking someone else to look at ten inkblot images. In each case,

这个独创性的测试是由一位瑞士的精神病学家赫尔曼·罗夏在1921年设计的。该测试需要两个人参与，其中一个人要求另一个人看

the interlocutor inquires of the viewer, "What might this be?", notes the response and attempts to draw conclusions.

十幅墨迹图形。每一个个案中，询问者都会问观察者，"这可能是什么呢?"，然后记录他们的回答，并试图从中得出推论。

The question has always been, of course, how reliable the connection is between the response to the blots (generally, people, animals or objects) and the alleged diagnosis. Over the years, many experiments have been done to test the link. Now Gregory Meyer of the University of Toledo and his colleagues have reviewed the data. Their results, which form the basis of a new manual on the topic, suggest the inkblot test does have real power.

当然，对此测试的疑问永远都落在对墨迹的回答(一般包括人物、动物或者物体)和所谓的诊断这两者之间的联系的可信度上。在过去的这些年里，已有很多实验来测试这个联系。现在托莱多大学的格雷戈里·迈耶和他的同事已经披露了相关数据，他们的成果已成为一本相关主题的新指南的基础，证明墨迹测试的确是有效的。

Dr Meyer's study is a review of 1,292 papers that report experimental attempts to link Rorschach responses with personality traits that have been established by other means. His main conclusion is that some of the ways the test has been used are, indeed, useless. He proposes, for example, axing the alleged connection between reporting mirrored images in a blot and the viewer's level of egocentricity. He would also get rid of the idea that if a viewer focuses on the details of an image rather than the broader picture, then he is likely to have an obsessive personality. A third traditional interpretation that does not pass muster, in Dr Meyer's view, is the suggestion that when a viewer sees things in a blot that the examiner thinks do not resemble the blot, that indicates impaired perception, which can lead to a diagnosis of psychosis. Dr Meyer would not get rid of this altogether. But he thinks the idea needs to be recalibrated.

迈耶博士的论文是一篇1292页的评论，该评论中介绍了一些实验，目的在于将罗夏墨迹的回答和已用其他方式创建的人格特征联系起来。他的主要结论是将这个测试用在某些方面确实是无效的。比如，他建议去掉从墨迹中看出的图像和观看者以自我为中心的程度之间的联系。他还摒弃了另外一个观点，即如果观察者将注意力放到一个图像的某些细节上而不是宏观的整体图片上，那么就推出这个人很可能有强迫性的人格。另一个在迈耶博士看来差强人意的传统解释是，当考察者认为一个观察者在一个墨迹上看出的东西不像那个墨迹，那么就意味着感知障碍，这会导致精神错乱的诊断。迈耶博士不会彻底否定这一观点，但是他认为应该要重新校核。

Some Rorschach diagnoses do seem to stand up, though. People who report seeing representations of passivity or helplessness in the blots are thought to have a dependent personality, meaning they rely on others to satisfy their needs. Some of the studies Dr Meyer looked at did indeed find that people who produce such responses are more likely to request guidance in a classroom, ask an experimenter for help when solving puzzles, or hold on to

但是，有些罗夏测试的诊断确实是站得住脚的。那些在墨迹中看到表征消极性或无助性的图像的人被认为具有依赖型人格，即他们依赖别人来满足自身的需求。迈耶博士做的一些研究确实发现作出此类回答的人更倾向于在课堂上要求指导，在解决难题的时候向有经验者求助，或者在被蒙上眼睛时紧紧抓住引路人。此外，一个观察者综合了一个墨迹的几个

a guide when they are blindfolded. And responses in which a viewer synthesises several elements in an inkblot to show how they are interrelated do seem to be correlated with intellect; such responses are found most often in people who also score highly on an unrelated psychological assessment, the Wechsler Adult Intelligence Scale.

要素并展示它们是如何相互联系的，这种反馈确实和智力相互关联。做出这类回答的大部分人都能在一项不相干的心理评估——韦氏成人智力测试中获得高分。

Dr Meyer disposes, too, of one perennial criticism of the Rorschach test—that it is culture-dependent. Studies in numerous countries come to broadly the same conclusions. A qualified thumbs-up, then, for inkblots. Perhaps the biggest threat to the test is that no one uses fountain pens any more, and so inkblots themselves have more or less become things of the past.

迈耶博士也处理了针对罗夏测试的一个长期存在的批判——文化依赖。在许多国家进行的研究大致上都得出了这些相同的结论，而这对墨迹测试来说是一个高度的认可。也许，对于该测试最大的威胁是没有人再用自来水笔了，所以墨迹本身就基本上变成了一种过去的东西。

Reading Comprehension 33

Babies Size Up the Social Scene
婴儿能判断社交情景

A new study suggests that babies acquire the skill of sizing up relationships between other people even before they learn to speak—that 10-month-old infants perceive social dominance and can predict who's likely to prevail when a conflict arises. In the past decade, developmental psychologists have shown that babies are remarkably perceptive about the social world around them. Before the end of their first year, for example, infants understand that people sometimes have competing goals, and they take notice of whether one individual helps or hinders another.

最新的研究表明，婴儿就能获得准确判断他人之间关系的能力，甚至早于学会说话：报告说十个月左右的婴儿就能够感知到社会优势，并预测出谁更可能在发生的冲突中获胜。在过去的十年中，发展心理学家已经证实了婴儿对周围世界的强烈感知能力。举例来说，在他们接近一岁的时候，婴儿已经能了解人们有时候会有竞争的目标，注意到一个人是在帮助还是在阻碍他人。

In the new study, Lotte Thomsen and colleagues investigated whether infants also have expectations about who's most likely to get their way when two individuals have conflicting goals. They brought into the lab 144

在新的研究中，洛特·汤姆森以及同事们调查婴儿是否也对竞争中更有可能获胜的人抱有一定的期望。他们将144名年龄在8至16个月之间的婴儿在母亲的陪同下请进实验室。坐

infants between 8 months and 16 months old, accompanied by their mothers. Seated on mom's lap, each baby watched videos starring two crude cartoon figures—each essentially a block with an eye and a mouth. (Psychologists often use simplified figures like these instead of more realistic ones to avoid confounding cues from facial expressions, gestures, or body posture.)

在母亲的膝盖上，每个宝宝都会观看由两个简单卡通形象扮演的视频——每个卡通形象都是长着一只眼睛和一张嘴巴的方块人。（心理学家通常用这些简化了的人物形象代替真实人物，以避免一些来自面部表情、手势、身体姿势的干扰因素。）

In one experiment, infants between 11 months and 16 months old watched a video in which a big blue block initially bounces across the screen from left to right. Next, a smaller green block crosses in the opposite direction. Then a conflict arises: Both blocks start across the screen and bump into each other in the middle, unable to pass. The dilemma could end one of two ways, with either the blue or the green block tipping forward, as if bowing down, and receding into the background to allow the other block to pass. When the little green block made way for the big blue block, infants looked at the screen for a few seconds after the clip ended before looking away. But when the little green block actually got its way, the infants stared at the screen for an additional 5 to 10 seconds on average. Thomsen and her colleagues, like many researchers who work with infants, interpret such extra attention as evidence that the infant has noticed that something is amiss—in this case, that their prediction that the large block should dominate the small block hasn't come true.

在一次实验中，一些11至16个月大的幼儿在观看视频，画面上是一个个头较大的蓝色方块人从屏幕左面跳到右面。接下来一个个头较小的绿色方块人从反方向穿过。于是竞争出现了：两个方块人都准备穿过屏幕并且在中间相撞，谁都无法通过。解决的方法有两种，任何一个方块人向前倾斜，好似在给对方鞠躬，并退到屏幕后方以让对方先通过。当绿色小方块人为蓝色大方块人让路时，婴儿在放映结束后几秒钟就把视线从屏幕上移开了。但是当绿色方块人先通过时，婴儿注视屏幕的时间平均比第一种情况长了5至10秒钟。汤姆森和他的同事与其他从事婴儿方面研究的研究人员一样，认为这多出的注视时间表明婴儿注意到有些地方不合理——即在这种情况下，婴儿对大方块人会支配小方块人的预期没有实现。

To try to rule out alternative explanations, researchers did several additional experiments including the possibility that the infants were reacting to the size difference between the blocks instead of their perceived social relationship. When they removed the eyes and mouths from both blocks, the difference in looking time vanished, suggesting that infants' expectations about which block should prevail apply only to objects with human features.

这些研究员作了许多额外的实验，以排除一些可能的其他解释，包括婴儿是对方块体积的差异作出了不同的反应而不是他们感受到了社会关系的差异。当研究人员将方块人的眼睛和嘴巴去掉时，婴儿在注视时间上的差异消失了，这证明了婴儿对哪个方块人会取得胜利的预测仅仅适合有人类特征的对象。

In another series of experiments with younger infants, Thomsen and colleagues found that the difference in looking time emerges between 8 months and 10 months, suggesting that this is when the ability to detect social dominance comes online.

在其他一些对象是年龄更小的婴儿的实验中，汤姆森和他的同事发现，注视时间的差异在8至10个月大的婴儿中开始显现，表明了这是判断社会关系的能力开始出现的年龄。

The result fits very nicely with the broader theme of showing that it seems to be part of our inherent human makeup to be attuned to the social world and the meaning of interactions between other individuals. And the asymmetry of power between individuals may be a fundamental social variable we are tuned to attend to.

实验结果很好地证明了，判断社会关系是人生来就有的能力，并且这种能力可以让人理解个体之间相互作用的意义。个体之间力量的不对等也许是我们需要调节和处理的社会基本可变因素之一。

Reading Comprehension 34

The Origins of Political Order
政治秩序的起源

Francis Fukuyama came to public notice in 1989 by predicting, in a famous article, "the end of history." He argued there that all people everywhere, following the arc of history toward its "end" or goal, would eventually aspire to liberty and construct a society grounded in liberal values. Since then people have ridiculed the prediction by pointing to current conflicts both within societies and between them. Yet the prediction is far from falsified, for Mr. Fukuyama had clearly conceded that centuries might pass before all societies found themselves on the same path. In the meantime, he noted, conflicts would inevitably erupt, even genocidal ones.

1989年，弗朗西斯·福山在他的成名作《历史的终点与最后一人》中预言，人类在历史发展的曲线中会趋向一个共同的"终点"或目标，那就是对自由的渴望，并最终建立起一个基于自由主义价值观的人类社会。从那时起，就一直有人在嘲笑这个预言，并指出在当前的社会内部及不同的社会之间存在着许多冲突。可是，福山的预言并非无中生有，他自己也明确地指出，世界各国还需要好几个世纪的发展才能最终走上大同之路。他说，在这段时间里，世界上还会不可避免地爆发出各种冲突，甚至是种族屠杀。

One question that hovered over the end-of-history argument was what political idea—and what real-life political structures—would best serve mankind's own destiny or "end." Hence the impetus behind "The Origins of Political Order," a sweeping survey that tries to explain

《历史的终点与最后一人》提出了一个问题，那就是什么样的政治理念，什么样的现实政治架构才能最好地为全人类的命运或"终点"服务？这是推动福山写作《政治秩序的起源：从史前人类到法国大革命》一书的动力，

why human beings act as they do in the political sphere. Magisterial in its learning and admirably immodest in its ambition, the book traces the history of political organization and principle from "prehuman times" up to the period of the French Revolution.

这本书试图全面地解释为何人类会在政治领域做出各种行为，并深入探讨了从史前人类起直至法国大革命时期的人类政治组织与政治理念。此书内容权威，写作志向深远宏大。

For Mr. Fukuyama, politics are decisive. The ways in which societies govern themselves, he believes, create paths that may last for centuries, even millennia. Unlike the libertarians, he does not believe the state is a second-order phenomenon, a mere enabler or protector of what people choose to do in civil society or, alternatively, a saboteur of their freedoms. On the contrary, the form the state takes is of first-order importance: It can allow for human flourishing or thwart it mercilessly.

在福山看来，政治起着决定性的作用。他认为，社会的统治方式会演变为不同的形式，并延续好几百年甚至是上千年。与自由主义者不同，他不认为国家是人类社会发展的次等现象——国家承担着公民的关爱者或保护者的角色，决定了人们能在社会中做什么，而换个角度看，国家也是个人自由的破坏者。相反，国家的组织形式是最重要的，它能让人们过上富裕幸福的生活，也可以无情地损害人们的生活。

By then the Industrial Revolution—even at its earliest stages—had unleashed the forces of production in ways hitherto unimaginable, allowing for abundance rather than scarcity, not least in the production of food. But the threshold proved to be more than a matter of escaping "the Malthusian trap" of hunger and overpopulation. In the years surrounding the French Revolution, Mr. Fukuyama believes, politics began to shape itself—at last—into an orderly and sustainable form.

当工业革命来临时，即使是在早期，它也让当时的社会释放出前所未有的生产力，物资充盈，不再贫乏，而且影响不只是在食物生产领域。福山认为，这一时代的重要性不仅是体现在社会避免了"马尔萨斯陷阱"中所说的饥饿与人口过剩。在法国大革命前后，政治体制开始塑造其自身，为了最终成为有序和可持续发展的形态。

Obviously, political order had been achieved before then, but in a fitful and incomplete way. In Mr. Fukuyama's view, a durable political order can arise, and societies can fully thrive, only when a state is formed, when the state itself operates according to a rule of law, and when the state becomes accountable—that is, when it must answer to its citizens. Until the threshold point around 1800, he says, all three properties rarely existed together.

显而易见的是，政治秩序早在这一时代之前就已形成，但它是不连续和不完善的。在福山看来，社会要形成可持续发展的政治秩序与充分茁壮成长的社会团体，就必须依靠三点：成型的国家、依法治理、负责任的政府——能响应民众呼声的政府。他认为，在1800年代之前，上述这三点基本上不曾共同存在过。

In ancient China, Mr. Fukuyama observes, we find a strong and authoritative state resting on the rule of law—a predictable set of rules and prohibitions (whether just or unjust, ultimately, is another question entirely). This

福山观察到，在古代中国，存在着依法治理的强大而权威的中央政府，并有着明确的法规与制度（至于这制度是否公正，就属于另一个问题了）。这并非是一蹴而就的成果，中国

achievement did not arise quickly, of course; it took centuries, and war was the crucible out of which it came. But it did last for nearly two millennia. Only intermittently, though, could Chinese subjects expect accountability from their rulers.

也花了好几个世纪时间，才从残酷的战乱中形成。这一成果延续了近2000年，虽然中间也有过中断，但中国的统治者们对他们的臣民还是负责的。

Mr. Fukuyama argues that China's despots and dynasties were in some sense accountable to their subjects by virtue of their grounding in Confucianism. This claim seems a bit forced, however. Confucianism may have restrained some rulers, but the restraint rested purely on the moral suasion of a religious idea, not on independent legal principle. A lack of genuinely accountable government, Mr. Fukuyama says, kept China in a sort of suspended animation. Chinese culture managed to produce great art, literature and theological reflection but no philosophy of freedom and ultimately no political evolution.

福山认为，中国的独裁君王与皇朝体制在某种程度上会对自己的臣民负责，因为他们的价值观建立在儒家思想之上。不过这个说法听起来有点勉强。要知道儒家思想可能会限制一些统治者，但这些限制只是局限于宗教思想的道德引导方面，对独立的法律制度没有作用。福山还说，中国缺乏真正对老百姓负责的政治体制，这让他们一直停留在僵化的状态。古代中国的文明产生了伟大的艺术、文学作品以及对形而上学的深刻思考，但没有形成自由的哲学思想，最终也没有出现政治演变。

Mr. Fukuyama notes that another major Asian society—India—only intermittently, across the centuries, achieved the semblance of a common, accountable statehood for the subcontinent. The barrier, he says, was the caste system and its ramifications, which protected subjects from the tyranny of an overbearing state by subjecting them instead to "the tyranny of cousins." The lesson of both China's and India's history, Mr. Fukuyama claims, is that "a better form of freedom emerges when there is a strong state and a strong society, two centers of power that are able to balance and offset each other."

福山还指出，亚洲的另一个大国——印度，在长达数个世纪的时间里，这块次大陆上也建立起了一个看上去像是共同体的负责任的国家体制，虽然中间也出现过一些间断。但他们的障碍是种姓制度及其产生的恶果，这项制度让印度的臣民不服从国家暴君的暴政，而是服从那些"暴君的表兄弟们"。福山认为，从中国与印度的历史中，我们可以吸取的教训是"自由社会较好的一个形式是：国家同时拥有一个强大的政权与一个强大的民间社会力量，这两者都成为权力的中心，它们能互相制约并保持平衡。"

Accountability is clearly the rarest and hardest property to achieve and yet the one that, for Mr. Fukuyama, makes the state something more than a stronghold for rough justice or "mere" authoritarian order. "Accountable government," he writes, "means that the rulers believe that they are responsible to the people they govern and put the people's interests above their own." This idea ultimately requires that rulers respect the basic rights of their subjects.

显然，对于政府来说，负责任依然是一个稀有而难得的品质，在福山看来，这让国家政权看来不仅仅只是一个简单的司法中心或者是"权威发令者"。他写道："负责任的政府，意味着统治者意识到他们要对人民负责，把人民的利益置于自己的利益之上。"这种观念要求统治者尊重人民的基本权利。

The idea of rights, he says, evolved most notably in Europe, though it took a long time for a full panoply of rights to take hold. The two most fundamental, he argues, are the right to property and the right to a fair trial. England in the 13th century, he claims, was the first place where these two rights were specifically acknowledged and where breaches could be challenged, often with success.

福山说，权利的观念在欧洲发展得最为显著，不过也是经过很长一段时间才发展成为一整套完整的权利法则的。他认为，其中最基本的两点就是财产权与公正审判权。13世纪的英格兰是最先明确承认这两项基本权利的地方，而那些违反这些权利的地方会遭到人民的挑战，且人民往往是胜利者。

It should be noted that, on the Continent, fundamental rights also arose and, resting on them, the idea of a "legal person," the foundation of contracts and of all later commercial law. But if Mr. Fukuyama is less attentive to continental developments during the medieval period, he is right to focus on England （and Scandinavia）as the place where far-sighted leaders first embedded accountable government. Ultimately, accountability took the form not only of fair courts but of the parliaments with which kings would famously struggle for centuries.

应该指出的是，当时的欧洲大陆上，基本权利的观念已经开始抬头，并由此形成"法人"的观念，这是随后出现的合同以及所有商业法律的基础。如果说福山对中世纪欧洲大陆的发展没那么留意的话，那么他把焦点对准英格兰（还有斯堪的纳维亚半岛）是正确的，在那里，有远见的领导者们首次引入了负责任的政府体制。最终，这些责任观念不仅形成了公平的法庭，而且造就了议会，同时也开启了随后数百年间国王与议会不停争斗的历史。

But there was no straight path from the early claims of rights-bearing citizens to the full modern state, Mr. Fukuyama notes. Unlike China, Europe was united only for brief periods, and the fragmentation helped to roil the status quo and drive political change. In short, rulers sought the means of enhancing their power and thereby thwarting their rivals and enemies, both within and without.

福山注意到，要从早期的权利分担的公民社会发展到现代国家，并没有捷径可走。与中国不同，欧洲只在很短的一段时期内是统一的，分裂的局面有助于改变现状并推动政治改革。简而言之，统治者们总在试图加强他们的力量，从而挫败他们在国内和国外的对手和敌人。

For a state to thrive in such circumstances of rivalry required, in Mr. Fuku yama's view, a form of "state-building." And here he allows economic considerations to enter the picture. The states best able to exploit their economic resources, he says, survived; those that didn't disappeared. The leading example here is monarchical France—a place where, one could argue, there was a rule of law and a form of accountable government, with each "estate" making claims for its rights and privileges. Even so, doom was its destiny.

在福山看来，一个国家在竞争的情况下想要蓬勃发展，就需要进行"国家建设"。在这里，他开始加入对经济因素的考虑。他说，那些幸存下来没有消失的国家就是因为它们能最好地利用其经济资源。君主制的法国是一个典型的例子，在法国，法律完备，政府也是负责任的，社会的每个阶层也都有其权利与特权。即使是这样，这个王朝仍走向了灭亡。

Behind the brilliant political theater of Versailles, Mr. Fukuyama says, and behind France's seemingly strict order of administration, confusion reigned. The French state taxed its citizens, but the elites, both the old aristocracy and the new bureaucratic bourgeoisie, found ways to avoid paying anything to the government. The same elites also failed to arrive at an idea of reform for a system in desperate need of it.

福山认为，在凡尔赛宫辉煌的政治舞台背后，在法国看似严格的管理秩序背后，是混乱的体制。法国政府对其公民征税，但社会的精英们，无论是旧贵族还是新官僚资产阶级，均以各种方式逃避任何政府收费。这些精英们同样也未能达成对现有制度进行迫切改革的一致想法。

The result was the collapse known as the French Revolution, which ushered in a terrifyingly more efficient version of the French state. This new model, able to tax and mobilize and punish at a level never before seen in Europe, shocked nearby governments into modernizing themselves in order to survive. Thus we arrive at the threshold of modernity and of the modern, technocratic, bureaucratic form of government that we are now so familiar with.

最终，法国大革命爆发了，这让法国成为了一个更加高效的国家。这种新的政府模式能够以欧洲前所未见的方式征集税收、动员人民与惩罚犯罪，让法国周边的国家无比震撼，被迫进行现代化改革以生存下来。这就是世界现代化出现的时期，从此形成了我们今天所熟悉的现代化、技术专家治理与官僚化的政府系统。

Mr. Fukuyama ends "The Origins of Political Order" on a sobering note. Today's liberal democracies, he says, especially the United States, have in the past two centuries managed to discover a sturdy equilibrium—balancing state power, the rule of law and citizen accountability. But current success, he warns, does not guarantee success in the future.

福山以一段发人深省的话作为《政治秩序的起源》的结束语。他说，今天的自由民主国家，尤其是美国，在过去两百年间成功地建立坚固的平衡制度——国家权力、法治和公民问责制三者互相制衡。但是，他又警告说，目前的成功并不保证未来的成功。

On the contrary, if there is any lesson of history, Mr. Fukuyama says, it is that the robust, masterful society of one era—China in the seventh century, say—may be the collapsed society of another. Future legitimacy depends, he notes, on "being able to maintain an adequate balance between strong state action when necessary and the kinds of individual freedoms that are the basis of its democratic legitimacy and that foster private-sector growth."

福山还说，相反地，如果要说我们从历史中能得出什么教训的话，那就是在某个时代中出现的健全而强大的国家——例如公元七世纪的中国，也可能成为另一个时期崩溃的社会。未来政府的合法性取决于"能够让一个强大的国家在采取必要的国家行动时，保持好国家与个人自由之间的适当平衡，这是保证国家民主合法性与促进私营企业发展的基础"。

Reading Comprehension 35

Women And the Arab Awakening
女性与阿拉伯觉醒

In Tunisia Lina Ben Mhenni, an activist, travelled round the country documenting protests on her blog, "A Tunisian Girl". Besides photographing the dead and wounded, she included pictures of herself with male protesters at sit-ins in the Kasbah in Tunis. Tawakul Karman, awarded the Nobel peace prize at the beginning of October, has been a leading figure in the pro-democracy demonstrations in Yemen, camping out for months in front of Sana'a University, calling for Ali Abdullah Saleh, Yemen's president, to step down. Defying their stereotype as victims of oppressive patriarchies, Arab women have made their presence a defining feature of the Arab spring.

在突尼斯，激进分子莉娜·本·莫海妮游遍全国，在自己的博客"一个突尼斯女孩"中真实记录下了全国各地的抗议活动。除了关于伤亡的照片外，博客上还有她和其他在突尼斯土城区(Kasbah)静坐示威的男性同伴的合影。于十月初被授予诺贝尔和平奖的塔瓦库·卡曼是也门争取民主示威游行活动的领军人物，她在萨那大学门口安营长达数月，要求也门总统阿里阿卜·杜拉·萨利赫下台。阿拉伯妇女正在挣脱父权制压迫下的传统形象，成为阿拉伯之春的一个决定性特征。

The position of women in the Arab world has long been difficult. In 2002 the first Arab Human Development Report cited the lack of women's rights as one of three factors, along with lack of political freedoms and poor education, that most hampered the region's progress. Amid the loud calls for democracy in the early days of the uprisings, little was said specifically about women's rights. But now that constitutions are being rewritten, many women in Egypt and Tunisia, whose revolutions are most advanced, hope to push their own liberation.

长期以来，女性在阿拉伯世界争取地位一直都很艰难。2002年第一份阿拉伯人权发展报告指出，女权的丧失，以及缺乏政治自由和教育水平低下成为阻碍阿拉伯世界进步的三大障碍。在争取民主的起义爆发的最初几天，渴望民主的响亮口号中几乎没有涉及女性权利。但是既然现在正在重新修订宪法，处于革命最前端的埃及和突尼斯的女性希望获得更多的自由。

In Egypt, the sight of women protesting is hardly new. In 1919 veiled women in Cairo marched against British rule, calling for independence. In 1957 Egypt became the first country in the Arab world to elect a woman to parliament, having allowed votes for women only the year before. During the rule of Gamal Abdel Nasser girls were encouraged to go to school, and women exhorted to join the workforce, as part of the general push

在埃及，女性参与抗议的情形已不新鲜。1919年脸蒙面纱的开罗妇女游行示威，反抗英国统治，要求独立。1957年埃及成为阿拉伯世界第一个选举女性成为议会成员的国家，而前一年它刚刚允许女性参与投票。在贾迈勒·阿卜杜勒·纳赛尔统治时期鼓励女孩们上学，鼓励妇女工作，这是经济发展的总体动力的一部分。1970年在安瓦尔·萨达特政权下，由于他

for economic development. In the 1970s under Anwar Sadat, and with encouragement from his wife Jehan, women made further gains. But since then progress has been stalled by the growing power of conservative religious groups.

的妻子吉安的鼓励，妇女权利进一步扩大。但是从那以后，女权运动由于保守宗教集团的势力日渐上升而停滞不前。

Today Egypt's women may work outside the home, go to school and university, and are free to vote and run in all elections. But women's literacy stands at just 58%, and only 23% of workers are women. The country's laws are a mixed bag. The constitution outlaws discrimination on the grounds of sex, but women are entitled to inherit only half as much as men. Husbands may divorce their wives in moments in front of a civil servant, but women endure lengthy court proceedings to do the same. A woman who remarries loses the right to custody of her children.

今天埃及妇女可以走出家门工作，上小学、中学和大学，自由投票，以及参加所有的选举。但是妇女非文盲的比例只占58%，工人中只有23%是妇女。国家相关法律混杂不一。宪法禁止性别歧视，但是女性只能继承男性继承财产的一半。丈夫跟妻子离婚只需要一个公务员和极少的时间即可，而妻子想要和丈夫离婚却不得不忍受冗长的法庭程序。此外，如果一个女人再婚就会失去对孩子的监护权。

Furthermore in the elections due in November 70% of MPs will be elected via party lists which must include at least one woman. This means, according to one government spokesman, that women will get at least 29% of seats in the new parliament. Quite how he came to this figure is unclear. Even if women are included in party lists, no order has been issued about how prominently they should appear. Many fear they will be placed so low that their presence will make little difference.

另外，在11月结束的选举中，70%的国会议员都会从党派的候选人名单中产生，每份名单至少包含一名女性。一名政府发言人表示，这意味着女性至少能获得新议会中29%的席位。不知道他是怎么得出这一数据的。即使党派的名单中包括女性，但并没有条款规定女性在其中的重要性。许多人担心女性会被置于过低的位置，使她们的言论行为都无足轻重。

But many others, especially those who have been campaigning for many decades, remain queasy. Fatma Khafagy, a founding member of the People's Socialist Alliance who is standing for parliament, is sceptical about the Brotherhood and their female associates. The Muslim Sisters take their orders from the Brothers, says Ms Khafagy, and all their leaders are men. She chafes at their emphasis on a traditional, family role for women: "Discrimination against women begins at home."

但是还有很多人，尤其是那些已经为争取权利活动了数十年的人，依旧疑虑重重。法蒂玛·哈法吉是拥护议会的“人民社会主义联盟”的创立者之一，她对兄弟会和他们的女性组织保持怀疑。哈法吉说，穆斯林姐妹会听从兄弟会的命令，而兄弟会所有的领导者都是男性。她为他们强调女性传统家庭角色而感到气恼：“对女性的歧视就是从家庭开始的。”

Much of the progress on women's rights in the Arab world has come as a result of declarations from above, rather than pressure from below. It has been largely an issue for the elites, and a hobby-horse for presidents' wives; and what is given with one hand may be taken back with the other. The recent decision of Saudi Arabia's King Abdullah to allow women to vote in municipal elections is a case in point. Kuwait has, at the emir's insistence, introduced female MPs, but its parliament has also trimmed women's rights in other ways, for example by introducing segregation in Kuwaiti universities.

多数阿拉伯世界女权的进步来自上层阶级的宣言而非下层人民的压力。它在很大程度上是精英阶层的问题和总统夫人的爱好；而统治者可能一手给了女性权利，另一手又把它收了回去。最近，沙特阿伯国王阿卜杜拉允许妇女在市政选举中投票就是一个不偏不倚的例子。科威特在其酋长的坚持下让女性进入议会，但是议会却在其他方面限制女性权利，比如在科威特的大学内实行男女隔离。

It is even more vital, then, that the new governments in Egypt and Tunisia are made aware of women at the outset. As they draft their new constitutions, they have an unparalleled opportunity to incorporate a broader interpretation of women's rights. If the old laws are not changed now, it will be many years before such a chance presents itself again. "We are in a scary situation," says Ms Hassan. "We don't know what the future holds." But change, she feels, must be coming.

更关键的是，埃及和突尼斯政府在一开始就意识到了女权运动的重要性。在起草新宪法时，他们有一个前所未有的机会来赋予女性更宽广的权利。如果旧法律现在不做出改变的话，就得等很多年才能再有这样的机会。"我们目前处于恐慌的境地，"哈桑女士说，"我们不知道未来会怎样。"但是她感到变革一定会到来。

Reading Comprehension 36

Economic Problems and Government Intervention
经济问题与政府干预

It is the *General Theory of Employment, Interest and Money* written in the depression years of the 1930's that has had such a massive effect in social, political and ideological terms. In this book, Keynes optimistically argues that downturns in the economy are short-term problems stemming from a lack of demand. Keynes offered a simple, though somewhat radical, solution: the government should boost short-term demand through public spending, and once the economy returns to

对社会、政治、意识形态方面造成重大影响的《就业、利息和货币通论》一书写成于发生经济大萧条的20世纪30年代。在这本书中，凯恩斯乐观地说道，经济衰退只是源自需求不足的短期问题。对此，他提出了一个简单但或许有些激进的解决方案：政府应当通过对公共事业的投入来提高短期的经济需求。一旦经济情况恢复，政府再通过增加税收和减少公共事业投入来填补其财政赤字。

buoyancy the government reclaims its budget deficit by increasing taxes and reducing public spending.

The underlying principle is straightforward enough: government spending should be inversely proportional to private trade: when trade is booming, government should spend little, when the economy slumps, public spending should go up. But what was radical about this proposal was the general principle that the government should intervene in the economy to control demand, an idea that has come to be known as "demand management policy".

这种解决方案之下的根本原则是相当明确的：政府投入应当与民间贸易成相反的比例，即当民间贸易繁荣时，政府应当减少投入；当经济衰退时，政府投入应当增加。但是这项提议的激进之处在于，认为政府应当干预经济并控制需求，这种理念后来被称为"需求管理政策"。

Through showing how government intervention could lead to a stable free market economy, Keynes' theory was seen at the time as the answer to Marx's prediction that the boom and bust cycle of capitalism would inevitably lead to socialism. However critics deplored the idea of government intervention for that it encouraged the anti-liberal idea that social problems should be solved by government, and indeed that government should look to academics to show them how to solve such problems. Nothing could have been more repugnant to the supporters of the classical "laissez-faire" economics of Adam Smith. On the classical view, the economy functions best when there is no interference from government. Smith believed that the natural economic order will, so long as it is not disturbed by governmental meddling, tend towards the maximum well-being of both the individual and society.

凯恩斯向人们展示出政府的干预怎样造就一个稳定而自由的市场经济，于是凯恩斯的理论被看成是回应了马克思对资本主义经济发展的预测，即资本主义经济中繁荣与萧条的周期循环必然导致社会主义的产生。但是，评论家们还是对政府进行干预的理念进行了谴责，因为它鼓励了某种反自由主义的思想，即社会问题应当由政府来解决，并且政府还应当在这些问题上求助于专家学者。对于经典的"放任自流"型经济政策（"laissez-faire" economics，由亚当·斯密提出）的支持者们来说，没有比这些看法更能激起他们的反感了。该观点认为，没有政府的干预，经济功能才能发挥完好。斯密认为，经济中蕴含的固有秩序在没有政府干预的情况下会对个人和社会产生最大的福利。

Reading Comprehension 37

Technology for World Food Shortage
解决世界性粮食短缺问题

The promise of delving long-term technological solutions to the problem of world food shortages seems

通过研制长期性技术来解决世界性粮食短缺问题似乎是一项难以完成的任务。这种方

difficult to fulfill. The proposals themselves were technically feasible, but they proved to be economically unviable and to yield food products culturally unacceptable to consumers. Recent innovations such as Antarctic krill, and the wheat-rye hybrid triticale seem promising, but it is too hasty to predict their ultimate fate.

式本身在技术上可行，但是在经济效益上和消费者的饮食文化接受度上都遭遇了“滑铁卢”。比如，近期的一些新发明诸如南极磷虾、（小麦和黑麦杂交的）黑小麦等貌似前景无限好，但是现在预言其最终命运还言之尚早。

One characteristic common to unsuccessful examples had aimed at the lack of technological adaption or cultural access to the marketing target——people whom they had been developed for. As well as the entire socio-cultural system, security of crop yield, practicality of storage, palatability, and costs became much more significant than previously realized by the advocates. For example, the better protein quality in tortillas made from opaque-2 maize will be of only limited benefit to a family on the margin of subsistence if the new maize is not culturally acceptable or is more vulnerable to insects.

这些失败的例子有一个共同的特点，那就是在技术上过于死板，以及与目标市场的饮食文化衔接不上。除了社会文化的这些因素之外，农作物的收成、贮藏的可行性、口感以及种植成本这些要素远比支持者们先前了解的意义重大。比如：一些由opaque-2型玉米做成的玉米饼含有质量更好的蛋白质，但是这种食物对于那些贫困家庭来说却没什么价值，原因在于这种新型玉米从文化上不被人们所接受，或者对于抵抗病虫害侵袭的能力比较低。

Indeed, the adoption of new food technologies depends on more than these technical and cultural considerations; economic factors and governmental policies strongly influence the ultimate success of any innovation as well. Although some economists regarded profitability as the key factor in guiding technical change—completely disregard the substantial effects of culture—they are correct in stressing the importance of profits. Only proved to be potentially profitable could those innovations be fully utilized by those large landowners and profitable-oriented ones, even at the expense of other segments of population in a country.

事实上，对于新食品技术的采纳更多地取决于政治和经济因素，而不仅仅是基于技术和文化上的考虑。虽然说很多经济学家们完全无视文化因素的作用，单纯地把盈利性作为技术变革的决定性因素，但是他们强调盈利的重要性是无可厚非的。只有证明新的技术能够带来经济利益，才能为大型土地所有者和利润导向型的企业所采用，哪怕这样会损害这个国家中另一部分人的利益。

Arguably, since large segments of the populations of many developing countries are close to the subsistence margin and essentially powerless, they tend to be the losers in this system unless aided by a government policy. Therefore, although technical advances in food production and processing will perhaps be needed to ensure food

可是，由于在很多发展中国家的人民都处于贫穷的状态，如果政府不帮助他们的话，他们将在这种环境下成为受损失者。所以，尽管一些技术改进的确能够提高食物生产和加工的效率，但是在发展中国家要想满足所有人的食物需求，有赖于平衡各类人群的经济能力。

availability, meeting food needs will depend much more on equalizing economic power among the various segments of the populations within the developing countries themselves.

Reading Comprehension 38

Statistics and Labor Market Problem
数据与劳动力市场问题

How many really suffer as a result of labor market problems? This is one of the most critical yet contentious social policy questions. In many ways, our social statistics exaggerate the degree of hardship. Unemployment does not have the same dire consequences today as it did in the 1930's when income and earnings were usually much closer to the margin of subsistence, and when there were no countervailing social welfare for those failing in the labor market. Increasing affluence, the rise of families with more than one wage earner, and improved social welfare protection have unquestionably mitigated the consequences of joblessness. Earnings and income data also overstate the dimensions of hardship. Among the millions with hourly earnings at or below the minimum wage level, the overwhelming majority are from multiple-earner, relatively affluent families. So the poverty statistics are by no means an accurate indicator of labor market pathologies.

到底有多少人因为劳动力市场的问题面临困境呢？这是最尖锐而又颇具争议的社会政策问题之一。我们的社会数据统计在很多方面夸大了实际的困难程度。现如今的失业情况和20世纪30年代比起来已经没那么悲惨了，在那个时候收入通常刚刚够维持生计，而且那时也没有为失业者准备的补偿性福利。毫无疑问，现如今人们日益增长的财富、更多的家庭中不止一个人有收入以及逐渐改善的社会福利保障缓解了失业带给人们的不利影响。此外我们的收入数据也夸大了困难程度。在数百万每小时工资刚刚达到甚至低于最低工资水平的人们当中，其实有很大一批人的家庭是相对富裕的，有多个挣钱养家的成员。所以，贫困数据对于反映劳动力市场的问题肯定是不准确的。

Yet there are also many ways our social statistics underestimate the degree of labor-market-related hardship. The unemployment counts exclude the millions of fully employed workers whose wages are so low that their families remain in poverty. For every person counted in the monthly unemployment tallies, there is another working part-time because of the inability to find full-time

但是，现在我们的社会数据其实在很多方面也低估了劳动力市场的困难程度。失业统计中没有把数百万虽然有工作但是工资太低难以养家的人算在内。另外，每有一个人记录在每月失业统计中，就有另一个人只有兼职工作，因为没有能力找到一份全职的工作，或者还有另一个人需要一份工作但没有被算在劳

work, or else outside the labor force but wanting a job. Finally, welfare in our country have always focused on the elderly, disabled, and dependent, neglecting the needs of the working poor, so that the dramatic expansion of cash and in-kind transfers does not necessarily mean that those failing in the labor market are adequately protected.

动力范围之内。最后，我们国家的社会福利往往只能顾及那些老弱病残、需要人照顾的群体，忽视了工作中的穷人的需求。因此，现金和实物援助的扩大并不意味着他们都能获得该有的照顾。

As a result, it is uncertain whether those suffer seriously as a result of labor market problems number in the hundreds of thousands, and, hence, whether high levels of joblessness can be tolerated or must be countered by job creation and economic stimulus. There is only one area of agreement in this debate—that the existing poverty, employment, and earnings statistics are inadequate for measuring the consequences of labor market problems.

基于此，我们搞不清楚那些拜劳动力市场问题所赐遭受苦难的人口数量是否达到了成百上千，也搞不清楚我们是否可以对高失业率置之不理，还是必须以经济刺激计划或者增加就业来解决这种现状。我们唯一可以确定的是：现有的这些贫困数据、就业数据、收入数据对于衡量劳动力市场的问题，是绝对不足的！

Reading Comprehension 39

Spinoza's Vision of Freedom, and Ours
斯宾诺莎和我们的自由观

Baruch Spinoza, the 17th-century Dutch thinker, may be among the more enigmatic philosophers in Western thought, but he also remains one of the most relevant, to his time and to ours. He was an eloquent proponent of a secular, democratic society, and was the strongest advocate for freedom and tolerance in the early modern period. The ultimate goal of his *Theological-Political Treatise*—published anonymously to great alarm in 1670—is enshrined both in the book's subtitle and in the argument of its final chapter: to show that the "freedom of philosophizing" not only can be granted "without detriment to public peace, to piety, and to the right of the sovereign, but also that it must be granted if these are to be preserved."

巴鲁克·斯宾诺莎是17世纪时的荷兰思想家，他可能是西方思想界中具有更多神秘色彩的哲学家之一，同时也是最契合当时以及当代社会诉求的思想家之一。他雄辩滔滔，力主一个世俗的、民主的社会，是人类文明现代化发轫时期自由与宽容的强力倡导者。他在1670年匿名发表的《神学政治论》堪称惊世骇俗之作；该书的小标题和最后一章的论述体现了其终极目的：为了阐明赋予人们"思想自由"对公共和平、虔诚和最高统治者的权利并无损害，不仅如此，若要保持它们就必须赋予人们这种自由。

Spinoza was incited to write the "Treatise" when he recognized that the Dutch Republic, and his own province of Holland in particular, was wavering from its uncommonly liberal and relatively tolerant traditions. In this work, Spinoza approaches the issue of individual liberty from several perspectives. To begin with, there is the question of belief, and especially the state's tolerance of the beliefs of its citizens. Spinoza argues that all individuals are to be absolutely free and unimpeded in their beliefs, by right and in fact. "It is impossible for the mind to be completely under another's control; for no one is able to transfer to another his natural right or faculty to reason freely and to form his own judgment on any matters whatsoever, nor can he be compelled to do so."

当时，斯宾诺莎发现，荷兰共和国，特别是他所在的荷兰行省，开始背离其独有的自由和相对宽容的传统精神，这种状况激发了他写作《神学政治论》。在这部著作中，斯宾诺莎对个人自由进行了多方面的阐述。首先是信仰问题，特别是国家对其公民信仰的宽容态度。斯宾诺莎认为，所有的个人都应享有绝对的、不受限制的信仰自由，这不仅是权利也是事实。"人的思想不可能完全任由他人操控；无论自愿或被迫，无人可将其自由思考并自行判断事物的天赋权利或能力让与他人。"

For this reason, any effort on the government's part to rule over the beliefs and opinions of citizens is bound to fail, and will ultimately serve to undermine its own authority. A sovereign is certainly free to try and limit what people think, but the result of such a policy, Spinoza predicts, would be only to create resentment and opposition to its rule.

基于此，政府一方任何辖制公民信仰和意见的努力均注定失败，并终将削弱其自身的权威。斯宾诺莎预言：最高统治者必会想方设法限制民众所想，但这种政策的结果只会催发人民对其统治的憎恶与反抗。

It can be argued that the state's tolerance of individual belief is not a difficult issue. As Spinoza points out, it is "impossible" for a person's mind to be under another's control, and this is a necessary reality that any government must accept. The more difficult case, the true test of a regime's commitment to toleration, concerns the liberty of citizens to express those beliefs, either in speech or in writing. And here Spinoza goes further than anyone else of his time: "Utter failure," he says, "will attend any attempt in a commonwealth to force men to speak only as prescribed by the sovereign despite their different and opposing opinions... The most tyrannical government will be one where the individual is denied the freedom to express and to communicate to others what he thinks, and a moderate government is one where this freedom is granted to every man."

人们可以争辩说，国家容许个人信仰并非难事。正如斯宾诺莎所指出的那样，人的思想"不可能"受到他人的辖制，任何政府都必须接受这个事实。但更难以做到的，而且对一个承诺宽容的政权构成真正考验的是，公民表达他们信仰的自由，无论是以公开演讲还是诉诸文字的方式。对此，斯宾诺莎比他同时代的人更进一步，声言："一国之内强令人们违背己见以发统治者意愿之语的任何企图，必将彻底失败……剥夺个人表达见解、与他人交流的自由的政府，是最暴虐的政府；温和的政府则允许每个人享有这种自由。"

Spinoza also argues for freedom of expression on utilitarian grounds—that it is necessary for the discovery of truth, economic progress and the growth of creativity. Without an open marketplace of ideas, science, philosophy and other disciplines are stifled in their development, to the technological, fiscal and even aesthetic detriment of society. As Spinoza puts it, "this freedom [of expressing one's ideas] is of the first importance in fostering the sciences and the arts, for it is only those whose judgment is free and unbiased who can attain success in these fields."

斯宾诺莎也从实用性的角度对言论自由加以论述，即它为发现真理、发展经济和培植创造性所必需。公开的思想空间的缺失将阻塞科学、哲学及其他学科的发展道路，从而对社会造成技术上、财政上乃至审美上的损害。正如斯宾诺莎所说，"这种(表达个人意见的)自由，在培养科学和艺术方面具有头等重要的作用，因为只有那些能够自由并无偏见地作出判断的人们，才可以在这些领域取得成功。"

Reading Comprehension 40

Why Time Seems to Slow Down
时光缘何放慢脚步

It is common to all that time flies when you're having fun, that when you are involved in something engaging the time seems to rocket by, even though that same event may feel long when you look back on it. The flip side, of course, is that boring events seem to drag on: a one-hour lecture of history can seem longer than the entire era being described.

我们都知道，快乐的时光总是短暂的。当我们玩得很开心时，当我们全身心投入某事之时，时光便如流水般飞逝；即使我们回头体味那些时光时，发觉耗时弥久。而另一方面，很显然地，那些无聊的事物似乎总是拖拽着时间。一个小时的历史讲座似乎可以比它讲的整个历史时期还要冗长。

An interesting paper was published exploring the role of your sense of entitlement on the perception of the passage of time. The basic idea is straightforward: at any given time, everyone feels some sense of entitlement. Standing on the line to check out at a big box retailer, you might feel particularly entitled to better service. So, a 10-minute wait for a slow check may feel like an hour. On the other hand, if you were sitting in a waiting room at the White House before having a chance to meet the president, you might consider yourself lucky to be there.

一篇有趣的论文探索了人的权利资格意识在感知时光流逝中的作用。文章的基本思路很简单：在任何给定时间，每个人都有某种权利资格的意识。当在一个大型零售店排队等待付款时，你尤其会感到有资格获得更好的服务。所以，在碰到结账慢吞吞的情况时，十分钟的等待都宛如一个小时的煎熬。然而，如果你获得了与总统见面的机会，正在白宫等候室里，你会认为这是一种运气。如果是那样，10分钟的等待便显得不那么长了。

In that case, a 10-minute wait might not feel so long.

In one study, the authors just looked at the correlation between people's general sense of entitlement and their perception of time. It turns out that there is a difference between people in how entitled they feel in general: some people generally feel more like they deserve to get things from the world than other people.

在一份研究中，研究人员仅仅观察了人们的总体权利资格意识与其时间感知之间的关系。结果表明，人们对于所获权利资格的感知在大体上是不同的：有些人认为自己应该比其他人从这个世界上获得的更多。

The authors gave people a number of questionnaires including one that measured the sense of entitlement. Then they had people do either a boring task (copying a matrix of letters) or a less boring task (using that same matrix of letters to find people's names). People did this task for exactly 10 minutes, and then they were asked how long the task took. When people did the relatively fun task, there was no relationship between the amount of time people felt they spent doing the task and their general sense of entitlement. In contrast, when people did the boring task, the more people generally feel entitled, the longer they felt they spent on the task.

研究人员给受试者提供了一些调查问卷，其中有一份就是衡量权利资格意识的。然后，他们让一些受试者做一种单调无趣的任务(抄写一个字母矩阵)，而让另一些受试者做一种不那么无趣的任务(用同样的字母矩阵来找出人名)。受试者用了整整10分钟完成了任务，然后被问及做这件任务所用的时间。当人们在做后一项相对有趣的任务时，其权利资格意识与其对时间消耗的感知没有关系。相反，当做前一项单调无趣的任务时，人们对自身权利资格的意识越强烈，感觉用在任务上的时间就会越多。

Now, you might think that being asked questions about yourself would be more interesting than answering questions about students in general. So, it could easily be the case that the survey would seem shorter when you are more engaged in the task. Thus, the sense of entitlement increased people's judgments of the time the survey took to complete.

现在，你可能会认为，回答关于自身的问题要比回答研究者的问题有趣。所以，很容易得出这样的结论：当你更投入地完成任务时，问卷就会显得短一些。因此，权利资格的意识增加了受试者对于完成问卷所需时间的判断。

What does all this mean? Time is one of our most precious resources. The greater your sense of entitlement, the more that you want to avoid wasting time. As a result, the more entitled you feel, the more pain you experience when your time is wasted. Even though nobody enjoys frustration, this mechanism is a good one to have. If we did not experience frustration when our time was being wasted, we might persist doing things that do not deserve our effort.

这说明了什么？时间是我们最珍贵的资源之一。你的权力资格意识愈强烈，你便愈加会避免浪费时光。其结果便是，你越感到自己有资格，在浪费时光时，你所经历的痛楚便越多。虽然没有人喜欢沮丧感，但拥有这种机制是有益的。假如，在浪费光阴时我们不感觉到沮丧，那么，我们便可能继续做一些不值得付出努力的事情了。

Reading Comprehension 41

Jung's Psychological Classification
荣格的心理学分类

Swiss psychologist and therapist, Jung was the disciple of Freud, but unlike Freud, Jung would divide the psyche into three parts: the ego, the personal unconscious and the collective unconscious. His reading of Freud, interjected with ideas from mythology, religion and philosophy, led him to posit a universal unconscious that revealed itself in symbolic form through dreams, mysticism and religion.

荣格是一位瑞士的心理学家和治疗师，他曾是弗洛伊德的弟子，但和弗洛伊德不同的是，荣格将人的心灵分为三个部分：自我、个人潜意识和集体潜意识。他阅读了弗洛伊德的作品，同时也吸收了来自神话、宗教和哲学的思想，这让他设想出一种通过梦、神秘主义和宗教体现在象征形式中的一种“普遍潜意识”。

The key to Jung's idea of a collective unconscious lies in the notion of an "archetype". According to Jung, the collective unconscious determines that our "experience" is conceived according to certain organizing principles, the archetypes. Jung outlined some of the most powerful archetypes that shape our lives and account for our behavior.

理解荣格“集体潜意识”的关键在于弄清“原型”（archetype）的概念。根据荣格的看法，集体潜意识决定了我们的经验是遵循某种组织原则——原型——来建构的。荣格描述了能够塑造我们的生活和解释我们的行为的几种最具影响力的原型。

One such archetype is the "mother" archetype. Although it is clear that having a mother is a necessary biological relationship, Jung's mother archetype refers to more than just the common relation that we all bear to some other human being. The "mother archetype" reflects a psychological need. What is significant about the mother archetype, Jung tells us, is that we all expect something or someone in our lives to fulfill the role of nurturing us and providing us with comfort in times of stress. This is an evolutionary need so it should come as no surprise that Jung says we come into the world ready to want mother, to seek her, to recognize and to deal with her. Ordinarily we project this need on to our biological mother. However, where Jung's theory comes into action in psychotherapy is in revealing the patterns of behavior people exhibit when the biological mother has not fulfilled

其中一个是“母亲原型”。尽管我们都清楚拥有一位母亲对建立生物亲缘关系是必要的，但荣格提出的“母亲原型”不仅仅指这种普通的生物联系。母亲原型反映出一种心理需要。荣格告诉我们，母亲原型的深远意义是指我们都希望在我们的生活中有某样东西或某个人能够完成养育我们和在我们承受压力时给我们以安慰这样的角色。这种需要是在进化过程中出现的，所以当荣格说，我们到达这个世界时就已经做好了期待母亲、寻找母亲、辨认母亲和与母亲相处的准备了，这丝毫不令人感到惊讶。通常，我们将这种需要投射在我们的生物学母亲身上。讲到这里，荣格的理论转向了精神分析的治疗领域，当生物学上的母亲没有完成“母亲原型”的角色时，分析师就开始对其子女的外在行为模式进行分析。例如，在此情

the archetypal role. For instance, someone whose biological mother did not fulfill the archetypical role may find themselves attracted to "mother-substitutes", the church, the army, national patriotism and so on.

况下，有些人可能会被“母亲的替代物”所吸引，如教堂、军队、爱国主义等等。

Besides these, Jung went on to distinguish between a number of different personality types, and invented the terms "introvert" and "extrovert" to describe two of the most basic types. These have become synonymous with being shy or being an exhibitionist, but Jung's explanation of these ideas was far more sophisticated. According to Jung, introverted personalities were those, such as himself, whose "ego" was turned more towards the internal and unconscious, whereas extroverts were orientated more towards outer reality and external activity. The distinction plays an important role in Jung's notion of the self. The self is the master archetype, that principle by which we structure our whole lives. Jung thought the self was in a constant process of development, which became fully realized when all aspects of our personalities are equally expressed. Thus to be overly introvert or overly extrovert represents an immaturity in development. However, if we develop normally, as we get older we tend to balance out the different aspects of our personality.

除此之外，荣格进一步区分了不同人格的类型，并且发明了“内向”和“外向”的术语来描述人格中最基本的两大类别。这两个术语似乎与害羞或爱出风头是同义词，但是荣格的解释要精密复杂得多。根据荣格的看法，内向者的自我更多朝向自己的内心和潜意识，而外向者的自我则更多朝向外部世界和外在活动。这种区分在荣格有关“自我”(self)的概念上起到了重要的作用。“自我”(self)是核心原型，通过此原则我们建构起整个生活。荣格认为自我处于一个不断发展的过程当中，当我们人格中的所有方面都均等地表现出来时，自我原型就完全实现了。因此，在人格发展中过度内向或过度外向都是不成熟的表现。但是，如果我们按照正常趋势发展的话，到我们年长时我们人格中的不同方面会趋向平衡。

社会科学类题源单词补充

分类	编码	真题原词	真题背景精确注释
法律	001	abolish	废止
法律	002	acquit	脱卸(债务)
法律	003	acquittal	释放
法律	004	alibi	不在犯罪现场的证据
法律	005	appeal	感染力；上诉
法律	006	apprehend	逮捕
法律	007	attorney	初级律师
法律	008	authentic	法律证实的
法律	009	bail	准许保释
法律	010	barrister	讼务律师
法律	011	commit	做(不好的事情)
法律	012	constitution	宪法
法律	013	constitutional	合乎宪法的;本质的
法律	014	convict	定罪
法律	015	conviction	定罪;信念
法律	016	culprit	犯罪者
法律	017	defendant	被告
法律	018	detain	使延迟
法律	019	edict	法令
法律	020	exculpate	开脱
法律	021	exonerate	免责
法律	022	felon	重罪犯
法律	023	felony	重罪
法律	024	forensic	庭辩的
法律	025	guilt	罪行
法律	026	illegal	不合法的
法律	027	illicit	违法的
法律	028	immure	监禁
法律	029	incarcerate	投入监狱
法律	030	inculpate	控告
法律	031	indict	控诉
法律	032	indictment	起诉
法律	033	infraction	违法
法律	034	intern	拘禁
法律	035	judicial	法庭的
法律	036	judiciary	法官

分类	编码	真题原词	真题背景精确注释
法律	037	jurisprudence	法理学
法律	038	legislate	制定法律
法律	039	litigant	诉讼人
法律	040	litigation	诉讼
法律	041	malefactor	罪犯
法律	042	maleficent	犯罪的
法律	043	manacle	枷锁
法律	044	mayhem	严重伤害罪
法律	045	nefarious	罪恶的，违法的
法律	046	ordinance	条例
法律	047	penalty	刑罚
法律	048	penology	监狱管理学
法律	049	perjure	作伪证
法律	050	perjury	伪证
法律	051	plaintiff	原告
法律	052	prosecute	检举
法律	053	reprieve	缓刑
法律	054	statute	法规
法律	055	statutory	法定的
法律	056	subpoena	传票
法律	057	treason	叛国罪
法律	058	tribunal	法庭
经济	001	accountant	会计师
经济	002	agent	代理经纪人
经济	003	antitrust law	反托拉斯法
经济	004	audit	审计
经济	005	bankrupt	破产
经济	006	borrowing	借款
经济	007	brokerage	佣金
经济	008	budget	预算
经济	009	capitalistic	资本的
经济	010	collateral	抵押品
经济	011	commercial	广告
经济	012	compound interest	复利
经济	013	consortium	财团
经济	014	consume	消费
经济	015	coupon	礼券
经济	016	currency	通货，货币
经济	017	default	拖欠债务
经济	018	deficit	赤字

分类	编码	真题原词	真题背景精确注释
经济	019	economic	经济学的
经济	020	economical	节约的
经济	021	economy	经济体
经济	022	financial crash	金融危机
经济	023	fiscal	政府财政的
经济	024	free market	自由市场经济
经济	025	GNP	国民生产总值
经济	026	import relief	进口援助
经济	027	inflation	通货膨胀
经济	028	interest rate	利率
经济	029	inventory	库存
经济	030	investment	投资
经济	031	invigorate	激励
经济	032	keynesian	凯恩斯主义
经济	033	laissez-faire capitalism	自由资本主义
经济	034	list price	标价
经济	035	managerial	经理人的
经济	036	margin	利润
经济	037	mark down	降价
经济	038	mark up	涨价
经济	039	mercantilist	重商主义者
经济	040	merchandise	商品
经济	041	monetary	货币的
经济	042	mortgage	抵押借款
经济	043	nickel	镍币
经济	044	outlet	销路
经济	045	output	输出
经济	046	pension	养老金
经济	047	per capita	人均的
经济	048	premium	保险金
经济	049	privatize	私有化
经济	050	proceeds	收入款项
经济	051	produce	农产品
经济	052	productivity	生产率
经济	053	profit	利润
经济	054	profitable	可获利的
经济	055	property	资产
经济	056	proxy	代理
经济	057	purchasing price	购买价
经济	058	quota	限额，定额

分类	编码	真题原词	真题背景精确注释
经济	059	rate	费用率；比率
经济	060	rating	信用额度
经济	061	real estate	房地产
经济	062	receipt	收据
经济	063	recession	经济衰退
经济	064	recurrent	周期性
经济	065	revenue	收入
经济	066	sale price	销售价
经济	067	simple interest	单利
经济	068	sluggish economy	经济疲软
经济	069	statistic	统计数据
经济	070	stipend	薪水
经济	071	stock	股票
经济	072	subcontract	分包合同
经济	073	subsidize	补助
经济	074	subsidy	津贴
经济	075	takeover	收购
经济	076	tariff	关税表
经济	077	transaction	交易
经济	078	treasury	国库券
经济	079	turnaround	转型
经济	080	turnover	营业额
经济	081	unemployment	失业
政治	001	allegiance	忠诚
政治	002	anachronistic	时代错误
政治	003	anarchy	无政府
政治	004	arbitrary	武断的
政治	005	ascendancy	统治力
政治	006	authoritarian	极权者
政治	007	autocrat	独裁者
政治	008	autonomy	自治
政治	009	ballot	投票
政治	010	bigot	顽固派
政治	011	bureaucracy	官僚政治
政治	012	cabal	阴谋集团
政治	013	cabinet	内阁
政治	014	candidacy	候选资格
政治	015	caucus	峰会
政治	016	centralization	集权
政治	017	coercion	高压政治

分类	编码	真题原词	真题背景精确注释
政治	018	commonwealth	政治集团
政治	019	filibuster	妨碍议事
政治	020	franchise	公民权
政治	021	gerontocracy	老人统治
政治	022	hegemony	领导权
政治	023	hierarchy	等级制度
政治	024	imperious	傲慢的，专横的
政治	025	interregnum	无王时期
政治	026	malfeasance	渎职
政治	027	matriarchy	母权制，妇女统治
政治	028	medieval	中世纪
政治	029	monarchy	君主制
政治	030	municipality	市政当局
政治	031	oligarchy	寡头政治
政治	032	oratory	演讲术
政治	033	plebeian	庶民
政治	034	plebiscite	全民投票
政治	035	plutocracy	富豪统治
政治	036	polis	城邦
政治	037	populist	平民党党员
政治	038	precinct	郡(辖区)
政治	039	regime	政治制度
政治	040	reign	王朝
政治	041	suffrage	选举权
政治	042	theocracy	神权政治
政治	043	tyranny	暴政
宗教	001	alter	祭坛
宗教	002	apostle	使徒
宗教	003	catholic	天主教徒
宗教	004	Centaur	半人半马(怪物)
宗教	005	christening	洗礼
宗教	006	congregation	宗教圣会
宗教	007	deity	神性
宗教	008	divinity	上帝
宗教	009	evangelist	福音传教者
宗教	010	Islamic law	伊斯兰教法
宗教	011	mass	弥撒
宗教	012	missionary	传教士
宗教	013	parish	教区
宗教	014	polytheist	多神论教徒

分类	编码	真题原词	真题背景精确注释
宗教	015	prophet	先知
宗教	016	Protestant	新教徒
宗教	017	rite	典礼
宗教	018	ritual	宗教仪式
宗教	019	saint	圣徒
宗教	020	sainthood	圣徒身份
宗教	021	salvation	灵魂超度
宗教	022	secularization	脱离宗教
宗教	023	sermon	布道
宗教	024	sin	原罪
宗教	025	theologian	神学家
宗教	026	throne	王座
宗教	027	trinity	基督三位一体

Note

后　记

本书的构思始于2009年，由笔者所撰写的一篇文章《解读新GRE考试阅读理解部分的改革》(http://edu.qq.com/a/20100322/000208.htm）发端而来，亲历了GRE考试的改革和变迁，在2011年5月笔者在中关村海淀剧院进行大规模备考复习讲座(http://v.youku.com/v_show/id_XMjc0MTA3MjUy.html)时逐渐成熟。王小丹老师和我一起负责主编新东方新GRE标准化教材的时候，小丹的聪明睿智使这种思想得到了前所未有的发展和延伸，再加上李政洁老师的耐心细致，当然还有窦中川老师中肯的建议以及孙春红老师和张茜老师的精心校对，融合成了摆在各位面前的这本书籍。

本书没有艰深晦涩的理论，没有让你摸不着头脑的抽象概念，而是非常具体、扎扎实实的干货。让大家看到新GRE考试的本来面目。具体来讲，当一篇GRE文章放到你的面前，你所看到的，不仅是诸多文章的共性(结构和套路)，还有它们的个性(主题和词汇)。美国教育考试服务中心(ETS)明确规定：阅读文章题材广泛，涵盖物理学、生物学、社会科学、艺术和人文等学科以及日常话题，源于各类学术性以及非学术性书籍和期刊(引自《GRE考试官方指南》第44页)。本书的前后两个部分使这一理念得到统合和具体化，是一本必读的考前用书。

前辈杨继老师在1999年撰写阅读教材后记中说过：终究有一天，人们会懂得一个道理：站在课堂上眉飞色舞的我们是最愚蠢的，而坐在课堂上洗耳恭听的你们是最聪慧的。非常欣赏他对现实这种客观冷静而又不带光环的态度。其实不必太把自己当回事儿，通过成就别人而彰显自己的价值，这就是我们的职责所在。看着数十万计的莘莘学子从我们的课堂走入北美最高等的学府深造对我们是一种最大的快慰。

胡　楠

2012年8月23日于中关村大河庄苑

新 GRE 阅读备考策略视频　by 胡楠

新东方大愚GRE精品图书推荐

《GRE考试官方指南》（附CD-ROM）

美国教育考试服务中心（ETS） 编著

- ◎ ETS官方独家授权版本，权威解析GRE考试
- ◎ 提供样题范例，帮助考生了解各题型的命题形式和要求
- ◎ 内含完整的全真试题，并配CD-ROM 1张，带给考生真实的考场体验

定价：88元　开本：16开　页码：448页

《GRE词汇精选》（最新版）（附MP3）

俞敏洪 编著

- ◎ 自1993年首版以来先后修订9次，收录迄今为止GRE考试的全部重要词汇，并给出精准释义
- ◎ 提供大量经典例句，结合语境加深对单词的理解与记忆
- ◎ 以“词根+联想”记忆法为主，辅以组合词、单词拆分、谐音等多种记忆方法，配以插图，轻松记忆
- ◎ 给出丰富的同义词，归纳常考搭配
- ◎ 提供返记菜单，便于查找定位
- ◎ 附赠600分钟MP3光盘1张，由专业人员朗读单词及中文释义

定价：58元　开本：16开　页码：488页

《GRE词汇精选：乱序版》（附MP3）

俞敏洪 编著

- ◎ “乱序”编排，提供科学单词记忆方法
- ◎ 给出丰富的同义词，归纳常考搭配
- ◎ 书内附赠600分钟MP3光盘一张

定价：59.8 元　开本：16开　页码：512页

《GRE词汇精选：便携版》

俞敏洪 编著

- ◎ 浓缩《GRE词汇精选》之精华，收词全面
- ◎ 提供“词根+联想”记忆法，实用有趣，轻松记忆
- ◎ 开本小巧，便于携带，方便考生随时随地记忆单词

定价：25 元　开本：32开　页码：448页

《GRE词汇逆序记忆小词典》

俞敏洪 黄颀 编著

- ◎ 《GRE词汇精选》（最新版）的姊妹篇
- ◎ 采用逆序编排体例，巧学助记
- ◎ 增添GRE考试最新词汇
- ◎ 附正序词汇索引，方便检测记忆效果
- ◎ 本书自1999年问世以来，畅销不衰

定价：15元　开本：32开　页码：308页

《GRE考试官方指南词汇必备》（附MP3）

余仁唐 编著

◎ 页码为序，合理编排方便查找
◎ 选词科学，根据语境精准释义
◎ 重点单词，循环出现加深记忆
◎ 一书多用，全面攻克GRE词汇

定价：25元　开本：32开　页码：264页

《GRE核心词汇考法精析》

陈琦 周书林 主编

◎ 7年实战经验沉淀，精炼3000必考词汇
◎ 直击GRE同反考法，星号标注最新词汇
◎ 权威韦氏英文解释，辅以经典英文例句
◎ 高分学员励志推荐，GRE考试高分必备

定价：55元　开本：16开　页码：464页

《新GRE高频词汇：句子填空》

杜昶旭 侯宇轩 编著

定价：48元 开本：16开 页码：384页

《新GRE高频词汇：阅读理解》

杜昶旭 侯宇轩 编著

定价：59元 开本：16开 页码：568页

◎ 科学统计20年GRE考试句子填空与阅读理解真题词汇
◎ 按照单词在考试中出现的频次从高到低排序
◎ 提供单词在GRE考试中考到的中、英文释义
◎ 提供与真题难度相当的例句及高质量中文翻译

《GRE阅读必备专业词汇》

包凡一 编著

◎ 真题为准，重点难点专业词汇一网打尽
◎ 直击考点，有的放矢掌握高频易考单词
◎ 话题分类，按照学科全面罗列各科词汇
◎ 小巧便携，方便随时随地复习与记忆

定价：15元　开本：32开　页码：280页

《词以类记：GRE词汇》（附MP3）

张红岩 编著

◎ 词以类记，按学科和意群精心归纳57个Word List
◎ 收词新、全，收集整理最新GRE重要词汇8400多个
◎ 多重记忆法综合运用，提高了有序储存的效率
◎ 听觉辅助记忆，1000分钟超长录音，另含词汇讲座内容

定价：55元　开本：16开　页码：532页